WHAT WAS SOCIALISM,

AND WHAT COMES NEXT?

EDITORS

Sherry B. Ortner, Nicholas B. Dirks, Geoff Eley

A LIST OF TITLES

IN THIS SERIES APPEARS

AT THE BACK OF

THE BOOK

PRINCETON STUDIES IN
CULTURE/POWER/HISTORY

WHAT WAS SOCIALISM, AND WHAT COMES NEXT?

Katherine Verdery

PRINCETON UNIVERSITY PRESS
PRINCETON, NEW JERSEY

COPYRIGHT © 1996 BY PRINCETON UNIVERSITY PRESS

PUBLISHED BY PRINCETON UNIVERSITY PRESS, 41 WILLIAM STREET,

PRINCETON, NEW JERSEY 08540

IN THE UNITED KINGDOM: PRINCETON UNIVERSITY PRESS,

CHICHESTER, WEST SUSSEX

LIBRARY OF CONGRESS CATALOGING-IN-PUBLICATION DATA

VERDERY, KATHERINE.

WHAT WAS SOCIALISM, AND WHAT COMES NEXT? / KATHERINE VERDERY.

P. CM.—(PRINCETON STUDIES IN CULTURE/POWER/HISTORY)

INCLUDES BIBLIOGRAPHICAL REFERENCES AND INDEX.

ISBN 0-691-01133-8 (CL. : ALK. PAPER). — ISBN 0-691-01132-X (PBK. : ALK. PAPER)

1. SOCIALISM—ROMANIA. 2. COMMUNISM—ROMANIA. 3. POST-COMMUNISM—

ROMANIA. 4. POST-COMMUNISM. I. TITLE. II. SERIES.

HX373.5.V47   1996

338.9498—DC20   95-32123

THIS BOOK HAS BEEN COMPOSED IN CALEDONIA

PRINCETON UNIVERSITY PRESS BOOKS ARE PRINTED ON ACID-FREE PAPER

AND MEET THE GUIDELINES FOR PERMANENCE AND DURABILITY OF THE

COMMITTEE ON PRODUCTION GUIDELINES FOR BOOK LONGEVITY OF

THE COUNCIL ON LIBRARY RESOURCES

PRINTED IN THE UNITED STATES OF AMERICA BY

PRINCETON ACADEMIC PRESS

1   3   5   7   9   10   8   6   4   2

1   3   5   7   9   10   8   6   4   2

(PBK.)

**TO MY MOTHER AND
THE MEMORY OF MY FATHER**

MELODY AND BASSO CONTINUO

OF MY LIFE'S MUSIC

Q: What is the definition of socialism?

A: The longest and most painful route from
capitalism to capitalism.

CONTENTS

INTRODUCTION   3

PART I: SOCIALISM   17

ONE
What Was Socialism, and Why Did It Fall?   19

TWO
The "Etatization" of Time in Ceauşescu's Romania   39

PART II: IDENTITIES: GENDER, NATION,
CIVIL SOCIETY   59

THREE
From Parent-State to Family Patriarchs: Gender and Nation
in Contemporary Eastern Europe   61

FOUR
Nationalism and National Sentiment in Postsocialist Romania   83

FIVE
Civil Society or Nation? "Europe" in the Symbolism of
Postsocialist Politics   104

PART III: PROCESSES: TRANSFORMING PROPERTY,
MARKETS, AND STATES   131

SIX
The Elasticity of Land: Problems of Property Restitution
in Transylvania   133

SEVEN
Faith, Hope, and Caritas in the Land of the Pyramids,
Romania, 1990–1994   168

EIGHT
A Transition from Socialism to Feudalism? Thoughts
on the Postsocialist State   204

Afterword   229

NOTES   235

INDEX   289

WHAT WAS SOCIALISM,
AND WHAT COMES NEXT?

INTRODUCTION

> Fate had it that when I found myself at the head of the state it
> was already clear that all was not well in the country. . . .
> Everything had to be changed radically. . . . The process of
> renovating the country and radical changes in the world econ-
> omy turned out to be far more complicated than could be
> expected. . . . However, work of historic significance has
> been accomplished. The totalitarian system . . . has
> been eliminated. . . . We live in a new world.
> *(Mikhail Gorbachev, resignation speech, 1991)*

THE TWENTIETH CENTURY might fairly be called the Bolshevik century. From the moment of the Soviet Union's emergence after the October Revolution, the presence of this new historical actor on the world stage affected every important event. Its birth changed the fortunes of World War I. The Allied victory in World War II owed much to the prodigious human and material capacities the Soviets were able to mobilize—despite the prior loss of many millions and vast resources from the purges, gulags, collectivization, and man-made famines of the 1930s.[1] So successful was the wartime effort that Stalin was able to bring into the Soviet sphere a number of other countries in Eastern Europe at the war's end. The presence of the Soviet Union in the world shaped not only international but internal politics everywhere, from Western European social-welfare policies to the many Third-World struggles that advanced under Soviet aegis. In the United States, fear of "Communism" and grudging respect for Soviet capabilities spurred violations of civil rights during the McCarthy period, a massive arms buildup, and substantial development from spin-off technology. Who could have foreseen that with Mikhail Gorbachev's resignation speech of 25 December 1991 so mighty an empire would simply vanish? Television cameras lingered on its final image: the small red table at which he had sat.

The Soviet Union's meek exit belies not only its tremendous power and influence during the twentieth century but also the positive meaning of

For thoughtful and sometimes strenuous reaction to an early form of this chapter, I offer my thanks to Michael Burawoy, Elizabeth Dunn, Ernestine Friedl, Michael Kennedy, Gail Kligman, Sidney Mintz, and Gale Stokes. I wish to note here as well a larger debt of gratitude to Elizabeth Dunn and Gale Stokes, for their generous help concerning the project of this book as a whole; to the International Research and Exchanges Board, for its largesse with funding; and to Mary Murrell and Lauren Oppenheim of Princeton University Press, for their work in expediting publication. All translations from Romanian in this book are my own.

socialism[2] for many who fought to produce and sustain it, both in the Soviet Union itself and in socialist-inspired liberation movements elsewhere. Although the people who created such movements were often few in number, they articulated the dissatisfactions of millions. Inequality, hunger, poverty, and exploitation—to these perennial features of the human condition socialism offered a response. It promised laboring people dignity and freedom, women equal pay for equal work, and national minorities equal rights in the state. By making these promises, it drew attention to major problems that capitalist liberal democracies had not adequately resolved.

Unfortunately, the execution of socialist programs encountered a number of snags; attempts to rectify them ended by corrupting its objectives, sometimes through monstrous, despicable policies that subjected hundreds of thousands to terror and death. These departures from the ideal led many committed Marxists to abandon their support of the left;[3] the expression "real" or "actually existing" socialism came into use, to distinguish its messy reality from its hopes and claims.[4] In addition to making socialism more difficult to support, real socialism's distasteful features made it harder to study. Criticism and exasperation came more readily than sympathy—and were more readily rewarded with notice. Those who sought to analyze it with an open mind could be dismissed as wild-eyed radicals or apologists of dictatorship. In the United States, one reason for this was the continuing legacy of the Cold War.

The Cold War and the Production of Knowledge

Some might argue that the twentieth century was not the Bolshevik but the American century, in which the United States became a global power, led the struggle of the free world against the Bolshevik menace, and emerged victorious. Although I am partial to neither the oversimplification nor the martial imagery of that account, there is no doubt that the Cold-War relationship between the two superpowers set the defining stamp on the century's second half. More than simply a superpower face-off having broad political repercussions, the Cold War was also a form of knowledge and a cognitive organization of the world.[5] It laid down the coordinates of a conceptual geography grounded in East vs. West and having implications for the further divide between North and South. Mediating the intersection of these two axes were socialism's appeal for many in the "Third World" and the challenges it posed to the First.

As an organization of thought, the Cold War affected both public perceptions and intellectual life. It shaped the work of the physicists and engineers who engaged in defense research, of the social scientists specializing in Kremlinology, of the novelists and cinematographers who produced spy thrillers. Inevitably, the Cold War as context fundamentally influenced all scholarship on "real socialism," and especially scholarship in the U.S.[6] Because the material in this book is a product of the Cold War, then, I might speak briefly about what it has meant to study Eastern Europe in that context. Without wishing to be overly autobiographical, I believe this sort of reflection appropriately frames the production of knowledge in which I have been engaged, as seen in the chapters that follow. I emphasize here both the institutional environment and the processes of personal identity formation to which the Cold War was central in my case, leaving aside other aspects of the North American academy or personal choices to which it seems extraneous.

I began preparing to work in Eastern Europe in 1971. In the most general sense, research there at that time was possible only because a Cold War was in progress and had awakened interest in the region, and because that war had abated somewhat into *détente*.[7] Détente brought with it the rise of funding organizations like the International Research and Exchanges Board (IREX), founded in 1968 expressly to mediate scholarly exchanges with the Soviet bloc, and the National Council for Soviet and East European Research (NCSEER, 1978).[8] Without détente, and without the desperate interest of socialist regimes in increased access to Western technology—the price for which was to let in scholars from the West—our research there would have been impossible. Similarly, between 1973 and 1989 ongoing scholarly access to the region depended on U.S. politicians' view that knowledge about socialist countries was of sufficient strategic importance to warrant federal funding for it.

Within my discipline, anthropology, there was little to incline one to work in Eastern Europe. On the contrary: in 1971, when I began to think about where I would go, Europe was not the place a budding anthropologist would choose. The great books dealt with Oceania, Africa, or Native America— with "primitives." Few anthropologists had worked in Europe (being "our own" society, it had low prestige), and one rarely found their publications on graduate syllabi. But anthropology has long rewarded an explorer principle: go to uncharted territory. Given that anthropological interest in Europe began relatively late, as of 1971 almost no fieldwork had been done in the eastern part of the continent—precisely because of the Cold War.[9] Eastern Europe was less known to anthropology than was New Guinea; this meant that any research there, even if not prestigious, would at least be "pioneering."

To allure of this professional kind one might add the romantic aura, the hint of danger, adventure, and the forbidden, that clung to the Iron Curtain and infused the numerous spy stories about those who penetrated it. To go behind the Iron Curtain would be to enter a heart of darkness different from that of Conrad's Africa or Malinowski's Melanesia, but a darkness nonetheless. That I was not immune to this allure emerges retrospectively from certain features of my early life. For example, I still actively recall the launching of Sputnik in 1957, when I was in the fourth grade. Although I surely did not understand its significance, I got the strong message that it was very important indeed; my recollection of Sputnik is so clear that I remember vividly the space of the classroom in which we were talking about it (just as many people remember exactly where they were when they learned the news of President Kennedy's assassination). Then there was my ill-fated attempt to teach myself Russian when I was twelve (it foundered when I got to declensions, something of which I had never heard). Again, a few years later, out of an infinite array of possible topics for my high school speech contest, the subject I picked was the evils of Soviet Communism.

Finally, there was my reaction to the map of Europe that a fellow graduate student acquired just as I was deliberating where to go for my dissertation research. As we pored over the wonderful place names in Hungary, Czechoslovakia, and Romania, I found myself becoming very excited. The closer we got to the Black Sea, the more excited I became: I was truly stirred at the prospect of working in a "Communist" country having all those terrific names. Because I had no specific research problem in mind (I just wanted to see what life "behind the Iron Curtain" would be like), nothing dictated my choice of a specific country to work in. I chose Romania from the wholly pragmatic consideration that at that moment, it was the only East European country in which one could do ethnographic fieldwork with relative ease. The reason was major upheavals in the other countries—in Poland in 1968 and 1970, in Czechoslovakia in 1968, in Hungary with its conflict-ridden shift to market mechanisms beginning in 1968—leading them to close themselves off, whereas the Romanian regime had recently chosen a path of greater openness.[10] Those upheavals bespoke a growing crisis in the socialist system, but the crisis was delayed in Romania; hence, that government permitted anthropological fieldwork—and, according to the Fulbright handbooks, even invited it.[11]

Notwithstanding this invitation, the Cold War placed a number of constraints on North Americans doing research there—on the kinds of topics we might pursue, the ways we thought about them, and our physical movements.[12] Concerning possible research topics, for example, I could not have submitted a proposal dealing with the organization of socialism; hence, my two proposed research projects were a regional analysis of social-status concepts and a study of the distribution of distinctive ethnographic microzones. When neither of those proved feasible for the village I had selected, I did a social history of Romanian-German ethnic relations—having been advised against a study of the local collective farm. Not only were my research topics constrained; so was the attitude I felt I could adopt in my work. I accumulated debts to the people I studied and to the government whose hospitality had permitted me to gather data; outright criticism seemed to be foreclosed. Fortunately, my village respondents' more or less positive assessment of socialism during the early 1970s made it easy to avoid public criticism, as did my own admiration for some of the achievements of the regime up to that point. It was only after the mid 1980s that my attitude became unequivocally negative.

Another constraint—one that greatly affected the anthropology of Eastern Europe—was the privileged place accorded the discipline of political science in creating knowledge about the region, owing to the strategic importance of the socialist world for U.S. politics. In the absence of a preexisting anthropological discourse on Europe more broadly, the hegemony of political science strongly influenced the way the anthropology of Eastern Europe developed. It proved all too easy, in retrospect, to solve the problem of how to find an audience by reacting to the issues posed in political science. This meant adopting much of the conceptual agenda of that powerful interlocutor[13]—nationalism, regime legitimacy, the planning process, development, the nature of power in socialist systems, and so forth—rather than defining a set of problems more directly informed by the intellectual traditions of anthropology.

A third constraint of research during the Cold War was on movement—a particular problem for anyone not residing in a major city, as anthropologists rarely do. For example, because I had inadvertently entered a military zone on my motorbike soon after I arrived, county authorities were convinced that I was a spy, and the proximity of the village where I lived to an armaments factory only confirmed this suspicion. My movements were closely monitored throughout the period between 1973 and 1989, sometimes to comic proportions (such as when I picked up a police tail during a trip to a hard-currency shop, and my truck-driver chauffeur—hauling a huge crane—sought to shake them off). Whenever a local cop or some politico wanted to score points with those higher up, he might "confirm" my reputation as a spy, noting that I continued to work year after year among people who commuted to the armaments factory. This reputation was so firmly entrenched that it followed me well into the 1990s. Thus the Cold War turned me into a resource that local authorities could use in pursuit of their own advancement, as well as a means to intimidate and seduce Romanian citizens into collaborating with the Secret Police.[14] During 1984–85, the surveillance placed not only on me but also on my respondents finally made it impossible for me to do fieldwork in rural areas at all.[15] In this way, regime repression altered my entire research program, compelling me to abandon ethnographic projects in villages for library research and interviews with urban intellectuals. The result of that work (*National Ideology under Social-*

ism[16]) had not been in my plans but was, in effect, forced on me by Romania's response to that moment in the Cold War.

The Cold War affected my research even in this new project, for some of the intellectuals I worked with thought of themselves as dissidents in their relation to the Romanian Communist Party. They were eager to talk with me, thereby attracting to their cause that most crucial of dissident resources: Western notice. The ongoing Cold War had made dissent within socialist countries a weapon in the hands of Western ones; dissidence would spark international protests and signature campaigns or other forms of pressure on socialist regimes. Thus although my topic—national ideology among Romanian intellectuals—turned out to be more sensitive than I had expected, I never lacked for willing respondents. This was true in part because both they and I were not merely "individuals" but points of intersection for the forces engaged in a much larger political struggle: that between "Communism" and "the free world."

The Cold War and Personal Identity

Those forces not only made me a privileged interlocutor for certain Romanians but in a peculiar way may also have acted even more deeply in my character, constituting my interest in Eastern Europe as in part an intrapsychic one. In saying this, and in exploring the Cold War's ramifications in personal identity, I do not mean to claim that other scholars' motives for studying socialism arose from similar causes but only to probe further for the structuring effects of the Cold War.[17] As I recall my excitement over the map of Eastern Europe, alongside the other early signs of my fascination with Russia, I see an idiosyncratic affinity between the anti-Communism of American society and certain aspects of my character. Through the Cold War, Soviet Communism came to represent the ultimate in Absolute Power and Authority—that was, after all, what totalitarianism meant—something I found at once frightening and captivating.

A moment of epiphany during my fieldwork in the disastrous mid-1980s, when Romania was about the last socialist country anyone would want to be in,[18] led me to wonder at the roots of the fascination. Having spent an exhilarating day with some Romanian friends getting around the endless obstacles the regime placed in everyone's way, I realized that despite the cold apartments and unavailable food and constant Securitate surveillance, I was having a good time, and it had to do with the satisfaction of defeating Absolute Authority. I realized all of a sudden that the Party's claims to total power over Romanian society were subverted every day by thoroughgoing anarchy, and somehow I found such an environment very invigorating. At that moment I saw "Communism's" special appeal for me as partly rooted in a projection: in studying totalitarianism, I had found an ostensibly neutral, scholarly sphere in which to externalize and explore my own internal admonitory voice. Had the Cold War not constructed "Communism" in this way—particularly in my most formative years, the 1950s[19]—such that the Soviet Union was Authority Incarnate, I might have found Eastern Europe less interesting. And had the U.S. government not defined this incarnate authority as the main threat to our national security, there might have been fewer material resources for pursuing my choice. For these reasons, I believe, my research into socialism was the direct product of the Cold War.

So, paradoxically, was my relation to Marxist theory, which has exercised much influence on my work. An interest in Marxism did not precede my research in Romania but rather emerged from it. I first went "behind the Iron Curtain" out of curiosity (enlivened by what I have said above) rather than from political or intellectual commitment to Marxist ideals. I wanted to see what life there would be like, not to offer a critique of either their system or ours. When I departed for the field in August 1973, I had read no Marx or Lenin (though my bibliography did include Eric Wolf's work on peasant exploitation)—further testimony, I would say, to the effects of the Cold War on North American intellectual life. As a result, the form in which I first came really to know Marxism was its institutionalized and propagandizing one, encountered through the Romanian media and my fieldwork.

Witnessing the chasm that separated this Marxism's expressed goals from the values and intentions of ordinary folk brought home to me how difficult was the task of revolutionary mobilization in the absence of extensive prior consciousness-raising. The point was made succinctly in a conversation one day with two women, members of the collective farm in the village I was studying. When they launched a contempt-ridden, culture-of-poverty diatribe against the "lazy" Gypsies who hung around the farm, I tried to counter with the social-structural critique of that idea. As I spoke, one of the women turned to the other and said, "*She's* more of a socialist than *we* are!" Repeated exposure to observations like this, together with Romanians' determined refusal to be made into "new socialist men" despite their ready acknowledgment that they derived some benefits from the system, served oddly to crystallize for me a new interest in socialism. Upon my return from the field, in 1975, I discovered dependency theory and related neo-Marxist writings, and I entered a department very respectful of Marx's intellectual heritage.[20] Reading and admiring *Capital* was thus the culmination, not the beginning, of my research into "real socialism." The result was a commitment to the critique of capitalist forms through the critical examination of socialist ones. In my own modest example, then, it might be said that the chickens of the Cold War came home to roost.

The Study of Postsocialism and the Themes of This Book

Although one might think that the collapse of the Soviet system would render nugatory any further interest in it, I am not of that opinion. The Soviet Union may be irretrievably gone, but the electoral victories of renamed Communist Parties in Poland, Hungary, Bulgaria, and elsewhere have shown that the Party is far from over. Indeed, exposure to the rigors of primitive capitalism has made a number of people in the region think twice about their rejection of socialism and their embrace of "the market." The former socialist world is still well worth watching, for several reasons.

This postsocialist moment offers at least three sets of opportunities, all having both scholarly and political significance. First is the opportunity to understand better what is actually happening in the region, if we can set aside the triumphalist assumption that free-market democracies are the inevitable outcome. How, in fact, are East Europeans managing their exit from socialism? Just what does it take to create capitalism and "free" markets? What sorts of human engineering, not to mention violence, chaos, and despair, does that entail? What are the hidden costs of establishing new nation-states? (The answers offered by former Yugoslavia and the Caucasus are disquieting, to say the least.) Do the electoral victories of the re-formed and renamed Communist Parties reflect simply their better organization based in long experience, or genuine public feeling about desirable political ends that they articulate better than others—or perhaps something altogether different, such as people's wish to be "villagers" rather than reverting to the "peasant" status that postsocialist parties would force on them?[21] Work on such questions would permit a more nuanced assessment both of our own "Western" trajectory and of the policies that might be appropriate toward one or another country of the region. To investigate these questions, I argue herein, requires a theoretically grounded understanding of the system that has crumbled and an ethnographic sensitivity to the particulars of what is emerging from its ruins. This does not mean that only anthropologists need apply,[22] but it does mean attempting to suspend judgment about the outcome. It also means acknowledging that such phenomena as "privatization," "markets," "civil society," and so on are objects of investigation saturated with ideological significance; we must question rather than mindlessly reinforce them.

A second opportunity, related to the first, is to broaden a critique of Western economic and political forms by seeing them through the eyes of those experiencing their construction. The forced pace of privatization, for example, reveals with special clarity the darker side of capitalism. Far from being mere demagoguery, nationalist objections to the plundering of these countries' wealth are reactions to visible processes of impoverishment; so too are populist revelations of "corruption." "Democracy" is being unmasked too, as the export of Western electoral practices makes their failings transparent, arousing shocked commentary—from Poles and East Germans, for instance, at the emphasis on sound bites and candidate packaging to the detriment of debate over principles and ideas. It is possible that as Romanians, Russians, Poles, Latvians, and others live through the effort to create liberal democracies and market economies, they will be driven to a criticism of these forms even more articulate than before, and perhaps to new imaginings of a more viable socialism.

Such new imaginings would be the more fruitful if coupled with the third opportunity of this postsocialist conjuncture: the fuller understanding of what actually existing socialism was. Whether one sees it as a system sui generis or as a peculiar and repellent version of capitalism, its features distinguished it from other sociopolitical organizations of human activity. Now that its archives are more open to inspection, we may learn a great deal that we did not know about how it functioned. This would enable thinking differently about how to avoid its mistakes, and that, in turn, would continue the thrust of some of the pre-1989 work on the region. For a number of scholars,[23] part of the impetus for studying socialism was to combat both the stereotypical, propagandizing notions of it so common in the U.S. media and also the utopian and idealized images held by Western leftists who had not experienced living in it; both contributed to a larger project of political critique. The goal of further study might be simply the ethnographic one of trying to grasp the variety of human social arrangements. More politically, the goal might be to consider possible futures and signal the problems with some of them; for critics of capitalism, knowledge and critique of the actual forms of socialism was and should remain a foremost priority, part of a persistent quest for viable alternatives to our own way of life. For both these goals, investigating socialism was a useful task. I believe it still is.

This book aims to encourage work on socialism and postsocialism in these directions. It is not primarily a book about Romania (the area of my research), even though much of my material comes from that country, but rather a book indicating how we might think about what socialism was and what comes after it. Some might argue that Romania is not a "typical" case and therefore is a poor guide for postsocialist studies, but I do not share this opinion. No socialist country was "typical"; each had its specificities, and each shared certain features with some but not all other countries of the bloc. To assume that conclusions drawn from one will apply to all would be unwise, but material from any of them can nevertheless raise questions that might prove fruitful elsewhere. That is my purpose here: to point to questions one might ask or approaches one might take in studying the several countries of the former Soviet bloc. To this end, I include chapters on the main themes of the "transition" literature—civil society, marketization, privatization, and nationalism. My treatment of these themes does not much resemble other things being written on them, however; I hope the differences will stimulate thought.

The chapters brought together here consist of essays written between 1988 and 1994. Unifying them is the theoretical model of socialism provided in chapter 1; the later chapters, concerning the "transition," presuppose this model even as they augment it or examine departures from the system it describes. That is, I see my overall theme as exploring how the operation of socialism influences what comes next. The first and second chapters treat the socialist period, while the remainder either span the divide between pre- and post-1989 or concentrate on developments subsequent to that year.

Chapter 1 is a compressed version of a longer analysis of the socialist system.[24] I present socialism as an ideal type, leaving aside for the moment its varied real-world manifestations; in like manner, it is often useful to speak analytically of "capitalism," for despite differences among countries like Canada, the Netherlands, and Australia, these cases also show important similarities. In offering a single model of socialism, I sought to synthesize work by East European scholars that would help organize our approach to socialist societies by stating the central principles that gave them coherence as a system of family resemblances. Like all ideal-type models, mine describes no actual socialist society perfectly. Moreover, it emphasizes the system's formal constitution rather more than the forms of resistance it engendered, which were among the most important sources of variation from one country to another (owing in part to differences in the countries' historical experiences). At best, the model signals certain social processes as fundamental while acknowledging both that these were not the only processes at work and that they were more fundamental to some socialist societies than to others. Parts of subsequent chapters fill out the discussion in chapter 1: these include further treatment of the "spoiler state" and how subjection was produced, of queues as a form of socialist accumulation, and of socialist temporality (chapter 2); socialism's gender regime (chapter 3); its "social schizophrenia" and the relation of a shortage economy to nationalism (chapter 4); and its property regime (chapter 6).

I believe that a model of this kind retains its heuristic utility even after 1989, for two reasons. First, it provides a framework for thinking further about the nature of socialism, from the new vantage point of its aftermath. Because the workings of a system often appear most clearly with its decomposition, we can expect to learn a great deal about socialism retrospectively. In thinking about these new insights, I find it helpful not to start the inquiry from scratch. Second, a heuristic model serves to indicate problem areas that might be particularly important and interesting in the "transition." The pervasiveness of intersegmental competition in the Party and state bureaucracies, for example, can be expected to give a special twist to programs of privatization.[25] The secondary but highly politicized role of consumption in socialism's political economy will surely make consumption an especially intriguing topic to follow.[26] Changes in the status of property and markets suggest other interesting questions, such as, How is the mix of "personal" and "depersonalized" being (re)configured in once-socialist societies? That is, how can we think about the juxtaposition of privatization in land, say— personalizing a once-collective good—with the kinds of *de*personalization characteristic of markets?[27] Another locus of significant change is the organization of labor in postsocialist factories, which will provide fascinating evidence about the relationship between workers' habits under "economies of shortage" and the kinds of behavior intended with the introduction of Western business practices and ideologies.[28]

In chapter 2 I take up a theme that appeared in chapter 1 and is echoed in chapter 7: the organization of time under socialism. Anthropologists and historians have explored differences in how time is organized and lived across different kinds of social orders. Following this lead, chapter 2 sketches the efforts of the Romanian Communist Party to organize and appropriate time and shows the effects of these policies for how human beings are made into social persons. I include this chapter because I believe that reorganizations of time will prove an especially significant and disconcerting aspect of postsocialism for those who live through its changes, and one likely to be ignored by those who study them. The postsocialist equivalent of E. P. Thompson's celebrated essay on the imposition of capitalist work rhythms is waiting to be written;[29] I hope to provoke someone to write it. The theme of socialist time appears again in chapter 7, as contributing to the millenarian attitudes of Romanian investors in the Caritas pyramid scheme.

Chapters 3 through 5 treat various facets of national identity: how it might relate to the transforming gender regimes of socialism and postsocialism, how the organization of socialism laid the groundwork for increased ethnic conflict after 1989, and how preconstituted nationalist discourses shape the political symbolism that can be used in building "civil society." For anyone familiar with Eastern Europe, there is no need to justify giving this much space to the theme of national identity, which is fundamental to politics and self-constitution throughout the region; perhaps nonspecialists might simply take my word for it.[30] Chapter 4 focuses directly on nationalism, while chapters 3 and 5 add to it two other themes—gender and civil society—significant in their own right.

Chapter 3 asks how gender and national identities intersected in socialism, suggesting that gendered imagery in national myths masculinizes the nation's lineage, feminizes territorial boundaries, and eroticizes national sentiment. In addition, the chapter presents preliminary data indicating that a new form of "patriarchy" has accompanied democratization, making the basic citizen of democracy *male*, as some feminists have suggested is true more generally. Clearly, research into postsocialist democratization must be attentive to gender. The way gender was organized under socialism figures importantly in other aspects of the transition as well; one reason is that the several ways in which gender equality was legislated served to reinforce the significance of gender difference even while ostensibly undermining it. This makes gender, like nationalism, a strengthened vehicle of postsocialist politics. The result, however, has not been—as it has with national identities— political mobilization behind gender-based political movements but rather an assault on feminism by nationalist ideologues, who see the health of the nation as dependent on women's subordinating their bodies and interests to the collective task of national "rebirth."

In chapter 4, I argue (along with others[31]) that postsocialist nationalism is best understood in terms of the workings of socialism, but unlike others I concentrate on its organization of the person, or self, and on the ethnic symbolism of postsocialist anxieties. As with gender, reinforcement of national identities during the socialist period privileges them as foci of organization in postsocialism, for reasons that chapter 4 only begins to indicate. A point this chapter touches upon—the link between nationalists and certain ex-Party apparatchiks—deserves further thought. One argument might be that nationalism is the form of political discourse preferred by all those who want to retain maximum power for the socialist state upon which they had become such adept parasites, and which openness to foreign capital would compromise. In other words, nationalists and ex-Communists share a defense not so much of the *nation* as of the *state*, which they wish to shield from foreign predation.

In chapter 5 I further explore a specific way in which national ideas have influenced post-1989 politics in Romania: through their effects on "civil society." In this chapter I treat civil society as a symbolic construct deployed in political argument, rather than as a "thing" to be "built." Such a procedure is one response to finding that the idea of civil society has proven to be both more complex and more slippery than it might seem.[32] I argue that in the Romanian case, the long-term prior development and institutionalization of the idea of "nation" has limited the political efficacy of ideas like "civil society." Although I realize that any analysis of politics must be attentive to more than just the properties of the symbols employed, examining as well the institutional situations and the balance of forces among competing parties, perhaps my discussion will encourage others to be more skeptical about what "civil society" may actually mean when various groups use it in political speech.

Chapter 6 examines a theme mentioned briefly in chapter 4 and more extensively in chapter 8: privatization. The kind of research supporting the chapter, village ethnography, restricts the form of privatization I can analyze to the decollectivization of agriculture. In this chapter I link problems of decollectivization with the way land was treated under socialism. Many of these points will be useful in thinking about decollectivization in other countries of the region, including the Baltic states. I show that although many critics charge the Romanian government with explicitly obstructing the return of land to its former owners, this task is so fraught with complexities that even the best government intentions might run aground on it. In so arguing, however, I do not contend that the Romanian government is in fact eager to see property restitution completed; instead, the maintenance of ambiguous property rights seems crucial to the post-1989 organization of power in that country (and quite possibly elsewhere). The material in this chapter might lead to two things the chapter itself does not attempt: a more vigorous critique of the very notion of property, and the relation of land restitution to ideas about the "nation" as a collective "possessive individual" (an entity that "has" a territory).[33]

In chapter 7 I analyze a remarkable occurrence of the early 1990s: the rise and fall of pyramid schemes, epitomized in the spectacular Romanian pyramid known as Caritas. This chapter engages another major theme of postsocialism—the development of markets—and treats it as part of the larger problem of cognitive transformation accompanying the end of the socialist system. In addition, the chapter describes some ways of accumulating both political capital (an aspect of the pluralization of politics) and also other kinds of wealth, and it offers some speculations about the sociopolitical structure of the transition (such as "mafias") that are taken up again in the final chapter. I treat Caritas, then, as a window onto multiple facets of life in postsocialist Romania, among them democracy, markets, privatization, and the accompanying changes in culture.

Finally, chapter 8 uses the metaphor of a transition to feudalism in order to explore the consequences of the party-state's decomposition. In investigating how state power is being altered and reconstituted, this chapter contributes to an emerging anthropology of the state. It revisits the question of privatization—seen now as both a symbolic construct and an arena for state formation—and discusses "mafia" similarly, as both a symbol and an actual process whereby power is privatized. Additionally, the chapter recapitulates from a different angle the point in chapter 5 about the politics of symbols, proposing that the metaphors and symbols we use *as analysts* in thinking about postsocialism may reveal (or suppress) important topics for investigation.

I have used the word "transition" several times and should say a word about my views of it. In my opinion, to assume that we are witnessing a transition from socialism to capitalism, democracy, or market economies is mistaken. I hold with Stark, Burawoy, Bunce, and others who see the decade of the 1990s as a time of *transformation* in the countries that have emerged from socialism; these transformations will produce a variety of forms, some of them perhaps approximating Western capitalist market economies and many of them not. Stark writes, for example, that the outcome of privatization in Hungary will be not *private* property but *recombinant* property, while Burawoy writes not of the *e*volution of a new system of industrial production in Russia but of its *in*volution.[34] Polities more closely resembling corporatist authoritarian regimes than liberal democracies are a distinct possibility in several countries (Romania, for instance), whereas military dictatorships should not be ruled out for others (perhaps Russia). When I use the word "transition," then, I put it in quotes so as to mock the naiveté of so much fashionable transitology. Similarly, the title of chapter 8 ("A Transition from Socialism to Feudalism?") marks my disagreement with the assumptions of that literature.

Taken as a whole, then, this volume constitutes a dissent from the prevailing directions of much transitological writing. It not only employs an understanding of socialism's workings that is far from widespread in scholarship about the region but also views the central concepts of work on postsocialism with a skeptical eye. This skepticism comes from being not at all sure about what those central concepts—private property, democracy, markets, citizenship and civil society—actually mean. They are symbols in the constitution of our own "Western" identity, and their real content becomes ever more elusive as we inspect how they are supposedly taking shape in the former Soviet bloc. Perhaps this is because the world in which these foundational concepts have defined "the West" is itself changing—something of which socialism's collapse is a symptom, not a cause. The changes of 1989 did more than disturb Western complacency about the "new world order" and preempt the imagined fraternity of a new European Union: they signaled that a thoroughgoing reorganization of the globe is in course. In that case, we might wonder at the effort to implant perhaps-obsolescent Western forms in "the East." This is what I mean by the final line in my first chapter: what comes next is anyone's guess.

PART ONE

SOCIALISM

1

WHAT WAS SOCIALISM, AND WHY DID IT FALL?

T HE STARTLING DISINTEGRATION of Communist Party rule in
Eastern Europe in 1989, and its somewhat lengthier unraveling in
the Soviet Union between 1985 and 1991, rank among the century's
most momentous occurrences. Especially because neither policy-makers
nor area specialists predicted them, these events will yield much analysis
after the fact, as scholars develop the hindsight necessary for understanding
what they failed to grasp before. In this chapter, I aim to stimulate discussion about why Soviet-style socialism fell. Because I believe answers to the
question require understanding how socialism "worked," I begin with an
analysis of this and then suggest how it intersected fatefully with certain
features of its world-system context.

What Was Socialism?

The socialist societies of Eastern Europe and the Soviet Union differed from
one another in significant respects—for instance, in the intensity, span, and
effectiveness of central control, in the extent of popular support or resistance, and in the degree and timing of efforts at reform. Notwithstanding
these differences within "formerly existing socialism,"[1] I follow theorists
such as Kornai in opting for a single analytical model of it.[2] The family resemblances among socialist countries were more important than their variety, for analytic purposes, much as we can best comprehend French, Japa-

This chapter was originally entitled "What Was Socialism, and What Comes Next?" and was
delivered as a lecture for the Center for Comparative Research in History, Society and Culture,
at the University of California, Davis, in January 1993. I am grateful to those who invited
me—William Hagen, G. William Skinner, and Carol A. Smith—as well as to members of the
Center's seminar, for a very stimulating discussion. I also received helpful advice from Ashraf
Ghani.

Earlier forms of the argument appeared in "Theorizing Socialism" and in my book *National
Ideology under Socialism: Identity and Cultural Politics in Ceauşescu's Romania* (Berkeley and
Los Angeles: University of California Press, 1991). The underlying conceptualization was developed in 1988; after 1989 I added some thoughts on how the model might illuminate the system's
collapse. Reprinted from *Contention: Debates in Society, Culture, and Science* 1, no. 3 (1993), by
permission of Indiana University Press.

nese, West German, and North American societies as variants of a single capitalist system. Acknowledging, then, that my description applies more fully to certain countries and time periods than to others, I treat them all under one umbrella.

For several decades, the analysis of socialism has been an international industry, employing both Western political scientists and Eastern dissidents. Since 1989 this industry has received a massive infusion of new raw materials, as once-secret files are opened and translations appear of research by local scholars (especially Polish and Hungarian) into their own declining socialist systems.[3] My taste in such theories is "indigenist": I have found most useful the analyses of East Europeans concerning the world in which they lived. The following summary owes much to that work, and it is subject to refinement and revision as new research appears.[4] Given temporal and spatial constraints, I will compress elements of a longer discussion, emphasizing how production was organized and the consequences of this for consumption and for markets.[5] I believe these themes afford the best entry into why Party rule crumbled much faster than anyone expected.

Production

From the earliest days of the "totalitarian" model, Americans' image of "Communism" was of an autocratic, all-powerful state inexorably imposing its harsh will on its subjects. Even after most area specialists ceased to use the term "totalitarian" in their writing, the image of totalitarian autocracy persisted with both the broader public and many politicians; indeed, it underpinned Ronald Reagan's view of the "evil empire" as late as the 1980s. Yet the image was by and large wrong. Communist Party states were not all-powerful: they were comparatively weak. Because socialism's leaders managed only partially and fitfully to win a positive and supporting attitude from their citizens—that is, to be seen as legitimate—the regimes were constantly undermined by internal resistance and hidden forms of sabotage *at all system levels.*[6] This contributed much to their final collapse. I will describe briefly some of the elements of socialist nontotalitarianism and signal a few places where resistance lay.[7]

Socialism's fragility begins with the system of "centralized planning," which the center neither adequately planned nor controlled. Central planners would draw up a plan with quantities of everything they wanted to see produced, known as targets. They would disaggregate the plan into pieces appropriate for execution and estimate how much investment and how many raw materials were needed if managers of firms were to fill their targets. Managers learned early on, however, that not only did the targets increase annually but the materials required often did not arrive on time or in the right amounts. So they would respond by bargaining their plan: demanding more investments and raw materials than the amounts actually necessary for their targets. Every manager, and every level of the bureaucracy, padded budgets and requests in hopes of having enough, in the actual moment of production. (A result of the bargaining process, of course, was that central planners always had faulty information about what was really required for production, and this impeded their ability to plan.) Then, if managers somehow ended up with more of some material than they needed, they hoarded it. Hoarded material had two uses: it could be kept for the next production cycle, or it could be exchanged with some other firm for something one's own firm lacked. These exchanges or barters of material were a crucial component of behavior within centralized planning.

A result of all the padding of budgets and hoarding of materials was widespread shortages, for which reason socialist economies are called economies of shortage.[8] Shortages were sometimes relative, as when sufficient quantities of materials and labor for a given level of output actually existed, but not where and when they were needed. Sometimes shortages were absolute, since relative shortage often resulted in lowered production, or—as in Romania—since items required for production or consumption were being exported. The causes of shortage were primarily that people lower down in the planning process were asking for more materials than they required and then hoarding whatever they got. Underlying their behavior was what economists call soft budget constraints—that is, if a firm was losing money, the center would bail it out. In our own economy, with certain exceptions (such as Chrysler and the savings and loan industry), budget constraints are hard: if you cannot make ends meet, you go under. But in socialist economies, it did not matter if firms asked for extra investment or hoarded raw materials; they paid no penalty for it.

A fictitious example will help to illustrate—say, a shoe factory that makes women's shoes and boots. Central planners set the factory's targets for the year at one hundred thousand pairs of shoes and twenty thousand pairs of boots, for which they think management will need ten tons of leather, a half ton of nails, and one thousand pounds of glue. The manager calculates what he would need under ideal conditions, if his workers worked consistently during three eight-hour shifts. He adds some for wastage, knowing the workers are lazy and the machines cut badly; some for theft, since workers are always stealing nails and glue; some to trade with other firms in case he comes up short on a crucial material at a crucial moment; and some more for the fact that the tannery always delivers less than requested. The manager thus refuses the plan assigned him, saying he cannot produce that number of shoes and boots unless he gets thirteen rather than ten tons of leather, a ton rather than a half-ton of nails, and two thousand rather than one thousand pounds of glue. Moreover, he says he needs two new power stitchers from Germany, without which he can produce nothing. In short, he has bargained his plan. Then when he gets some part of these goods, he stockpiles them or trades excess glue to the manager of a coat factory in exchange for some extra pigskin. If leather supplies still prove insufficient, he will make fewer boots and more shoes, or more footwear of small size, so as to use less leather; never mind if women's feet get cold in winter, or women with big feet can find nothing to wear.

With all this padding and hoarding, it is clear why shortage was endemic to socialist systems, and why the main problem for firms was not whether they could meet (or generate) demand but whether they could procure adequate supplies. So whereas the chief problem of economic actors in Western economies is to get profits by selling things, the chief problem for socialism's economic actors was to procure things. Capitalist firms compete with each other for markets in which they will make a profit; socialist firms competed to maximize their bargaining power with suppliers higher up. In our society, the problem is other sellers, and to outcompete them you have to befriend the buyer. Thus our clerks and shop owners smile and give the customer friendly service because they want business; customers can be grouchy, but it will only make the clerk try harder. In socialism, the locus of competition was elsewhere: your competitor was other buyers, other procurers; and to outcompete them you needed to befriend those higher up who supplied you. Thus in socialism it was not the clerk—the provider, or "seller"—who was friendly (they were usually grouchy) but the procurers, the customers, who sought to ingratiate themselves with smiles, bribes, or favors. The work of procuring generated whole networks of cozy relations among economic managers and their bureaucrats, clerks and their customers. We would call this corruption, but that is because getting supplies is not a problem for capitalists: the problem is getting sales. In a word, for capitalists salesmanship is at a premium; for socialist managers, the premium was on acquisitionsmanship, or procurement.

So far I have been describing the clientelism and bargaining that undercut the Party center's effective control. A similar weakness in vertical power relations emerges from the way socialist production and shortage bred workers' oppositional consciousness and resistance. Among the many things in short supply in socialist systems was labor. Managers hoarded labor, just like any other raw material, because they never knew how many workers they would need. Fifty workers working three eight-hour shifts six days a week might be enough to meet a firm's targets—*if* all the materials were on hand all month long. But this never happened. Many of those workers would stand idle for part of the month, and in the last ten days when most of the materials were finally on hand the firm would need 75 workers working overtime to complete the plan. The manager therefore kept 75 workers on the books, even though most of the time he needed fewer; and since all other managers were doing the same, labor was scarce. This provided a convenient if unplanned support for the regimes' guaranteed employment.

An important result of labor's scarcity was that managers of firms had relatively little leverage over their workers. Furthermore, because supply shortages caused so much uncertainty in the production process, managers had to turn over to workers much control over this process, lest work come to a standstill.[9] That is, structurally speaking, workers under socialism had a somewhat more powerful position relative to management than do workers in capitalism. Just as managers' bargaining with bureaucrats undercut central power, so labor's position in production undercut that of management.

More than this, the very organization of the workplace bred opposition to Party rule. Through the Party-controlled trade union and the frequent merger of Party and management functions, Party directives were continually felt in the production process—and, from workers' viewpoint, they were felt as unnecessary and disruptive. Union officials either meddled unhelpfully or contributed nothing, only to claim credit for production results that workers knew were their own. Workers participated disdainfully—as sociologist Michael Burawoy found in his studies of Hungarian factories—in Party-organized production rituals, such as work-unit competitions, voluntary workdays, and production campaigns; they resented these coerced expressions of their supposed commitment to a wonderful socialism.[10] Thus instead of securing workers' consent, workplace rituals sharpened their consciousness and resistance. Against an official "cult of work" used to motivate cadres and workers toward fulfilling the plan, many workers developed an oppositional cult of nonwork, imitating the Party bosses and trying to do as little as possible for their paycheck. Cadres often found no way around this internal sabotage, which by reducing productivity deepened the problems of socialist economies to the point of crisis.

The very forms of Party rule in the workplace, then, tended to focus, politicize, and turn against it the popular discontent that capitalist societies more successfully disperse, depoliticize, and deflect. In this way, socialism produced a split between "us" and "them," workers and Party leaders, founded on a lively consciousness that "they" are exploiting "us." This consciousness was yet another thing that undermined socialist regimes. To phrase it in Gramscian terms, the lived experience of people in socialism precluded its utopian discourse from becoming hegemonic—precluded, that is, the softening of coercion with consent.[11]

Ruling Communist Parties developed a variety of mechanisms to try to obscure this fact of their nature from their subjects, mechanisms designed to produce docile subject dispositions and to ensure that discontent did not become outright opposition. I will briefly discuss two of these mechanisms: the apparatus of surveillance, and redistribution of the social product.

Surveillance and Paternalistic Redistribution

In each country, some equivalent of the KGB was instrumental in maintaining surveillance, with varying degrees of intensity and success. Particularly effective were the Secret Police in the Soviet Union, East Germany, and Romania, but networks of informers and collaborators operated to some extent in all. These formed a highly elaborate "production" system parallel to the system for producing goods—a system producing paper, which contained real and falsified histories of the people over whom the Party ruled. Let us call the immediate product "dossiers," or "files," though the ultimate product was political subjects and subject dispositions useful to the regime. This parallel production system was at least as important as the system for producing goods, for producers of files were much better paid than producers of goods. My image of this parallel production system comes from the memoirs of Romanian political prisoner Herbert Zilber:

> The first great socialist industry was that of the production of files. . . . This new industry has an army of workers: the informers. It works with ultramodern electronic equipment (microphones, tape recorders, etc.), plus an army of typists with their typewriters. Without all this, socialism could not have survived. . . . In the socialist bloc, people and things exist only through their files. All our existence is in the hands of him who possesses files and is constituted by him who constructs them. Real people are but the reflection of their files.[12]

The work of producing files (and thereby political subjects) created an atmosphere of distrust and suspicion dividing people from one another. One never knew whom one could trust, who might be informing on one to the police about one's attitudes toward the regime or one's having an American to dinner. Declarations might also be false. Informers with a denunciation against someone else were never asked what might be their motive for informing; their perhaps-envious words entered directly into constituting another person's file—thus another person's sociopolitical being. Moreover, like all other parts of the bureaucracy, the police too padded their "production" figures, for the fact of an entry into the file was often more important than its veracity.[13] The existence of this shadowy system of production could have grave effects on the people "processed" through it, and the assumption that it was omnipresent contributed much to its success, in some countries, in suppressing unwanted opposition.

If surveillance was the negative face of these regimes' problematic legitimation, its positive face was their promises of social redistribution and welfare. At the center of both the Party's official ideology and its efforts to secure popular support was "socialist paternalism," which justified Party rule with the claim that the Party would take care of everyone's needs by collecting the total social product and then making available whatever people needed—cheap food, jobs, medical care, affordable housing, education, and so on. Party authorities claimed, as well, that they were better able to assess and fill these needs than were individuals or families, who would always tend to want more than their share. Herein lay the Party's paternalism: it acted like a father who gives handouts to the children as he sees fit. The Benevolent Father Party educated people to express needs it would then fill, and discouraged them from taking the initiative that would enable them to fill these needs on their own. The promises—socialism's basic social contract—did not go unnoticed, and as long as economic conditions permitted their partial fulfillment, certain socialist regimes gained legitimacy as a result. But this proved impossible to sustain.

Beyond its effects on people's attitudes, paternalism had important consequences for the entire system of production discussed previously and for consumption; here I shift to the question of why consumption was so central in the resistance to socialism. A Party that pretends to meet its citizens' needs through redistribution and that insists on doing so exclusively—that is, without enlisting their independent efforts—must control a tremendous fund of resources to redistribute. Nationalizing the means of production helped provide this, and so did a relentlessly "productionist" orientation, with ever-increased production plans and exhortations to greater effort.

The promise of redistribution was an additional reason, besides my earlier argument about shortages, why socialism worked differently from capitalism. Socialism's inner drive was to accumulate not profits, like capitalist ones, but distributable resources. This is more than simply a drive for autarchy, reducing dependency on the outside: it aims to increase dependency of those within. Striving to accumulate resources for redistribution involves things for which profit is totally irrelevant. In capitalism, those who run lemonade stands endeavor to serve thirsty customers in ways that make a profit and outcompete other lemonade stand owners. In socialism, the point was not profit but the relationship between thirsty persons and the one with the lemonade—the Party center, which appropriated from producers the various ingredients (lemons, sugar, water) and then mixed the lemonade to reward them with, as it saw fit. Whether someone made a profit was irrelevant: the transaction underscored the center's paternalistic superiority over its citizens—that is, its capacity to decide who got more lemonade and who got less.

Controlling the ingredients fortified the center's capacity to redistribute things. But this capacity would be even greater if the center controlled not only the lemons, sugar, and water but the things they come from: the lemon trees, the ground for growing sugar beets and the factories that process them, the wells and the well-digging machinery. That is, most valuable of all to the socialist bureaucracy was to get its hands not just on resources but on resources that generated *other* usable resources, resources that were themselves further productive. Socialist regimes wanted not just eggs but the goose that lays them. Thus if capitalism's inner logic rests on accumulating surplus value, the inner logic of socialism was to accumulate means of production.[14]

The emphasis on keeping resources at the center for redistribution is one reason why items produced in socialist countries so often proved uncompetitive on the world market. Basically, most of these goods were not being made to be sold competitively: they were being either centrally accumulated or redistributed at low prices—effectively given away. Thus whether a dress was pretty and well made or ugly and missewn was irrelevant, since profit was not at issue: the dress would be "given away" at a subsidized price, not sold. In fact, the whole point was *not* to sell things: the center wanted to keep as much as possible under its control, because that was how it had redistributive power; and it wanted to give away the rest, because that was how it confirmed its legitimacy with the public. Selling things competitively was therefore beside the point. So too were ideas of "efficient" production, which for a capitalist would enhance profits by wasting less material or reducing wages. But whatever goes into calculating a profit—costs of material or labor inputs, or sales of goods—was unimportant in socialism until very late in the game. Instead, "efficiency" was understood to mean "the full use of existing resources," "the maximization of given capacities" rather than of results, all so as to redirect resources to a goal greater than satisfying the population's needs.[15] In other words, what was rational in socialism differed from capitalist rationality. Both are stupid in their own way, but differently so.

Consumption

Socialism's redistributive emphasis leads to one of the great paradoxes of a paternalist regime claiming to satisfy needs. Having constantly to amass means of production so as to enhance redistributive power caused Party leaders to prefer heavy industry (steel mills, machine construction) at the expense of consumer industry (processed foods, or shoes). After all, once a consumer got hold of something, the center no longer controlled it; central power was less served by giving things away than by producing things it could continue to control. The central fund derived more from setting up a factory to make construction equipment than from a shoe factory or a chocolate works. In short, these systems had a basic tension between what was necessary to legitimate them—redistributing things to the masses—and what was necessary to their power—accumulating things at the center. The tension was mitigated where people took pride in their economy's development (that is, building heavy industry might also bring legitimacy), but my experience is that the legitimating effects of redistribution were more important by far.

Each country addressed this tension in its own way. For example, Hungary after 1968 and Poland in the 1970s gave things away more, while Romania and Czechoslovakia accumulated things more; but the basic tension existed everywhere. The socialist social contract guaranteed people food and clothing but did not promise (as capitalist systems do) quality, ready availability, and choice. Thus the system's mode of operation tended to sacrifice consumption, in favor of production and controlling the products. This paradoxical neglect of consumption contributed to the long lines about which we heard so much (and we heard about them, of course, because we live in a system to which consumption is crucial).

In emphasizing this neglect of consumption as against building up the central resource base, I have so far been speaking of the *formally* organized economy of socialism—some call it the "first" or "official" economy. But this is not the whole story. Since the center would not supply what people needed, they struggled to do so themselves, developing in the process a huge repertoire of strategies for obtaining consumer goods and services. These strategies, called the "second" or "informal" economy, spanned a wide range from the quasi-legal to the definitely illegal.[16] In most socialist countries it was not illegal to moonlight for extra pay—by doing carpentry, say—but people doing so often stole materials or illegally used tools from their workplace; or they might manipulate state goods to sell on the side. Clerks in stores might earn favors or extra money, for example, by saving scarce goods to sell to special customers, who tipped them or did some important favor in return. Also part of the second economy was the so-called "private plot" of collective farm peasants, who held it legally and in theory could do what they wanted with it—grow food for their own table or to sell in the market at state-controlled prices. But although the plot itself was legal, people obtained high outputs from it not just by virtue of hard work but also by stealing from the collective farm: fertilizer and herbicides, fodder for their pigs or cows, work time for their own weeding or harvesting, tractor time and fuel for plowing their plot, and so on. The second economy, then, which provisioned a large part of consumer needs, was parasitic upon the state economy and inseparable from it. It developed precisely because the state economy tended to ignore consumption. To grasp the interconnection of the two economies is crucial, lest one think that simply dismantling the state sector will automatically enable entrepreneurship—already present in embryo—to flourish. On the contrary: parts of the second economy will wither and die if deprived of the support of the official, state economy.

It is clear from what I have said that whereas consumption in our own society is considered primarily a socioeconomic question, the relative neglect of consumer interests in socialism made consumption deeply political. In Romania in the 1980s (an extreme case), to kill and eat your own calf was a political act, because the government prohibited killing calves: you were supposed to sell them cheap to the state farm, for export. Romanian villagers who fed me veal (having assured themselves of my complicity) did so with special satisfaction. It was also illegal for urbanites to go and buy forty kilograms of potatoes directly from the villagers who grew potatoes on their private plot, because the authorities suspected that villagers would charge more than the state-set price, thus enriching themselves. So Romanian policemen routinely stopped cars riding low on the chassis and confiscated produce they found inside.

Consumption became politicized in yet another way: the very definition of "needs" became a matter for resistance and dispute. "Needs," as we should know from our own experience, are not given: they are created, developed, expanded—the work especially of the advertising business. It is advertising's job to convince us that we need things we didn't know we needed, or that if we feel unhappy, it's because we need something (a shrink, or a beer, or a Marlboro, or a man). Our need requires only a name, and it can be satisfied with a product or service. Naming troubled states, labeling them as needs, and finding commodities to fill them is at the heart of our economy. Socialism, by contrast, which rested not on devising infinite kinds of things to sell people but on claiming to satisfy people's *basic* needs, had a very unadorned definition of them—in keeping with socialist egalitarianism. Indeed, some Hungarian dissidents wrote of socialism's relationship to needs as a "dictatorship."[17] As long as the food offered was edible or the clothes available covered you and kept you warm, that should be sufficient. If you had trouble finding even these, that just meant you were not looking hard enough. No planner presumed to investigate what kinds of goods people wanted, or worked to name new needs for newly created products and newly developed markets.

At the same time, however, regime policies paradoxically made consumption a problem. Even as the regimes prevented people from consuming by not making goods available, they insisted that under socialism, the standard of living would constantly improve. This stimulated consumer appetites, perhaps with an eye to fostering increased effort and tying people into the system. Moreover, socialist ideology presented consumption as a "right." The system's organization exacerbated consumer desire further by frustrating it and thereby making it the focus of effort, resistance, and discontent. Anthropologist John Borneman sees in the relation between desire and goods a major contrast between capitalism and socialism. Capitalism, he says, repeatedly renders desire concrete and specific, and offers specific—if ever-changing—goods to satisfy it. Socialism, in contrast, aroused desire *without* focalizing it, and kept it alive by deprivation.[18]

As people became increasingly alienated from socialism and critical of its achievements, then, the politicization of consumption also made them challenge official definitions of their needs. They did so not just by creating a second economy to grow food or make clothes or work after hours but also, sometimes, by public protest. Poland's Communist leaders fell to such protest at least twice, in 1970 and in 1980, when Polish workers insisted on having more food than government price increases would permit them. Less immediately disruptive were forms of protest in which people used consumption styles to forge resistant social identities. The black markets in Western goods that sprang up everywhere enabled alienated consumers to express their contempt for their governments through the kinds of things they chose to buy. You could spend an entire month's salary on a pair of blue jeans, for instance, but it was worth it: wearing them signified that you could get something the system said you didn't need and shouldn't have. Thus consumption goods and objects conferred an identity that set you off from socialism, enabling you to differentiate yourself as an individual in the face of relentless pressures to homogenize everyone's capacities and tastes into an undifferentiated collectivity. Acquiring objects became a way of constituting your selfhood against a deeply unpopular regime.

Bureaucratic Factionalism and Markets

Before turning to why these systems fell, I wish to address one more issue: politicking in the Party bureaucracy. Although this took different and specific forms in the different countries, it is important to mention the issue, for socialism's collapse owed much to shifts in the balance among factions that emerged within the Party apparatus. Even before 1989, researchers were pointing to several forms of intra-Party division. Polish sociologist Jadwiga Staniszkis, writing specifically of the moment of transition, speaks of three factions—the globalists, the populists, and the middle-level bureaucracy; others, writing more generally, distinguish between "strategic" and "operative" elites, the state bureaucracy and the "global monopoly," the bureaucracy and the Party elite, "in-house" and "out-of-house" Party workers, and so forth.[19] One way of thinking about these various divisions is that they distinguish ownership from management, or the people who oversaw the paperwork of administration from those "out in the field," intervening in actual social life.[20] We might then look for conflicting tendencies based in the different interests of these groups—such as conflicts between the central "owners" or paperworkers, on one hand, who might persist in policies that accumulated means of production without concern for things like productivity and output, and the bureaucratic managers of the allocative process or its fieldworkers, on the other, who *had* to be concerned with such things. Although the power of the system itself rested on continued accumulation, such tendencies if unchecked could obstruct the work of those who had actually to deliver resources or redistribute them. Without actual investments and hard material resources, lower-level units could not produce the means of production upon which both bureaucracy and center relied. If productive activity were so stifled by "overadministration" that nothing got produced, this would jeopardize the redistributive bureaucracy's power and prestige.

Thus when central accumulation of means of production began to threaten the capacity of lower-level units to produce; when persistent imbalances between investment in heavy industry and in light industry, between allocations for investment and for consumption, and so on, diminished the stock of distributable goods; and when the center's attempts to keep enterprises from meddling with surplus appropriation obstructed the process of production itself—this is when pressure arose for a shift of emphasis. The pressure was partly from those in the wider society to whom not enough was being allocated and partly from bureaucrats themselves whose prestige and, increasingly, prospects of retaining power depended on having more goods to allocate. One then heard of decentralization, of the rate of growth, of productivity—in a word, of matters of output, rather than the inputs that lay at the core of bureaucratic performance. This is generally referred to as the language of "reform."

For those groups who became concerned with questions of output and productivity, the solutions almost always involved introducing mechanisms such as profitability criteria and freer markets. This meant, however, introducing a subordinate rationality discrepant with the system's inner logic and thereby threatening continued Party rule. Market forces create problems for socialism in part for reasons treated implicitly or explicitly above in contrasting capitalism's demand-constrained economies with socialism's economy of shortage (its lack of interest, for example, in the salability of its products). But more broadly, markets create problems because they move goods horizontally rather than vertically toward the center, as all redistributive systems require. Markets also presuppose that individual interest and the "invisible hand," rather than the guiding hand of the Party, secure the common good.[21] Because these horizontal movements and individualizing premises subverted socialism's hierarchical organization, market mechanisms had been suppressed. Reformers introducing them were opening Pandora's box.

Why Did It Fall?

My discussion of socialism's workings already points to several reasons for its collapse; I might now address the question more comprehensively. To do this requires, in my view, linking the properties of its internal organization (discussed above) with properties of its external environment, as well as with shorter-term "event history." This means examining the specific conjuncture of two systems—"capitalist" and "socialist," to use ideal types—one encompassing the other.[22]

In event-history terms, the proximate cause of the fall of East European and Soviet socialism was an act of the Hungarian government: its dismantling of the barbed wire between Hungary and Austria, on the eve of a visit by President George Bush, and its later renouncing the treaty with the GDR that would have prevented East German emigration through Hungary. This culmination of Hungary's long-term strategy of opening up to the West gave an unexpected opportunity for some East German tourists to extend their Hungarian vacations into West Germany; the end result, given that Gorbachev refused to bolster the East German government with Soviet troops in this crisis, was to bring down the Berlin Wall. To understand the conjuncture in which Hungary could open its borders and Gorbachev could refuse Honecker his troops requires setting in motion the static model I have given above and placing it in its international context. This includes asking how socialism's encounter with a changing world capitalism produced or aggravated factional divisions within Communist Parties.

International Solutions to Internal Problems

My discussion of socialism indicated several points of tension in its workings that affected the system's capacity for extended reproduction. Throughout their existence, these regimes sought to manage such tensions in different ways, ranging from Hungary's major market reforms in the 1960s to Romania's rejection of reform and its heightened coercive extraction. In all cases, managing these tensions involved decisions that to a greater or lesser degree opened socialist political economies to Western capital. The impetus for this opening—critical to socialism's demise—came chiefly from within, as Party leaders attempted to solve their structural problems without major structural reform. Their attitude in doing so was reminiscent of a "plunder mentality" that sees the external environment as a source of booty to be used as needed in maintaining one's own system, without thought for the cost. This attitude was visible in the tendency of socialist governments to treat foreign trade as a residual sector, used to supplement budgets without being made an integral part of them.[23] Because of how this opportunistic recourse to the external environment brought socialism into tighter relationship with capitalism, it had fateful consequences.

The critical intersection occurred not in 1989 or 1987 but in the late 1960s and early 1970s, when global capitalism entered the cyclical crisis from which it is still struggling to extricate itself. Among capitalists' possible responses to the crisis (devaluation, structural reorganization, etc.), an early one was to lend abroad; facilitating this option were the massive quantities of petrodollars that were invested in Western banks, following changes in OPEC policy in 1973. By lending, Western countries enabled the recipients to purchase capital equipment or to build long-term infrastructure, thereby expanding the overseas markets for Western products.[24]

The loans became available just at the moment when all across the socialist bloc, the first significant round of structural reforms had been proposed, halfheartedly implemented, and, because profitability and market criteria fit so poorly with the rationale of socialism, largely abandoned. Reluctance to proceed with reforms owed much, as well, to Czechoslovakia's Prague Spring, from which the Party apparatus all across the region had been able to see the dangers that reform posed for its monopoly on power. Instead of reforming the system from within, then, most Party leaderships opted to meet their problems by a greater articulation with the surrounding economy: importing Western capital and using it to buy advanced technology (or, as in Poland, to subsidize consumption), in hopes of improving economic performance. Borrowing thus became a substitute for extensive internal changes that would have jeopardized the Party's monopoly over society and subverted the inner mechanisms of socialism. In this way, the internal cycles of two contrasting systems suddenly meshed.

The intent, as with all the international borrowing of the period, was to pay off the loans by exporting manufactured goods into the world market. By the mid-1970s it was clear, however, that the world market could not absorb sufficient amounts of socialism's products to enable repayment, and at the same time, rising interest rates added staggeringly to the debt service. With the 1979–80 decision of the Western banking establishment not to lend more money to socialist countries, the latter were thrown into complete disarray. I have already mentioned several features that made socialist economies inapt competitors in the international export market. The "plunder" stance toward external economies, the system's fundamental organization against notions of salability of its products, the shortage economy's premium on acquisitionsmanship rather than on salesmanship, the neglect of consumption and of producing to satisfy consumer needs with diverse high-quality products—all this meant that an adequate response to the hard-currency crisis would have catastrophic effects on socialism's inner mechanisms. To this was added the fact that socialist economies were "outdated": as Jowitt put it, "After 70 years of murderous effort, the Soviet Union had created a German industry of the 1880s in the 1980s."[25]

In these circumstances, the balance of power tilted toward the faction within the Communist Party of the Soviet Union that had long argued for structural reforms, the introduction of market mechanisms, and profit incentives, even at the cost of the Party's "leading role." The choice, as Gorbachev and his faction saw it, was to try to preserve either the Soviet Union and its empire (by reforms that would increase its economic performance and political legitimacy) or collective property and the Party monopoly. Gorbachev was ready to sacrifice the latter to save the former but ended by losing both.

While Western attention was riveted on the speeches of policy-makers in the Kremlin, the more significant aspects of reform, however, were in the often-unauthorized behavior of bureaucrats who were busily creating new property forms on their own. Staniszkis describes the growth of what she calls "political capitalism," as bureaucrats spontaneously created their own profit-based companies from within the state economic bureaucracy. Significantly for my argument that socialism's articulation with world capitalism was crucial to its fall, the examples she singles out to illustrate these trends are all at the interface of socialist economies with the outside world—in particular, new companies mediating the export trade and state procurement of Western computers.[26] In fact, she sees as critical the factional split between the groups who managed socialism's interface with the outside world (such as those in foreign policy, counterintelligence, and foreign trade) and those who managed it internally (such as the Party's middle-level executive apparatus and the KGB).[27] Forms of privatization already taking place as early as 1987 in Poland and similar processes as early as 1984 in Hungary[28] show the emerging contours of what Staniszkis sees as the reformists' goal: a dual economy. One part of this economy was to be centrally administered, as before, and the other part was to be reformed through market/profit mechanisms and selective privatization of state property. The two were to coexist symbiotically.[29]

These forms of "political capitalism" arose in part by economic managers' exploiting the shortages endemic to socialism—shortages now aggravated to crisis proportions. In the new hope of making a profit, "political capitalists" (I call them "entrepratchiks") were willing to put into circulation reserves known only to them—which they would otherwise have hoarded—thus alleviating shortages, to their own gain. As a result, even antireformist Soviet and Polish bureaucrats found themselves acquiescing in entrepratchiks' activities, without which, in Staniszkis's words, "the official structure of the economic administration was absolutely unsteerable."[30] Contributing to their tolerance was rampant bureaucratic anarchy, a loss of control by those higher up, rooted in the "inability of superiors to supply their subordinates (managers of lower level) with the means to construct a strategy of survival."[31] Because superiors could no longer guarantee deliveries and investments, they were forced to accept whatever solutions enterprising subordinates could devise—even at the cost of illicit profits from state reserves. Entrepratchiks soon began to regard the state's accumulations much as Preobrazhensky had once urged Soviet leaders to regard agriculture: as a source of primitive accumulation. They came to find increasingly attractive the idea of further "privatization," so important to Western lenders.

It is possible (though unlikely) that socialist regimes would not have collapsed if their hard-currency crisis and the consequent intersection with capitalism had occurred at a different point in capitalism's cyclicity. The specifics of capitalism's own crisis management, however, proved unman-

ageable for socialist systems. Without wanting to present recent capitalism's "flexible specialization" as either unitary or fully dominant (its forms
differ from place to place, and it coexists with other socioeconomic forms),
I find in the literature about it a number of characteristics even more inimical to socialism than was the earlier "Fordist" variant, which Soviet production partly imitated. These characteristics include: small-batch production;
just-in-time inventory; an accelerated pace of innovation; tremendous reductions in the turnover time of capital via automation and electronics; a
much-increased turnover time in consumption, as well, with a concomitant
rise in techniques of need-creation and an increased emphasis on the production of events rather than goods; coordination of the economy by finance
capital; instantaneous access to accurate information and analysis; and an
overall decentralization that increases managerial control (at the expense of
higher-level bodies) over labor.[32]

How is socialism to mesh with this?—socialism with its emphasis on
large-scale heroic production of means of production, its resources frozen by
hoarding—no just-in-time here!—its lack of a systemic impetus toward innovation, the irrelevance to it of notions like "turnover time," its neglect of
consumption and its flat-footed definition of "needs," its constipated and
secretive flows of information (except for rumors!) in which the center could
have no confidence, and the perpetual struggle to retain central control over
all phases of the production process? Thus, I submit, it is not simply socialism's embrace with capitalism that brought about its fall but the fact that it
happened to embrace a capitalism of a newly "flexible" sort. David Harvey's
schematic comparison of "Fordist modernity" with "flexible post-modernity"
clarifies things further: socialist systems have much more in common with
his "Fordist" column than with his "flexible" one.[33]

Let me add one more thought linking the era of flexible specialization
with socialism's collapse. Increasing numbers of scholars note that accompanying the change in capitalism is a change in the nature of state power:
specifically, a number of the state's functions are being undermined.[34] The
international weapons trade has made a mockery of the state's monopoly on
the means of violence. The extraordinary mobility of capital means that as it
moves from areas of higher to areas of lower taxation, many states lose some
of their revenue and industrial base, and this constrains their ability to attract capital or shape its flows. Capital flight can now discipline all nation-
state governments.[35] The coordination of global capitalism by finance capital
places a premium on capital mobility, to which rigid state boundaries are an
obstacle. And the new computerized possibilities for speculative trading
have generated strong pressures to release the capital immobilized in state
structures and institutions by diminishing their extent.[36]

This has two consequences for the collapse of socialism. First, groups inside socialist countries whose structural situation facilitated their fuller participation in the global economy now had reasons to expand their state's receptivity to capital—that is, to promote reform. Second, the control that socialist states exerted over capital flows into their countries may have made them special targets for international financial interests, eager to increase their opportunities by undermining socialist states. These internal and international groups each found their chance in the interest of the other. It is in any case clear from the politics of international lending agencies that they aim to reduce the power of socialist states, for they insist upon privatization of state property—the basis of these states' power and revenue. Privatization is pushed even in the face of some economists' objections that "too much effort is being invested in privatization, and too little in creating and fostering the development of new private firms"—whose entry privatization may actually impede.[37]

No Time for Socialism

Rather than explore further how flexible specialization compelled changes in socialism, I wish to summarize my argument by linking it to notions of time. Time, as anthropologists have shown, is a fundamental dimension of human affairs, taking different forms in different kinds of society. The Western notion of a linear, irreversible time consisting of equivalent and divisible units, for instance, is but one possible way of conceptualizing time and living it. A given cultural construction of time ramifies throughout its social order. Its calendars, schedules, and rhythms establish the very grounds of daily life (which is why elites, especially revolutionary ones, often manipulate them), undergird power and inequality, and affect how people make themselves as social beings.

Capitalism exists only as a function of time—and of a specific conception of it. Efforts to increase profits by increasing the velocity of capital circulation are at its very heart. Thus each major reorganization of capitalism has entailed, in Harvey's terms, "time-space compression": a shrinking of the time horizons of private and public decision-making, whose consequences encompass ever-wider spaces owing to changed communications and transport technology.[38] The basic logic of socialism, by contrast, placed no premium on increasing turnover time and capital circulation. Although the rhetoric of Stalinism emphasized socialism as a highly dynamic system, for the most part Soviet leaders acted as if time were on their side. (When Khrushchev said, "We will bury you," he was not too specific about the date.) Indeed, I have argued that in 1980s Romania, far from being speeded up, time was being gradually slowed down, flattened, immobilized, and rendered nonlinear.[39]

Like the reorganization of capitalism at the end of the nineteenth century, the present reorganization entails a time-space compression, which we all feel as a mammoth speedup. Yet the socialism with which it intersected had no such time-compressing dynamic. In this light, the significance of Gorbachev's perestroika was its recognition that socialism's temporality was unsustainable in a capitalist world. Perestroika reversed Soviet ideas as to whose time-definition and rhythms were dominant and where dynamism lay: no longer within the socialist system but outside it, in the West. Gorbachev's rhetoric from the mid-1980s is full of words about time: the Soviet Union needs to "catch up," to "accelerate" its development, to shed its "sluggishness" and "inertia" and leave behind the "era of stagnation." For him, change has suddenly become an "urgent" necessity.

> [By] the latter half of the seventies . . . the country began to lose momentum. . . . Elements of stagnation . . . began to appear. . . . A kind of "braking mechanism" affect[ed] social and economic development. . . . The inertia of extensive economic development was leading to an economic deadlock and stagnation.[40]

These are the words of a man snatched by the compression of space and time.

Even as he spoke, new time/space–compressing technologies were wreaking havoc on the possible rhythms of his and other leaders' control of politics, as Radio Free Europe made their words at once domestic *and* international. Soviet leaders could no longer create room for themselves by saying one thing for domestic consumption and something else for the outside world: they were now prisoners of simultaneity. The role of Western information technology in undermining socialism was evident in the spread of Solidarity's strikes in 1980, news of which was telephoned out to the West and rebroadcast instantly into Poland via Radio Free Europe and the BBC, mobilizing millions of Poles against their Party. The revolutions of 1989 were mediated similarly.

I am suggesting, then, that the collapse of socialism came in part from the massive rupture produced by its collision with capitalism's speedup. If so, it would be especially useful to know something more about the life-experience of those people who worked at the interface of these two temporal systems and could not help realizing how different was capitalism's time from their own. Bureaucrats under pressure to increase foreign trade and foreign revenues, or importers of computer equipment, would have discovered that failure to adapt to alien notions of increased turnover time could cost them hard currency. They would have directly experienced time-annihilating Western technologies, which effected a banking transaction in milliseconds as opposed to the paper-laden hours and days needed by their own financial system. Did the rise of "profitability" criteria in the command economy owe something to such people's dual placement? Did they come to experience differently their sense of themselves as agents? My point, in short, is that the fall of socialism lies not simply in the intersection of two systems' temporal cycles but rather in the collision of two differently constituted temporal orders, together with the notions of person and activity proper to them.

If socialist economies had not opened themselves to capital import and to debt servicing, perhaps their collision with capitalist speedup would have been less jarring—or would at least have occurred on more equal terms. But the capitalist definition of time prevailed, as socialist debtors bowed to its dictates (even while postponing them), thereby aggravating factional conflicts within the elite. Because its leaders accepted Western temporal hegemony, socialism's messianic time proved apocalyptic. The irony is that had debtor regimes refused the definitions imposed from without—had they united to default simultaneously on their Western loans (which in 1981 stood at over \$90 billion[41])—they might well have brought down the world financial system and realized Khrushchev's threatening prophecy overnight. That this did not happen shows how vital a thing was capitalists' monopoly on the definition of social reality.

What Comes Next?

The outcome of the confluence between socialist and capitalist systemic crises is far more complicated than "capitalism triumphant," however. Ken Jowitt captures this with an unexpected metaphor, that of biological extinction and its attendant erasure of formerly existing boundaries among forms of life. In his brilliant essay "The Leninist Extinction," he pursues the metaphor's implications as follows:

> [One feature] of mass extinctions . . . is that they typically affect more than one species. In this respect, the collapse of European Leninism may be seen more as a political volcano than as an asteroid. A volcano's eruption initially affects a circumscribed area (in this case limited to Leninist regimes), but, depending on its force, the effects gradually but dramatically become global. The Leninist volcano of 1989 will have a comparable effect on liberal and "Third World" biota around the globe.[42]

After describing the new regime "species" that have emerged with changed forms of government in Poland, Hungary, Romania, and elsewhere, as well as other new forms of political life arising out of Yugoslavia and the Soviet Union, he ponders the larger question of the end of the Cold War:

> For half a century we have thought in terms of East and West, and now there is no East as such. The primary axis of international politics has "disappeared." Thermonuclear Russia hasn't, but the Soviet Union/Empire most certainly has.

Its "extinction" radically revises the framework within which the West, the United States itself, the Third World, and the countries of Eastern Europe, the former Russian Empire, and many nations in Asia have bounded and defined themselves.

The Leninist Extinction will force the United States [not to mention all those others] to reexamine the meaning of its national identity.[43]

What the Leninist Extinction confronts us with, then, is a conceptual vacuum. Jowitt concludes by invoking the biblical story of Genesis ("the world was without form, and void"), whose theme is bounding and naming new entities, as the "narrative" most appropriate to the immediate future.

In my view, not only is Jowitt absolutely right but one could go even further. It is not just new political identities, including our own, that we will have the task of bounding and naming—a task which, if the example of Bosnia is any indication, is of awesome magnitude. It is also the entire conceptual arsenal through which Western institutions and social science disciplines have been defined in this century. As one reads scholarship on the postsocialist processes of "privatization," the creation of "property rights," the development of "democracy" or "civil society" or "constitutions"—in short, the proposed building of a "liberal state"—profound confusion sets in. One begins to see that these terms do not label useful concepts: they are elements in a massive political and ideological upheaval that is by no means restricted to the "East."

If this is true, then everything we know is up for grabs, and "what comes next" is anyone's guess.

2

THE "ETATIZATION" OF TIME IN

CEAUŞESCU'S ROMANIA

THAT THE NATURE of time differs in different social orders has been a staple of anthropological analysis at least since Evans-Pritchard's work on the Nuer and Leach's classic paper on the symbolic representation of time.[1] Accordingly, anthropologists have catalogued the variant organizations of time in other cultures; they have also examined what happens when the bearers of non-Western or noncapitalist temporalities confront the new organizations of time brought to them by capitalist commodity production.[2] Such treatments of time as a social construction do not always make explicit, however, the political context within which time is experienced and the politics through which it is culturally "made." That is, to see time as culturally variable, with different conceptions of it functionally fitted to one or another social environment, is only part of the story. These conceptions themselves are forged through conflicts that involve, on one hand, social actors who seek to create or impose new temporal disciplines—either as elements of new productive arrangements or as the projects of revolutionary political regimes—and, on the other, the persons subjected to these transformative projects. In a word, the social construction of time must be seen as a political process.

In this chapter I explore temporal politics through an example in which regime policies created struggles over time, as people were subjected to and resisted new temporal organizations. The example is Romania of the 1980s,

This chapter was first prepared for a meeting of the American Ethnological Society in March 1989—thus before the end of Party rule—and revised slightly thereafter. I had not conducted fieldwork explicitly on the subject of time but marshaled ethnographic data from various field trips on other topics (pursued chiefly before the collapse of socialism, plus a brief visit in 1990) to make the argument. I am much indebted to Ashraf Ghani for extensive discussions that led me to frame this chapter as I have and for suggesting many of its central ideas. Thanks also to Pavel Campeanu, Gail Kligman, and Henry Rutz for comments on an earlier version. Three research grants from the International Research and Exchanges Board (IREX) supported my fieldwork in 1984–85, 1987, and 1988, which produced the data I report here.

The volume in which this chapter was initially published had made the relation between "structure" and "intention" its organizing theme, hence the centrality of these notions here. Reprinted from *The Politics of Time*, ed. Henry Rutz, American Ethnological Society Monograph Series no. 4 (Washington, D.C.: American Anthropological Association, 1992), by permission of the American Anthropological Association. Not for further reproduction.

prior to the violent overthrow of Communist Party leader Nicolae Ceaușescu in December 1989.[3] Both directly, through policies expressly aimed at the marking of time, and indirectly, through policies aimed at solving other problems but implicating people's use of time, the Romanian Party leadership gradually expropriated Romanians of much of their control over time. I call this process "etatization," a term borrowed from Romanian writer Norman Manea, who uses the word *etatizare* (literally, "the process of statizing") to describe the fate of people's private time in his native country.[4] While some might wish to render this as "*nationalization*," I prefer the more cumbersome "etatization" because in Romania the "state" and the "nation" have not necessarily been isomorphic: the activities of the state-occupying regime have often been at odds with what some would see as the interests of other inhabitants, the nation or "people." Although I will not make this distinction the basis of my argument,[5] one might phrase the struggle over time in Romania as, precisely, a struggle between "etatization" and "nationalization"—that is, a struggle between the state and the people for claims upon time.

I concentrate here on the "etatization" part of this struggle: the ways in which the Romanian state seized time from the purposes many Romanians wanted to pursue. There are a number of means through which time can be seized—rituals, calendars, decrees (such as curfews), workday schedules, and so on. My discussion focuses on the vehicle through which these devices organize time: the body, site of many possible uses of time, only some of which can be actualized. To phrase it differently, I treat time as a medium of activity that is lodged in and manifested through human bodies; that is, I emphasize not alternative *representations* of time but alternative *utilizations* of it. While acknowledging time's cultural element, I presuppose that there is an irreducible durative aspect in the passage of time no matter how it is constructed. Thus at a given level of technology, an individual can accomplish only so much in the space between successive midnights. If political decisions force more activity onto individuals within this space without increasing their technical capacities, then certain purposes or projects will go unrealized, and this prospect may provoke resistance. While my premise may seem a failure to problematize time as a cultural construct, I hold that, to the contrary, struggles over time *are* what construct it culturally, producing and altering its meanings as groups contend over them.

To "mark time" in a particular way is to propose a particular use or deployment of bodies that subtracts them from other possible uses. Alternative deployments of bodies in time reveal for us the seizure of time by power, which I will illustrate with some ways in which the Romanian state seized time by compelling people's bodies into particular activities.[6] Bodies subjected to such seizure had a few options, in response. They could voluntarily acquiesce in it, acknowledging the state's right to make this claim and accepting the hegemonic order within which it was exercised. They could acquiesce in form only, compelled to do so by the way in which time was seized and alternative uses precluded, but not necessarily agreeing with the claim made on them. Or they could resist the seizure of time, seeking to withdraw themselves for purposes other than those proposed from above. Many Romanians in Ceauşescu's era chose the second and third options. Whenever possible, they preferred to use their bodies in time toward reproducing households and local relations rather than toward promoting the power of the Romanian state and its ruling Communist Party.

In my examples, I distinguish loosely between the fates of time-invested bodies in urban and in rural settings, without further specifying their class situation. I also consider how time is related to the sense of self. Because social senses of self are intricately bound up with temporal investments in certain kinds of activity, incursions upon these activities have consequences for how the self is conceived and experienced. Therefore, I also describe briefly how the state's seizure of time encroached upon people's self-conceptions.

The Forms and Mechanisms of Etatization: Intention and Structure

I organize my argument in terms of the relation between structure and intention, viewing the etatization of time in Romania as the joint result of intentional projects of state-makers, unintended consequences of actions aimed at other problems, and structural properties of Romanian socialism as a social order sui generis. For my ethnographic examples to make sense, I should first characterize Romanian socialism in the decade of the 1980s, in terms of both the projects its leaders pursued and the inner logic of the social order itself, an inner logic only partly related to the leaders' intentional projects.[7] The tendencies I discuss antedated the 1980s but became especially visible then, as economic crisis sharpened their contours.

To a greater degree than in any other East European state, coercion combined with attempts at ideological persuasion were the basis of rule in Ceauşescu's Romania. This distinguished that regime from others in the region, in which material incentives generally played a greater role. The most extreme contrast in the bloc was between the virtual police state of Romania and relatively liberal Hungary, with its low level of police control and its high standard of living. Because the Ceauşescu leadership determined to reduce noxious "foreign interference" by repaying the foreign debt ahead of schedule, it imposed increasingly severe austerity measures beginning in 1980. These included massive exports of foodstuffs and other necessities, and significant reductions of imported goods and fuel, to slow the drain of hard currency. Expecting popular opposition, the regime intensified its apparatus of surveillance and repression. Persons who raised a protest were expelled or isolated by round-the-clock police watch; strikes or riots were put down by force; increasing numbers of persons were drawn into the net of collaboration, reporting to the Secret Police on the activities of their friends and associates. Under these circumstances, resistance tended to take covert forms,[8] such as theft of public property, laxity in work discipline, and constant complaining within one's intimate circle.

The exercise of coercion accompanied concerted efforts to raise popular consciousness in support of Party rule. Under Ceauşescu, activists strove to create a "new socialist man," a clearly intentional project that involved wholly new ways of constituting the person. Some of this, as I will show, was to be accomplished through new temporal markings. Another element of persuasion under Ceauşescu involved overt nationalism, partially (though far from wholly) explainable as an explicit quest for legitimacy.[9] National heroes were exalted, workers' energies were coaxed forth in the name of industrialization as a national goal, national enemies were built up in more or less veiled ways to mobilize the Romanian populace behind its Party's protective front. Previously inculcated national sentiments made this a lively field of activity, although not one of uniform agreement.

The intentions and projects of Romania's Communist Party leadership moved in sometimes coordinate, sometimes contradictory relation with a set of systemic tendencies that were not consciously planned. These tendencies resulted from the overall organization of socialism's political economy, with its collective rather than private ownership of the means of production, its central allocations, and its centralized management of productive activity. Basic to the workings of socialist firms, as described in chapter 1, were "soft budget constraints": firms that did poorly would be bailed out, and financial penalties for what capitalists would see as "irrational" and "inefficient" behavior (excess inventory, overemployment, overinvestment) were minimal.[10] In consequence, they did not develop the internal disciplinary mechanisms more often found in capitalist ones. Firms learned to hoard materials and labor, overstating both their material requirements for production and their investment needs. Thus these systems had expansionist tendencies that were not just inherent in growth-oriented central plans but were also generated *from below*. Hoarding made for unpredictable deliveries of inputs, which caused irregular production rhythms, with periods of slackness giving way to periods of frantic activity ("storming") when a delivery of materials finally enabled effort toward meeting production goals.

Central decisions together with hierarchical interactions between planners and producing firms, then, resulted in "economies of shortage" that generated "scarcity" in Romania, a scarcity primarily of supplies rather than of demand (the scarcity central to capitalism).[11] Time was implicated in such scarcity in several ways, but particularly as the medium through which labor would act in production to make up for the nonoptimal distribution of the other productive resources. Once enough materials were brought together to produce something, the task of the authorities was to seize enough labor time from workers to make up for earlier periods of shortage-enforced idleness. But precisely those periods of enforced idleness motivated the authorities to further seizures of time, for "idle" time might be deployed toward other objectives, and power might be served by interfering with them.[12]

Two examples will show how the Romanian Party seized time in order to increase the production of goods within the system of shortage I have described. The examples come from the period 1984–88, a period in which relative shortage was greatly exacerbated by massive exports of foodstuffs and reduced imports of fuel. Thus the "normal" systemic shortage was conjoined with explicit policies that worsened it.

One villager who commuted daily by train to an urban factory job complained to me of the irregularity of his work time. On some days he would hang around the factory doing very little, on others he would commute two hours to work only to be sent home owing to insufficient electricity; on still others he was required to work overtime, for which he was not paid. He would pay himself for the overtime by cutting work to help his mother plow, sow, weed, or harvest on the private plot they held as members of the collective farm. For such work, the mother would withdraw her labor time from the collective, whose requirements she had filled by bailing and stacking hay during the winter months, when her household economy could better tolerate her absence. Mother and son together produced enough food on their private plot to maintain four or five pigs, a number of sheep, and a good standard of living for their three-person household.

Beginning in about 1983, however, the state sought ways to move some of this "private" product into state warehouses rather than peasant cellars. At first, villagers were given a list of items and amounts—a pig, some chickens, one hundred kilograms of potatoes, and so on—that they were required to contract to the state from their plot, in exchange for a minimal payment. When this proved inadequate, each rural family was told not just how much of various goods to *contract* but exactly how much of each to *plant* on the private plot. Upon delivery of the contracted amounts, the family would receive coupons entitling them to buy bread at the village store; without the coupon they could get no bread. Because private plots were too small to grow cereals, purchased bread was most villagers' only option. The new contract requirements therefore effectively seized the labor time that had been given over to household production for household consumption; it added the products of that labor time to the meager output of state and collective farms. In this way, the authorities recouped a portion of the enforced idleness of their factory worker, as well.

Comparable seizures of time were also found in village households whose adults all commuted to work in the city. Such commuter households were assigned a quota of agricultural production alongside their regular jobs; failure to meet the quota might mean confiscation of their private plot. Because the private plot guaranteeing them something to eat was the main reason these workers had not moved to the city altogether, the sanction was an effective one: without the plot, household consumption would suffer. To keep their plot, commuters now had to pay a substantial "tribute" in extra work. Both these examples rest, of course, on the much earlier decision by the Party to collectivize land, enabling later seizures of the labor time embodied in rural folk.

These examples show rural households compelled into the state's definition of their use of time. The source of compulsion in both instances was the state's leverage with respect to household consumption, which villagers wished to protect. To these specific instances one could add many other ways in which central planning, shortage, and export combined to reduce individuals' control over their schedules to a bare minimum. Zerubavel, in a discussion of scheduling control, observes that "every scheduling process implies a combination of personal and environmental elements, the proportion between which is very significant sociologically."[13] Using the examples he adduces (from North American society), over what sorts of items had Romanians lost scheduling control by the late 1980s?

Urban dwellers could generally choose the time when they would use the bathroom, but their choice of when to flush or wash up was constrained by whether or not the public water supply had been turned off. Buckets of water stored in apartments might compensate, but not for bathing, which (if one wanted one's water hot) depended on having gas to heat the water. People could not choose the time when they would heat water or cook their meals, since the gas was generally turned off at precisely the times of normal use, so as to prevent excess consumption. Urban housewives often arose at 4:00 a.m. to cook, that being the only time they could light the stove. Unless one walked, no one could choose when to arrive at work, since public transportation was wholly unreliable (owing to measures to conserve use of gasoline), and the ration of gasoline for private cars was so derisory that cars did not provide an alternative for daily movement.

Although the natural environment usually controls when farmers must sow their crop, Romanian farmers were not permitted to plant by the timing optimal for nature: if tractors received no fuel allotment, there might be no planting until well into November or June. Village women lost control over when they would iron or do the laundry, for fuel conservation measures included turning off the electricity delivered to rural areas for large portions of each day—generally according to an unannounced schedule. Village women who commuted to urban jobs often found that there was no electricity when they returned home, and they were obliged to do the washing by hand. Electricity outages also prevented villagers from choosing when they would watch the two hours of television to which Romanian air time had been reduced. The state infringed even upon the most intimate decisions concerning when to make love, for the official desire for (and shortage of) more numerous laboring bodies led to a pro-natalist policy that prohibited all forms of contraception as well as abortion. This forced the "scheduling" of intimacy back onto the rhythms of nature.

To Zerubavel's strategic question, then, concerning who is authorized to schedule parts of the time of other people, we can reply that in Ceauşescu's Romania, national and local political authorities scheduled (or, better said, precluded the scheduling of) an extraordinary amount of others' time. Behind these appropriations of scheduling lay political decisions about how to manage austerity so as to repay the foreign debt. It is impossible to prove that an additional conscious intention was to deprive the populace of control over its schedules, but this was indeed an effect of the policies pursued.

Many of the regime's seizures of time were explicitly aimed at increasing production; yet these and other policies also had the effect, whether consciously intended or not, of producing not *goods for* the state but *subjection to* it. To clarify this I must introduce another structural element of Romania's redistributive economy. Redistribution, Eric Wolf reminds us, is less a type of society than a class of strategies implemented through various means.[14] Redistributors must accumulate things to redistribute, which form their "funds of power." A redistributive system delivers power into the hands of those persons or bureaucratic segments that dispose of large pools of resources to allocate. From the highest levels of the planning apparatus on down, therefore, actors strive to bring as many resources as possible under their control.

In socialist redistribution, it was generally the Party and state apparatuses that disposed of the greatest means for redistribution. The practices of socialist bureaucrats thus tended to augment the resources under the global disposition of the apparatus of power, a tendency Fehér, Heller, and Márkus see as the basic "law of motion" of socialist societies.[15] Particularly important, in their analysis, was that resources not fall out of central control into consumption but expand the basis of production for the apparatus. In other words, these systems accumulated *means of production*, above all.[16] Competitive processes within socialism's all-encompassing bureaucracy thus made inputs count more than production or outputs.[17] Inputs, however, might be both absolute and relative—relative, that is, to the resources commanded by other actors. To the extent that the resources of other actors could be incapacitated, the pool at the center would be enhanced. Jan Gross, from whom I draw this proposition, argues that Stalin's "spoiler state" produced its power by incapacitating those actual or potential loci of power that were independent of the state-sponsored organization. This regime's power came from ensuring that no one else could get things done or associate together for other purposes.[18]

This relative conception of power seems to me to illuminate a number of seizures of time in Ceauşescu's Romania. Their immediate "cause" was, again, a shortage economy strained to the utmost by austerity measures and exports; the effect was an astounding immobilization of bodies that stopped the time contained in them, rendered them impotent, and subtracted them from other activities by filling up all their time with a few basic activities, such as essential provisioning and elementary movements to and from work. My examples show us how shortages of certain items were converted into a seizure of citizens' time, but rarely for producing goods that might *alleviate* shortage. These seizures instead produced incapacity, and therefore enhanced power.

The most obvious example, all too often signaled in the Western press, was the immobilization of bodies in food lines. I see this as a state-imposed seizure of time because it was precisely the state-directed export of foodstuffs, alongside the state-supported crisis in agriculture, that raised to epic proportions in Romania a phenomenon also present in several other socialist countries. More generally, it was socialist policy to suppress the market mechanism (which, in Western economies, eliminates lines by differentiating people's ability to pay). Urban in its habitat, the food line seized and flattened the time of all urbanites except those having access to special stores (the Party elite and Secret Police). Meat, eggs, flour, oil, butter, sugar, and bread were rationed in most Romanian cities; they arrived unreliably and required an interminable wait when they did. During the 1980s other food items, such as potatoes and vegetables, came to be in shorter supply than usual, as well. Depending on one's occupation, some of the time immobilized by provisioning might be subtracted from one's job—office clerks, for example, were notorious for being absent from their desks when food hit the local store—but people like schoolteachers or factory workers had to add onto already-long working days the two or three hours required to get something to eat.

In a brilliant discussion of socialism's queues (of which the food line is the prototype), Campeanu offers additional insights through which we can tie the immobilization of bodies in food lines to the enhancement of central power.[19] Queues, he suggests, function as agents of accumulation. They do this, first, by reducing the opportunity for money to be spent; this forces accumulation on a populace that would spend but is not permitted to. Moreover, by rationing consumption, queues prevent resources from being drawn out of the central fund of use values administered by the state, which (according to the argument of Fehér et al. mentioned earlier) would reduce the reserves that form the basis of its control. Queues thus maintain the center's fund of power. Second, Campeanu argues, queues serve the larger processes of central accumulation through the unequal exchange that is their essence. The state is entitled to buy labor at its nominal price, but labor must buy the goods necessary for its reproduction at their nominal prices *plus* "prices" attached to time spent in line and to good or bad luck (i.e., being served before supplies run out). Thus the value of the labor force becomes paradoxically inferior to the value of the goods necessary to it, as waiting drives up the cost of consuming without affecting the price labor must be paid in the form of a wage. In other words, by making consumption too costly, queues enable a transfer of resources into accumulation. This forced accumulation is achieved by converting some of the "price" into waiting time[20]—that is, by disabling consumption as consumers' bodies are immobilized in lines.

Was there not some "cost" to the state, as well as to consumers, of immobilizing people in food lines? It must be remembered that socialist systems did not rest on the extraction of profits based in workers' labor time (a process quintessentially rooted *in time*). "Time wasted," for a capitalist, is profit lost. In socialist systems, which accumulated not profits but means of production, "time wasted" did not have this same significance. Time spent standing in lines was not a cost to the socialist state. This same time spent in a general strike, however, would have been costly indeed, for it would have revealed basic disagreement with the Party's definition of "the general welfare" and would thereby have undermined that central pillar of the Party's legitimacy—its claim to special knowledge of how society should be managed.[21]

Still other seizures of time derived from official priorities in allocating fuel, already alluded to. Some of the petroleum produced in or imported by Romania was exported for hard currency; beginning in 1984, this was facilitated by prohibiting the use of private cars for most of the winter. The remaining gasoline was preferentially allocated, first, to the chemical industry and other major industrial production; then to transporting goods destined for export; after that, to peak periods in agriculture; and only last to public transportation. Villagers who had to take a bus to town or to the train might wait for hours in the cold, or end by walking six to eight kilometers to the train station; residents of urban centers formed gigantic swarms at infrequently served bus stops; many urbanites preferred to walk long distances to work rather than be trampled in the melee. Vastly curtailed train schedules immobilized people for hours on end as they waited for connections. Trains were so crowded that most people had to stand, making it impossible to use the time to read or work (the more so because trains were unlighted after dark). No one has attempted to calculate the amount of time seized by the state-produced fuel shortage. Among friends with whom I discussed it, anywhere from one to four hours had been added on to the work day, hours that could be put to no other purpose (except, for some, to the exercise of walking).

The fuel shortage was converted into an additional "time tax" for residents of villages: it increased their labor. Labor-intensive agricultural production returned to replace mechanized agriculture, as tractors and harvesters were sidelined by insufficient fuel.[22] Tractor drivers sought to conserve their tiny fuel allotments by making the furrow shallow rather than deep and by increasing the spaces between rows. This produced more weeds as well as an inferior crop yield. Exports of petroleum reduced production of herbicides, which meant that the bountiful weed harvest had to be weeded by hand. The greater demand for labor in villages was part of the motive for taxing commuters with farm work, as mentioned earlier; added to the effects of reduced electricity upon the work of both urban and rural women, it greatly lengthened the working day for all.

Although the austerity measures responsible for these conversions of shortage into a "time tax" were not entirely the state's "fault," the peremptoriness with which they were executed lends credence to the notion that power was constituting itself through the effects of austerity. An exchange in the correspondence column of an urban newspaper illustrates this nicely:

> [Query from a reader]: "For some time now, tickets are no longer being sold in advance for long-distance bus trips out of Iaşi. Why is this?"
> [Reply]: "As the Bus Company director informs us, new dispositions from the Ministry of Transport stipulate that tickets should not be sold in advance, and for this reason the bus ticket bureau has gone out of service."[23]

As an answer to the question "why," the response leaves something to be desired, showing just how uninterested the authorities were in justifying the seizure of time. The distribution of time implied in the exchange was this: persons wanting to take a bus to another city would get up hours in advance of the scheduled departure (for one could never be sure how many others would be wanting to travel on the same day) and go stand in line before the booth that would open for ticket sales just prior to the departure hour. As usually happened in Romania, friends of the ticket-seller would have gotten tickets ahead, meaning that even those whose position in the line might lead them to think there were enough seats left for them could be disappointed, returning home empty-handed many hours later.

As this example shows particularly well, such seizures of time did more than simply immobilize bodies for hours, destroying their capacity for alternative uses of time. Also destroyed was all possibility for lower-level initiative and planning.[24] This was surely an advantage to those central planners for whom initiatives from below were always inconvenient; one cannot easily imagine such destruction of initiative, however, as the conscious motivation of the policy. The central appropriation of planning and initiative was furthered by a monopoly over knowledge that might have allowed people to use their time "rationally"—that is, otherwise. Not knowing when the bus might come, when cars might be allowed to circulate again, when the exam for medical specializations would be given, or when food would appear in stores, bodies were transfixed, suspended in a void that obviated all projects and plans but the most flexible and spontaneous.

The preceding examples illustrate how a shortage of resources, especially fuel, was converted into a seizure of time that immobilized it for any other use. I would add to these an additional set of examples in which the "time tax" exacted of people came not from conversions of shortage but from the simple display of power, which was by that very fact further enhanced. In a modest form, this was what happened in most of the interminable Party or workplace meetings that occupied much time for persons in virtually every setting; because meetings also sometimes accomplished organizational business, however, I do not count them. I refer, rather, to displays such as the mobilization of bodies from schools and factories to line the route, chanting and waving, whenever Romanian president Nicolae Ceauşescu took a trip or received a foreign guest. Delays in the hour of arrival seized more of the waiting crowd's time. (It was not just Ceauşescu who was greeted by the appropriation of bodies and the time they contained: so also were other "important" figures, including even the writer of these lines, who as part of a group of Honored Guests helped to appropriate the entire afternoon of a welcoming committee of schoolchildren.[25]) Every year on 23 August, Romania's national "independence" day, hundreds of thousands of people were massed as early as 6:00 A.M. for parades that actually began around 10:00 or 11:00. Because experience proved that parades could turn into riots, as of about 1987 these crowds were massed somewhat later, in closely guarded stadiums—to which, of course, they walked. There they witnessed precision drills, whose preparation had required many hours from those who performed them.

Here, then, is the ultimate "etatization" of time, seized by power for the celebration of itself. Tens of thousands of Romanians waited, daily, in contexts in which they could do nothing else: time that might have gone to counterhegemonic purposes had been expropriated.[26] Schwartz calls this "ritual waiting," whose cause is not scarcity in the time of someone being awaited. Ritual waiting serves, rather, to underscore the social distance between those who wait and whoever is responsible for the waiting.[27]

The various seizures of time in Romania were not distributed evenly across the landscape, for it was urbanites who waited the most: for transport, for food, for parades, for visiting dignitaries, for light, for hot water, for cooking gas. Villagers waited for buses and trains and light, but rarely for preorganized demonstrations, parades, or Honored Guests; their "time tax" came in the form of ever-greater claims upon their labor. The persons most removed from such encroachment were uncollectivized peasants living in the hills and not commuting to city jobs. Perhaps not surprisingly, these people were prime targets of Ceaușescu's infamous "settlement systematization" plan, which, by destroying their individual houses and settling them in apartment buildings, would bring them more fully under control, more vulnerable to seizure of their time.

What does all this suggest about the relation between intentionality and structure, and between "system logic" and contradiction, in the etatization of time? Without the possibility of interviewing high Party officials, one cannot say how many of the effects I have mentioned were consciously planned as such by Party leaders. I find it difficult to believe, however, that the austerity program behind so much of the etatization of time was intended to produce subjection: it was intended first of all to pay off foreign creditors. That its consequences for subjection may have been perceived (and even desired) is very possible. Those consequences emerged, however, as side-effects of other policies carried out within a system governed by tendencies peculiar to it (the dynamics of a shortage economy based on centralized bureaucratic allocations).

This is nonetheless not to say that "system logic" is inexorable, or that the effects to which I have pointed were characteristic of socialism everywhere. Specific policies of specific leaderships made a difference, setting up contradictory tendencies and exacerbating them. So did the environmental conditions peculiar to one or another socialist country. The command structure of socialism in East Germany, for example, was similar to that of Romania; yet its proximity to West Germany required East German leaders to maintain a standard of living closer to that of the West, which, together with subtle investment flows from West Germans, resulted in productivity and consumption higher than Romania's. The "economic crisis" that so exacerbated Romania's shortage came in part from the leadership's desire to pay off the foreign debt, instead of rescheduling it as did leaders in Poland. Romania in the 1980s gives us an excellent example of the extremes to which political decisions could push the "logic" of socialism, producing a form of gridlock rather than processes analyzable as somehow functionally "rational."[28] This extreme case reveals potentials not generally evident, through which we can improve our grasp of sociopolitical processes under socialism and their relation to time.

Spheres of Encroachment and Resistance

What was the Romanian state seizing time *from*? What activities was it incapacitating, whether by intention or by chance? To what other uses did people continue to put the reduced time left to them? To ask this question is also to ask where struggles against etatization were most evident—that is, where it issued in resistance to the state's encroachment. I will mention three areas particularly assaulted by the etatization of time: independent earnings, household consumption, and sociability. Each of these also constituted a focus of resistant deployment of time, resistances that—given the degree of coercion mobilized against them—were nearly invisible but nonetheless real.[29]

The widespread shortages of virtually everything, coupled with cleverly disguised reductions on incomes in people's regular jobs, pushed everyone into secondary and often illegal forms of earning (particularly lucrative for the consumer services rationed by queues). For example, waiters or clerks in food stores were in great demand as sources of food. They filched meat, potatoes, bread, and other items from their restaurants or shops, selling them at exorbitant prices to people who might have been so foolish as to invite an American, say, to dinner. (These practices naturally reduced the food available in shops and restaurants.) Gas-station attendants, in exchange for a huge tip, some Kent cigarettes, or a kilogram of pork, would sometimes put extra gas into the tank. Ticket-sellers at the railway station, if properly rewarded, might "find" tickets for crowded trains. People with cars would hang around hotels to provide black-market taxi service at twice the normal fare (demand for them was high, since the fuel allotments to regular taxis were so small that they were rarely to be found when needed). Drivers for the forestry service ripped off truckloads of wood to sell to peasant villagers and American anthropologists.

The sources of secondary income were legion, but the state's seizure of time pushed them in the direction of "hit-and-run" strategies requiring little time and few formal skills, rather than the moonlighting, spare-time sewing, extended house building,[30] and other sources of skilled earning for which people no longer had enough time. It was difficult for a schoolteacher to find a few extra hours for tutoring after she had stood in several lines and walked to and from work, or for a secretary to take home the professor's manuscript to type for extra pay. In consequence, Romanians built up their unofficial earnings not as much from parallel *productive* endeavors as from *scavenging*.[31] The authorities did everything in their power to punish behaviors like those I have mentioned, for outside earnings not only diminished the state's revenues but also mitigated people's utter dependence on their state wage, reducing the state's leverage over them.[32]

Examples of outside earnings merge directly into the second locus of struggle between a time-seizing state and resistant households. The forms of the state's seizure of time encroached particularly on the consumption standards of households, whose members reacted by trying to seize some of it back in one way or another. Theft from the harvests of the collective farm was one prime instance. Another was ever-more-sophisticated ways of killing calves at birth or shortly thereafter; this relieved the villager of the obligation to sacrifice milk to the calf and to produce six months' worth of fodder for it, as the state insisted, and also (though this was not the first aim) afforded the household an illegal taste of veal. (The killing had to be sophisticated because all such deaths had to be vet-certified as "natural" if one were to avoid a heavy fine.)

The extent to which foodstuffs—repositories of the time and labor of village peasants and commuters—focused the struggle over time was brought home to me in October of 1988, as I drove into the village of my 1984 fieldwork to pay a visit. Both early in the day when I arrived and late at night when I left, local authorities were out in the fields with those workers they had managed to round up for the potato and corn harvests, and the streets were crawling with policemen shining powerful flashlights on every vehicle that might divert corn or potatoes into some storehouse other than that of the collective farm. Whether on that night or on some other, numerous villagers would "recover" sacks of corn and potatoes from the collective farm, thereby recouping some of what they had been obligated to contract from their private plots. This enabled them and their urban relatives to eat better than they "ought" to. It also enabled a few other urbanites to avoid standing in food lines in October for the winter's supply of potatoes because—using the extra gas they had bribed from the gas-station attendant—they would drive their cars directly to a village and pay five times the market price to buy forty kilograms of potatoes from some peasant. The practice naturally furthered urban food shortages and was one reason why policemen randomly stopped cars to spot-check for transport of food, which they would confiscate. Such events further illustrate my claim that the apparatus of coercion was central to Ceauşescu's regime and to its capacity to seize time.

In addition to the state's seizure of time from secondary earnings and from household consumption, state policies threatened a third area: sociability, or the reproduction of local social relations. It was one thing to struggle for the resources necessary to maintaining one's household; to find enough food to entertain friends and relatives, however, was something else. In urban centers the decrease in socializing (upon which many people remarked to me spontaneously) was the direct result of unavailable food and drink. In villages, somewhat better provisioned with these items, incursions on sociability came from state attempts to mobilize village labor on Sundays and holidays and from strict rationing of certain substances essential to providing hospitality: sugar, butter, and flour. Romanian villagers mark Christmas, Easter, Sundays, saints' days, and a variety of other occasions with visiting sustained by cakes and wine or brandy (sugar is essential to making all these, butter and flour to making the cakes). The various seizures of villagers' time lengthened the hours that women had to spend providing these items of hospitality; rationing lengthened the time for procuring the ingredients;

being mobilized to weed on Sunday reduced the time for visiting; and exhaustion from the various taxes on time often reduced villagers' interest in socializing. In both urban and rural contexts, then, for different reasons, human connections were beginning to suffer from the etatization of time.

This tendency was significant for a number of reasons, not least the attenuation of social ties that might be mobilized in overt resistance to the regime. The chaos during and after Ceauşescu's overthrow gave indirect witness to the social disorganization his rule had produced. I wish to focus, however, on the implications of attenuated sociability for people's self-conceptions. This will enable me to discuss more broadly the ways in which the appropriations of time inherent in the state's projects were gradually eroding older conceptions of the person. Through these examples we can see how attention to temporality reveals links between state power and the constitution of self.

The State and the Self

I understand the "self" as an ideological construct whereby individuals are situationally linked to their social environments through normative statements setting them off *as* individuals from the world around them; thus understood, individuals are the sites of many possible selves, anchored differently in different situations. The self has been an object of intense interest for the organizations individuals inhabit, such as states and religions. Historically, the attempt to redefine the self in ways suitable for one organization— such as the state—and detrimental to another—such as the church—has been a locus of major social contention. Temporality can be deeply implicated in definitions and redefinitions of the self, as selves become defined or redefined in part through temporal patterns that mark them as persons of a particular kind.

For example, the periodicities of the major religions distinguish different kinds of persons.[33] A person is marked as Protestant by attending weekly church services on Sunday and by observing certain religious festivals, such as Christmas or Easter; a person is marked as Roman Catholic, in contrast, by attending mass not only on Sundays (if not, indeed, daily) but also on the holy days of obligation (All Souls Day, feast of the Immaculate Conception, the Assumption, etc.), more numerous than the holy days of Protestants. A person is marked as Orthodox by these rhythms of worship and also by the observance of myriad saints' days (which some Catholics also observe, but in smaller number). A person is marked as Muslim by multiple prayer rituals within each day, by religious festivals different from those of Christians, by special observance of Fridays rather than Sundays, and by the pilgrimage, which gives a distinctive rhythm to an Islamic life.[34] Jews, meanwhile, have long differed from both Christians and Muslims by special observance of Saturdays, as well as by a wholly different set of periodicities and sacred days.[35]

In seeking to create the new socialist man, the Romanian state moved to establish new temporal punctuations that would alter the sense of personal identity tied to the ritual markings of the week, the year, and larger periods. In contrast with the religious rhythms just mentioned, the identity of the new socialist man was to be marked by *non*observance of a fixed holy day, his day(s) of leisure distributed at random across the week.[36] Party meetings scattered irregularly throughout the week also marked socialist man as *a*rhythmic, within short periodicities. Over longer ones, his annual cycle was to be punctuated not by religious festivals but by secular ones—for example, New Year's, May Day, Women's Day[37]—and, increasingly, by national ones—Romanian independence day, the four hundredth anniversary of the enthronement of this or that prince, the birthday of this or that Romanian hero. Many of these latter observances, however, unlike those of religious calendars, differed from one year to the next: this year the two hundredth anniversary of the enthronement of Prince X, next year the four hundredth anniversary of the birthday of Hero Y. The arhythmia of these ritual temporalities echoed that of socialist production patterns, with their unpredictable alterations of slackness and "storming" to fill production quotas. If, as Zerubavel suggests, one effect of temporal regularity is to create the background expectancies upon which our sense of the "normal" is erected,[38] a possible consequence of socialism's arhythmia would have been to keep people permanently off balance, to undermine the sense of a "normal" order and to institute *uncertainty* as the rule.

The new periodicities aimed to supplant older ones that marked persons as Romanian Orthodox. This was met, however, by resistant self-conceptions, particularly over the suppression of religious holidays and, in the villages, over the Party's attempt to extract work on Sundays. Christmas was a major battleground, as factory directors announced that workers absent on Christmas day would not receive their annual bonus, while workers pulled strings to get formal medical statements that they had been absent for "illness." Peasants, harangued to present themselves for Sunday work, would hide if they saw their brigade-leader coming; or they would show up at the farm, having arranged to be called home for some "emergency" after half an hour. A similar tug-of-war took place between villagers and local Party officials whenever one of the many Orthodox saints' days fell on a normal workday. The Party defined this time as suitable for labor; villagers and the priest, by contrast, defined it as "dangerous," insisting that work done on such days would bear no fruit or even bring disaster. Behind these different interpretations lay something deeper, however: the definition of the self as secular member of a broad social(ist) collectivity, or as Romanian Orthodox member of a narrow household one.

In the context of variant self-conceptions, the erosion of sociability discussed earlier was very significant. Sociable gatherings would have cemented close solidary networks that might resist both the officially emphasized large-scale collectivism and the creeping atomization that regime policies produced. That is, sociability served to reproduce groupings intermediate between individuals and the social whole. The etatization of time prevented this, just as many other aspects of Party policy eroded the space intermediate between individuals and the state. In so doing, it incapacitated a major part of Romanians' conception of self, for in their view, to be Romanian—to be a person—is to offer hospitality.[39] If one does not have the wherewithal to do this, one is diminished as a human being. Some anecdotal evidence will support this claim. First, one hapless host upon whom a friend thrust me unannounced was complaining that it was impossible to entertain one's friends any more because one had nothing to offer them. To my matter-of-fact suggestion that maybe the food crisis would detach the idea of sociability from the offering of food, he stared at me open-mouthed, in shock. "Then we would be like Germans!" he said, "a people with a completely different nature!" This gentleman's self-conception was not unique; I encountered it often in my initial fieldwork in a German-Romanian village, where the offering of food was a principal indicator by which Romanians thought themselves distinct from Germans.[40] Second, like this man but in more exaggerated form, others upon whom I chanced without invitation presented their "paltry" offerings of food with a self-abasement I found unbearable.

Such instances brought home to me in a very direct way how shortages of food, the diminution of time that was associated with them, and the other "time taxes" that made provisioning so difficult had assaulted many people's self-image. The erosion of sociability meant more than the decline of a certain social order, marked by social observance of particular ritual occasions that reproduced solidarity among friends and family: it meant the erosion of their very conception of themselves as human beings.

Reports of friends suggested an additional assault on self-conception from the state's seizures of time. In one report, a friend had heard that eggs were to be distributed for unused ration coupons. Having a hungry eighteen-year-old son, she thought that by waiting at the store with a jar she might be able to get a few broken eggs without a ration card. She explained her idea to the clerk, who found one broken egg; after an hour another broken egg appeared. Another hour turned up no broken eggs, and customers had stopped coming. My friend approached the clerk in the now-empty store, suggesting that she simply break another couple of eggs and that would be the end of it. The suggestion evoked loud and anxious protests: what would happen if someone reported her, and so on. At length the clerk "found" one more broken egg, bringing the yield for two hours' waiting to three broken eggs. As my friend left the store, she burst into tears, feeling—in her words— utterly humiliated. The experience of humiliation, of a destruction of dignity, was common for those who had waited for hours to accomplish (or fail to accomplish) some basic task. Being immobilized for some meager return, during which time one could not do anything else one might find rewarding, was the ultimate experience of impotence. It created the power sought by the regime, as people were prevented from experiencing themselves as efficacious.

Such seizures of time were therefore crucial in the expropriation of initiative mentioned earlier; they were basic to producing subjects who would not see themselves as independent agents. They contributed to the "passive nature" by which many observers, including Romanians themselves, explained the lack of overt resistance to the Ceauşescu regime, as well as to the feeling many expressed to me that Communist rule was "ruining Romanians' character." The etatization of time shows how intricate—and how intricately temporal—were the links between sweeping state policies and people's sense of self, the latter being eroded by and defended from forces both intentional and systemic.

Finally, these links between the self and the etatization of time help us to understand better the regime's profound lack of legitimacy, amply illustrated in the manifestations of public hatred that accompanied the overthrow of Ceauşescu. These links become more perceptible if we define time in terms of bodies, as I have done here. By insinuating itself and its temporalities into people's projects and impeding those projects through the medium of people's very bodies, this regime reproduced every day people's alienation from it.[41] By stripping individuals of the resources necessary for creating and articulating social selves, it confronted them repeatedly with their failures of self-realization. As their bodies were forced to make histories not of their choosing and their selves became increasingly fractured, they experienced daily the illegitimacy of the state to whose purposes their bodies were bent.

Perhaps the contrasting trajectories of regime and social body from which these alienations emerged helps to explain the contrast between two different expressions of time, which increasingly characterized the pronouncements of regime and citizens during the 1980s. Pronouncements emanating from the top of society became more and more messianic, invoking amid images of ever-greater grandeur the radiant future whose perfect realization was just at hand; farmers and factory workers, meanwhile, increasingly invoked the Apocalypse.[42] For the Party leadership, time was in a process of culminating, of becoming *for all time*. For everyone else, however, time was running out. In December of 1989, it finally did—for the leadership, as well.

The preceding discussion suggests that the etatization of time in socialist Romania was quite a different matter from seizures of time at one or another stage in the development of capitalism. Although some of the time seized in Romania was put to the production of goods, much of it went instead to displaying power, to producing subjection, to *depriving* bodies of activity that might produce goods. Early capitalism seized the rhythms of the body and the working day, and it transformed them; it stretched out into a linear progression of equivalent daily units what had once been the repetitive annual cycles of an agrarian order.[43] The state in Ceauşescu's Romania seized time differently. First, it generated an arhythmia of unpunctuated and irregular now-frenetic, now-idle work, a spastically unpredictable time that made all planning by average citizens impossible. Second, within this arhythmia, it flattened time out in an experience of endless waiting.[44] Campeanu expresses this admirably: "Becoming is replaced by unending repetition. Eviscerated of its substance, history itself becomes atemporal. Perpetual movement gives way to perpetual immobility. . . . History . . . loses the quality of duration."[45] The loss of the durative element in time is wonderfully captured in the following Romanian joke: "What do we celebrate on 8 May 1821? One hundred years until the founding of the Romanian Communist Party."

"Capitalist" time must be rendered progressive and linear so that it can be forever speeded up—as Harvey puts it, "The circulation of capital makes time the fundamental dimension of human existence."[46] Time in Ceauşescu's Romania, by contrast, stood still, the medium for producing not profits but subjection, for immobilizing persons in the Party's grip. The overthrow of this regime reopens Romania to the temporal movements of commodity production, consumption, time-based work discipline, and initiating selves.

PART TWO

IDENTITIES: GENDER, NATION,

CIVIL SOCIETY

3

FROM PARENT-STATE TO FAMILY PATRIARCHS:

GENDER AND NATION IN CONTEMPORARY

EASTERN EUROPE

ASTERN EUROPE has been for the past half-century a major proving ground for experiments in both the social organization of gender and the attempted redefinition of national identity. Early pronouncements by socialist regimes in favor of gender equality, together with policies to increase women's participation in the work force, led optimists to expect important gains for women; the internationalist bias of Soviet socialism[1] promised to resolve the "national question," making national conflicts obsolete; and the Party's broadly homogenizing goals bade fair to erase difference of almost every kind from the social landscape. Had these promises borne fruit, socialism would have given "gender" and "nationalism" a wholly novel articulation.

Although socialism clearly did not liberate women or put an end to national sentiment, it did reshape them and (thus) their interconnections. My objective in this chapter is to offer some thoughts on how these two aspects of "difference" intersected under socialism and on what changes we might look for in the postsocialist period. I aim to raise issues for discussion rather than present a finished argument. I begin by defining what I mean by the terms "gender" and "nation," then sketch the gender regime of socialism, give some examples of gendered national discourse in socialist Romania, and look briefly at what has been happening with nationalism and gender since 1989 in certain Eastern European countries.

Gender had not been a subject of my work until I was asked to contribute a paper for a conference on gender and nationalism, organized by Catherine Hall and Judith Walkowitz and held in Bellagio in July 1992. I am grateful to the organizers and participants, as well as to members of the Johns Hopkins Women's Studies Seminar, for stimulating comment that assisted my revision. I could not have written the paper without the assistance of Gail Kligman, who provided much of the material on which it is based. Mary Poovey, Emily Martin, Kirstie McClure, and Lauren Sobel also offered helpful advice.

The data used in the analysis come exclusively from primary and secondary written texts, not from ethnographic research. This chapter first appeared in *East European Politics and Societies* 8 (1994) and is reprinted with the permission of the American Council of Learned Societies.

Concepts

I take "nation" and "gender" to be cultural constructs used both in academic writing and in everyday life (even, occasionally, with some overlap in those two registers). As constructs, they are made up—arbitrary—but through their utilization in social life they become socially real and seemingly natural. Both constructs are basic means of social classification. Each names a particular way of organizing social difference, a dimension along which categories indicating difference (male, female; Catalan, French, Polish) are arrayed. Each also implies both homogeneity and difference simultaneously, creating putative internal homogeneities that can be contrasted with one another *as* differences. Thus a given "nation" has no meaning except in a world of other, different nations, but a great deal of social effort has historically been expended on defining any given nation as distinctive by virtue of qualities *all* its members are presumed to share. The same can be said of gender or gender roles. Gender and nation exist in part as an aspect of subjective experience (national or gender "identities," for instance)—as a subjectivity that orients persons in specific, distinctive ways according to the nationness and gender attributed to or adopted by them. This subjectivity is, in turn, the joint product of prevailing cultural understandings and people's social situations. To examine the intersection of nation and gender is to ask how either of them implicates the other, in the way they are socially elaborated or lived.

Gender, as a construct, mediates the relation between bodies, as anatomical or biological givens, and social meanings about them. It is a symbol system by which bodies enter into sociality.[2] In this sense, gender can be seen as a fundamental organizer of the connection between nature and culture. Most gender systems construct a very small number of categories— usually two, "feminine" and "masculine" (with alternative forms generally seen as acceptable or deviant permutations of these). In making bodies social, gender enters into organizations of power and inequality to produce what R. W. Connell calls gender regimes, which consist of a gender division of labor, a gendered structure of power, and a structure of cathexis.[3] The term "patriarchy" refers to gender regimes whose inbuilt inequalities favor the occupants of masculine gender roles.

Nation, as a construct, mediates the relation between subjects and states (which are themselves social constructs too). It is a cultural relation intended to link a state with its subjects and to distinguish them from the subjects of other states. I use the term "nationalism" to refer to activity (including discourse) or sentiment that posits such a relation as important, whether it be oriented toward an existing state and its regime or toward some other state/ regime, envisioned as more suited to the nation's interests. The subjectivities integral to "nation" are fundamental elements of the basic political form of modern times, the nation-state. To the extent that the modern nation-state is defined in relation to a geographical territory, "nation" parallels "gender" in linking the physical "body" of the state to a set of meanings and affects, thus rendering physical space sociopolitical.[4] And because such events as war and military service involve the state directly in the bodies of its (male) subjects, the standard rhetoric of nation-states effectively ties together control over subject bodies and that over territory.

Actual nations are potentially infinite in number; the grounds for defining them, however, are more limited. Eric Hobsbawm mentions several of the meanings nation has had since ancient times, but for the modern world he identifies two main senses of it. These are 1) a relation known as citizenship, in which the nation comprises all those whose common political participation ostensibly undergirds collective sovereignty, and 2) a relation known as ethnicity, in which the nation comprises all those of supposedly common language, history, or broader "cultural" identity.[5] The latter is the meaning most often invoked with the term "nationalism" (which I sometimes sharpen by calling it "ethnonationalism," to signal the ethnic meaning). I would add to these a third form of cultural relation between state and subject, the form attempted under socialism—in Romania, frequently using the expression "socialist nation." It emphasized a quasi-familial dependency I will call "socialist paternalism." Instead of political rights or ethnocultural similarity, it posited a moral tie linking subjects with the state through their rights to a share in the redistributed social product. Subjects were presumed to be neither politically active, as with citizenship, nor ethnically similar to each other: they were presumed to be grateful recipients—like small children in a family—of benefits their rulers decided upon for them.[6] The subject disposition this produced was dependency, rather than the agency cultivated by citizenship or the solidarity of ethnonationalism. Sharing a kinship-familial metaphor, socialist paternalism and ethnonationalism as state-subject relations have a certain affinity. Indeed, in official discourses of Ceauşescu's Romania in the 1970s and 1980s, the two meanings are virtually impossible to disentangle.

Nation in these three (or other) senses can implicate gender in a variety of ways. Citizenship and political rights, for example, can be understood as applying differentially to women and men—or, to phrase it the other way around, notions of "male" and "female" can be elaborated in such a way that they intersect unequally with citizenship.[7] In many societies, women are citizens only by virtue of their ties to husbands and fathers; a man marrying a foreign woman makes her his nation's citizen, but a woman marrying a foreign man loses her rights; the offspring of men, but not of women, automatically become citizens; and so on. Similarly, ethnonational symbols may be thought of in gendered terms.[8] Other (weaker) nations may be "feminized" (and raped), and a national identity may be defined and protected by sequestering or defending "our" women from the allegedly insatiable sexuality of other nations' men.[9] Finally, socialist paternalism implicated gender by seeking to eradicate male/female differences to an unprecedented degree, casting onto the state certain tasks associated with household gender roles. From these examples, it is clear that both gender and nation are essential to the hegemonic projects of modern state-building, and that a prime vehicle for symbolizing and organizing their interface is the family.

The Gender Regime of Socialism

Although the socialist states of Eastern Europe and the Soviet Union differed from one another in important ways, I treat them as forming a broad class of societies more similar to one another, in certain organizational respects, than to other societies. I have presented in chapter 1 my analysis of the "workings" of socialism as a system—without, however, considering the place of gender in this.[10] In the following brief summary, I draw upon scholarship by Joanna Goven, Gail Kligman, Maxine Molyneux, and others, whose work helps to clarify the gender regime peculiar to socialism.[11]

Socialist systems legitimated themselves with the claim that they redistributed the social product in the interests of the general welfare.[12] Using this premise, socialist paternalism constructed its "nation" on an implicit view of society as a family, headed by a "wise" Party that, in a paternal guise, made all the family's allocative decisions as to who should produce what and who should receive what reward—thus a "parent-state." As Preobrazhensky put it, "The family must be replaced by the Communist Party."[13] While socialism resembled many other political systems in emphasizing the family as a basic element in the polity, I believe that it went further than most in seeing society not simply as like a family but as itself a family, with the Party as parent. Socialist society thus resembled the classic *zadruga*:[14] as an extended family, it was composed of individual nuclear families, but these were bound into a larger familial organization of patriarchal authority with the "father" Party at its head.[15] We might call the result a "zadruga-state."

Peculiar to the zadruga-state, as Goven and Dölling show, was a substantial reorganization of gender roles within its nuclear families, increasing the degree of gender equality in them.[16] The reason was that socialist regimes pushed an industrialization program that was (perforce) labor-intensive and capital-poor, necessarily requiring the labor power of everyone regardless of sex. More than any ideological commitment, this fact produced socialism's emphasis on gender equality and the policies that facilitated it. These included generous maternal leaves, child-care, and (except in Romania after 1966) liberal access to abortion, which enabled women to exercise greater control than before over this aspect of their lives.[17] Among the consequences of women's participation in the labor force was increased relative authority within family units, even as various state policies and the state's usurpation of allocative decisions undercut the familial authority of men.

While many commentators have remarked upon the ensuing "double" or even "triple burden" of housework, mothering, and wage work borne by women—that is, husbands assumed no more of the first two of these than before—it is nonetheless true that socialism also reorganized household tasks to some extent. First, relatively youthful retirement served to make unpaid household labor increasingly the responsibility of pensioners (as opposed to housewives), who stood in food lines, cared for grandchildren, cooked for their working offspring, and so on.[18] That is, social reproduction was to a degree "geriatrized." It nonetheless remained heavily feminized, partly because the tasks were considered women's work but also because pensioners were disproportionately female, owing to the sex imbalance in the elder age groups. (Hence the feminization of food lines.) Second, the zadruga-state's interest in their labor power led it to take upon itself some of women's "traditional" nurturing and care-giving roles. Policy statements underscored this: for example, the Central Committee of the Romanian Communist Party would periodically emit decrees that ordered local Party organizations to help protect and consolidate the family by ensuring good working conditions for women, providing more public eating facilities, and increasing industrial production of semiprepared foods and labor-saving devices for housework.[19] These policies plus the health system show how socialist regimes moved to assume aspects of the child care, housework, medical care-giving, and care of the elderly that in other societies were chiefly the job of women.

The zadruga-state could go further still, however: it might seek to "etatize" even the labor of birth itself. The most extreme forms of this appeared in pro-natalist Romanian policies of the 1970s and 1980s, discussed in detail by Kligman, which treated women's bodies as no more than instruments of the state's reproductive requirements. Obligatory gynecological exams were to ensure that pregnancies had not been terminated, and doctors were held responsible for natality rates in their districts, their salaries docked if birth rates were lower than expected. Thus not just women but also male doctors became agents of biological reproduction in socialist Romania.[20] Childless persons, both women and men, paid a "celibacy tax"—further evidence that birth was not solely women's affair. As Ceauşescu put it, "The fetus is the socialist property of the whole society."[21] In support of this premise, his and others' speeches repeatedly pointed to increases in the numbers of kindergartens, day-care centers, and maternity facilities and in the size of family subsidies.

In sum, socialism visibly reconfigured male and female household roles.

One might say that it broke open the nuclear family, socialized significant elements of reproduction even while leaving women responsible for the rest, and usurped certain patriarchal functions and responsibilities, thereby altering the relation between gendered "domestic" and "public" spheres familiar from nineteenth-century capitalism.[22] Biological reproduction now permeated the public sphere rather than being confined to the domestic one. At the same time, the space in which both men and women realized pride and self-respect increasingly came to be the domestic rather than the public sphere, as they expressed their resistance to socialism through family-based income-generating activities (the so-called "second economy").[23] In a word, families within the zadruga-state differed in fundamental respects from the organization of domestic and family life common over the past century in Western countries.

Not only were gender roles reconfigured; in many socialist policies, one sees a long-term goal of gradually homogenizing the entire "zadruga family" under its Party's wise patriarchal leadership.[24] The members of society were to form a homogeneous fraternity, tied to the "father" Party above them; differences such as those between male and female were to be effaced within a new set of discriminations—between good and bad Party members, or Party members and others—while women were expected, like men, to "militate" for the building of a socialist society and to be "heroines" of socialist labor.[25] Even when describing motherhood as women's supreme mission, for example, speeches by Ceauşescu and others simultaneously presented it as a "profession" (*meserie*) requiring a "qualification" (*calificare*); this use of terms drawn from industry helped to equalize "male" and "female" forms of work.[26]

In addition, women, like everyone in the society, had become dependents, wards of a paternalist regime that made the most important decisions in "the whole family's" interests. The dependent attitude the Party expected of this homogenized populace appears vividly in the Romanian media during the 1980s, which frequently invoked the "boundless gratitude" and "profound appreciation" of Romanians for the "parental care" and "exceptionally valuable guidance" of the Party and its leaders.[27] Horváth and Szakolczai's fascinating work on Hungarian Party activists gives further evidence of how cadres perceived the population they served as helpless, infantilized, and dependent—and worked to make it more so.[28]

Despite reorganizations of family roles and these tendencies toward homogenization, the structure of power and the larger division of labor in the socialist family remained decidedly gendered. As we might guess from imagery of the socialist family's wise Party "father," the state apparatus was heavily masculine. The core sectors of socialism—the bureaucracy itself, heavy industry, the army, and the apparatus of repression—were almost wholly male, especially at the apex, and were represented as such. In the state bureaucracy, women overwhelmingly held clerical and secretarial functions (as is true virtually everywhere). Women were indeed brought into political office, but generally at lower levels and in areas deemed appropriately female: education, health care, and culture.[29] Thus although these "female" roles had been to some degree taken out of the hands of mothers in nuclear families, they remained feminized in the broader division of labor of the zadruga-state.

Comparable gendering can be seen in the composition of the labor force. For example, in Romanian industry in 1985, 42 percent of the labor force was female, but women formed 80 percent of textile workers, 50 percent of those in electronics, and 30 percent of workers in machine construction; among white-collar occupations, women formed 43 percent of persons employed in science but 65 percent of employees in the more "feminine" jobs in culture, education, and the arts, and 75 percent of health care workers.[30] Like all socialist regimes, the Romanian one fostered a cult of heavy industrial production whose hero-workers were overwhelmingly represented as male, while agricultural production and activities related to consumption, including employment in the service sector, tended to be carried out by women and to be symbolized as such (to the extent that these production-oriented regimes gave any space to representing those activities).[31]

In addition to this persistent gendering of the power structure and the societal division of labor, a gradual refeminization of nurturance seems to have been underway during the 1980s (if not before). The reasons differed from one Eastern European country to another. In Hungary, for example, Gal reports that Party policy had begun pushing women out of the labor force and back into housework, so as to reduce the enormous cost of child care and care of the elderly.[32] Expansion of the "second economy" further reinforced "traditional" gender norms, associating men with the primary wage and women with supplementary work.[33] In Romania the impetus came partly from these cost concerns but more directly from the state's pro-natalist policy, which communicated a very mixed message concerning women's roles.[34] On the one hand, Party literature presented women as doing everything that men did: fulfilling the plan, solving problems, providing political leadership, and being a dynamic element of Romanian socialism. On the other, despite claims about the "fetus as social property," the press emphasized that mothering was the special task and privilege of women. Countless articles extolled women's noble mission as rearers of children and guardians of the nation's future. Some derived the strength of the mother-child bond from the fact that mothers stay at home to take care of the house and raise children, while fathers leave for work and for military service (with women constituting about 40 percent of the labor force, this description applied to exceedingly few families).[35]

Predictably, the implications of such emphases spilled over into the wider division of labor. For example, in 1973, the Central Committee of the Romanian Communist Party commanded enterprises to create good working conditions for women, so they could give more time to rearing children, and suggested the following provisions: extending work into the home, developing four-hour shifts and regular half-time positions for women employees, and providing early retirement for women with several children. The decree further observed that because women are best suited to certain kinds of work—those requiring low physical effort, such as electronics, optics, chemistry, food processing, commerce, and so on—the Party would establish a "nomenclatura" (special list) of jobs for which women would have first priority.[36] Thus the feminization of certain kinds of work was further institutionalized, in the name of mothering.

The message about women and childbearing became ever more insistent in Romania throughout the 1980s, as the birth rate continued to stagnate despite the unavailability of contraception and stringent penalties for abortion. Party literature now spoke of the Party's support of the "most beautiful traditions of the Romanian people: motherhood, and the bearing and raising of many children."[37] To document this new "Romanian tradition" of large families, there were articles such as the lengthy interview with two well-known historians, published in the Party daily under the headline "The Home with Many Children, Sign of a Good Citizen's Sense of Responsibility for the Future of the Nation."[38] In it, the two scholars discussed historical research proving that since its very beginning millennia ago, Romanian society had the family unit as its basic cell, preserver of its traditions and element of its progress. One asserted, in a blatant justification of patriarchy, that "only with the founding of a family does a man acquire his true social identity."[39] As these historians saw it, what had enabled Romanians not to be obliterated through centuries of war and invasion was their large families, producing a dense population that supported the rise of defensive medieval Romanian states. In a word, the family with many children was a fundamental aspect of Romanians' historical continuity since the time of the Dacians, over two thousand years ago.[40] We see here how Ceauşescu's socialist nation intersected with the ethnonation precisely on the issue of women's "nurturant nature."

Although Romania's pro-natalism was extreme, the tendencies it revealed were nonetheless evident elsewhere in Eastern Europe: a socialization of reproduction, in tension with various factors reinforcing patriarchal family norms, and a persistent gendering of power and of the work force. These features of socialism have several consequences for gender and nation in the postsocialist era. The most important of them is that the zadruga-state's incursions into women's nurturant roles opened both socialism and women to accusations of having jointly destroyed the ethnonation, the national character, and "traditional" national values. Nationalist politics in the post-

socialist period thus focuses on driving women back into their "proper" nurturant roles, recaptured from the deficiently mothering state, so as to reverse the damage to the nation. Work on the abortion controversy in Poland,
Hungary, and Croatia (to be discussed in the final section of this chapter)
shows precisely this line of assault on the positions women acquired under
socialism.

The Gendering of Nationalism in Socialism: Examples from Romania

Regime emphasis on building a "socialist nation" did not mean total erasure
of nation in the ethnic sense. This was particularly true of Romania, where
to a degree unparalleled elsewhere, Party leaders themselves embraced the
(ethno)national idea.[41] From the forms this embrace took, we see even more
clearly how thoroughgoing was the patriarchy of the zadruga-state, even as
it emasculated its nuclear-household heads and empowered women.

Nation as Tradition

The national idea has lain at the center of Romanian politics for two centuries or more. It shares with other ethnonationalisms in Eastern Europe (as
well as elsewhere) an obsession with Romania's territorial borders: with
where "the nation" ends, territorially speaking. There has been trouble on
nearly all borders but particularly on the western one with Hungary, for
many Hungarians contest Romanian sovereignty over multiethnic Transylvania, to which each side has an arsenal of "proofs" of rightful ownership.[42]
For Romanians, these center on arguments from ethnography and folklore—showing an unbroken Romanian peasant tradition—and from history
and archeology—showing unbroken Romanian continuity of settlement
from time immemorial.[43] Both arguments are served by the existence of regions where "tradition" still "lives"—where peasants still walk around in the
same garb as can be seen on Trajan's column, for example, or sing Christmas
carols mentioning events registered in antiquity.[44] The region par excellence
of this "living tradition" is Maramureş, in northern Transylvania. Its "tradition," and national rhetoric more broadly, are interwoven with gender.

From the official point of view—in the Ceauşescu regime's discourse
about tradition and in how its invented traditions were organized—tradition
was not gendered; it was equally male and female. But as Kligman's research
in Maramureş shows, tradition was effectively feminized.[45] This is partly
because regime investment policies drew Maramureş men out of the rural
labor force into industry or into seasonal labor migration, thus leaving peasant agriculture overwhelmingly female.[46] Therefore women were perforce

the bearers of a "traditional" livelihood, since they were the ones who stayed at home in conditions from which state policies had excluded economic "modernity." Moreover, the regime's very marginalization of Maramureş made it a locus of resistance to the political center. The tenacity of local custom became a sign of its resistance and produced an identity distinct from the regime's image of Romania as a "multilaterally developed" industrializing society. In women's centrality to life-cycle rituals and in their consumption styles ("traditional" clothing, food preparation, house decor, etc.) women reproduced this resistant localism more than did men. As Kligman puts it, "Women are now the practical tenders of tradition—for their families, their villages, and the state."[47] Her data show that in Ceauşescu's Romania, "modernity" in the form of industrial wage work was produced and figured by men, "tradition" by women.[48] This feminized tradition is, of course, crucial to Romanian claims to that territory.

Nation as Patrilineage

Nationalist texts from the Ceauşescu years also show a gendering of the "nation" and of "tradition," but in rather different ways from those just discussed. The Maramureş peasantry stabilized only a part of Romanian national identity (a very important part, of course, since it made Transylvania "Romanian" by the putative longevity of the region's folk customs); other parts of this identity rest on national history.[49] Not only Ceauşescu's speeches but all manner of newspaper articles, for example, included lengthy references to Romanian history. These nearly always presented that history as an endless sequence of male heroes, strung out one after another, almost like a series of "begats," and producing the impression of the nation as a temporally deep patrilineage. Here are parts of such a text, published in English under the title "Great Figures in the History of Romanian Genius":[50]

> A Romanian, and especially a foreigner who would make a study of the great figures in the history of the Romanian spirit, according to Carlyle's vision of the "hero," of "geniuses," of the great "makers of history," may not understand the precise way in which the history of the Romanian spirit took shape. . . . More than in the West, such figures acquire general collective features and, one after the other, enter "history," "tradition" and "folklore." Hence the response they arouse in the people, the assimilation of their message by ever broader sections of the Romanian people. The Romanians lack the egocentric vision of the great personalities. The[se] become "great" first by redeemed, recuperated collectivity. . . .
>
> One of the earliest figures of South-Eastern European dimensions, the Ruling Prince Neagoe Basarab, represents a synthesis between the Byzantine and

Romanian spirit, owing to the twofold cultural and architectural work he helped advance: *The Teachings of Ruling Prince Neagoe Basarab to His Son Teodosie*, and the church built at Curtea de Arges, a superb 16th century architectural monument. The Teachings, more especially, those contemporary with the work of Machiavelli, are a handbook of political and practical wisdom, dealing with ethic thinking, military art and pedagogy. The Romanian political spirit had reached the stage of theoretical, crystallized and codified presentation. It was a decisive step forward in the art of governing, in the relationships between the ruling prince and his subjects, in moral principles, at the opposite pole of "Machiavellism." Influenced by the Christian lore . . . the Romanian spirit constantly rejected cynicism and political amorality.

Two great, pre-eminently political figures, who lived in the 15th and 16th centuries respectively, embodied and gave memorable expression—traditional now—to the spirit of independence and resistance to foreign aggression, against invaders. One must never forget that this highly patriotic feature has left a deep imprint upon the entire history of the Romanian national spirit, where it can be traced as an uninterrupted presence.

Through the battles he won and the military defeats he suffered, through the foundation of citadels and churches, through his feudal yet uninterrupted cultural activity, Stephen the Great, the Ruling Prince of Moldavia, is the symbol of a great personality always present in legends, in folklore, in the great tradition of the Romanian people. The end of his rule marked the end of the independent political life of Moldavia. . . . His activity also belongs to the European resistance against the Turkish invasion. There is much truth in the thesis holding that the West was defended against the many waves of invasion by the fight waged by the peoples living in the East and South-East of Europe. The Romanian spirit, viewed in a historical light, possesses some of the legitimate pride stemming from a vocation and a feeling for the necessity of courage and sacrifice, in an area of expansion and passage to Central Europe or to Constantinople.

Michael the Brave is an epic figure . . . possessing a vision that exceeded by far the historical conditions of the epoch. His opposition to the Turks marked by a memorable date, the battle of Calugareni (1595), which he won under epic conditions—is a daring attempt at unifying the three Romanian lands (Walachia, Moldavia and Transylvania) under one single rule. The unification was achieved—though ephemerally—through a rapid campaign and his political acumen, and, though short-lived, it has lasted ever since in the national history of the Romanians. Thus, the awareness of the unity of the Romanian people, of its common origin and language, . . . became a reality for the first time. A spiritual tradition became an historical fact. . . . Treacherously murdered by his chance allies, Michael the Brave illustrates and consolidates through his death one more historical constant of the Romanian spirit: the value and significance of sacrifice, of the supreme sacrifice for the triumph of a lofty or common cause. One should not overlook the fact that masterpieces of Romanian folk poetry . . . belong to the same *ethos* of accepted, creative death, through the natural agreement between individual destiny and hostile forces.

All through the history of the Romanian people, the social and national awareness has brought about actions of equal symbolic value. When conditions of social and national oppression in Transylvania, at the end of the eighteenth century, led in 1784 to the outbreak of the great peasant uprising headed by Horea, Closca and Crisan, the execution of the three national heroes added one more foundation stone that helped build the edifice of the Romanian spirit. It was the contribution of spontaneous, "anonymous" heroes, genuine representatives of the oppressed masses of people. By means of such popular, anti-feudal explosions, the Romanian spirit, under highly unfavorable social conditions, asserted periodically its dignity, the dream of a juster and better life, of a more prosperous life. Due to its national and social fights against serfdom, the people acquired the awareness of its liberty, of its national and human rights, and demanded the abolishment of oppression and social discrimination. . . .

The 1821 revolt led by Tudor Vladimirescu, openly national [and] antifeudal . . . , gave a regenerating impulse to the social and national claims, an ethic consciousness once again marked by the supreme sacrifice of the leader of the revolt. Tudor Vladimirescu too was to die, murdered like his forerunners and fellow-sufferers in their collective sacrifice.

The 1848 Revolution in all the Romanian Principalities is the first expression of the bourgeois democratic spirit, accompanied by a great national and social elan. It was dominated by the pure image of Nicolae Balcescu, who stands out most clearly as an ideologist, historian and politician possessing a vast European vision. . . . Nicolae Balcescu contributed his fervour, an ardent revolutionary spirit, a radical democratic consciousness, complete devotion to the cause. The modern democratic Romanian political spirit won in him its first ideal exemplary figure. . . .

The figure of the national poet Mihai Eminescu possesses the same shaping quality and spiritual significance as any promoter, social or political, of the Romanian historical awareness. Eminescu gave powerful expression to the national consciousness of the Romanians, he also gave Romanian poetry its true dimensions, he transformed the Romanian language into an exceptional means of expression and fixed in the hearts and minds of millions of Romanian people the effigy of the "poet" and of the "genius," thus the encounter with great Art, with Poetry. Through such a representative, the Romanian spirit was not only enriched, but it also became universal, more subtle and purified. . . .

The prominent representatives of the Romanian culture and spirit mentioned so far constitute a brief selection from a large number of personalities whose names echo solemnly in the remoter or more recent history of the Romanian people.

In line with the great humanistic traditions of the Romanian people, in the vast context of historical revolutionary transformations in Romania, the outstanding personality of Nicolae Ceausescu expresses, in a striking militant hypostasis of a modern, independent, fully sovereign socialist country, the loftiest aspirations of the Romanian spirit.[51]

This text, as suggested earlier, presents Romania as an extended patrilineage of "heroes" living "exemplary" biographies. Their biographies all emphasize heroism and triumph, along with victimization and sacrifice—things they share as individuals with the nation that unites them, "Romania." The passage constructs a national self that is collective and has collective rather than individual interests—that is, it constructs the nation as a "collective individual."[52] This collective individual acts as an entity: it does things, fights for its freedom, asserts its dignity, participates in world culture, possesses legitimate pride, rejects cynicism, and so forth. Such a collective individual generally also *possesses*: it "has" a culture and a bounded territory and a character or spirit.[53] The one presented here seems to consist largely of "sons" (sometimes with their fathers), culminating in Ceaușescu, who was usually referred to as the "most beloved son of the nation." The excerpt's complete silence on *female* "geniuses" eloquently renders men the dynamic, active, heroic principle. (In school manuals during the socialist period, some effort went into finding the occasional exemplary female, but they rarely appear in Ceaușescu's speeches or articles in the popular press, except in women's publications.)[54]

There is nothing especially unusual in this. As George Mosse has shown, much nationalism rests on homosocial masculine bonding.[55] It suggests a peculiar kind of lineage, however, one that reproduces itself without recourse to females or even to sex. In this excerpt, emphasis falls primarily on the national spirit and its reproduction through culture (created by men) or through men's creative death—that is, women may create life in this world, but more fundamental to the nation's continuity is its life eternal, ensured through culture, heroic deeds, and qualities of the spirit: the realm of men.[56] The theme of sacrifice and creative death in this excerpt permeates both Romanian historiography and important Romanian folk tales (not to mention other nationalisms).

There are interesting parallels between this image of a collective Romanian nation reproduced without women's intervention and the biblical creation story Carole Pateman sees as the originary myth for models of patriarchal civil society (the myth that stands at the root of the citizenship meaning of "nation"). Adam—like the zadruga-state and like the eponymous ancestors of Romanians—is both mother and father, representing the procreative power of a male complete in himself; Eve springs from him, after all. Thus woman's procreative capacity is "denied and appropriated by *men* as the ability to give *political birth*, to be the originators of a new form of political order."[57] These parallels show a patriarchal imagery underlying both ethnonational and citizen nation, collective entities nurtured and midwifed by the heroic deeds and sacrifices of men.

Nation as Lover/Beloved

The patrilineages of this kind of history writing do more than simply procreate the nation. They also provide the source of sentiments necessary to procreating it, and here they join with other elements of national culture such as poetry and art. In exploring this issue, I follow Connell's suggestion that an essential component of any gender regime is its structure of cathexis, or gender patterning of emotional attachments.[58] I see this as providing a clue to a problem I do not find persuasively treated in literature on nationalism: how national sentiment becomes cathected—how subjects come to feel themselves national.[59]

Let me illustrate by means of a second excerpt (henceforth referred to as "excerpt 2," the one above being "excerpt 1"). It comes from a long essay by Romanian poet and writer Ion Lăncrănjan, in his book *A Word about Transylvania*.[60] Unlike the previous one, this text was produced not for an international audience but for a local one. It offers a self-definition of Romania and Romanians implicitly against Hungary and Hungarians. Its context was increasing friction between Romania and Hungary, evident in writing by historians throughout the 1980s and probably related to the increasingly divergent strategies of the Ceauşescu and Kádár regimes—ever-greater coercion vs. ever-greater market forces.[61] Accompanying this friction was evidence of heightened attachment (on the Romanian side) to the idea of "Romania" and to the contested soil of Transylvania.[62] These two themes are apparent in excerpt 2:

Patriotism—A Vital Necessity
Only One Love

As a child, you think the world begins and ends with the threshold of the house where you were born, with the edge of the village or town in which you first saw the light of day, with the light that first set the boundaries of your sight. As an adolescent, you think that your first love is your only true and great love, in comparison with which the stars in the sky grow pale and the lilies fade, along with everything that is alive and mortal, for, or so you then think, only this love of yours, around which everything else turns, even the land and the waters, is undying. Things change after that, you realize the world is bigger and more comprehensive, and loves succeed one another endlessly, yet over them all there arises out of nothing, when you aren't even aware of it, a single and inextinguishable love[63]—love of your country [*patria*], love of your native land and of the places of your birth and of the nation [*neam*][64] you come from, that unstinting love that overpowers, time and again, that grows and opens itself to the light as you yourself grow and are clarified in and toward the world, a love that intersects with and fraternizes with your first love and with all your other loves, for only those who are capable of love are able to love their country and their people, only those who are good and generous, only those who know the weightiness of speech and the earthquake of self-abandon can raise themselves up to the height of this profound and powerful sentiment.

We will see, if we look back, that the most notable sons of the Romanian people, the most enlightened and gifted, the best and most just, the most honest and sincere, the most daring, passed through the fire of this sentiment, gave themselves to it without restraint, gave themselves in fact to the country and the people they were descended from. The life and work of Eminescu,[65] for instance, are inconceivable without this self-giving, without this sacred love, which his genius purified for all time, raising it up into the undying light of eternity, and in its light he himself was pulverized, without stopping to waver, without awaiting sustenance or payment from somewhere, carrying everything through as if preordained to happen thus so that our country, Romania, and our ancestral language, our culture, in its entirety, might acquire a new and deeper self-awareness. The pathos of the life of this great poet, whose feet trod all the regions inhabited by Romanians so as to hear their speech and know their aspirations and legends, his tremendous labor, of inestimable value, everything that this superb man wrote and did, stood under the sign of his great and earth-shaking love, for in his unique and exemplary case, things took a dramatic if not indeed tragic turn, so deep was his ardor, so pure, so unhesitating, so total, that it was transformed at last into an undying flame.

The same things can be said also about Bălcescu, about Iorga, and about Sadoveanu.[66] Bălcescu, especially, can be compared only with Eminescu, for the same fire consumed him, too; he too put above everything, above satisfactions and glory, his love for his people and his country, where he would have wanted to die but where he did not manage to return, dying instead in the loneliness of strangers and entering thus into eternity. The other two men, Iorga and Sadoveanu, seem less legendary, being closer to us in time. But the pathos of their lives also stood under the sign of love of their country and people, which both of them served in their own ways, with self-abnegation.

Nor should we forget, besides the example of these notable men and of so many others—the always-fresh and ever-unsullied example of the man of the people, the example of the people itself, for it was the parent and the teacher of all, it ascended the "Golgothas" of the centuries, bleeding and gnashing its teeth, believing so much in its own star, having such strength in its manner of being—its beauty, and sensibility, and intelligence, and vivacity, and love, and

longing—that it overcame everything in the end: centuries of hostility, subjuga-
tion, and dependency, being itself that which its most important men were: the
people of an earth-shaking, profound, and pure love. . . .

Love, any love, raises up and purifies, and love of country, love of your places
of birth, of your people, gives another meaning to everything, raising everything up onto the high platform of all accomplishments, making of yesterday's
child a daring and clear-headed man, transforming the adolescent into a hero,
as has so often happened, as will happen again, and as ought to happen.

Romania—Eye of the World

Romania is my natal land, the land of my dreams, the land of my longing. . . .
Romania is my land of origin, it is the old song of the flute and the quiet whisper
of the plowed field that is almost ripe; . . . it is the far-away and almost forgotten
tinkling of the shepherd's pipe that brightens the mountainsides of an eve-
ning—it is the land with the name of a girl and the fiery soul of a fiery man! . . .

Romania is the land that paid with sweat and tears—and often, much too
often, with blood—for whole days and years of its tumultuous history, it is the
land across which came massive waves of fire and smoke, it is the land that
always refound its being in its own soil, in its mountain springs, in the quiet of
its glades, in the fascinating journey through its fascinating landscapes, in its
just and honest judgment, owing to which no one can push you aside or destroy
you if you rely on what is yours, if by your work and your struggle you have
become one with the soil on which you tread!. . .

Romania is the land whose boundaries give it the shape of the sun, "plump,"
as our unforgettable poet Blaga would have said; it is a land with so much
beauty, so rich and so good, so generous and credulous and endowed so bounti-
fully—that you can't capture it in words, you can't paint it on paper in all its true
and radiant splendor, you keep missing something: a leaf that is dying, a flower
opening its corolla toward the sky, the rumbling of a mountain storm or the
endless calm of the sea, the deep breathing, barely perceptible and barely felt,
of the plain at sunset, the peaceful song of the regions between the Carpathians
and the East, the silver trill of the swallow!

Romania is the land of some unforgettable men, the land of Bălcescu, the
land of Horea and Iancu, of Michael the Brave and Stephen the Great, the land
of the Basarabs, of Gelu and the Mușatins,[67] the land that never let itself be
conquered, that met difficulty with quiet and patience—and how often that
was! . . .

Romania is a hardworking and capable land, exceedingly capable, with the
most diverse and unexpected inclinations, and even if it was also often sad, in
a distant and not-so-distant past, the reason is that the fruits of this indus-
triousness were often taken from it, outright or indirectly through the usual
base perfidy, and it was left more often than not only with tears and weeping. . .

Romania is the land of the truest independence, a land now geared into a profound process of renewal, it is a land penetrated from one end to the other by the manly, powerful, and rising hum of machines; it is a land that adds to its old jewels other, more valuable ones, a land that makes the strong waters into current and electric light, a land in which fires burn constantly—at the [steel mills in] Hunedoara, Galaţi, Reşiţa and other places! . . .

Romania is the land of friendship, a hospitable land full of understanding and of respect for everyone, eager to assimilate all that is good and beautiful, wanting only to be respected, understood, and appreciated justly for its hard work! . . .

Romania is the eye of the world, an eye that is clear and watchful, sensitive to the finest nuances of the light, deep and vibrant, with rustling eyelashes of rustling grain stalks, with melancholy eyelids and with rough hiding places of a rough audacity, with the clearness of great and calm waters, with undreamt-of openings toward the future! . . .

Romania is my natal land, the land of my origin, with which I am so much and so fervently in love that if I should happen to die who knows where, in a distant and foreign place, I would rise up again on my feet and I would walk back here, to my country, to these loved and known places! But let us not speak of death, now when it is more appropriate than ever to speak of life, of that which was and will remain imperishable in the soul of this land with the name of a girl and the rough steadfastness of a rough man![68]

These two essays, like the one preceding them, construct a collective individual made up of sons and unforgettable men, and they emphasize heroism and self-sacrifice, triumph and victimization. But they also do something more: they explicitly work on sentiment. The excerpts show clearly how central gender is to eroticizing the nation: male heroes burn with ardor for a feminized "Romania" who has eyelids and eyelashes, is "plump," has the "name of a girl," and is overtly linked with a man's first adolescent *amour*. Whereas the unstated emotional underpinnings of national solidarity in excerpt 1 are a simple admiration of heroes or, at best, loyalty to a kinship line, the love appropriate between a son and his father, in excerpt 2 this becomes an (almost incestuous) erotic attachment between "Romania" and her "sons."

To create the basis for this erotic attachment requires identifying two separate elements that can be joined. In this text, "Romania" becomes divided into two components: a container or receptacle (a kind of house) and the thing contained, the residents. Each has gender connotations and is linked with additional oppositions. The container is feminine and the residents masculine, the space of "Romania" is feminine and the temporally deep lineage of its inhabitants (those "unforgettable men") masculine, the body is feminine and the soul masculine. That is, space is feminized and time masculinized, and "Romania" is given a female body and a male soul (the "fiery soul of a fiery man"). The homeland becomes the inactive female object of sentiment, while the male subject is a historically acting subject, themes very common in modern conceptions of identity.[69] Thus we cannot say that this collective individual "the Romanian nation" is strictly masculine, as appeared to be so in excerpt 1: here it is an active (masculine) principle intimately tied to a (passive) feminine space—territory—which the masculine principle will defend.[70]

The feminization of space deserves further comment. In Romanian historiography, where national victimization is a central theme, this victimization often has a spatial dimension: the barbarian violates Romania's borders, rapes her,[71] mutilates her. The Soviet annexation of Bessarabia is widely referred to as the rape of Bessarabia, and the temporary annexation of Transylvania by Hungary in 1940–44 is seen as a bodily mutilation. (Similarly, when Hungary lost Transylvania after 1918, images of this showed the beloved motherland's "white and virginal but mutilated and bleeding body," and politicians spoke of a "revered body . . . torn asunder and ravaged by barbarians.")[72] The most obvious basis for seeing this violated space as feminine is the (Western) association of the female with body and nature, as in landscape. One thinks of all those metaphors of men plowing the fields, as well as the images—ubiquitous in so much celebrated art—of prostrate female nudes, like material nature the passive object of the active gaze and actions of men.

This association, one not confined to the case at hand, achieves two things. First, it naturalizes/genders the question of territorial boundaries, so vexed in the nineteenth- and twentieth-century history of Eastern Europe. It makes these boundaries like the skin of the female body, fixed yet violable, in need of armed defense by inevitably masculine militaries ("sons" defending their "motherland," their "mothers," and their "beloveds"—conveniently conflated). Second, it establishes a gendered structure of cathexis, a set of sentiments, to support this armed defense.

We therefore see in excerpt 2 the outlines of a set of antinomies familiar in Western thought and especially in Romanticism:

$$\frac{\text{woman}}{\text{man}} \sim \frac{\text{beloved}}{\text{lover}} \sim \frac{\text{body}}{\text{soul}} \sim \frac{\text{nature}}{\text{culture}} \sim \frac{\text{land}}{\text{people}} \sim \frac{\text{space}}{\text{time}} \sim \frac{\text{birth}}{\text{(creative) death}}$$

That is, we see something paralleling the values of a "traditional bourgeois" gender regime, and this organization sustains a cathexis of the national sentiment as like, but better than, one's first love. Does the excerpt reveal a form of resistance (perhaps unacknowledged) to socialism's reconfiguration of household gender roles by usurping male authority and empowering women, in relative terms, as allies of the state? Or does it reveal, rather, the "deep structure" of a higher-order patriarchy, essential to the zadruga-state? That a text permeated with the preceding antinomies can exist at the heart of this zadruga-state, written by one of Ceauşescu's favorite poets, indicates that however radical socialism may have been in reorganizing family structures and roles at one level, at another its paternalism dovetailed perfectly with patriarchal forms central to national ideas elsewhere in the West. What happens to these two levels of gender organization with the fall of socialism, and how does the national idea figure in the outcome?

Postsocialist Nationalism and Antifeminism: Examples from Hungary, Poland, and Croatia

With the end of socialism, the prior differences among the countries of Eastern Europe have been accentuated, yet one unsettling commonality is evident in nearly all: increasingly visible ethnonationalism, coupled with antifeminist and pro-natalist politicking. Much of it centers on the issue of abortion.[73] Only in Romania is there (so far) no active antiabortion movement, because the earlier ban on abortion there has made people all too aware of the costs; but even in Romania, Kligman detects the same "retraditionalization"—a return to "traditional values," family life, and religion, with women's place once again to be in the home.[74] Elsewhere, abortion was more or less readily available, and as is clear from recent work, nationalism and opposition to abortion are working hand in hand, together with assaults on the position of women in the labor force and in public life.[75] As a male Hungarian worker told anthropologist Eva Huseby-Darvas, "The ideal situation would be if from now on all women could stay home as Hungarian mothers should, and if men could, once again, earn enough to support their family."[76]

The connection is strikingly visible in slogans such as "The Unborn Are Also Croats" and "Abortion Is Genocide."[77] It appears also in political arguments about the "seventeen million murdered fetal Polish citizens" or the "five million Hungarians" dead in "our Hungarian Holocaust," killed by the thirty-five years of the Communists' liberal abortion policies and the selfish women who took advantage of them—and still want to.[78] In Croatia, conservative groups, funded by private sources, the Catholic Church, and international pro-life organizations, are taking the liberal abortion law to court with arguments about the family as the fundamental unit of a nation; their feminist opponents are treated as subversives.[79] Nationalists in Hungary have gone so far as to compare the aborted Hungarians with the (many fewer) dead from Hungary's worst historical military disasters (the Turkish defeat in 1526, the battle of Stalingrad in World War II) and to erect, in the town of Abasár, an "Embryo Memorial" to those sacrificed Hungarians.[80] They refer to pro-abortion feminists as "murderers of mothers" and hold women responsible for the "death of the nation."[81]

The most extended analysis of these trends is Joanna Goven's, based on data from Hungary.[82] Her argument, more complex than I can summarize here, roots this reaction in the way the pre-1989 opposition to socialism reinforced "traditional" family roles, and this is now exaggerated as the opposition takes over the running of society. New political movements are reversing women's gains under socialism and their increased control (except in Romania) over reproductive decisions. In other words, the zadruga-state's usurpation of familial-patriarchal authority is now giving way to policies and attitudes aimed at recovering that lost authority for men in nuclear families. The politics of this involves "othering" women as allies of the Communists.[83] Because Communism proved itself the enemy both of nature, by trying to make humans be what was "contrary" to their acquisitive and deeply gendered "nature," and of the nation, which it almost killed off by permitting birth rates to fall, the women who became its allies (or at least careerist, feminist women) must therefore be enemies of the nation, too. So a nationalist politics now proposes to reshape the nation against the debilitating "mothering" of socialism. This entails reconfiguring the family yet again, compelling women back into the nurturing and care-giving roles "natural" to their sex and restoring to men their "natural" family authority.

Goven offers some stunning material to illustrate this. She cites political texts that speak of the need for Hungarian men to become real men again instead of the wimps that socialism had made them; if they do, then women will automatically want to be their subordinates once more.[84] Numerous writings express concern with or disapproval of the "matriarchy" that had become all too common in Hungary.[85] They argue that "socialist mothering" made men weak and lacking in authority, and to alter this requires restoring autonomy to the family and authority to the father: mothers should be dependent not on society but on their husbands.[86] Essentialism pervades these writings, with their emphasis on "natural differences" that suit women to homemaking functions. Even more important are texts decrying the aggressiveness (especially in sexual matters) that socialism encouraged in women, and above all their destructive aggressiveness within the family; women, such texts complain, have ceased to be affectionate and understanding.[87] I see this as further confirmation that what is at issue is precisely women's nurturing and emotional roles, weakened by socialism's having assumed them so women could work.

Thus, Goven's data suggest, political pluralism and the restoration of capitalism in Hungary are bound up with the reimposition of certain "bourgeois" family norms. This is the more necessary as the welfare state of socialism is forced to shuffle off many of its functions: there is no longer enough money for all those day-care centers and kindergartens, for lengthy maternity leaves and family allocations—in a word, for socialized reproduction. Nurturance must re-devolve onto women, then, and politics must assist this by reining in all those aggressive Hungarian wives and mothers so derelict in their duty to the nation.[88] Here, for example, is Kata Beke, Hungary's first secretary of education under the HDF government in 1990: "In the rich store of historical examples . . . the European model of marriage has proven to be the most successful and resilient. Because it corresponds to humanity's two-sexed nature, to the set of complementary differences hidden in our genes. Because only here [in Europe] can a new generation grow up in a normal—that is, two-sexed—world."[89] Only if gender polarity is restored, argue political groups across the spectrum, will Hungary again become a healthy society.

There is some evidence that although many women wish to continue working, others are eager for this restoration and do not resent the loss of their place in the labor force and political life. For them, work was a necessity, not something they sought; Party activism was a torment that a certain number had to bear because the Party insisted on proving its egalitarianism with "quotas." For many, the home was always a haven from an oppressive state; they are content to return there now, if only their husbands can earn the proverbial family wage. Many women indeed saw socialism as contrary to nature, because it treated as equal two sexes that they believe are "by nature" wholly different.[90] Many see the end of socialism as necessarily a restoration of the natural order of things, in which gender essentialism and the natural role of mothering have a crucial place.[91] It is chiefly the abortion question that has mobilized a few of them to defend what they had come to see as a right.

If Hungary is any indication, postsocialist Eastern Europe reveals how tightly interwoven are "socialism" and "capitalism" with specific—and variant—organizations of gender; and these in turn are bound up with the national idea. The end of socialism means the end of a state that assumes significant costs of biological and social reproduction, instead of assigning most of these costs to individual households, as capitalist systems have done. If, as some scholars argue, the gender organization of the capitalist household cheapens the costs of labor for capital by defining certain necessary tasks— "housework"—as nonwork (and therefore not remunerating them), then the economies of postsocialist Eastern Europe will be viable only with a comparable cheapening.[92] Thus the end of socialism necessarily means making once again invisible, by feminizing them and reinserting them into households, those tasks that became too costly when rendered visible and assumed by the state. The chief alternative Eastern Europe's women might anticipate is what has happened in more advanced economies: the commodification of household tasks into services (day care, cleaning, meal provision, etc.) for which a working couple pays something closer to their real cost than is paid when these are "housework." Until the commodity economy becomes as pervasive in Eastern Europe as it is now in the developed world, however, postsocialist Eastern Europe will be returning to the housewife-based domestic economy that was superseded at least in part by both social-ism and advanced capitalism.

A crucial means for this return will be the new democratic politics, which is proving to be—for quite different reasons from one place to another—"misogynist."[93] And central to this, as Goven's Hungarian data show, is eth-nonationalism. It is not difficult to see why. Post-1989 political forms are still being legitimated through "anti-Communism": through being the opposite of what the Communists did. Because Communist Parties all across Eastern Europe mostly toed the Soviet internationalist line in public, national senti-ment became a form of anti-Communism. This resistant aura to nationalism makes it an obvious means of reversing the damage Communists did to the nation they suppressed. To the extent that women are seen as having benefited from socialism or as having had the socialist state as their ally, feminism becomes socialist and can be attacked as antinational. The separate threads come together, as has been shown, in the issue of abortion. It owes its force partly to a vital symbol of socialism's demise: the idea of the nation's rebirth. The nation cannot be reborn if fetuses—and the nation with them—are condemned to death.[94] The nation cannot return to health if its women refuse to bear and nurture its "fetal citizens." The nation's recovery from socialism requires, then, a new patriarchy, instituted through a new demo-cratic politics that serves the national idea.

One of several ironies here is that Western policy-makers accustomed to thinking of nationalism, with its irrational "tribal" passions, as not in keeping with a modern Western political economy are suddenly finding that the best promoters of the Westernizing, anti-Communist values they hope to foster are local nationalists. Western liberalism has always found ethnonationalism suspect, for it restricts the "demos" of democratic participation to the mem-bers of a chosen people, excluding the ethnic "others" from full citizenship. This challenge to the notion of universal citizenship, which liberal political theory would place at the heart of democratic politics, is now lodging itself at the center of Eastern European "democracy." As the transition from so-cialism proceeds, scholars should be especially attentive to how nationalist politics integrates gender, what alternative forms of national imagery will be offered and by whom, and how the politics around issues like abortion will produce distinctive forms of democracy and capitalism in which nation and gender are intertwined in novel ways.

4

NATIONALISM AND NATIONAL SENTIMENT IN

POSTSOCIALIST ROMANIA

FOR WESTERN OBSERVERS, a striking concomitant of the end of Communist Party rule was the sudden appearance of national movements and national sentiments. We were not alone in our surprise: even more taken aback were Party leaders, somehow persuaded by their own propaganda that Party rule had resolved the so-called national question. That this was far from true was evident all across the region, from separatism in Slovenia, Croatia, Slovakia, and the Baltic and other Soviet republics, to bloodshed between Romania's Hungarians and Romanians and between Bulgaria's Turks and Bulgarians, to Gypsy-bashing in Czechoslovakia, Hungary, Romania, Poland, and Bulgaria, and widespread anti-Semitism—even in countries like Poland, where there are virtually no Jews. From no country was evidence of national conflict absent. Why?

The most common explanation by U.S. journalists and politicians has been that the end of "Communism"[1] took the lid off ancient hatreds that Party rule had suppressed. Indeed, so insistent is the ancient-hatred theory that alternative accounts are shut out.[2] It combines with an apparent view of the socialist period as in every respect an aberration whose end restores business as usual, a more normal order of "irrational tribal" passions in a part of the world long regarded as backward. Because asserting temporal distance, such as by calling something "ancient," is a classic means of establishing the thing so called as inferior,[3] this and the imagery of "tribalism" and "irrationality" make the explanation immediately suspect as ideology, not analysis.[4]

The first version of this chapter was delivered in February 1992 in my Lewis Henry Morgan Lectures, University of Rochester. Early versions were presented as lectures at George Washington University and Duke University as well. I am grateful for suggestions from the organizers and audiences on those occasions, as well as to the following people for comments on earlier drafts: John Borneman, József Böröcz, Gerald Creed, Susan Gal, Ashraf Ghani, Ewa Hauser, Robert Hayden, Gail Kligman, Melvin Kohn, and Andrew Lass. The examples given are from secondary literature on Eastern Europe and from ethnographic research, both prior to and immediately after 1989.

Reprinted from *Slavic Review* 52 (1993), with the permission of the American Association for the Advancement of Slavic Studies.

In this chapter I offer several alternatives to ancient hatred as an explanation of nationalism and national sentiment in postsocialist Eastern Europe. I suggest that to see socialism as having "suppressed" national conflict is a mistake, as is an understanding of present conflicts that ignores the effects of the dismantling of socialism. Although causes rooted in history have indeed been exceedingly important, I prefer to emphasize how the organization of socialism enhanced national consciousness and how aspects of the supposed exit to democratic politics and market economies aggravate it further. My discussion does not present a unified explanation but includes several, for nationalism in the region has many causes, ranging from the macrosocial to matters of personal identity. It is, in other words, overdetermined, and the relevant causes vary from one country to another. I give only cursory treatment to some of them, particularly those already covered in other literatures, so as to focus more fully on those illuminated by anthropology. Although I draw most of my examples from Romania, I will bring in other countries of the region as I proceed.

I might begin by recapitulating what I mean by "nation" and "nationalism," as discussed in chapter 3. "Nation" is a name for the relationship that links a state (actual or potential) with its subjects.[5] Historically, the idea of "nation" has meant a relationship of at least two kinds: first, a citizenship relation, in which the nation is the collective sovereign emanating from common political participation; and second, a relation known as ethnicity, in which the nation comprises all those of supposedly common language, history, or broader "cultural" identity.[6] The "citizenship" meaning of nation seems to have originated in the centers of liberal democracy, where it only sometimes coexists (as, for example, in France) with the "ethnic" meaning of nation. The latter is the meaning most common in Eastern Europe and is the one usually associated with "nationalism"—by which I mean the invocation of putative cultural or linguistic sameness toward political ends and the sentiment that responds to such invocation.

Because *no* state is ethnically uniform, the two meanings are potentially at odds: within given state borders, the number of potential citizen participants usually exceeds the membership of any ethnic nation (although this does not mean that all potential citizens are always recognized as such). Therefore, how a given polity defines the relationship between "ethnic nation" and "citizenship" deeply affects its form of democracy. Nationalism is of such consequence for democratic prospects in Eastern Europe because some groups make tactical use of a nationalism that would exclude large numbers of others from citizenship rights and political protection. This *ex*clusive tactical nationalism can also be *in*clusive, if it seeks to include members of the ethnic nation living in other states; in this case, it can threaten international peace. These potentials for exclusion and for war give nationalism a bad name among Western (especially North American) liberals, who have trouble studying it with sympathy.

Nationalism, History, and Socialist Policies

Let me briefly take up three of the reasons for nationalism specifically relating to socialist and presocialist times in Romania and more broadly elsewhere in Eastern Europe. The first is the obvious historical reason: the national idea is playing so vital a role in postsocialist politics because it had played a vital role in politics for well over a century. Eighteenth-and nineteenth-century national movements consolidated the meaning of nation as ethnic, for in many cases it was as ethnics that people had felt excluded from the prerogatives of citizenly status, monopolized by other nations. The Romanian movement in Transylvania is a good example. Later, during the 1920s and 1930s, in all East European countries ideas about "nation" became deeply embedded not only in political discourse but also in many institutions—economic, scientific, political, and literary. Although the early years of socialist internationalism suppressed this form of discourse, it gradually crept back in, to greater or lesser degrees and more or less covertly, in every country.[7] This occurred in part because of the legitimating value of "nation" and in part because talk of national interests gave ready expression to the anti-imperial feelings of many East Europeans (including many of their Party elites), against Soviet or Russian domination.

In a word, nineteenth-century national movements and the twentieth-century history of East European states were so effective in inculcating the national idea that the years of Communist Party rule could not completely expunge it. Indeed, it would have been impossible for party-states in an international system of *nation*-states to eradicate overnight so basic an element of modern political subjectivity. "Nation" in its ethnic meaning had entered firmly into people's political and social identities and their senses of self. This history is in some ways the precondition for all my other arguments in this chapter, yet it is neither "ancient" (these national identities being fairly modern) nor sufficient to explain present conflicts. No set of issues simply hangs around for forty years awaiting resurrection. Much has happened in the meantime.

A second reason why national ideas are now important applies chiefly to the Soviet Union and Yugoslavia, the two long-term "federations" in the region. In these two states, the main national groups each had their own republics: the principle of national difference was constitutionally enshrined. Leaders of nationalities held power as such, in their republics. More important, this was so in a social environment that the party-state had worked assiduously to cleanse of *other* organizational forms that might compete with its own initiatives. When a system of that sort begins to decentralize and to encourage more initiative from lower-level units, the only units having the organizational history and experience to respond are nationalities.[8] Weakening at the center thus empowers national elites first of all.

Some of them (those in Croatia and Slovenia, for example) at once began refusing to drain their budgets for subsidies to backward regions; others (such as those in Lithuania and Estonia) began complaining about their earlier forcible incorporation into the Soviet empire. Precisely because the Soviet regime had destroyed all other bases for political organization while constitutionally enshrining the national basis, national sentiment emerged to overwhelm federal politics. This form of federal organization—installed by the Bolsheviks and by Tito—can properly be said to have been *part of socialism*; it reinforced rather than undermined ethnic difference, and as Soviet anthropologist Valery Tishkov and others argue, it was the proximate cause of the dissolution of the Soviet and Yugoslav federations.[9] It was significant in the breakup of Czechoslovakia as well, where a comparable reification of nationality had existed since 1968. One can even see echoes of it in the Party-membership ethnic quotas of other, nonfederated socialist states, like Romania and Bulgaria.[10]

Third, there were additional features of socialism that made national ideas salient for average citizens, especially in those countries, regions, or republics having significant numbers of ethnic groups that were intermingled rather than territorially separated. In chapter 1 I have described socialism as a system of organized shortage. Basic to these societies was competition for access to scarce resources, with social actors constantly striving to put their hands on resources in very short supply. The more highly centralized such a system was—the more it resembled Romania or the Soviet Union rather than Hungary or Yugoslavia,[11] for example—the more severe the shortage was, and the more active the competition was likely to be. Under these circumstances, any device that increased one's chance of obtaining what one needed had a functional role to play. Shortage-alleviating devices included the ever-present use of personal ties and "bribery." I believe that another such mechanism was ethnic preference: the tightening of ethnic boundaries, or the use of ethnicity as a basis for personalistic connections. In its most exclusive form, this expels competitors from the networks that supply a shortage economy, giving members of one group an edge over claimants from "other" groups.[12]

Let me give a concrete if trivial example to show how ethnicity might work in regulating shortage. In Transylvania, where the mix of Romania's ethnic groups is greatest, one sometimes finds ethnic occupational specializations—quite common in multiethnic settings. In the city of Cluj, for instance, where hairdressing is almost wholly in the hands of Hungarians, I noticed during my 1984–85 visit that several of my middle-aged Romanian women friends appeared rather often with their hair visibly grizzled at the roots, a lapse in self-presentation wholly out of keeping with their usual style. Finally one of them begged me to get her some hair coloring on my next trip West, for with the many restrictions on hot water and on imports of virtually everything, including hair dye, her beautician could no longer service all the regular customers but only special friends. I doubt that in such circumstances every Hungarian beautician consciously served only her Hungarian friends. Rather, ethnicity excludes "naturally," as one restricts one's services to one's closest associates; and it is a commonplace that in situations of ethnic antagonism, such as that between Transylvania's Romanians and Hungarians, it is very likely that special friends will be of one's own ethnic group.

In other words, ethnonational identifications were one of several particularizing forces spawned by the system of centralized command. This makes them an analogue of the second economy and, like it, a form of resistance integrally tied to the organization of socialism. Given the premium this organization placed on all forms of particularism, to see Party rule as having "kept the lid" on a nationalism now free to "reassert itself" is, I believe, quite mistaken.

National Sentiment and Transition Politics

So far I have suggested three of several forces that were at work, in both presocialist and socialist times, to keep the national idea alive despite the Party's formal disapproval of it. The forces I have named had varying impact. Constitutionally enshrined national republics existed only in the Soviet Union, Yugoslavia, and post-1968 Czechoslovakia; and ethnicity was useful in reducing shortage mainly where ethnic groups were intermingled, such as in Romania, Bulgaria, Slovakia, and some Soviet republics. I will now discuss the several ways in which the processes of exiting from socialism create or reinforce nationalism and national consciousness: how "privatization" and other aspects of "constitutionalism" provoke national conflicts; how multiparty politics enables certain groups (often, those privileged under socialism) to make use of the national idea; and how Party rule created political subjectivities in ways that are now susceptible to the symbols inherent in national appeals.

There are many features of the proposed dismantling of socialism that aggravate relations between social groups. All have in common the fact that political and economic processes that the party-state had taken out of local hands are now being restored—not to the same hands as had relinquished them, of course, and here is part of the problem. A prime example is privatization. Although the principle holds for privatization in any form, I will illustrate it with privatization of land. Except in Poland and Yugoslavia, the expropriation of land and the formation of collectives virtually eliminated competition for land among local groups, whether these were defined as clans, as ethnic groups, or as families. After collectivization, the most they could compete for (and this they did) was bureaucratic access to regulate the benefits that might be derived from now-common property. But privatization restores the possibility of competition over land, and it does so after decades of population shifts, resettlings, expulsions, and changes in ownership that preclude a simple restoration of the *status quo ante* and precipitate conflict.

For example, in Aurel Vlaicu (Binţinţi), the village of my 1974 fieldwork, prior to 1940 the wealthiest farmers were Germans.[13] When they were deported to Siberia in 1945 for war-reparations labor, their considerable lands were expropriated and given to poor villagers of Romanian ethnicity. These people, in turn, were the ones compelled to donate the land to the collective farm. Beginning in 1991, the collective farm (although not the state farm nearby) was to be disbanded. Germans, expecting to receive the maximum allowable under the law—ten hectares per family—were astonished and enraged to learn, in July of that year, that they had been given not rights to land but shares in the state farm, whereas the recipients of the amounts once owned by Germans would be the Romanians to whom the land had been given in 1945. Germans as a group took the decision to court, alleging ethnic discrimination. They won, but that was not the end of the matter: Romanian villagers contested the judgment, and ethnic antagonism has escalated between two groups that had mostly gotten along quite peaceably since the collective was formed thirty years ago. It is in this context that one now hears what I never heard before: Romanians in the village saying—after a full century of cohabitation with Germans—"Why don't you Germans leave? What more do you want here? The land is ours."[14]

This case is simple by comparison with those in areas such as the Caucasus, where ethnic intermixtures and successions of ownership are infinitely more complex.[15] Throughout the region, it was often nationalities who had been expelled or deported (as with the Germans above) or who had temporarily fled (as many Romanians did from northern Transylvania after 1940). Thus it is as nationalities that they contest the redistribution of lands being proposed. If property had remained collective, this source of ethnic conflict would not arise; hence, we are looking at conflicts whose cause is clearly postsocialist. That they are heated owes much to the uncertain future of local economies, in which the prospects for unemployment make access to land the last guarantee of survival.

Other aspects of the transition have similar consequences for somewhat different reasons. Arutiunov has described, for example, the struggle between groups in Abkhazia, where Abkhazians (who form a minority) were struggling to achieve a legislative and particularly a judicial majority.[16] There, as in all formerly socialist societies constructing new constitutions and new supposedly independent judiciaries, it became a matter of great moment *which* nationality would control the judicial apparatus. This was not simply to enable corruption of the judiciary (though that may be part of it); it was to guarantee that judges would acknowledge the importance of the customary law that still regulates behavior—far more than does constitutional law—throughout the area. Arutiunov gives the example of a man who killed his brother-in-law for an insult to his honor; the local chief of police acknowledged the justice of the killing, and even though he knew it "should" be punished according to formal law, he delayed doing so. Without such a flexible judiciary, Abkhazians would find themselves at the mercy of other groups' notions of justice, a fate they dearly hope to avoid. Analogous situations may well obtain in other parts of the former Soviet bloc, wherever the formation of new political entities has produced a new judicial apparatus, which groups with conflicting stakes in judicial outcomes can struggle to control.

Even more significant are the new constitutions and citizenship laws that have been developed, both for existing states and for the states newly created from the former federations (Croatia, Slovenia, Estonia, Slovakia, etc.). In nearly every case, the premise of these constitutions is that state sovereignty resides in a majority ethnonation, not in individual citizens. Robert Hayden has pointed to the problems attendant upon these practices in his article on constitutional nationalism.[17] A good example is the temporary citizenship rulings in Estonia that barred more than a third of the population from participating in the 1992 elections. Even in the preexisting states constitution writing has been inflammatory, as ethnonational groups strove to create conditions favorable to them in the new constitutional order. The drafting of the Romanian constitution, for example, provided just such a conflict-ridden moment between Romanians and the Hungarian minority.[18] As for why "citizenly" rights are defined in ethnic terms, I would invoke both the preformed ethnic identities of earlier nation building and the constitutional reification of nationality in the socialist period, under circumstances that obstructed the formation of "civic" or other countervailing identifications.

Further sources of intergroup conflict emerge from the electoral process and the groups that come into competition in it. In Romania, these include some extreme nationalist organizations, such as the "Romanian Hearth" (*Vatra Românească*), its associated political Party of Romanian National Unity (PUNR), and the "Greater Romania" Party (PRM). These groups have not hesitated to use xenophobic, anti-Semitic, anti-Gypsy, and anti-Hungarian rhetoric, inflaming public opinion against other nationalities. They have also adopted the time-honored language of opposition to Europe, used since the mid-nineteenth century all over the region to resist both penetration by Western capital and the dislocating introduction of Western political forms. In its 1990s form, this discourse inveighs against the "return to Europe" proposed by those favoring market reform, privatization, and democracy.

Together the parties named here won just under 12 percent of the seats in the Romanian parliament in the September 1992 elections, but this understates their influence, since they formed the most important bloc of swing votes and their natural political allies have been the parties of former Communist apparatchiks.[19]

Who are these nationalists, socially speaking? Many in Romania's political opposition are convinced that they are the former old guard—above all, ex–Communist Party politicians and members of the Secret Police (sometimes collectively known in Romania as the "Red Right" plus "Green Left," or more concisely as the "National-Communists").[20] Extreme nationalism joins with the moderate nationalism of some in Romania's governing party, the FDSN (later PDSR), the chief party of former Communist bureaucrats. Romanian president Ion Iliescu, for instance, celebrated Romania's national holiday in 1991 by sharing a toast with extreme nationalist stalwarts,[21] all of them apparatchiks of yore.

The equation "nationalism equals Securitate plus Communists" appears often in various newspapers of the Romanian opposition. These argue that the former Securitate and its successor organization are sowing discord among Romania's national groups, blaming Gypsies, Jews, and Hungarians for all the country's woes instead of acknowledging that Party rule itself, in which they so signally collaborated, is responsible for present problems. They see the Securitate and former Party elite as seeking to undercut democratic processes by convincing the public that opposition means anarchy. The opposition also charges these old-regime groups with fanning popular anxiety by spreading rumors of a possible revision of the borders, which would return part of Transylvania to Hungary. Anti-European and nationalist rhetoric has been associated with the old elite elsewhere as well, such as in Hungary, Poland, and Slovakia.[22]

That the opposition interprets things in this way is partly, of course, in the nature of its political struggle. Because the Romanian public generally reviles the name of Communism (though not necessarily everything one might associate with its platform), opposition leaders can capitalize on this by labeling their opponents "Communists" and "Securitate." Any group who charges that the governing party or its nationalist allies are disguised Securitate and crypto-Communists thereby undermines those others' legitimate claim to power, while presenting itself as the true defender of an anti-Communist national interest. In other words, these charges and countercharges are part of the larger process of reconstituting political legitimacies, of seeking to construct moral authority for one's own party and undermine that of others.

This said, however, it is likely that the equation of nationalists with members of Romania's old regime has some truth.[23] It is supported first of all by the reaction of both nationalists and the ruling party to the Soviet putsch in

August 1991: they spoke up in favor of it, as one would expect of persons whose fates were tied to the centralized, repression-based system the Soviet putsch leaders represented and were trying to reinstall.[24] And who else but the old elite would argue, as the Romanian Hearth has, for returning the confiscated funds and patrimony of the former Communist Party and for renationalizing industries now being spun off from state control?

Public opinion largely prevented these groups from arguing their case by defending the Communist Party itself. Moreover, although the language of marketization and reform is used by all, the political opposition has monopolized it, leaving old apparatchiks few rhetorical alternatives but the time-honored "defense of the nation."[25] The electoral process has given this rhetorical form certain advantages, too, particularly in zones with large percentages of Hungarians. In such areas, the degree of fragmentation among Romania's political parties (144 competed in the September 1992 elections[26]) means that ethnically Romanian politicians risk losing elections to Hungarian candidates, for nearly all Hungarians vote with a single Hungarian party. Gerald Creed has made a similar argument for Turkish areas in Bulgaria.[27] Following the changes of 1989, in both Romania and Bulgaria the largest national minorities (Hungarians and Turks, respectively) each formed a political party and voted for it in a compact bloc;[28] a Romanian or Bulgarian politician living in those regions would stand a chance of winning only if he could persuade all voters of his own nationality that their group is under terrible threat from the other group. The extreme nationalist Romanian Hearth organization originated in just such a region, and the pattern of election of nationalist-party Romanian mayors has conformed closely to this picture.

If such elites find cause for worry in democratization, some—especially those in the less developed countries and regions—also find it in market reforms. There may be a connection between nationalism and the former Party apparatus wherever relative economic backwardness obstructs the possibilities for enrichment through the market. Former members of the apparatus in such regions—that is, in Romania, Bulgaria, Slovakia, and the less developed parts of the former Soviet Union—have rather poor prospects for transforming themselves into the new propertied class of "entrepratchiks," as is happening in the more developed Baltic states, the Czech Republic, Poland, and Hungary.[29] Even in those latter regions, however, some former apparatchiks who are losing ground to others more "enterprising" than themselves may defend their turf nationalistically. In all these cases, the opposition to market reforms appears as a defense of national values.

It is easy to see why the former elite might be nationalists, genuinely resenting "Europe" and Europeanizing reforms. Although members of the Secret Police and other Communist apparatchiks remained particularly strong in Romania, where the structures and personnel of the Ceauşescu regime were minimally displaced, they also exist, weakened to varying degrees, in all postsocialist countries. Many of them do not see a ready place for themselves in a democratic, market-based society. Among the allies of these old political elites are some intellectuals whom change also injures— writers, poets, artists, and historians[30] accustomed to the socialist regime's support of culture. Unlike the technical intelligentsia, many of these intellectuals find themselves sinking in a market economy. They have every reason to oppose market reforms and to be genuinely concerned for the market's deleterious effects on the quality of the nation's cultural values.[31] Such intellectuals and members of the former ruling apparatus, in often-fortuitous alliance, have been especially powerful opponents of "democracy" and the market—and especially effective proponents of nationalism—because they have long experience with disseminating their ideas and disrupting the ideas of others. When they oppose reform in the name of national values, they have an immense potential audience: all those ordinary people whom markets and privatization injure, such as the many workers in Romania (and the other countries of the region) who have lost their jobs in a transforming economy.[32]

The association between nationalism and those variously privileged under socialism does not hold for every country, or even for all of any one country. Macedonian leader Gligorov is both a nationalist and a former Communist; in Hungary the nationalist leaders were not Communists; and while old Communists were the most active advocates of Slovak independence, in the Czech regions the association is weaker.[33] Which groups use national rhetoric for political advantage depends partly on what alternatives other groups have already appropriated. Not all nationalists are former Communists, nor all ex-Communists nationalists. My remarks are intended to point to one group that in some places makes use of the electoral process to retain power by tactical use of a national rhetoric, offering to others who find contemporary changes bewildering and painful a way of thinking about their plight. To see nationalism here as resulting from ancient hatreds is clearly inadequate.

National Identity and Socialism's Divided Self

All my arguments so far are inadequate, however, to explain why the ideas such groups use—to considerable effect—are national ideas rather than any others. I will explore two possible answers: similarities between national ideology and certain policies of the Communist Party, and ways in which "anti-Communism" became an identity that feeds national identities.

Throughout the region, Communist Parties pursued policies designed to narrow both the gaps between and the sources of antagonism among social groups and to create social homogeneity. These policies included things like measures to decrease income inequalities and gender-based discrimination, and efforts to assimilate groups such as the Gypsies.[34] They aimed to minimize the differentiation of social interests and to make everyone equally dependent on state handouts. The regimes presented this as a moral imperative, making morality (rather than political interest) the basis of political community. By homogenizing the social field, the Party could justifiably claim to represent and serve the interests of society as a whole, a collective subject from which it had ostensibly effaced meaningful differences.[35] (Note the contrast with classic liberal democracy, in which parties generally claim to represent the interests of specific groups.) Such homogenizations were in the service of neither an ethnic nor a citizen "nation" but of a socialist nation that, as I argued in chapter 3, was a kind of extended family. The party-state reinforced its claim to speak for society-as-a-whole by purging the landscape of other organizations that might independently articulate specific interests or grievances.

Claude Lefort calls the result "the representation of the People-as-One," built on a denial that society consists of divisions. In consequence of such policies, he says, "In the so-called socialist world, there can be no other division than that between the people and its enemies."[36] Communist Parties constructed their identity by defining and setting themselves off from an enemy: class enemies, the enemy in the bourgeois West, enemies at the border (such as Nazism), and the enemies within, the dissidents.[37] They created a dichotomized universe, dividing the world into the Good and the Bad, Communism and Capitalism, proletarians and kulaks, Party members and those who resisted the Party's dictates. Their emphasis on the People-as-One, combined with the insistence on the moral basis of political community, facilitated establishing the community's boundaries by expelling its enemies. In consequence, dissidents and kulaks were exiled, sent to labor camps, or interned in mental hospitals, so as to maintain a clean, uncontaminated, morally pure community.[38]

A public that found itself ill-served by Party rule took up this same dichotomizing, but in reverse: opposition and resistance were good, and the regime was bad. The grounds for community remained, however, moral (in this case, opposing the regime), and the universe remained black and white, but with opposite values from those of the Party. The political opposition, too, saw itself as representing the collective subject "society as a whole," whose unified interest the Party had betrayed. Organizations like Solidarity and the Czech Civic Forum brought this attitude across into the postsocialist era.[39]

I have tried to make clear how kindred are the central elements of socialist rule, particularly the emphasis on the interests of the whole, with nationalism. They share both a fundamental essentialism (identities are fixed, unchanging) and a totalizing impulse. As Jan Urban puts it, "Nationalism is a totalitarian ideology."[40] In its most extreme forms, it too rests on a moral community defined by sameness rather than by difference: others who are "like us." Many East Europeans are used to thinking in terms of secure moral dichotomies between black and white, good and evil. For those who also understand democracy not as institutionalized disagreement and compromise but as consensus—and they are many—a powerful longing for a morally pure unity can easily solidify around the idea of the nation and the expulsion of polluting aliens: those who are not of the "People-as-One."[41] This is the easier because socialist homogenization left a relatively undifferentiated social field that nationalists can claim to represent on behalf of the nation as a whole. But the *meaning* of "nation" has shifted: it has become ethnic.

Let me sharpen this point further by recalling that the result of people's gradual alienation from and moral repudiation of Party rule was the opening up, in each country, of a yawning chasm between "us" and "them." "They" were always doing something nasty to "us"; "we" suffered hardship while "they" wallowed in privileges and luxury goods and built fancy houses. Even though the categories "we" and "they" might be elastic, their occupants changing from one situation to another, this elasticity does not weaken the basic split—us and them. In socialist countries the split was pervasive: between public and private, official and unofficial, "first" and "second."

The pervasive us/them split precluded legitimation, but it also did far more: it formed people's very identities.[42] Anthropologists who study the concepts of "person," "self," and "identity" generally note some sort of fit between these and the social environment. All regimes enter in some way into persons, constituting identities; in socialism these were split. Countless East Europeans have described the "social schizophrenia" or "duplicity" that became their way of life: you developed a public self that could sit at interminable meetings and read aloud the most arrant inanities (even while covertly signaling distance from these inanities as you read), and then at home or among close friends you revealed your "real" self—a self that was, of course, relentlessly critical of what "they" were doing. Like the second economy, which worked only in parasitic relation to the first, this "real" self was meaningful and coherent only in relation to the public or official self. In other words, people's sense of identity and personhood was not independent but required the "enemy" Party, the "them," to complete it. Bipolarity, in short, became constitutive of the social person.

The end of Party rule, however, produced a crisis in this self-conception: the "them" against which so many had delineated their "selves" had vanished. Senses of self had been built up and perpetuated for decades with the certainty that the enemy was the Communists; now they were gone. As a group of East European social scientists visiting Washington in the fall of 1991 told their host, "We had to find a *new* enemy."[43] That enemy, I suggest, became "the *other* others"—other nationalities, who existed in greater or smaller numbers in every one of these states.[44] As anthropologists have known since the path-breaking work of Fredrik Barth,[45] the essence of ethnic identities is a dichotomization into "us" and "them," through a process analogous to moral dichotomization in socialism: both produce identities based in an attribution of difference that yields opposed status groups. Easing the shift from the oppositional identities of Communism to those of ethnicity was the fact that many East Europeans were already seeing the Communists not just as "them" but as aliens, opposed to the whole (ethno)nation.[46] Their alienness was posited both by linking them with Russians and Jews (Jews having been overrepresented in the early Communist movements) and in other ways. For example, well before Romanian dictator Ceauşescu's overthrow but even more so after it, rumors circulated that Ceauşescu was "not really Romanian" but Tatar, Turkish, Armenian, or even Gypsy,[47] and during the 1980s I heard many Romanians claim that the Securitate were a *different race of people*, physically recognizable as such.[48] This image of an alien Party, parasitic upon the nation and now deservedly expelled from it, feeds readily into a search for other enemies of the nation to expel.

What ends does this hypothesis serve, when so many other things, including the pre-Communist history of national conflicts, already account for nationalism?[49] First, historical enmities must be reproduced into the present: their continuity cannot be simply presupposed. Second, part of what makes nationality so powerful is that it exists not just at the level of political rhetoric, interest groups, and constitutionalism but as a basic element of people's self-conception. Scholars should therefore not stop at macrolevel explorations but also explore the sources of national sentiment in individual identities (as I sought to do in chapter 3). My experience in Romania convinces me that among that regime's most notable consequences for personal identity was the dichotomizing of self against other. And third, something beyond concrete intergroup antagonisms is required if one is to account for how there can be hatred of groups like Jews and Gypsies in countries where they are almost nonexistent. Other causes must be at work. I suggest that one of these causes is that people's identities are still being defined, as before, in strict relation to unacceptable others whom one excludes from one's moral community.[50]

In making this suggestion, I hope to serve the broader goal of understanding how ethnic sentiment becomes entangled with other kinds of subjectivity. Anthropological common wisdom would suggest that Romanians should not have precisely the same personality configurations or "stable individual identities" as North Americans. In other words, Romanians and others formed within socialist political economies were constituted as subjects in ways rather different from people in other kinds of social worlds. To my knowledge, however, no one has offered a convincing analysis of what we might see as a distinctive "socialist identity structure."[51] The result may well *not* be "an identity," and it may not be normatively assumed to be stable, as *our* "identities" are supposed to be. Self-actualization in socialist Romania seems to me, rather, to have been much more situationally determined than North Americans find acceptable, such that people could say one thing in one context and another in another context and not be judged deceitful or forgetful or mad. Within this kind of contextually determined "self," I believe, there is a fundamental reflex toward microexperiences of solidarity and opposition: of "myself" as part of a larger entity, "us," collectively defined against "them." The ubiquitous (and now sadly absent) jokes of the socialist period are a superb example of this: little oppositional moments, enacted repeatedly in daily rituals of sociality, whose humor lay precisely in the sociality and the expressed opposition to "them." And I have been arguing that the categorical distinction among different *kinds* of "them" is very labile, moving readily from "Communist" aliens to "ethnic" ones.

A slightly different angle on this same problem—of the subjectivities in which ethnic dichotomization may be embedded—is manifest in a particular feature of the way national historiography constructed national selves, in Romania and other East European countries. All across the region, local historiographies represented the nation as an innocent victim, victimized nearly always by other nations rather than by its own members (never mind that co-nationals often did do the victimizing—to wit, the Ceauşescus). Poland appears time and again in Polish historical works as the "Christ of nations," whom the nations around it unjustly crucified, carving it up for over a century; generations of Czechs have been raised with the image of their nation as martyr. Hungary's and Romania's historians have presented their nations as suffering for the salvation of Western civilization, sacrificed on an Ottoman altar so the glory of Western Christendom might endure. Hungarians also view themselves as having been constantly thwarted by others— Habsburgs, Russians, and so on—from achieving their God-given mission to become a great civilizing power.[52] Bulgarian and Romanian historians see their people's "darkest" period in the time of direct Turkish rule, claiming that the Turks did everything possible to ruin the nation's economy and culture. Famous Romanian émigré Mircea Eliade wrote in 1953, "Few peoples can claim that they had so much ill fortune in history as the Romanian people."[53] (An impious Romanian writer calls this "the lacrimogenesis of the Romanian people."[54]) In every East European country, most people saw the Communist regime as the imposition of a foreign power, the Soviet Union. For those who suffered under Party rule, this was merely the latest in a long series of victimizations by other nations.

Given many people's frustrated and discouraging lives over the past forty years, how natural it is to explain their victimization in national terms. How automatic a reflex it is to accuse the Gypsies of getting rich "without work-ing," when one seems unable to make ends meet despite all one's efforts, or the Jews for having "brought Communism in the first place" and for the ongoing financial machinations that (many Romanians believe) thwart eco-nomic recovery. The contrast between the anarchy of Romania's political scene and the apparent discipline and militancy of the political party of the Hungarians makes it easy for Romanians to believe in a Hungarian plot to recover Transylvania with another mutilation of Romania, as happened in 1940. The postrevolutionary vogue for prison memoirs, exposing in excruci-ating detail people's suffering under the (as they see it) Russian-Jewish Communist Party, contributes further to this sense of a history of national victims.

I believe this experience of a self as both national and victim—of a self that has been victimized by history just as one's nation has been—disposes many Romanians to accept nationalist demagogy: "Oh, wretched Roma-nians, your troubles have always come from the scheming of aliens in your midst. Expel them and all will be well." No matter which social groups make use of this rhetoric, it takes root because of the way the national and self identity of many Romanians emphasizes unjust suffering, in a present in which suffering remains deeply real—and still unjust. The historiographical construction of national selves dovetailed nicely, then, with the practices and experiences of socialism, which tended to "other" (as class enemies, as saboteurs, as traitors) those seen as responsible for social problems.

Here, I believe, are the seeds of people's receptivity to an anti-Western, antimodernist, archnationalist political discourse that blames other national groups for whatever is going wrong. Thus I see "scapegoating" explanations of ethnic conflict as too simplistic. More precisely, socialism produced a characteristic organization of the self—one characterized by an internalized opposition to external "aliens," seen as "them";[55] it also produced specific conditions from which scapegoating emerged as an effective political tactic, one that uses stereotypes of other nationalities as means to explain social problems.

Ethnic Symbolism

I will now explore a related issue: what the symbolism behind ethnic stereo-types reveals about those who employ them. My examples are Romanians' use of stereotypes of Gypsies and Jews and of the "Hungarian problem" in Romania's current political context. I will suggest that images of these groups have become important symbols for discussing particular kinds of social dislocation attendant on the exit from socialism.[56]

The principal group singled out as a symbol of dislocation all across the region is the Gypsies; actual or "merely" verbal Gypsy-bashing is prevalent even in Poland, where Gypsies are few in number. No matter: public sentiment is whipped up against them nonetheless, along with other groups merged with them in people's minds (in Poland, Romanians; in Hungary, Arabs; and so on). The forms of the stereotypes suggest that the problem is not Gypsies per se but markets and the dislocations of economic reform, which Gypsies are made to symbolize.

Gypsy-bashing begins in their somewhat greater visibility in the flourishing petty commerce that has accompanied market reforms (paralleling the trade practiced by nomadic Gypsies, under socialism), although they are far from the only ones engaged in it. In Romania, this traffic is called *bişniţă* (from "business"); it involves goods that are produced by the seller, and also goods acquired illicitly from warehouses that usually supply state stores. In either case the prices charged can be quite high. Numerous Romanians, from the most refined intellectual on through unskilled laborers, account for the problems they face as caused by *bişniţă* and the Gypsies who supposedly monopolize it. Almost any conversation in Romania, in cities as well as in villages, can turn into an impassioned attack on Gypsies: it is said that they steal goods from warehouses, or bribe the person in charge, walk off with whole months' production, and either sell things on the street at a frightful markup (eating into salaries already weakened by rampant inflation) or cart them off to Hungary and Yugoslavia, so that when the innocent buyer goes to the store for something there is nothing to be found.

Many Romanians criticize Gypsies not only for their putative monopoly of trade but also for theft and laziness, long-standing stereotypes now mobilized more insistently than ever. Under socialism, of course, no one worked hard, and everyone stole. Now, however, inflation increasingly drives people to hold two or even three jobs and thus to be enraged at "lazy" Gypsies, who must be living by "theft" since many appear to have no other work; and many Romanians also see as a form of theft the profits gained from trade. Theft, I believe, is a potent notion in Romania and across the whole region, in part because inflation and the dizzying rate of change have left people acutely conscious of a hole in their pockets. The "real" reasons have to do with government pricing and taxation policies, the uneven and disorienting effects of the market, IMF-imposed austerities, joblessness from closing inefficient firms, privatization, reduced subsidies, and a host of other things. To see all this as a problem of "theft" is a helpful simplification. It is solidly rooted in the ideas of the socialist period: the productionist view that trade is bad and work is good (i.e., exchange is inferior to production), that it generates inequality, that it is illegal because it is "like" the black market, that Gypsies aggravate shortage, and that for all these reasons they are criminals deserving punishment. As market reforms exaggerate all these problems of socialism, anger focuses on Gypsies, who have become their symbol.

The same symbolization of Gypsies appears in every East European country. But more is at stake than "representation." How seriously should we take the attitudes people express toward Gypsies? In a taxi ride in Bucharest during the summer of 1991 my driver mentioned a Gypsy neighborhood that had been recently attacked and burned; to my expression of alarm at this, he replied calmly, "There's only one solution to the Gypsy problem: mass extermination." Another friend said on another occasion, "Hitler had the right idea about Gypsies." Yet other friends to whom I reported these exchanges told me I was taking them too literally—told me, in effect, that I was inappropriately assuming a one-to-one relation between language and its behavioral referent, between signifier and signified. Are the comments I have quoted just "verbal inflation," then, a sign of the desperation and lack of control people are experiencing but not a cause for alarm? Gypsy areas in several villages and towns in Romania, Poland, and other East European countries have been attacked, the houses burned and the inhabitants beaten or killed. After the residents of a certain Romanian village drove out its Gypsy members, a man offered the justification that they had "expelled not Gypsies but thieves."[57] Is this a passing moment of intolerance, or the beginning of pogroms? We do not really know. We know only that these attitudes indicate significant resistance toward the effects of market reforms, for which Gypsies are getting the blame.

Similar questions can be asked and similar points made about anti-Semitism, except that the stereotypes are different. In Hungary, Poland, Russia, the Czech and Slovak Republics, and Romania, anti-Semitic talk has raised much concern—even in countries like Poland where there are almost no members of that group. How can there be anti-Semitism without Jews? They seem everywhere to symbolize two things: socialism and cosmopolitan Westernism. The association with socialism stems from the fact that in many East European countries, the Communist Party initially had disproportionate numbers of Jews among its members and its leaders. Thus people who are angry at socialism for their wrecked lives see Jews as responsible for the whole disastrous experiment (never mind that Poles, Czechs, or Romanians were also in charge). But long before Party rule, Jews in this region were also seen as cosmopolitan, urban, and Westernized. Whenever Western influence has brought trouble, Jews have become its symbol.[58] Whereas intolerance of Gypsies suggests problems related specifically to the market, anti-Semitism suggests a broader hostility to things of "the West," including democracy and private property, as well as markets; and it embraces themes of concern to a broad array of groups, distressed either at past injustices under socialism or at present dislocations. To say that one dislikes Jews is easier and less revealing than to say one dislikes democracy or international lending institutions. One can make this statement employing Jews as a symbol even if there are few actual Jews around.[59]

My last example of how the dislocations of the moment may be symbolized by means of other nationalities concerns the way Romania's nationalists foment anti-Hungarian sentiment, employing the language of "purification," of expelling "enemies," and of the "People-as-One." Here is an example:

> Romanians, Hungarian fascism is attacking us openly. . . . *In twenty-four hours we must ban by law all anti-Romanian groupings: the Hungarian Democratic Union of Romania and Soros Foundation, as well as their stooges, the Civic Alliance Party, Group for Social Dialogue,* Literary Romania, *Democratic Convention! Romanians, don't be afraid of the wild beast of Hungarian revisionism; we have put its nose out of joint a few times already, and now we'll crush it decisively and without pity! They want autonomy? Expel them!*[60]

In many of their writings they invoke the problem of Transylvania, playing upon the collective trauma Romanians experienced when the northern part of that region was briefly returned to Hungary, between 1940 and 1944. Although the majority of the population is Romanian, many Romanians fear that Hungary wants to repossess the territory; nationalists exploit this fear. Their language continually emphasizes not just these aliens' defilement of sacred Romanian soil but the image of Romania's territorial dismemberment. A book written to warn Romanians of the impending danger, for example, shows on its cover a map of Romania being menaced from the northwest by a giant set of teeth, about to take a huge bite out of the country's pleasingly rounded shape.[61]

Although in electoral terms nationalist groups polled "only" 12 percent of the vote in the September 1992 elections, my conversations over three summers suggest that many Romanians, especially those in Transylvania, found their rhetoric compelling. This is partly from real, recollected experiences of 1940–44 but also, I believe, from what as a result of those events "Hungary" has come to symbolize. In the post-1989 context—one in which many feel utterly confused, in which a bewildering party politics collides with a thirst for consensus, in which intolerance of opposing views strains long-standing friendships and even marriages, and in which inflation causes new rounds of panic every week—Hungarians and Hungary have come to represent the loss of a feeling of wholeness. The "Hungarian problem" symbolizes the fragmentation, the feeling of flying apart, of chaos and loss of control, that accompanies the collapse of the only thing that held Romanians together: Party rule and their opposition to it. An abstract feeling of social fragmentation gains a concrete object when the Hungarian party demands group autonomy,[62] when Hungary's Prime Minister Antall pronounces himself leader of "all the world's Hungarians," and when conferences in Hungary raise the question of repossessing northern Transylvania:[63] in other words, when Romanian national sentiments collide with the nationalism of Hungarians. If attitudes toward Gypsies express anxiety at the ravages of the market and economic reform, then, anti-Hungarianism consolidates self and wholeness against the newly deepened fragmentation of social life, which is both a legacy of socialism and a product of the transition itself.

Conclusion

I have proposed a number of factors contributing to the salience of national sentiment in Romania. They include tactical resort to national ideas and symbols, often by people formerly privileged under socialism and eager to retain that privilege; competition over newly privatized land or over the newly decentralized institutions of new political entities; and a broad socie-tal receptivity to "national" explanations, owing to affinities between the "self" of socialism and a psychic economy in which other national groups become symbols, used for explanation and blame. By emphasizing so many sources of nationalism and national sentiment in Romania and in the rest of the region as well, I have meant to argue that these phenomena are heavily overdetermined. There are no parsimonious explanations for them: Occam's Razor here sacrifices understanding instead of yielding it. Their determi-nants lie equally in the historical and structural situations of groups in the polity, in calculations of advantage and the rhetorics that promote them, in social constructions of "self" and "person," and in people's representations of their life circumstances in which images of other social groups serve as pri-mary symbols.

Such multiple determination should not be a surprise, for "nation" as a construct stands at the root of the central political subjectivity of modern times: that which inserts people into "nation-states." Building nation-states has entailed processes of internal homogenization and differentiation[64]— homogenizing the population that is subject to a single sovereignty and dif-ferentiating it from those of other sovereignties. It has also entailed creating loyalties and identifications suited to the early-modern state's penchant for war; this was achieved by entering directly into social persons and forming identities that linked them unambiguously with "their" encompassing polity. The cultural construct that has accomplished these tasks in modern times has been "nation." It is an idea with a venerable lineage, owing to its root meaning of "birth"—a notion crucial to making the arbitrary constructs of the social order appear natural.[65]

In its march across the globe, however, "nation" has been wrongly thought to mean a single thing, whereas its meanings have in fact been sev-eral. Upgraded from its medieval meaning of "feudal estate," it took on the meaning of "citizen"; with this, it became the foundational concept of modern state sovereignties in the Western world. This concept did not make equal sense everywhere, however: in some places, great masses of people lacked citizenship and its concomitant sovereignty, and in others (such as "Germany") political fragmentation produced sovereign entities that were laughably small. The ideas through which such situations would be reversed were those of Herder, who argued that it was not a unified political will that made true nations but "shared" history, language, culture, and sentiment. This, said Herder, should constitute a "nation": a community of birth, a "natural" entity, rather than the artificial constructs (states) made by conquest and political calculus. Herder's ethnic concept of nation migrated from "Germany" into the national movements of peoples throughout Eastern Europe (as well as elsewhere in the world), becoming the principal idiom of politics there.

Given this history, then, my argument cannot be that socialism *caused* present sentiments and conflicts, only that it perpetuated and intensified national feeling, whereas a different outcome was also possible. Just as the meaning of nation has shifted historically, it might also have shifted under the impress of socialism. I have proposed here that this is precisely what did not happen. The Communist Party's manner of entry into Eastern Europe and its mode of operation had much to do with this outcome; they fed the anti-imperial sentiments of satellite nations, politically reified national identities in the mistaken belief that these were mere epiphenomena of class difference, bred widespread resistance to Party rule, eliminated organizational forms (besides the Party) that might have shaped other identities, and institutionalized competition for which ethnic difference was a handy resource. Thus Party rule enhanced the salience of the national idea. In Romania in particular, I have suggested elsewhere, the encounters between the national idea and a monolithic socialism resulted, through a complementary schismogenesis, in a more monolithic nationalism.[66] Instead of nudging national sentiments in a new direction, then, socialism strengthened them in ways that were not readily apparent until the changed political circumstances of the "transition" gave them new space.

One might object that by excluding similar national phenomena in the nonsocialist world, such as Sri Lanka (or even an increasingly xenophobic Western Europe), my account is weakened.[67] This objection assumes that just because something we call "nationalism" occurs in many places, it is the same phenomenon in all of them—that similarity of form implies similarity of both content and cause. I disagree. Social scientists too often lump together "nationalisms" that are quite different, seeking a single explanation where very diverse forces are at work. That the world community is organized so as to produce nation-states and therefore nations (though this may now be changing) does not mean those nations have everywhere the same lineage. To the contrary: it is their particularities that deserve exploration, lest we misconstrue their origins and significance. Nation is first of all a political symbol. As such, its meanings are as varied as its multiple histories and as numerous as the social-structural positions from which it can be both utilized and read.

There is no better illustration of this truth than the fateful consequences of Woodrow Wilson's failure to recognize it. By seeing "nation" as having a single, universal sense and by promoting "national self-determination" as the route to a peaceful world order, Wilson (in the words of Eugene Hammel) "legitimized the ethnic nation-state and confused its creation with democracy."[68] The persistence of such simplistic views perpetuates the confusion. It will not do to overlook the presence of nationalism in Eastern Europe's new polities on the assumption that any political movement opposed to Communism is thereby "democratic," or to abdicate thoughtful policy in the belief that national conflicts erupt from some atavistic, primordial urge no one can influence. As I have argued here, socialism and its aftermath have influenced them mightily, in ways we should continue to explore.

5

CIVIL SOCIETY OR NATION? "EUROPE" IN THE SYMBOLISM OF POSTSOCIALIST POLITICS

> Romania today has two possible directions before it: Bolshevist
> Asiatism or Western, European standards. Between these, [we]
> see only one choice: Europe, to which we already belong
> by all our traditions since 1848.
> *(Leaders of new civil-society party)*
>
> The temptation of the Common European Home is a utopia
> every bit as damaging as Communism.
> *(Romanian nationalist senator)*[1]

FOLLOWING THE COLLAPSE of Party rule in the Soviet bloc, a theme central both to scholarship about the region and to politics and discourse inside it has been the creation of democratic polities with robust civil societies. In some countries the idea of civil society antedated the revolutions, having energized dissident opposition to socialist regimes. The same dissidents, or movements fashioned after their example, brought the notion of civil society into post-1989 political symbolism and activity. Everywhere, it came closely intertwined with the idea of "Europe." "Europe" was a vivid presence in the talk of dissidents; it remains, for many, the overarching symbol of the end of Party rule, signifying all the Western forms socialism suppressed—forms such as civil society. To build civil society, then, is to return to Europe. To talk of building civil society, like talk of returning to Europe, indicates one's adherence to an entire program of social change (or at least one's opposition to someone else's program). In this sense, "civil society" in post-1989 Eastern Europe is as much a feature of political discourse and symbolism as of societal organization.

Written for a conference in the spring of 1993, this chapter rests on a selective reading of Romanian newspapers from 1992 and the early part of 1993, supplemented by brief field trips in the summers of 1990–92. It builds upon the analysis of intellectuals and political discourse in my *National Ideology under Socialism: Identity and Cultural Politics in Ceaușescu's Romania* (Berkeley and Los Angeles: University of California Press, 1991). Special thanks to Elizabeth Dunn for lengthy conversations that helped to clarify my argument in this chapter, and to Sorin Antohi, Michael Kennedy, Kirstie McClure, and Ron Suny for helpful comment.

Because "civil society" and "Europe" enter contexts (both political and semantic) very different from one formerly socialist country to another, these ideas have a varied career. Their political contexts range from Poland, where the Solidarity movement had opened a large space for non-Party politics, to Romania, Bulgaria, and Albania, where such a space was almost nonexistent. And the field of meanings within which these symbols interact includes a number of other central symbols, more or less vigorous, such as socialist values (equality, welfare), "bourgeois" notions (prosperity, initiative), and patriotic ideals (nation, anti-imperialism). The strength of these symbols affects the fate not only of ideas about civil society and Europe but also of the political programs they signify.

In this chapter I examine the fortunes of a pro-European, civil-society rhetoric in postsocialist Romania. Focusing on a small group of politicians and intellectuals who see themselves as partisans of Europe and civil society, I follow their talk about these in a few critical moments during 1991–93; I also note the counteruse of "Europe" by some of their political opponents. In Romanian political discourse during this period, "Europe" means, for its civil-society advocates, the source of the political and economic forms Romania should adopt; for others, it means a neoimperialist menace threatening Romania's independence. That is, "Europe" represents either aid and salvation or imperial domination. But for all who use it, to speak of "Europe" is (as has been true for two centuries) at one and the same time a statement of political intentions and a statement of national identity. Democracy, private property, civil society, and Europe: it is around these symbols that "Romanianness"—including policies toward foreign capital, new property regimes, and new political arrangements—will be redefined. The stakes of the redefinition are not only rhetorical: from it will emerge the very forms and symbols of Romanian politics in the future.

As is clear, for the purposes of this discussion I take Europe, democracy, civil society, and nation as key symbolic operators, elements in ideological fields, rather than as organizational realities. While recognizing that politics is far more than symbolism and discourse, I believe that for the former Soviet bloc these aspects have not yet received the attention they warrant. Therefore, instead of asking (as some would) "Do we have resurgent nationalism in Romania?" or "Is Romania developing civil society?" I ask what a political economy of the symbolism around these notions can reveal about that country's postsocialist politics. I look at how the overwhelming presence of the master-symbol "nation" in Romania's political space limits what opposition intellectuals and politicians can do with symbols like "civil society," "democracy," and "Europe," and I find them compelled to address the national idea despite their aim of constructing, instead, a new political object: a democratic society of European form.

Teleological Elites and Moral Capital

In order to link the preceding symbols with political processes in Romania, I use the notion of "moral capital," seen as a type of political capital having special currency in Eastern Europe and the former Soviet Union. Central to rule in modern states are their regimes of legitimation and control;[2] an important ingredient in these is the kinds of symbols that rulers and others are able to mobilize. Those symbols, in turn, define and help to build the political capital of the actors who wield them. Efforts to introduce new symbols, redefine old ones, and monopolize their definitions are thus integral both to building political capital by aspirant political elites and to producing new regimes of legitimation where the old ones have collapsed.

The end of Party rule throughout Eastern Europe opened a struggle for relegitimation, while also changing the definition of what counts as political resources and undermining prior accumulations of them. To take the most obvious example, position in the Party apparatus ceased to provide political capital. Definitions of alternative sources did not emerge *de novo*, however. One of their parameters was a lengthy history in which elite status had been understood in a certain way, a way that paradoxically accommodated Communist elites rather well. Following Iván Szelényi, I refer to these elites as "teleological elites."[3] For such people, the conduct of politics and intellectual life, as well as their place in these, was defined first and foremost in terms of the pursuit and defense of certain values rather than the mastery and institutionalization of certain procedures. This is to invoke, of course, Weber's celebrated distinction between two kinds of rationality—*Wertrationalität* and *Zweckrationalität*, the rationalities of ends and of means. Although one can never wholly separate ends from means or create satisfactory ideal types based on them, I nonetheless find it helpful to see East European elites as having typically privileged a "wertrational" orientation, one that reached its climax with the teleological elites of the Communist Party. (The hackneyed phrase "The end justifies the means" says it all.) Composing these elites were both producers of culture—"intellectuals"—and politicians, jointly arguing about values, about the knowledge necessary for implementing them, and about the politics appropriate to doing so. Because people of elite status in the eastern part of Europe have moved back and forth between intellectual and political work while participating in a common discourse, I do not distinguish here between politicians and intellectuals.[4]

A corollary of the teleological orientation is that certain kinds of symbolic capital have tended to prevail over other kinds as political resources: specifically, moral capital—a capital rooted in defining certain values as correct and upholding them—has held an edge over what we might call technical or expert capital, rooted in certain competencies and the mastery of procedures and techniques. Moral capital is present, of course, in the claims of elites in other systems too; differently defined, it often plays a role in U.S. elections, for instance. In emphasizing moral capital here, I wish merely to underscore that a certain language of claims—moral claims, often intertwined with national values—has had especially great resonance in East European politics. While Communist Party leaders surely did not ignore technical questions, their first concern was to establish a monopoly on the definition of virtue, of purity, of social entitlement and obligation. These are not chiefly technical or procedural matters (although procedures may be implied in the answers to them).[5] And these concerns established the grounds for social and political action within the societies over which Communist Parties ruled.

As time passed and Communist Parties found it increasingly difficult to legitimate themselves—as resistant subjects perceived their overbearing elites more and more as "them"—there arose in each socialist country various forms and degrees of organized opposition. This opposition sought to establish its credibility on grounds already set by the past and by Party rule itself: morality. Although some intellectuals sought to challenge the Party on grounds of competence, claiming that as intellectuals, they were better qualified to determine the country's direction, even this claim rested on a teleological foundation: better qualified to determine ultimate values for the society.[6] Overall, opposition leaders took their stand on the morality of opposition to the regime, and of opposition as the only morality acceptable.[7] Making morality the only criterion that counts then entailed accumulating moral capital with which to challenge the morality of the Party.

How did dissidents accumulate moral capital? That is, how did people with no formal political power acquire politically salient authority—something crucial to their role in politics both before and after the end of Party rule? There were several routes for doing so. Two of them involved elaborating and defending ideas about civil society and national values. Partisans of "civil society" generally presented it as a sphere free of politics,[8] therefore morally superior to the corrupt politics of the Party and central to any quest for greater democracy. Those who defended "nation" imagined it as a pure value and object of loyalty that the Communists had betrayed, hence moral superiority would lie in restoring it to its rightful place at the center of politics. As concepts, "civil society" and "nation" were sometimes coterminous, sometimes developed in tandem, and sometimes set in contrast to one another; the mix differed from case to case.[9] So, too, did the robustness of the idea of civil society, which tended to be stronger in Poland, Czechoslovakia, and Hungary, for example, than in Romania and Bulgaria.

An additional and very important means of accumulating moral capital through resistance was the idea of suffering. This might take any number of forms, resulting from the Party's harassment, persecution, imprisonment, or torture of those who claimed to defend civil society or nation against it. Crucial in establishing this form of moral capital during the socialist period was notice by "the West" (West European countries and the United States) in the context of the Cold War. Given Western hostility to Communism, persons who resisted Communist tyranny and suffered for it gained visibility and renown. They might come to the attention of their countrymen, despite censorship, through foreign broadcasts enhancing their moral stature as pioneers of freedom. By 1989 it was chiefly dissident intellectuals who gained this kind of renown—people like Václav Havel and Jan Patočka in Czechoslovakia, Doina Cornea in Romania, Jacek Kuron and Adam Michnik in Poland, and György Konrád and Iván Szelényi in Hungary.

In speaking thus about suffering and moral capital, I do not wish for an instant to diminish the reality and significance of that suffering, which was in many cases terrible and permanently crippling. My aim is only to underscore the way in which otherwise powerless opponents of increasingly unpopular regimes acquired, precisely because their powerlessness invited persecution, a kind of political resource. Their persecution, suffering, and consequent moral capital rested on the defense of moral and national values long defended by Eastern Europe's teleological elites; they rested, as well, on the morality claims of the Party itself, which set the agenda for the counterdefinitions its opponents might offer. That the suffering of the latter was real only fortified the moral capital it built.

The political resource contained in resistance-based suffering was to carry over into the postsocialist period. Doubtless the most stunning instance of the moral-turned-political capital inherent in persecution was Havel's unparalleled ascent from political prisoner to Czechoslovak president. Others who gained political stature from their previous persecution include, of course, Poland's Wałęsa; Romania's Ion Iliescu sought to capitalize on this same resource by presenting himself as the victim of his opposition to Ceauşescu's policies, which had led to his demotion and exile to Party posts in the provinces. In the anti-Communist climate of 1990, when widespread euphoria at the end of Party rule accompanied moves to excise the Party and all it stood for from public life, the sufferings it had caused became grounds for visibility and respect for increasing numbers of people. For example, in Romania the suffering of longtime political prisoner Corneliu Coposu helped to constitute his moral authority as head of the resuscitated National Peasant Party, while the persecuted members of the Association of Former Political Prisoners gave that organization considerable clout in the newly forming political opposition. Candidates for political office in such organizations, or participants wanting the microphone at their meetings, might justify themselves with the capital of suffering (expulsion from the workplace, jail, ostracism, etc.) they had accumulated from their refusals to serve the regime.[10] To show that one had suffered under the Communists became in Romania a major claim, entitling one to the right to be heard in the political sphere. To argue that one had suffered for the Romanian nation or for a democratic civil order—that is, to join the two sets of morality arguments, civil society (or nation) with suffering—might strengthen one's moral authority further.[11]

The remainder of this chapter illustrates some of these points with specific reference to Romanian political/intellectual discourse between 1991 and early 1993. This was a period in which the mass political movement that had arisen in late December 1989 as the "National Salvation Front" and then become a political party, winning the May 1990 elections, was consolidating its hold on power and clarifying its self-definition. It split into two factions, led respectively by President Iliescu and former Prime Minister Roman; these later became separate parties, known by their acronyms as FDSN and FSN (they later changed their names again to PDSR and PD).[12] Reflecting a division between older reformist Party apparatchiks and younger technocrats, this schism created room for the further development both of opposition movements and parties and of nationalist ones.[13] The latter were to benefit from the increased vulnerability of the ruling PDSR following the September 1992 elections, when that party could no longer carry a parliamentary vote on its own and needed allies. Thus 1991–93 constituted a critical moment in the reconfiguration of Romania's political field.

In assessing what the political opposition was able to accomplish in this critical interval, one must bear in mind that there had been little effective opposition in Romania, in contrast with other bloc countries. The idea of "civil society" had far less purchase there than elsewhere; instead, dissidents had been likely to protest through veiled references to "Europe" and through defending a certain idea of Romania[14]—that is, through the idea of "nation" and the defense of its values. Moreover, an especially vigorous development of Romanian national ideology over the past two hundred years, amid repeated struggles to define and control the symbol "Romanian nation," had endowed that particular symbol with great force.[15] Under Ceauşescu, it had buttressed indigenist (rather than Europeanizing) definitions of Romanian identity: Romanians as autochthones, as sui generis, rather than as Europeans and heirs of Rome. This recent history constrained what one could accomplish politically with ideas about "civil society" and "Europe" after 1989.

Romania after the "Revolution"

In the political field that took shape after Romania's so-called revolution, initial advantage went, as elsewhere, to the handful of former dissident intellectuals. Party opponents such as Doina Cornea and poet Mircea Dinescu endowed the emerging National Salvation Front with tremendous moral authority, helping to sanctify its other, Party-based aspirants to leadership.

These included veteran Communists who had signed a letter of protest to Ceaușescu in March 1989, and a number of second-tier Party bureaucrats claiming (like Iliescu) that their careers had suffered for their refusal to be Ceaușescu's toadies. After 22 December 1989, these variously defined "dissidents" found themselves presidents and presidential councilors, ambassadors, and government ministers. Talk of "civil society," "democracy," and a "return to Europe" echoed loudly through the corridors of power, as the newly ascendant opposition imitated the style of speech of their analogues in Poland, Czechoslovakia, and Hungary, empowered shortly before.

But the timing of Romania's revolution had enabled its Party elites to learn from the fates of Party leaders elsewhere, just as the demonstrating crowds in Czechoslovakia and Bulgaria had learned from the encouraging experience of prior demonstrators in East Germany.[16] From the initial chaos of the revolution, members of the former Party apparatus managed to preserve, over the next several years, far more of the structures of rule than was true in the former bloc countries to the northwest. The National Salvation Front and most of its civil-society dissident allies soon came to a parting of the ways (indeed, as of February 1993 the government was actually bringing treason charges against Doina Cornea for undermining the state).[17] In the September 1992 elections, the Front's conservative faction—Iliescu's group of old-time Party bureaucrats—even promoted an *anti*reform political program and raised questions about the desirability of privatizing agriculture or large state firms. This faction won the largest single bloc of votes. Its political allies in a new governing coalition were several small parties—the Agrarianists and the Socialist Labor Party (the former Communist Party) as well as two nationalist parties, the Greater Romania Party (PRM) and the Party of Romanian National Unity (PUNR).

Given Romanians' dismal experience with "Communism," however, that coalition could not overtly constitute its rule *as Communists*. During two electoral campaigns, Iliescu was repeatedly challenged to explain his relationship to the Party and the doctrines of Marxism-Leninism; he replied that he was no longer a Communist. Thus in its struggle for relegitimation, Iliescu's party (the PDSR) proceeded along two lines: it insisted on its own definition of democracy, thereby contesting the opposition's use of this symbol, and it placed itself ever more openly on the side of the nationalist PRM and PUNR. That is, it began to stake its legitimacy on defense of "the nation," producing the curious spectacle of a "National-Communist" alliance of ex-Communists and nationalists. This legitimation strategy resulted in part from the opposition's earlier capture of the symbols "democracy" and "civil society" and in part from widespread revulsion at alternative values such as "socialism," but it also accorded well with the political goals of the PDSR.[18]

I should clarify what I mean by the term "opposition." The word is very imprecise, because the groups that might qualify for it kept changing colors and sides. I use "opposition" as Romanians do, to mean all those Romanian politicians taking a position overtly opposed to that of the party (or parties) of government—anyone who regularly criticized Iliescu in the press, for instance. The opposition's unity was far from reliable. Some of the oppositional parties joined the so-called Democratic Convention, an umbrella party formed in hopes of beating the National Salvation Front; these groups nonetheless quarreled often among themselves, as well as with other groups or people (such as the National Liberal Party) who were not part of the Convention but usually voted anti-PDSR. In the space of two years (1991–93), parties divided, disappeared, changed names, and reconfigured their political coalitions; members left their party to join another, disavowed their party program while remaining in parliament as its supposed representatives, and mended fences with former enemies only to split from their closest friends. In such an unstable political landscape, the referent of "opposition" is itself highly unstable. The term therefore refers to a quite miscellaneous collection of personages, orientations, and interests, defined only through their criticism of the ruling coalition.

As the PDSR consolidated its power, the opposition groups lost the advantage they had enjoyed immediately after the revolution.[19] Their inexperience and ineptitude made it easy for the PDSR to diminish their credibility with the public and to undermine their moral capital. Although the Democratic Convention won 27 percent of the 1992 national vote by defining itself as "anti-Communist," this was considerably less than expected. Opposition groups remained all too vulnerable to the nationalist accusation that in talking of Europe they were not anti-Communist but antipatriotic, servants of "foreign powers" (i.e., Europe, Hungary), lackeys of the American Embassy, and traitors who aim to "sell the country" and who should be expelled from Romania's new democracy. Their disadvantage was not only rhetorical but also institutional, for the balance of electoral forces in parliament meant that they could not carry any vote unless a few in the governing coalition defected.[20] Moreover, the government maintained control over the allocation of radio frequencies, licenses for TV broadcasting, and access to television programming. The opposition's ability to disseminate its ideas was thus increasingly hostage to vertiginous rises in the price of paper—produced under state monopoly.

The coordinates of the field of action discussed in the following pages, then, were these: the governing coalition held most of the cards, institutionally speaking, and utilized the most powerful rhetorical symbol, while both the opposition's rhetoric and its political position were weak. The illegitimacy of socialist rhetoric (though not of all its ideals) forced the options it might have voiced into other channels of political expression—talk of civil society and nation being the main alternatives. In seeking to show how their

political disadvantage compelled opposition forces to modify and even abandon their civil-society discourse, I focus on three groups: members of two
civil-society organizations known as the Civic Alliance (AC) and the Group
for Social Dialogue (GDS), which overlapped with a third, the Civic Alliance
political party (PAC). These groups, together with members of the National
Peasant Party, had formed the core of the Democratic Convention, building
its strength by drawing other parties into it; their allies included the party of
Romania's Hungarians. Although the various groups represented very diverse orientations and interests, all were resolute opponents of both Iliescu's
PDSR and its nationalist allies.

The Struggle to Define Central Political Symbols

I begin with some brief examples of the political symbols central to Romanian politics at that time and of the rhetoric defining the field of their use.
These symbols include "democracy," "nation" and "the national interest,"
and "patriotic."[21]

From the very outset, opposition groups defined themselves as the au-
thoritative defenders of "democracy," repeatedly labeling the PDSR and the
nationalists "antidemocratic." The PDSR contested both the definition and
the label. Shortly after the revolution, Iliescu asserted as his aim the building of "original democracy," in which, it soon became clear, opposition was
expected to suppress its disagreement for the good of the whole. "Original
democracy" was government by consensus rather than by a process of institutionalized disagreement and compromise (as the opposition defined it).
Thus a contrast emerged between the "original democracy" of the PDSR
and what the opposition defended as "true" or "authentic" or "real" democracy. The opposition's version was far from universally accepted: in brief
visits during the summers of 1990–92, I spoke with many Romanians who
thought democracy should be consensus and accused the opposition parties
of obstructing the country's forward march by disagreeing with the government, instead of "pitching in and helping to get us out of this impasse."

In asserting a definition of "democracy," people might also claim to defend the "Romanian nation." An example comes from a 1990 letter to the
prime minister, in which two nationalist writers well placed under
Ceauşescu seek permission to start a nationalist magazine:

> We would not have emerged from our self-imposed silence had we not been
> more and more revolted by the scandalously antinational character of certain
> publications. . . . These publications have become a sort of agent of denunci-
> ation, maintaining a climate of tension and terror over the people of good faith
> of this country. This isn't good. We cannot remain passive before the attempt of
> these hypocrites, ulcerated with political ambitions for aggrandizement and

enrichment, to destabilize the country—and worse—and to enslave it to foreign powers. . . . We see that the most perilous politics (draped in the garb of democracy, naturally!) comes from the [opposition] publications . . . manipulated openly and diabolically by the same old pig-sty at Radio Free Europe. All these people were traitors before and still are today.[22]

These writers abjure the so-called democracy of ambitious traitors (namely, anyone who disagrees), and they imply that the national interest would be better served by patriotic consensus.

Such accusations drove opposition groups to offer and defend their own understandings of what constitutes "patriotism," "anti-Romanian activity," and "national interest"—preoccupations we might not otherwise expect in people aiming to build civil society. PRM senator C. V. Tudor's chief initiative during the winter of 1993 was to introduce a law punishing "anti-Romanian activity" (meant to include most of what the political opposition was advocating). In a commentary on this initiative, one opposition member listed a number of things *he* would consider to be "anti-Romanian activity," such as: injustices committed against the Romanian people, its biological degradation, Romania's drop in living standards during the 1980s to the bottom of the list in Europe, the death of Romanian babies in freezing and underequipped maternity wards, the falsification of the national history, the killing of women from self-induced illegal abortions and of thousands of Romanians from the cold and hunger throughout the Ceaușescu period—in a word, the actions of the Romanian Communist Party, which C. V. Tudor and his nationalist friends were busily rehabilitating.[23] In addition, other opposition writings frequently questioned the "patriotism" of those in power and accused them of ruining Romania in all manner of ways—by wrecking the economy, corrupting power, and creating a dismal image of Romania in the eyes of Europe and the world (the epitomal "anti-Romanian act"). And just as the nationalists complained that the opposition wanted to "sell" the country to "foreigners," the president of the Democratic Convention countered that the PDSR was "playing the game of those foreign forces hostile to Romania"[24]—meaning not the Westerners whom nationalists objected to, but Russia.

Besides compelling their opposition enemies to counterdefinitions of "anti-Romanian activity," the government's nationalist allies forced them to elaborate an alternative understanding of the "national interest" and of how this interest related to foreign interests. A 1993 editorial in the opposition paper 22, entitled "Are These Our National Interests?" shows this nicely.[25] In it, the author affirms that three years after the so-called Romanian revolution, the original structures and personnel of the former regime have achieved a nearly complete restoration, and its beneficiaries now defend their actions as being in the nation's interests. How can this be, the editorial asks, when they wish to return to the policies that put Romania in last place in Eastern Europe and left the population with grave protein deficits, when the new powerholders are perpetuating the economic disaster and eliminating all opportunity and all hope? "Can this be in the national interests, I wonder?" The author asks the same question concerning the government's use of anti-Americanism and anti-Westernism, which will necessarily force Romania back under the heel of Moscow—"but is this in the national interest of Romanians," when all our greatest misfortunes have come not from the West but from the East? Can it be in the national interest to push the country into the arms of the Russians, "who have never known any relation of 'collaboration' except to subjugate the weaker partner?" Repeating these questions again and again, the author makes plain that the government's definition of the national interest is deeply suspect.

A final example of argument over national symbols shows an opposition paper contesting government spokesman Paul Everac's definition of "national pride." Everac had appeared in a special TV editorial in which he complained that Romanians' sense of national pride was slipping, since everyone seemed to be motivated only by abject cupidity and by chasing after a few pairs of used trousers from foreign aid packets. He decried the contraband in foreign cigarettes as degrading to Romanians. With this, he opened himself to attack from a columnist for 22, who asked, "Where was our national pride when we were importing collectivization? . . . And when we were importing all the idiot theses of Stalin . . . ? And when we put up with all Ceauşescu's gibberish and pronounced it words of genius? Where was the national pride when we stood in lines from the crack of dawn for a cup of milk?"[26] Everac had also sought to shore up the national pride by affirming that one of the ancestors of Romanians—the Roman emperor Trajan—was the genitor of Europe itself. To this the same columnist retorted, "This means either that we have *European* pride—which is more comprehensive—or that we are trying in our way to rediscover our founding father, or more exactly, the European part of our inheritance. Who took it, since we no longer have it, Mr. Everac doesn't bother to tell us. The moment when we lost Europe was placed under erasure just like the moment when we lost Bessarabia and Bucovina."[27] These lines are reminiscent of the dissident accusation against Ceauşescu, that he was tearing Romanians from their European inheritance and trying to move the country into Africa.[28] To complete the parallel, another news item observed that President Iliescu had expressed criticism of the Romans' "greed and plundering" of other nations; by this he distanced Romania from both its imperialist forebears and "Europe's" similar tendencies of today.[29] These alternative views show us a government defending Romanian "independence" against a pro-Europe opposition, each offering a different image of where Romania's "inheritance" truly lies and who (Europe, Russia) represents the greater danger.

In such company, the opposition did not have the luxury of ignoring the "nation" so as to build up "civil society." They were compelled to respond to the agenda set by those promoting national values. Significantly, however, each time they did so, they further reinforced the idea of nation and jeopardized the prospects for the civil society they wished to promote.

The Situational Constraints on "Civil Society": Three Cases

Having shown something of the alternative visions offered for Romania's "democracy" and its "national interest," I will now present three cases to illustrate how the presence of the symbol "nation" dominated the space for symbolic maneuver on the part of those defending a pro-Western vision of Romania's future. In the first case we see how vulnerable is a concept of civil society when defined independently of "the nation." The case concerns the founding congress of the Civic Alliance Party, in June 1991, and involves only members of that group—largely but not exclusively Romanian in membership—in dialogue among themselves. The second case involves (mostly Romanian) members of the Group for Social Dialogue in conversation with members of the Hungarian Democratic Union of Romania (UDMR), the party supported by virtually all Romania's Hungarians. Since that party was included in the Democratic Convention, for which all members of the Group for Social Dialogue voted, the second case enlarges the field of social allegiances by explicitly engaging Hungarians—who are nonetheless, in broad party terms, political fellow travelers. The third case enlarges the field still further, to include with Civic Alliance/Democratic Convention spokesmen the PDSR and its nationalist allies. In that case, the issue being debated was the composition of the Romanian delegation to the Council of Europe, which was considering Romania's possible membership. In all three cases, "Europe" plays a central role in defining the political options, and the symbol "nation" constrains the efficacy of "civil society."

Civic Front or Ethnic Front? The Congress of the Civic Alliance Party

As described by one of its founders, the group "Civic Alliance" was formed on 15 November 1990, "as a movement to build civil society."[30] Another active member put it thus: "The Civic Alliance is the only group that could constitute a legitimate power in Romania: its principle of action is alliance and its basic moving force is civic consciousness." And a third: "The problem of democracy is first of all a civic problem—about freedom for one's beliefs, one's ethnic identity, one's politics."[31] The group also claimed to stand for national reconciliation, for bringing the country's various ethnic groups together and dispelling the organized confusion and hate sown by the nationalists and PDSR. These statements leave no doubt as to the relative place of civic and ethnic symbols in the group's charter.

In July 1991, this organization held a conference with a view to forming a political party, to be called the Civic Alliance Party, or PAC.[32] Its aim, in the approximate words of the organizer who read its proposed statute, was to

> contribute to the democratization of Romanian society and to offer a new image of Romania to the world. Romania today has two possible directions before it: Bolshevist Asiatism or Western, European standards. Between these, the PAC sees only one choice: Europe, to which we already belong by all our traditions since 1848. All the best periods of our history have been periods of Europeanizing. The PAC wants to send Europe a Europeanizing message, to offer a credible partner for Romania's neighbors and for Europe, and to express our decisive break with the past. We must follow our neighbors in breaking down the structures of Soviet type; we must break the ties with the Soviet Union that are keeping us from Europe—ties like the mutual assistance treaty President Iliescu recently signed with Gorbachev. Among our goals must be the separation of powers in the state and an independent judiciary that meets European standards.
>
> The stakes of the Civic Alliance Party are not power but Romania. We cannot be a party of only one nationality; we must embrace all Romania's groups. We cannot work to divide Romanian society but must press for a countrywide social dialogue. We must respect the right of self-determination, which includes asking people where they want to live and then working out any conflicts in this by international treaty. [He had said earlier that the nationalities issue is a false problem, stirred up by a government that wants to draw attention from the real problems it cannot solve.] Our aim must be to build a secure Romania, with a law-governed state and a powerful civil society.[33]

As the conference unfolded, however, it became clear that different people among the organizers and delegates were proposing two potentially contradictory notions: 1) the PAC must be a civic party that would not be limited to any one nationality and would address the problem of national-minority rights in a fair-minded way; and 2) a vital element in the party platform must be to re-create the "Greater Romania" of the 1930s, by bringing back into Romania "our brothers" in newly independent Moldova (a region that between 1918 and 1940 was Romanian Bessarabia, and thereafter Soviet Moldavia). Among the opening speeches of the conference were greetings from groups in Moldova, urging the PAC to be a party of "national reintegration."[34] This objective, initially raised by only a few of the Bucharest organizers, came with increasing insistence from the provincial delegates, some of whom even proposed writing into Romania's constitution the intention to reincorporate Moldova. The Moldovan question became still more urgent when a special announcement was made, to great consternation, that there had been severe flooding in Moldova and tens of thousands of people had lost their homes. In response, the congress voted to urge the government to help Moldova, "since we are one people." Nobody mentioned the 35 percent of the population of Moldova who are ethnic Russians, Gagauz, Ukrainians, and others; only "our Romanian brothers" seemed to count.

The Moldovan question raised significant problems for a party claiming to emphasize the civic over the national and to embrace Romania's minorities. That nothing was said about the status of Moldova's non-Romanian 35 percent was sure to be galling to potential non-Romanian minority supporters of PAC (the country's Hungarians, Germans, etc.), concerned at what this national preoccupation implied for their own status in Romania. None of the enthusiasts of reintegration thought to acknowledge the parallel between Moldova and Transylvania, both regions containing sizable ethnic minorities who might prefer to be in some other state or might want guarantees of their civic status in Romania. The Moldovan question showed how feeble were the PAC's civic sentiments, so readily overshadowed by national feeling. As speaker after speaker invoked Moldova, the problems of how to build civil society or integrate minorities into it faded from view.

More was at issue, however, than a groundswell of fraternal feeling in response to natural disaster: the groundswell itself affected the political calculus of the party organizers and the very commitment of some of them to the "civic alliance" inscribed in their name. These effects of the Moldovan question and its consequences for negotiating a definition of "civic" that would not also be "ethnic" came blatantly to the fore during the morning of the second day.[35] Perceiving the drift of comments from the hall, some of the organizers unilaterally decided that it would be wise to scratch a planned reading of the proposed statement on the rights of minorities. They reasoned that if the PAC kept its minorities plank, it would alienate many of the voters who, like the group's own delegates, were sensitive to the national idea; in particular, it would alienate Romanian voters in Transylvania, where ethnic issues were especially acute. Since those were precisely the Romanians most likely to be interested in other aspects of the PAC platform, the sticky tactical question now became how far the PAC should go to attract those votes, at the expense of what the party's organizers had initially agreed should be its multiethnic principles—principles in accord with their conception of a European-style civic society. The person who had been chosen to read the minorities statement at the congress was furious and complained (in private) that all the organizers with ethics were being pushed out by a new mafia, peddling nationalism and monarchism rather than the moral and civic principles for which the group was supposed to stand.

After heated backstage discussion, it was finally agreed that the statement on minorities would be read after all, but in a very undesirable slot—the time when most people were marking off their ballots to elect leaders of the new party and the hall was buzzing with conversation. Thus few actually heard a document that was dedicated to Europe, civic life, and the supersession of national differences by these larger values. It spoke of a Romania integrated into Europe and adhering to the Helsinki norms for the protection of minorities; it decried recrudescent xenophobia and chauvinism in Romania, as well as the governing PDSR's complicity in this; it invoked Romanian traditions of cooperation and peaceful cohabitation with other groups. It emphasized that national rights are a fundamental human right and a foundation of democracy, affirming that "no nation can be indifferent to the fate of the minorities with which it lives." While underscoring that minorities had the obligation to be loyal citizens of Romania and to defend its constitution and laws, the statement called for tolerance and for the rights of minorities to respect and to equality with all other Romanian citizens (including the right to oppose assimilation, to use their language, etc.), and it granted minorities the right to appeal to international organizations if these guarantees were not observed.

The statement received almost no reaction from a thoroughly inattentive audience.

The problem of the PAC's relations with minorities dogged its footsteps on into the larger political arena. Included among the parties to the Democratic Convention was the UDMR, the party of Romania's Hungarians. It had polled 7 percent in the previous elections and could be expected to do so again—a solid bloc of votes the Convention would surely need if it were to match the voting strength of the PDSR. But the inclusion of the UDMR enabled the PDSR and its allies to accuse the Convention of being "anti-Romanian" and those in the PAC, in particular, of having "sold out to the Hungarians." In Transylvania, the anti-PDSR vote was evenly divided between the Convention (which had expected to sweep that region) and the nationalist PUNR.[36] This greatly diminished the Convention's parliamentary strength and vindicated the calculation of those in the PAC leadership who had wanted to suppress the statement on minorities and, even at the expense of civic values, ride nationalism to victory.

Are Civic Rights Individual or Collective? Relations with the UDMR

Following the national elections in September–October 1992, in which the Convention failed to win the presidency or its expected number of parliamentary seats both despite and because of its electoral alliance with the Hungarian Party, the opposition was unpleasantly surprised by a UDMR declaration in favor of Hungarian autonomy. This document, called the "Cluj Declaration," emerged from a power struggle within the UDMR between its radical and moderate factions. The Cluj Declaration angered many among the Hungarians' erstwhile allies, who were unprepared for it, did not know how to interpret it, and saw in it a further erosion of the opposition's political chances. Indeed, the nationalist Romanian parties immediately launched an attack on the Hungarians and their opposition allies.

In this context of anxiety and offense, members of the Group for Social Dialogue (GDS) invited members of the UDMR to a roundtable discussion, later published in the group's newspaper, 22.[37] The Group for Social Dialogue had been the very first civil-society organization founded in late December 1989; most of its members later joined the (much larger) Civic Alliance, some also taking leadership positions in the PAC. In setting up a roundtable with the UDMR, the GDS aimed to discuss what the Hungarians meant by "autonomy" and why they insisted on a definition of "rights" as collective rather than individual. This second point revealed fundamental differences between the Hungarians present and their Romanian interlocutors, differences having major implications for their joint effort to build "democracy" and "civil society"—even though the common premise of all was that they were building democracy and the PDSR was not. Their differences echoed as well in their invocations of "Europe."

In the Cluj Declaration, Hungarians insisted that they are members not simply of a national minority but of a community; this entitles them to request autonomy like other communities—religious ones, territorial ones, and so on—allowing them to resolve without external interference any matters relating to their community identity: education, language maintenance, culture, and so on. They also claimed that the jural entities guaranteed equal rights in the Constitution should be not just individuals but communities as well. The heart of their disagreement with Romanians from the GDS was that the latter were perplexed about why Hungarians saw a constitutional guarantee of individual rights as insufficient protection: why did there need to be collective guarantees? What sort of rights did the Hungarians claim that went beyond the guarantees of individual rights to freedom of expression, of association, and so forth?

Although the long-term implications of the different views include substantially different understandings of such important matters as citizenship, I believe the crux of the disagreement was more immediately strategic: the GDS and other opposition groups would be able to support the Hungarians only if they could do so in the context of a "democratic movement" seeking better definition, and better enforcement, of individual rights under the law. As one Romanian participant put it, "Your arguments so far refer to shortcomings in the existing legislation. . . . From this it follows that we have to improve the laws and, even more, their enforcement. Why, then, haven't you oriented yourselves to these things that interest you directly and that are also of general interest? Why do you think there is another route to your goals than the general route toward democracy?"[38] By the end of the discussion, the Romanian participants were saying outright that the Hungarians' declaration had put obstacles in the path of democratization and had fanned the flames of Romanian nationalism, pushing the PDSR into the arms of the Romanian nationalist parties.[39] Some saw the Hungarians' move as corrupting the proper definition of democracy, as "introducing into a discussion about democratic rights, about democracy, an extrademocratic criterion, an anthropological criterion—the *ethnie*."[40] Beneath this talk, the Romanians were saying that if Hungarians insisted on collective rights, to support them would be politically disastrous.

Two of the many important points that emerged from this discussion concerned how to build civil society and undermine the power of the governing coalition, and what lessons "Europe" might hold for the treatment of national-minority problems. First, the Hungarians argued that their claim to autonomy was a significant move toward decentralization and, as such, would diminish the center's power. As one of them put it, "In our opinion, two political conceptions collide here, two modes of seeing things: a political conception whose values emphasize decentralization and autonomy, and a political conception according the state a tutelary role that impedes the initiative of the structures of civil society. To put forward the idea of autonomy is not a problem between Hungarians and Romanians" (but rather one between state and civil society).[41]

To this, one of the Romanians replied that it would be almost impossible to discuss decentralization in Romania because Romanians see this as imperiling Transylvania's place in a unified Romanian state: any "local autonomy" might lead to Transylvania's spinning out of Romania's orbit, becoming either an autonomous entity or an annex of Hungary.[42] Therefore, only with great difficulty could Hungarians and Romanians discuss local autonomy without arousing this fear.[43] Preferable for the Romanian participants was constant pressure on the government for individual civil rights, whose exercise would constrain the state. We see here two irreconcilable strategies and rationales[44] for breaking the PDSR's lock on power, with each group seeing its strategy as central to building "democracy" or "civil society." In both strategies, however, national concerns distort the space within which civic ones can be pursued.

Second, while Romanians and non-Romanians in the roundtable used "Europe" equally to illuminate the political options, they differed on *how* "Europe" might do this. A non-Romanian position on the matter came from one of the GDS's own members, an ethnic German, who argued as follows:

To think of the state as unitary, national, sovereign, and so on is anachronistic. If we think this way, it's only because we're unsure of our identity as Romanians. . . . The underlying question is always, Is Transylvania ours or not? From this flow certain discussions that are in fact old-fashioned, that concern territoriality, which is a deep instinct but doesn't necessarily define humanity's essence. In the world today, especially in Europe, the struggle is for group rights, community rights. This is a reality, and we can't exempt ourselves from it. If we bridle at this idea it's because we haven't gotten into Europe yet. We have to get into Europe, and then discuss the problem at a European level.[45]

Thus to be "European"—a goal to which all participants in the roundtable were committed—is to renounce "anachronistic" attachments to territoriality and to defend group rights.

In 1990s Romania, however, this program would be politically suicidal, losing the opposition virtually all its Romanian voters.[46] The Romanian partners to the discussion were thus understandably reluctant to adopt the defense of collective rights. One of them challenged this "argument from Europe" with another argument, also "from Europe":[47]

> Over the past few years, the Council of Europe has been working on an international document about collective rights. But progress has been unimpressive because, it seems, the concept has many complexities that must somehow be resolved. The [Hungarians'] position has surprised us, then, and at least for those of us who occupy ourselves rather more with questions of human rights and the rights of minorities, it raises a lot of problems. To put collective rights above individual ones means to overturn a structure, a whole conceptualization of the relation between individual and community that is fundamental to the new conception of democracy on which postwar Europe was built. In this sense, we would end up giving priority to certain rights of the state, of the "general" collective, even over communal and individual rights. . . . How does the UDMR conceptually defend this asymmetry between collective and individual rights?[48]

Here Europe is seen as having laid the foundations for democracy with a certain conception of the relation between individual and collective that is not yet quite as anachronistic as the first speaker claims. The second speaker sees democracy as based in individual civil rights, posited as the ongoing legacy of Europe that he thinks Romanian politics should make its own. In these arguments we see how tightly interwoven are "civic" and "national" ideas even within civil-society groups like the GDS. Hungarians claim that their ethnic autonomy will create space for more civil society, but Romanians see it as jeopardizing their own national unity; Romanian civic individualism, in turn, strikes Hungarians as insensitive to Hungarian national concerns.

Absent from the words of the debate but nourishing the strong passions at its heart were also, I believe, feelings about the morality of suffering and the claims it would enfranchise. Several of the Romanians in the debate had suffered persecution as individuals for their opposition to the Party; their consequent moral standing was evident in the respect they enjoyed within the GDS. Arguments for individual civic rights sprang from their courageous individual defense of such rights. Many Hungarians, by contrast, saw the entire Ceauşescu period as a terrible assault on their collective national being: they had felt ever-more-stringent regulations against their language, schools, publications, and so on as attacks on their very existence as Hungarians (and hence as humans), and they had viewed Ceauşescu's much-publicized village destruction program of 1988–89 as genocide. This collective suffering deserved recognition and redress, as well as guarantees against its recurrence. Given the context of the discussion and the effort of all participants to keep it cordial, the language of justification-by-suffering was almost absent. Even so, however, one Hungarian replied as follows to a Romanian's saying that their aim should be to make the government respect constitutional guarantees for individual and general liberties: "Of course! But don't you agree that we [Hungarians] suffer more, because we live not only in the general context but through what is specific to us?"[49] Here relative suffering is used to force a rank-ordering of the desirable civic rights.

The GDS's roundtable highlights, I believe, how difficult it was for the Romanian opposition to consolidate itself as a democratic force in a political field so mined by the national idea and past national conflicts. If the opposition could not contemplate local autonomy as a means of decentralizing and thus of reconfiguring power because to do so would invite charges of treason and national dismemberment, and if there could be no defense of democracy except through individual rights—through a set of rights central to building up political subjectivities that may now be obsolescent—then the opposition was sorely constrained in its challenge to the ruling coalition. No defense of individual rights can respond adequately to the homogenizing ideology of nationalism, so closely akin to Party policies that homogenized the social landscape and predisposed people toward homogenizing rather than pluralizing discourses.[50]

On the same playing field as the GDS and UDMR were other groups eager to seize the homogenizing initiative. Consider the following, written in defense of nationalist (PUNR) mayor Gheorghe Funar, of the Transylvanian city of Cluj:

> What would be the consequences if Funar were removed from his post as mayor? . . . The whole of Transylvania would fall into the rapacious and bloody hands of the horthyists of the UDMR. . . . The UDMR would become the principal political force in Transylvania and would dictate to the overwhelming majority of the population. Statues, monuments, and Romanian cemeteries would be profaned, horthyism would revive, the Orthodox Church would reel before a Vatican offensive, all Transylvania would tremble. . . . The government can fall, the president can fall, for as it is he is mostly an ornament, but Funar

cannot be allowed to fall. . . . Political regimes are ephemeral and pursue only narrow interests. The basis of success must be the union of all Romanians irrespective of their religious faith or political preferences.[51]

For pro-Funar nationalists, the homogenizing discourse of anti-Hungarian Romanian chauvinism proved a potent political resource, gaining them votes and political office in the country's ethnically mixed regions. "Europe" has nothing to offer these people.[52] Similar if less exaggerated views also came from President Iliescu. He defined Europe's position on the national question thus:

We are criticized in relation to democratic norms concerning national minorities, when the only policy toward minorities in Western countries is to assimilate them, not to assure their rights. Do people in France talk about minorities and their right to use their mother tongue and to organize schools in German? Does anyone suggest creating a [German-language] university in Strasbourg? . . . If we were to follow the example of the West, we would have to promote a politics of assimilating the nationalities, of liquidating all schools in their mother tongues, of prohibiting any language other than the language of state. In France, French is used throughout the administration and system of justice, no? This is what it would mean to follow the Western example.[53]

For Iliescu, Europe indeed sets a standard for Romania—one of denying minorities any special status. To complete the field, here is the opinion—quoted at greater length in chapter 4—of nationalist (PRM) senator C. V. Tudor, staunch critic of "Europe" and advocate of a consensual view of democracy from which Hungarians and their friends should be banned as traitors:[54]

Romanians, Hungarian fascism is attacking us openly. The political paranoia of Budapest has entered its final phase. . . . So we have been right, over the past two years, to sound the alarm against Hungarian terrorism. *In twenty-four hours we must ban by law all anti-Romanian groupings: the Hungarian Democratic Union of Romania and Soros Foundation, as well as their [opposition] stooges . . . ! They want autonomy? Expel them!*[55]

Under circumstances in which writers of lines like these are easily elected, no political opposition to such forces can count on success if it allies with minorities and guarantees their rights. We see, then, the hegemony of "nation" as a political symbol.

The themes of the roundtable between the GDS and UDMR have a coda. In January 1993 the UDMR held its party congress and elected new party leaders, amid a fierce factional struggle. In advance of the congress, observers anticipated that the radical nationalist faction, led by bishop László Tökés, might take over the UDMR, an outcome that would gravely compromise its place in the opposition coalition. The Romanian groups in the Democratic Convention therefore mobilized themselves, sending its highest-ranking members to the congress. Their speeches all conveyed the message: you are not alone; we share a common struggle to build a more democratic Romania.[56] Not only did the levels of applause for the speeches of the Convention leaders show unexpected support for the moderate line within the UDMR, which went on to win the leadership, but the troubling phrases about "collective rights" were removed (at least for the moment) from the party's program, which mentioned only local autonomy and personal rights. The opposition's Romanian parties saw the result as a victory for the spirit of interethnic collaboration and a good omen for the Convention's future.[57] (Unfortunately, however, this was not to last, for by late 1994 the UDMR was once again agitating for local autonomy, and the Convention's refusal to back it up led to its leaving the antigovernment coalition in 1995.)

Romania Goes to Europe: Who Will Represent Us?

My third and final case concerns discussions around the parliamentary delegation that was to represent Romania at the Council of Europe. Despite the fulminations of the PDSR and its nationalist allies against "selling the country to foreigners" and "neo-imperialism," as of February 1993 the Romanian government was petitioning the Council of Europe for admittance. Maneuvering began in parliament to select the delegates who would travel to Strasbourg to present the case. As Romania's staunchest supporters of the idea of Europe, members of the opposition had somehow expected they would be the delegates. Instead, they found themselves outflanked by the PDSR and its allies. These parties not only managed to secure a disproportionate number of places on the delegation but also gave those places to several nostalgic apologists of the Ceauşescu era, who were overtly antagonistic to integration with Europe and critical of international organizations. They were people who had often condemned in their writings the "aberrant regulations" of international accords that would have Romania as their victim, a Romania "besieged in the heart of a terrible plot"[58]—in which they saw the opposition as a partner. As one of them put it, "Before our very eyes, these people [the opposition] are selling the country piece by piece."[59]

Some opposition commentators immediately suspected that the maneuvering over the delegation was itself a plot: to prevent Romania's acceptance into Europe by sending people who would compromise the country's credibility in Europe's eyes. The resulting denial of membership would then "force" the government into the alliance it actually preferred—with the East. As one journalist summarized this view, "The gravest suspicion that pollutes our political life is that President Iliescu, supported by the former Securitate . . . , intends to alienate Romania from Western Europe and throw it again into the orbit of Slavic imperialism."[60] (The same journalist also believed that the game was in fact more duplicitous, with those in power wanting integration into Europe on terms that would legitimate them and their behavior—that is, integration despite the presence of vociferous nationalists and Ceaușescu nostalgics among the delegates. As sign of its newly "Europeanizing" interest, the PDSR was right then rushing through parliament approval for an EC loan despite its stringent provisions.) Another commentator suggested that the government might think the "love-me-with-all-my-warts" strategy would work because the success of the international boycott of Serbia hinged on Romania's compliance in policing the Danube. For this reason, the PDSR could expect the Europeans to close their eyes to some of Romania's uglier characteristics.[61]

Opposition commentary on the delegation to Europe clearly revealed a battle to shape Europe's image of Romania, with the PDSR and nationalists on one side and various opposition parties on the other. Commenting on one nationalist's view that "we want to offer the West another image of Romania," an opposition journalist worried that the PDSR-stacked delegation "will surely make use of the occasion to tell Europe that in Romania there is no minority problem and no National-Communist current."[62] The president of the Civic Alliance Party, Senator Nicolae Manolescu, nuanced the picture:

> The Front [i.e., PDSR] found that it had to choose between sending, let's say, a "correct" delegation to the Council of Europe—one that would enhance our chances of gaining membership—and preserving its problematic parliamentary majority. If the Front chose Europe, it risked a rupture with [its two nationalist allies], which would wipe out its majority. . . . In these conditions they didn't want to sacrifice a working majority for a possible European membership. . . . We, of course, put the following question: in a matter concerning the national interest, why didn't they accept a consensus across party lines? In both the Senate and the House the opposition proposed a [delegation based on] national consensus. But this consensus was rejected in a way that, in my opinion, shows how an opportunistic political calculation to maintain their political majority is more important to the Front than the national interest. . . . [We are nonetheless not boycotting the delegation] because we can't let those in power claim that the opposition is sabotaging Romania's entry into Europe.[63]

In this comment, the quintessential pro-European party spokesman finds himself compelled to invoke the "national interest" (by which he means international assistance, and which the PDSR has jeopardized in a crassly "antipatriotic gesture)";[64] meanwhile, the government has repeatedly accused the opposition of sabotaging the "national interest" whenever Romania lost a vote in the U.S. Congress, or in Europe. The issue of the delegation to Europe also reveals, however, some constraints on the behavior of the

PDSR itself. Although the government knew it could not survive without loans, it was reluctant to pay the political price of accepting them over the objections of its nationalist allies, who saw integration into Europe as a national catastrophe and the Council of Europe itself as "playing the game of an international conspiracy directed from Budapest."[65] How to win the next elections if Romania's economic situation remained so parlous? And how to improve the economic situation except by Western assistance? At least one observer saw in this dilemma the cause of further fissures in the PDSR itself, between two currents—one choosing European integration and the other resisting it so as to maintain firmer internal dominance.[66] The case shows how complex a symbol "Europe" has become, in the world of Romanian realpolitik.

Conclusions

The preceding cases illustrate how certain notions—such as Europe, Asia, foreign domination, democracy, national interest, and civil society—were deployed in Romanian politics during 1991–93. They were deployed as having *moral* significance, based in their implications for the fate of the Romanian nation—an idea seen by all as having ultimate value. Because each of these symbols legitimated a different program and different actors aspiring to power, the different moral claims made by using one or another of them had consequences for the power they helped to consolidate. These various symbols were participating, then, in maintaining or transforming the political, economic, and social structures that have characterized Romania for the past half-century.

In hopes of transforming these structures, some in Romania availed themselves of a global political discourse about rights, democracy, civility, the West, and Europe. This discourse marshals allies in Western Europe and the U.S., thereby possibly mobilizing a stream of resources for Romania's transformation. But as was clear from the 1992 election results, it was less successful in marshaling supporters inside Romania, especially in the villages, where nearly half the population resides. Analysis of the election results showed that the Democratic Convention's greatest strength was among people with higher education (three times as many voted for the Convention as for the PDSR) and in major urban centers, but that it was weak in rural areas, where six times as many voters preferred the PDSR.[67] It was also weaker than it should have been in the most Westernized, developed, "European" part of the country: Transylvania, where long-term co-residence with Hungarians and Germans has both Europeanized Romanians and traumatized them on the ethnic question. There, many who rejected the "Bolshevist Asiatism" of the PDSR voted not for the Convention—too cozy with

Hungarians—but, instead, for the Party of Romanian National Unity (Transylvanians elected a full 84 percent of that party's members of parliament).

Aside from the obvious ethnic problem for Transylvanians, why is it that "Europe" and all it implies have been relatively uninteresting to many in the Romanian electorate? This is a complicated question. Its answer involves matters such as the symbolic economy of power, unemployment and the reduced social welfare inherent in Western-style reforms, and the institutional and organizational advantages of the governing coalition. To begin with, "Europe" is an urban intellectuals' conceit; they have not done enough to translate it positively into the life terms of everyone else. Romania's entry into the "civilized" world is important in the self-conception of intellectuals, for whom culture and civilization are of the essence;[68] but these have rather little import for the daily existence of many villagers, for instance, either toiling with rudimentary equipment on tiny patches of land or commuting long hours to work in distant factories. What have Europe and civil society to do with this? For village residents, the defenders of "Europe" have not managed to constitute its symbols as meaningful objects of political action.

Worse still, the effects of Europeanization that villagers have indeed understood are not necessarily an appealing prospect. As several ethnographers have reported, although some East European villagers are eager for privatization of land, others fear that this will divide their communities into rich and poor, make them proprietors without giving them adequate means for producing, possibly subject them to unpayable levels of taxation and force them out of agriculture altogether, and even spell the end of collective farm pensions.[69] In Romania, the PDSR argued convincingly that an electoral victory by the opposition would mean restoring an older era of large estates and landless peasants. More than a few villagers saw the arguments of urban "civil-society" intellectual/politicians as potentially catastrophic—like the previous round of urban-based initiatives toward them: collectivization.

Aside from not having managed to create a program appealing to rural residents, the opposition was handicapped by the legacy of socialism's relative homogenization of the social field and its language of equality and unity (see chapter 4). Despite people's widespread dissatisfaction with Party rule, some of the Party's moral claims have remained attractive. These include the idea that social solidarity is valuable and that it rests on a shared social condition, to which great differences in wealth are inimical. Many Romanians (to say nothing of others in the region) are deeply suspicious of the differentiation of social interests that is expected to accompany the growth of a democratic polity and market economy.[70] Their resistance to the possibility of social division has set limits, I believe, to the opposition's civil-society talk, compelling them to present civil society as a unified moral realm, separate from politics and the state—just as it was once the unified moral realm of opposition to the Party—rather than as a domain of multiple and competing interests, integral to democratic politics.[71] Such an emphasis on unity makes their discourse more consonant not only with popular preferences for equality but also with discourses about the always-unitary "nation." Only if market-based differentiation advances the fortunes of enough Romanians to breed an interest in "pluralism" might the unity and homogenization evoked by the idea of "nation" begin to seem less attractive than symbols of other kinds.

This outcome is not what one might have predicted from the jubilation around ideas of Europe and civil society in December 1989, which suggested that these symbols would now overpower "nation." Given the extent to which Ceauşescu had overused the latter, it was a reasonable calculation that other symbols would have more force in post-Ceauşescu politics; newly empowered anti-Communists would have seen no risks, in 1990, to imitating the democratic and civil-society rhetoric of their analogues in Hungary and Czechoslovakia. As it happened, this calculation proved erroneous. The Romanian Communist Party, in alliance with some of the same nationalists who now support the PDSR, had substantially strengthened the already potent political symbol, "nation," increasing its capacity to structure fields of discourse. In making use of it in post-1989 struggles, the PDSR and their nationalist allies were wielding the most powerful weapon in the symbolic arsenal of Romanian politics.[72] Owing to its force and to continued disquiet over social differentiation, the more closely opposition groups approximate "nation" in elaborating their rhetoric, the greater will be their political success over at least the short to medium run. This would mean less talk of Europe, and a more distant relation with Hungarians—in short, less of what initially made the political opposition an admirable and novel force in Romanian politics, from a certain (North American) point of view.

In a discussion of intellectuals in India, Nicholas Dirks observes that the globalization of the discourses upon which Third World intellectuals draw has the effect of obscuring the conditions of production and the meanings of symbols at their points of origin.[73] Dirks's insight requires that any analysis of the politics of discourse pay special attention to both the local and the global aspects of the conditions of production through which symbols are "processed," as well as of the resources utilized in doing so. This paper has shown that in 1990s Romanian political discourse, there is a tremendous discrepancy between the local and the global situations and resources of the main participants. The opposition has the more powerful international resources, congealed in their references to Europe and civil society. But within Romania, the "National-Communists" monopolize both the institutional resources and the most potent political symbol, and their use of it puts their opponents on the defensive. Their pressure, which is also the pressure of a certain historically constituted discourse and of its master symbol, "nation," compels all other political actors in Romania to "nationalize" their political instruments—and in so doing, to strengthen "nation" as a political symbol even further. The pressure is felt not just at the level of discourse: it affects political strategy also, as my examples have shown. And it requires that for the opposition, "Europe" and the "civil society" it implies must mean first of all something national—a conception of Romania as a civilized, European country rather than a backwater of Slavdom. Only secondarily can it mean the forms and practices of a pluralist politics.

PART THREE

PROCESSES: TRANSFORMING PROPERTY,

MARKETS, AND STATES

6

THE ELASTICITY OF LAND: PROBLEMS OF PROPERTY

RESTITUTION IN TRANSYLVANIA

Land doesn't expand, and it doesn't contract; we'll find
your piece of it.
(Judge in a court case over land)

"Hey! Since when did my garden shrink?" "It didn't
shrink, it stretched."
*(Two neighbors arguing over the boundary
between their gardens)*

The day will come when a man will go out into his field and
not know where it begins or ends.
*(Biblical reference by villagers to the imminent
end of the world)*

IN MEMORY OF IOAN ALUAŞ

IN FEBRUARY 1991, the Romanian parliament passed a law for the restoration of land to its former owners. Known as Law 18/1991, the Law on Agricultural Land Resources (*Legea Fondului Funciar*) liquidated collective farms and returned their lands to the households that had given them over at collectivization (1959–62).[1] The former owners recover not merely usufruct, or use rights, but full rights of ownership. A North American urbanite might imagine (as I did myself) that this process would unfold something as follows. Land was collectivized by putting together all peasant farms in a village and working them in common. Therefore, because a field and its constituent parcels are fixed goods—like a table with so many

Written in August 1994, this chapter resulted from nine months' ethnographic research on property restitution in Transylvania (September 1993–June 1994). My research was supported by a grant from the International Research and Exchanges Board (IREX), with funds from the National Endowment for the Humanities, the United States Information Agency and the U.S. Department of State, which administers the Russian, Eurasian, and East European Research Program (Title VIII). These organizations might well disagree with my views.

I am grateful to Ashraf Ghani, Gail Kligman, Paul Nadasdy, and Michel-Rolph Trouillot for helpful comment, and to C.T., B.I., and B.A. for teaching me most of what I know about property place mats on it, marking where each piece begins and ends—to restore those parcels to their original owners is only a matter of determining the coordinates of the place mats prior to 1959 and reattributing them to whoever had them at the time. This should not be a complicated matter.

Whoever thinks thus is mistaken. In this chapter I will show that collectives were not formed simply by putting together peasant farms, that land is not fixed but exceedingly elastic, that collectivization was more a matter of unraveling the place mats than of simply taking them up, and that the better image of decollectivization comes not from the judge quoted at the top of this chapter but from villagers' biblical images of apocalypse. Transylvanians will probably never see the full restoration of their earlier rights to land.

There are a number of reasons why property restitution might prove more complicated than its backers—including Western governments and lending institutions—had imagined. To begin with, 30 percent of Romania's agricultural land was in state farms (IASs), not collective farms (CAPs), and Law 18 disbands only the latter.[2] The state justifies this decision as necessary to ensure that food is still produced (on the state farms) while the collectives are being dismantled. But this leaves many prior landowners locked out of properties that happen to be located in state farms, and they have resisted both by suits and by forcible occupations. More problematically, Law 18 re-creates the property situation as of 1959 for a society existing some thirty years later. Thus it reconstitutes the farms of households that were viable units thirty years ago but whose members have now died, emigrated, married, and otherwise substantially changed their relationship to land. The result has been conflicts among kin, among members of different ethnic groups, between villagers who had land before and those who did not, and between village residents who remained in the village and those who emigrated to an easier life in town. Law 18 has thus produced a degree of upheaval and tension in rural areas nearly as disruptive as that of collectivization itself.

I will concentrate less on these two sources of difficulty in the application of Law 18 than on a third: the present consequences of socialism's operation and especially of its treatment of land. By erasing the grid of property from the landscape, by removing the boundaries that immobilized land—by removing, as it were, the tacks that held the place mats to specific sites on the table—socialism engendered a landscape with elastic qualities. Given the

---

restitution in Transylvania. I also owe a debt to officials of Geoagiu commune for facilitating my work and to the Aurel Vlaicu land commission, whose members graciously accepted my company during some of their rounds. Ioan Aluaş, to whom I have dedicated this chapter, was my research collaborator in the Department of Sociology in Cluj and first made me aware of the elasticity of land. He helped me launch the project but died while it was in progress.

This chapter is reprinted from *Slavic Review* 53 (1994), by permission of the American Association for the Advancement of Slavic Studies.

political decision to restore prior ownership rather than simply to distribute land, this elasticity kindles dissension and opens wide spaces for maneuver by the village and commune elites charged with reimposing a grid.

Unlike earlier times and places in which seemingly unbounded land became the object of possession, however (one thinks of the enclosures, or the colonization of the Americas), this elasticity confronts a social memory of a landscape with edges, with owners, a landscape corseted by the spatial grid of a rationalizing economy and state. Property restitution is therefore, like Kundera's proverbial struggle of memory against forgetting, a struggle of certain groups and persons to tie property down against others who would keep its edges flexible, uncertain, amorphous. It is a struggle of particularization against abstraction, of specific clods of earth against aggregate figures on paper, and of particular individuals and families, reasserting thereby their specificity against a collectivist order that had sought to efface it. The story of property restitution is a story of forming (or failing to form) potentially new kinds of persons, along with new social identities based in property and possessing. This story is part of the larger drama of transforming Romania's class structure, economy, and system of state power.

In what follows, I speak often of land that moves, stretches, evaporates—of land that acts.[3] This locution is apt. In early 1990s Romania, not only land but social life itself has lost its moorings. People's conceptions of their world, the parameters of their long-standing survival strategies, their sense of who is friend and who enemy, the social context in which they had defined themselves and anchored their lives—all have been overthrown. Social institutions are in a process of redefinition and flux, and once-recognizable groupings and structural positions have lost contour. "The state" is not the state of before, nor the courts, nor the police, and political parties are still little more than shifting conglomerates of friends and their networks. It is not yet clear either to participants or to analysts what structures will ground social action in the future. In such fluid circumstances, when the slots that define the possibilities for human agency are up for grabs, the few things that appear solid—such as land—suddenly take on new importance. But even this solidity turns out, as I will show, to be an illusion. By revealing it as such, I hope to capture the sense of profound dislocation that prevails in the Transylvanian countryside.

The Law on Agricultural Land Resources

In contrast to property restitution in some other postsocialist contexts such as Albania, Russia, and Armenia, but as in Bulgaria, Slovakia, and the Czech Republic, Romania's Law 18 does not just distribute land to villagers who live on it and have worked it: it attempts to re-create the property regime that existed before collectivization.[4] There are a few exceptions to fully re-constituting the status quo ante. 1) No owner will receive more than ten hectares. 2) The minimum holding to be reconstituted is one-half hectare. 3) People with land in the area of state farms (IASs), rather than the CAPs, will receive not land but dividends from the proceeds of those farms. 4) Although owners are "as a rule" (*de regulă*) to receive land on their "former sites" (*vechile amplasamente*)—that is, the precise parcels they had owned be-fore[5]—where construction or other changes in land use obviate this they will get equivalent pieces elsewhere.

One need not be resident in a village to receive land, then, nor does one receive it in some proportion to one's capacity to work it.[6] Moreover, people who worked for decades on a collective farm but had given it no land might get nothing at all. Restitution for some thus means deprivation for others. The law specifies that such people should receive up to one-half hectare if there is land in excess of the claims of former owners; it even invites land commissions to *create* excess land by subtracting a fixed percentage—the "reduction coefficient"—from the reconstituted holdings; and it gives com-missions the option of consolidating parcels instead of reproducing the frag-mented property structure of the 1930s. These provisions, together with the ten-hectare limit, mean that Law 18 aims not quite at full property restitu-tion but, rather, at restitution touched with agrarian reform. Because many Transylvanian villages have no excess land, however (the reduction co-efficient having been misapplied), and because field consolidation is infre-quent, agrarian reform has faltered.

How did it happen that Romania is partly resuscitating the past in this way, seeking to lift out whole chunks of the Communist period as if it had never occurred? This is a complex question, since similar decisions were made in other East-bloc countries for varying political reasons. In all of them, however, the collapse of Communist Parties that many had believed eternal showed people that their understanding of their past was grievously mistaken; as a result, they have sought a more secure, usable past to give compass to their trajectories, and the pre-Communist order is the readiest available.

Important in refashioning the past, in Romania as elsewhere, was wide-spread popular revulsion to "Communism" and all it stood for. That senti-ment was politically articulated by different groups in different countries. In the Romanian case, its spokesmen were the reanimated "historical par-ties" of the interwar years, most particularly the Liberal and National Peas-ant parties. These were revivified in 1990 by some of their now-aged former members, many of whom the Communists had jailed, while confiscating their property.[7] Jail and confiscation, in the anti-Communist public mood of 1990–91, became significant moral/political assets and qualified the programs of the historical parties as touchstones of anti-Communism.[8] Thus their call to restore property that had been either confiscated outright or coerced from its owners gained wide resonance.[9] Anti-Communist feeling was so pervasive that even the former Communists of the governing National Salvation Front were forced into the clamor to restore property to its former owners. They had sought initially to preempt this demand by giving one-half hectare to everyone living in rural areas, regardless of prior ownership status. But at that political moment in Romania, it was impossible to reverse course: the influence of the historical parties had given the idea of property restitution, rather than simple redistribution, too much momentum.

Law 18 was nevertheless a political compromise. Although all agreed to premise the law on restitution rather than land reform, the governing party managed—over the objections of the historical parties—to impose a limit of ten hectares on reconstituted holdings.[10] The change was crucial. Justified as a measure to promote social equity (to permit giving land to as many people as possible, including those who had worked in the collectives but had not owned land), its effect was to preclude the re-creation of a viable, propertied middle class in agriculture, one that might exert certain kinds of pressure on the state.[11] The passage of this limit by the parliament indicates the balance of forces in Romanian politics at the time: anti-Communist groups allied with an older class of owners (represented by the historical parties) lost out to the newer class of apparatchiks, the political base of the National Salvation Front.

This is especially clear in the discrepancy between amounts one can inherit and amounts one can thereafter acquire. Regardless of the number of heirs, no farm existing in the 1950s can be reconstituted with more than ten hectares—that is, if a father had twenty hectares in 1958 and then died, leaving two sons, they will not each receive ten hectares but must instead split a single ten-hectare farm. The law stipulates that once people have received land, however, they may freely "acquire by any legal means" up to a limit of one hundred hectares. Certain groups of people were better situated than others to obtain land after 1991, either because they had more money to buy it or because they had the means to make fraudulent acquisition appear legal. These included newly elected mayors, plus the rural agrarian elite of the Communist period—for example, agronomists and presidents of collective farms, heads of state farms, heads of the agricultural machinery stations, all of whom have the edge in building a new social position, by contrast to the now-handicapped pre-Communist elite. From this we see the "entrepratchik" character of the governing party, which accepted certain anti-Communist reforms while modifying them to the advantage of the former Communist Party apparatus.

This group pushed its advantage further in the 1992 electoral campaign by arguing to rural inhabitants that a victory by the historical parties would mean re-creating the large estates of the gentry and ensuring poverty for the rest. For most villagers, then, a vote for Iliescu and his party[12] meant a vote to acquire property rather than give it to the rich of pre-Communist times. Iliescu's party therefore gained significant political capital by accepting the compromise of land restitution but modifying it in crucial respects, which won it an overwhelming vote in rural areas.

The passage of Law 18 in February 1991 launched the dissolution of collective farms all across the country and the restoration of individual private landownership. Agents of the latter were to be land commissions working at three administrative levels: the county, its constituent communes, and their constituent villages. Of these three, the most important were the commune commissions, charged with determining the amounts of land each village's households were to receive and with resolving disputes wherever possible. Problem cases would go to the county land commission or to the courts. The actual measuring and assignment of specific parcels to their newly established owners was the job of commissions working in each village, subsets of the commune commission. Administratively, there is a sharp break between the county commissions and those of the commune and village: the former exercises almost no control over the latter two, which are run by the commune mayor. He therefore has great power over how property restitution proceeds.

I watched the unfolding of this process between September 1993 and June 1994 from the vantage point of the Transylvanian village Aurel Vlaicu, located in the commune of Geoagiu in Hunedoara county.[13] The location is significant, for Transylvania's property history and structure are very different from those of Romania's other parts, owing to the region's prior inclusion in the Habsburg Empire. During the 1860s, the Austrians introduced property registration into Transylvania. Because the parts of present-day Romania that were not under Austrian occupation instituted land records much later and in more provisional form, anyone there who now wishes to prove ownership has fewer, and more unreliable, sources than do Transylvanians. The latter therefore have greater hopes both of reestablishing ownership and of resisting usurpation by local authorities. For this reason, what I observed in Vlaicu is not always true of land restitution across Romania as a whole.[14] Some features of it are, nevertheless, such as the hiding of land and the socialist treatment of property, both of which have rendered Romania's landed surface flexible and unstable.

Elastic Surfaces

As I listened to villagers in Vlaicu, accompanied the village land commission on its rounds, and attended court cases about land in the county capital, Deva, I found my mental map of a fixed landscape—a table with place mats—becoming destabilized. Parcels and whole fields seemed to stretch and shrink; a rigid surface was becoming pliable, more like a canvas. It was as if the earth heaved and sank, expanding and diminishing the area contained within a set of two-dimensional coordinates. But Vlaicu does not sit on a fault line. How then to understand the unexpected elasticity of its land, elasticity against which some farming families struggle to impose their claims while others extend it further? How can bits of the earth's surface migrate, expand, disappear, shrink, and otherwise behave as anything but firmly fixed in place?

A Terraphagous River

For the inhabitants of Vlaicu, perhaps the most dramatic sites for these permutations lie along the river Mureş. Like all rivers a kind of living thing, the Mureş periodically breaches its confines and becomes a mover of earth. In the past fifty years it has meandered fifty meters southward into village land, biting off people's fields and disgorging them onto the opposite shore or somewhere far downstream. A man—I'll call him Ion—whose parents once worked a parcel in the fertile plain near the river finds today that his claim to that parcel makes him not a farmer but a swimmer. While Ion might reasonably claim instead a parcel on the opposite shore, filled out by alluvial deposits, that shore belongs to another village, Homorod. From a cadastral point of view, the fields there do not exist: they have no topographic numbers. From a practical point of view, however, they exist very much: their rich and productive soil invites tillage by whoever can impose himself successfully upon them—in all likelihood, the local officials who speculate the situation, expelling the untitled and installing themselves. Thus Ion's hope of recovering elsewhere what the river tore away will likely be frustrated. His family parcel is nowhere: it has simply vanished.

Two things suggest that the river's inconstancy is a political matter, that the elasticities and possibilities inherent in it have political correlates. The first has to do with maps. As of 1994, the best maps of village terrain are those made in the 1880s, when Austro-Hungarian authorities commassed the myriad, minuscule parcels of Transylvania's peasants. But the quadrant of Vlaicu's map that contains the migrant Mureş has disappeared from the archive. As the archivist explained to me, the river's disregard for property had produced serious conflicts between Homorod and Vlaicu, and the maps borrowed to compose the differences had somehow disappeared. A careless moment? Or were they inconvenient in the illusion of fixity they offered, in the constraints they placed on creative impropriation?

The second hint as to the river's politics lies in the contrasting nature of property and ownership on its two banks, for Homorod and Vlaicu are two very different kinds of villages. Homorod, on the northern shore, was never collectivized. Although the Communist Party found ways to insinuate itself into hill villages like Homorod, it did not transform them as radically as it did collectivized villages like Vlaicu. Homorod's hillside fields remained the undisturbed private property, then, of those who had owned them for generations. But in Vlaicu, on the southern bank, private ownership was erased. Individual strips were torn forcibly from their proprietors and massed into huge blocks, owned in theory and in law by the members collectively and managed in practice by representatives of the Communist Party and the Romanian state. Thus to the north, individualized private interests defending private possession; to the south, collectivized public interests pressing the goals of a socialist Romania. And between them an unsettlingly nomadic river.

The Mureş—at this bend in its course, at least—seems to have been a partisan of possessive individualism rather than of collective weal. It has eaten the lands of the collective while burping them up for individual owners on the opposite bank. Indeed, it has done so literally with a vengeance, for the fields in Vlaicu that the Mureş has carried away were precisely those that landless Homorodeni obtained in the land reform of 1921, only to lose them to collectivization—even though Homorod itself was not touched. When Vlaicu's collective was formed in 1959, it offered Homorodeni who owned fertile parcels in the floodplain other, less productive lands "in exchange," in locations less suited to mechanized farming (and thus of no use to Vlaicu's CAP). A terraphagous Mureş has avenged them.

It is just possible that the Mureş has not meandered unaided and that the difference in the status of property on either side influenced its course. An agronomist from Vlaicu explained to me that in the 1960s Homorodeni had profited from local road construction to turn the Mureş to their service. As private owners with a particular interest to defend, and as producers of the brandy that lubricates all social relations and that comes mainly from the hills, Homorodeni had bribed the construction crews to dump excess gravel and landfill on *their* side of the river, thus protecting its shores from erosion and encouraging the river southward. On the Vlaicu side, by contrast, there was no "owner" who would be concerned with erosion and would work against it with plantings or jetties that might check the river's appetite for fresh soil.

Thus did nature and two distinctive forms of ownership combine to move the earth. Surfaces expanded in one place and shrank in another, making the landscape elastic and confounding Vlaicu's land commission with vanished parcels, reconstituted elsewhere, to be usurped by people from other places. This very fact, however, required that other land in Vlaicu also be elastic so as to accommodate the claims of those the river had dispossessed. To what extent and by what means have Vlaicu's fields stretched to oblige this need?

Stretching Land

One day in March 1994 the three nonlocal members of Vlaicu's land commission—the commune mayor, an agronomist, and the topographer assigned from Deva—joined its three local members for a working session.
Instead of handling the complaints of the villagers who had flocked to see
them, however, the mayor told them to come back the following day. He had
a more urgent task: finding some land for claimants from a neighboring village. To this end he asked the topographer to measure on the map the surface area of a particular section of Vlaicu's fields. The topographer moved his
ruler around on the map for a bit, made some calculations and announced,
"24.7 hectares." "Not enough," replied the mayor. "How much do we need?"
"28.4 hectares." The topographer busied himself with the ruler again and a
few minutes later announced, "28.2. Close enough?" "Fine," replied the
mayor. A 24-hectare field had just grown to 28. This episode entered my
field notes under the rubric "stretching land."

I was not privy to other such incidents of stretching, but I learned of ways
in which the village's arable surface area as of 1959 had been expanded. The
most important was a consequence of the socialist regime's incessant demand that production be ever increased. Target figures were constantly
raised, requiring local mayors and collective farm presidents to find new
sources of output. In agriculture, this meant efforts to bring new lands into
cultivation by filling swamps, plowing pasture to make it arable, draining
wetlands, and so on. As a result, some villagers whose fields had ended in
marshes or pasture in 1959 now find that the arable surface is bigger—and
no one else claims it. Their fields have stretched.

This is particularly evident along one street in Vlaicu, where gardens had
abutted a swamp. During the 1980s, the collective had cleared the swamp of
brush and trees and had bulldozed soil into it to create arable land. The
surface area thus gained augments the total available for redistribution to
settle villagers' claims. People who repossessed their gardens after 1989 now
enjoy many more square meters of garden than what they or their parents
had before. Hence one man's observation that he owed his newly measured
garden to the collective. And thus the reply one villager offered another who
was complaining about the measurements being proposed for his garden:
"Hey! Since when did my garden shrink?" "It didn't shrink, it stretched."

Perhaps the most elastic zone in the village's surface in 1993–94 was the
land occupied by state farms. Property restitution in Romania to date affects
only collectives;[15] state farms (IASs, containing 30 percent of the land) have
been declared shareholding companies. They cultivate the land as state enterprises but pay the former landowners dividends, set by the Ministry of
Agriculture as minimally the cash equivalent of three hundred kilograms of
wheat per share (i.e., per hectare) owned.[16] Early in the decollectivization

process, dividends from IASs were paid to many people whose family land did not lie in the actual territory of the state farms, including persons whose land had been confiscated by or forcibly donated to the state (in contrast to the communal property of collective farms, formed from "voluntary" donations[17]). As initially conceptualized, their parcels were to create a reserve land fund for distribution to landless persons who had worked in the CAPs; meanwhile, the victims of confiscation and forced giving were to be compensated with dividends from the state farm corporation. Thus some parcels of land would count doubly: as the specific property awarded to a villager (or usurped by some official) *and* as an abstract amount to be compensated in IAS dividends to the land's original owner.

Between 1991 and 1994, IASs became veritable rubber sacks, their capacities stretched in some cases well beyond those implied by the farm's actual surfaces. The director of a farm might receive from a mayor a list of shareholders whose shares, when totaled, exceeded the areas actually available, as mayors temporarily stuffed into the IAS "rubber sack" anyone whose case presented problems. Because it was not the land itself but its product that was being divided—a product much more divisible, manipulable, and convertible than are actual land surfaces—the capacity for stretching land via dividends in the IASs thus considerably expanded the possible surface area of villages. (As dividend-hungry shareholders—and, in some cases, profit-conscious IAS directors—increasingly insist that only persons whose land actually falls within the perimeter of IASs should receive dividends, their elasticity declines.)

The IAS stretches land in another way, too. Either through confusion or by design, some villagers count twice the areas written on their property affidavit (*adeverință*).[18] Let's say Nicolae's affidavit gives him three hectares. He knows that two of them are in the state farm and he collects two hectares' worth of dividends. But in addition, he tells the village post-CAP agricultural association[19] that he wants it to work all his land, which his affidavit shows to be three hectares. The association pays him three hectares' worth of produce, and the IAS gives him two hectares' worth of dividends: thus Nicolae effectively has *five* hectares. This kind of fraud or error caused the Vlaicu association significant losses until its accountant realized what was happening.[20] She then cooperated with the IAS director to prevent such duplications (and thus to rigidify the landscape).

Hidden Land

Some of the current stretching of land is the simple reflex of earlier shrinkages. Peasants everywhere have always hidden land from authorities; but beginning particularly in the 1950s, Romanian peasants did so with desperation.[21] In 1948, partly to force villagers into collectivizing and partly to assure the postwar state an adequate food supply for its industrial ambitions, the Party assigned each peasant household a delivery quota whose magnitude increased exponentially with the size of the holding.[22] The difference between owning four hectares and owning five could be the difference between having and not having enough to eat for the winter. For those with too much land, one way to handle the problem was to donate or sell parcels to friends or relatives, with the secret understanding that the sale was merely a fiction. This has created myriad difficulties for property restitution, as those who donated their pretend purchases to the CAP are now reluctant to give them back to the real owner.

But this practice did not shrink the total land available. Another one, however, did just that: declaring less than one actually held. Because the quotas were set according to agricultural registers based not on existing cadastres but on self-declaration, there was ample opportunity to hide land. One Vlaicu clerk of those years was a notorious drunk and could readily be persuaded, for a bottle of brandy, to reduce the recorded size of one's holdings. (A sociologist from another village told me that his mother had *seven* different recorded figures for the area of her farm, each figure responding to a particular need of the time, and each the result of liberal applications of brandy.) Any holding thus dipped in brandy shrank the hectarage of not just that person but the entire settlement, thereby invalidating the areas reported in official figures from the 1950s. Such shrinkages have effects in the present, as owners of shrunken fields often find it difficult now to stretch them back out to their former dimensions. The extra land involved, however, helps to make the village's total area more elastic.

Following collectivization in 1959–62, authorities further concealed the land that peasants had hidden before. Local officials, pushed to increase their production figures, found it very convenient that peasants had hidden land:[23] it enabled them to swell their productivity by planting and harvesting areas that were officially recorded as smaller than they actually were. If a collective farm sowed 200 hectares and harvested 600 tons, the productivity would be 3000 kilograms per hectare; but if higher officials thought there were only 150 hectares producing the same 600 tons, the yield would be a much more impressive 4000 kilograms per hectare. The difference might mean a bonus or a promotion for the mayor or farm president. During my fieldwork in Vlaicu in the 1970s, I repeatedly heard that nearby Romos village had the highest productivity in the county. In 1994 I learned that Romos also had 100 hectares or more of land hidden by local authorities (something they were able to do, I was told, because someone from Romos headed the county cadastral office where the figures were kept). Thus even as commune mayors and collective farm presidents created land by clearing and draining, they also hid some from higher authorities. The category "un-productive land" was, I hear, an especially good hiding place.[24]

This practice was apparently not limited to communes and collective farms. The late Professor Ioan Aluaş of Cluj told me that during the 1970s Ceauşescu became enraged when satellite maps showed massive discrepancies between the surfaces recorded from the air and those reported from below. Aluaş, working on a sociology research contract, was asked to discover what had happened to some of the land missing from the reported statistics of one county. In a conversation with the county's First Secretary, he was told to stop looking for the missing land "because we need it to be missing." Aluaş believed that official collusion in hiding land extended to the top levels of the Ministry of Agriculture, a parallel to the hoarding of raw materials that occurred in all branches of both the Romanian and other socialist economies.[25] This phantom land bedevils the process of impropriation as people discover that the figures they have used to request return of their parental holdings understate those holdings, but without other forms of proof they may not regain all that once was theirs. On the other hand, what some thought would be a four-hectare farm may suddenly mushroom into five.

Shifting Perimeters

We see from these examples that the area of the village itself is in question. Just how big *is* Aurel Vlaicu? Just how many hectares *are* there to be redistributed? The more one pursues this matter, the more elusive it becomes. The uncertainty is itself a further source of the land's capacity to stretch: if no one knows for sure exactly how big Vlaicu is, then there is no fixed limit to how many claimants can be stuffed into its perimeter. Only when villagers seek to occupy their land and find that somehow there isn't enough for everyone are the limits of this elasticity revealed.

Consider the following figures. As of the 1895 agricultural census, the total area of Vlaicu (then Benczencz) was given as 2,301 yokes[26] (1,324 hectares), 1,414 (814 hectares) of them arable. Almost the same figure (2,296 yokes) recurs in a source from 1921,[27] and in a 1941 agricultural census the surface is given as 1,414 arable yokes (814 hectares). So far so good. For the more extensive 1948 agricultural census, taken with an eye to collectivization, two different listings of the raw data give the total surface area as 2,235 yokes (1,287 hectares) and 1,122 hectares; one puts the arable surface area at 920 hectares, the other at 808.[28] The total at the end of collectivization was reportedly 1,309 hectares, of which 948 were arable.[29] The same source lists the total area of the newly formed collective farm as 652 hectares, 84 of them located *in other villages*—superb illustration of the capacity of collectives to stretch the landscape. Figures available for the 1980s show the area variously as 1,657 hectares (1,028 arable)[30] and 1,439 hectares (988 arable).[31] The land commission determined in 1991 that it had either 599 or 631 hectares available for redistribution; this was later revised to 759 hectares,[32] reflecting the return to Vlaicu of a number of fields that had been given to the collective in neighboring Gelmar (though not all the fields so given).[33] The totals for redistribution exclude land now held in various state farms, which, according to one list I saw from 1991, totals 801 hectares (683 arable),[34] but the agronomist who discussed this figure with me did not think it accurate. Thus 814 arable hectares, 920, 808, 948, 1,028, 988, 759—which is it?

Between 1895 and 1994, the borders of the village were periodically changed. Large fields were transferred to landless peasants from nearby villages in the 1921 land reform; reflecting this, the maps used by Vlaicu's CAP in the 1970s showed a smaller area than those from earlier in the century. Another substantial area was moved from Vlaicu's CAP to Gelmar in the 1960s. State farms straddled the borders of adjacent villages, making figures for their sizes useless to a researcher seeking to replicate earlier statistics. How big is Vlaicu really? People I asked estimated its arable surface as anywhere from 600 to 800 hectares. I, for one, have no idea how big it really is.

Under these circumstances, it is hardly surprising that talk of "stretching" and "shrinking" is widespread. Contrary to the judge in my epigraph, who stated in court, "The land doesn't expand, and it doesn't contract; we'll find your piece of it," people in Vlaicu speak of land that changes size and shape. "Hey! Since when did my garden shrink?" "If it rains a bit more, maybe the surface will stretch out a little." "Why do they keep remeasuring the land every year? Do they think it contracts and expands in the meantime?" "That's what you're doing, Mr. Topographer, stretching land. You don't shrink it much, but you do stretch it out." "How can a bigger piece of land get littler?" "The land commission gave land to everyone who asked for it, but if you put all this land end to end it would reach to Budapest." The land begins to take on plastic properties: it pulsates and heaves, oozes out at the borders, and evaporates into nothing. "I can't understand where my land has gone! It was there on Monday, but by Wednesday it had vanished!" (Even newspapers sometimes use this language: note the headline "Are Hectares Evaporating?"[35]) Land reproduces spontaneously, too, in surprising ways: "Vasile's family had only five hectares, and now look: his holdings amount to twice that." For some, it seems land can be moved around at will. "That guy brought his holding down from the hillside into the plain." "Mrs. S. was here the other day, trying to move her land from Vinerea village over to Vlaicu." It can actually migrate quite far, as with the land of a friend from town who said, "When my parents worked our land, it was right there in the village; now they tell me it's in the state farm fifty miles away."

The Property Regime of Socialism and
the Roots of Social Conflict

How is it that seemingly fixed surfaces have become so pliable? Some of the many answers to this question have been suggested in the preceding—land reclamation by mayors and CAP presidents, the hiding of land by both peasants and officials, and so on. There are additional reasons for the present elasticity, and they have to do with how the past regime treated the properties under its charge. First and most obviously, collective farms were worked in huge blocks, not in the maze of tiny fields of the 1930s. To create these huge blocks one had to obliterate all distinguishing characteristics from the landscape: trees and hedgerows were cut down, boundary stones between fields removed. To rationalize and reorganize cultivation, CAPs bulldozed old ditches and dug new ones; plowed over dirt paths and roadways and carved out roads more suited to the new, expanded use of fields; plowed crosswise across what had been tens of strips plowed lengthwise—this alters the land's very conformation. Most of the signs whereby people had recognized their property disappeared. If a farmer's fields once began at a particular willow tree, that tree was now gone.

In consequence, decollectivization has become a war between competing social memories (and memory, as is well known, is exceedingly elastic). It is a war fought on very shifting sands, for the surface is now wholly relativized. I asked many people whether, when it came time to repossess their family land, they had known where it was. Most of the older people said yes, but when asked to describe how I might know when I got to their field, nearly all could give only a relative response, such as: "Well, the first parcel next to the road in Hillside Field is Iosif's, the second is my cousin Petru's, and the third is mine." It was the rare answer that invoked a fixed reference point—a tree still standing after thirty years, the crossbars of the railway signal. Thus fields have drifted from their original moorings in space. Even reference to the roads or ditches was not certain, for these too had changed in the meantime. "Stoian never had *two* roads on his land; one of them should be plowed up." "It's not right to measure my garden by the ditch along here, because that ditch was in a different place thirty years ago." Such were the complaints of Vlaiceni to the village land commission. Its meetings were filled with shouting and acrimony, as people contradicted one another's memories of how the land lay in the past.

The vehicles of memory include written records that often complicate rather than solve the problem. Under the Austrian land registry system introduced in the 1860s, each household was listed with all the parcels to which it had rights; thenceforth, any transaction involving any parcel was to be entered into this register (*Cartea Funciară*) at the notary's office. For those whose parents or grandparents had gone to the trouble and expense of registering their property, an entry in the Land Register now serves as near-definitive proof of ownership, even if it does not accord with other declarations. But not everyone entered property into the Land Register. Poorer peasants during the 1930s and 1940s might simply not have bothered, since registration cost money. Especially in the 1950s, when peasants were buying or getting rid of land on the sly, they might have sold it with a handwritten document and two witnesses but not entered the transaction officially. Most important of all, after 1948 the new Communist power consistently ignored land registration; they had abolished most private landed property and had no use for its proofs. Although some people still went to register the purchase of a house or garden, the collective farm's extensive modifications in ownership and usufruct rights went unrecorded.

It is not that the socialist regime ceased to acknowledge property at all. To the contrary: within socialist property as a whole, the distinction between state property and the property designated as collective was enshrined in law, if not fully in practice. The property of collectives was marked by its "volitional" character, the "free consent" behind the donations that formed them.[36] It was also distinct in belonging collectively only to the group of persons who had actually donated the land and assets; other forms of socialist property, by contrast, belonged to the "people as a whole," not to some subset of it.[37] Thus while those other forms could be managed by representatives of the "people as a whole," namely the Romanian Communist Party, collective farms were in theory to be managed only by the representatives of that small group who had donated land to them. Theoretically, the state was not supposed to *determine* activity within collectives; it could only suggest, guide, or recommend.[38] The distinction between the two forms of property underlies Romania's procedure in returning land: collective farm property goes back to those who donated it, but state farms remain (at least temporarily) as state-directed enterprises.

In practice, officials often disregarded the distinction between forms of socialist property, giving orders to CAP presidents and forcing policies on farms in the name of a higher rationality. A 1974 law textbook implies that one result of this gap between theory and practice was debate as to whether the acts emitted by collectives—which were nonstatal entities—have the same jural status and consequences as those of statal entities.[39] The answer to this question is of great moment for property restitution and for the confusion it breeds, owing to the ways in which local authorities allocated property rights and exchanged property between state and collective farms.

Socialist Property and the Allocation of Use Rights

Collective farms were empowered to assign property rights to their members, particularly in two forms: 1) house-lots, and 2) use rights to the so-called private (or usufruct) plots held by CAP members. Village offspring

who wanted to build houses, persons moving into the village from elsewhere, or villagers with peripheral houses who wanted to move closer to the
center might apply to the CAP for a lot on which to build. The parcel granted
might even include a garden large enough to serve as a private plot. Although this parcel was inevitably the former possession of some proprietor,
with the socialization of land such details ceased to matter. As villagers recover their property rights, those who once owned the land on which others
have built houses lose the right to one thousand square meters of that land—
the space occupied by the house and a small garden—but can claim the rest
of it, and they can also claim an equivalent of the one thousand square meters in some other part of the village. Similarly, if they are gracious enough
to leave the owner of the house the entire garden behind it, beyond the
specified one thousand square meters, they can also claim that whole area
elsewhere.

These provisions have two important consequences, one for social relations and one for the elasticity of land. First, the interests of people living on
house-lots allocated by the CAP are set in opposition to those of the former
owners. Where the landowner claims all beyond the one thousand square
meters the law allows, the householder may be left with inadequate land to
sustain livelihood. Because people who received CAP house-lots were usually from other villages and did not bring land into the CAP, they receive no
land now except for that around their houses. Many of them have lost the
industrial jobs for which they moved into Vlaicu (with its proximity to transport and several factory towns); losing their household gardens is thus potentially catastrophic. The conflict over household gardens is one cause of
the heightened hostility between "locals" and "inmigrants" (*băştinaşi* and
"*venituri*"), a hostility many of the latter see as a new form of class conflict.
The result of their landlessness is that they have no choice but to sharecrop
on the fields of the new proprietors, if they are to have anything to eat. It is
a prospect they do not relish: as several of these inmigrants said to me, "We
don't want to be serfs to the local 'nobility'!"

The second consequence of the house-lot–garden problem is that the surface of Vlaicu must indeed be elastic, because it must accommodate the
claims of landowners to equivalent land elsewhere. For every ten households given the minimal one thousand square meters, an extra hectare of
land must materialize out of nowhere to be given the former owners. For
every expanded garden left to its new occupants, even more land must be
found. Those villagers who have magnanimously left larger gardens to
householders on their land do not seem to realize that their choice implies
an elastic surface; they simply assume that land will be found elsewhere.[40]
The situation is even more complex if, as in Vlaicu, the land of the house-lots
is now claimed by three different owners, two of whom can expect compensatory parcels. This situation arises where land was confiscated in the land

reform of 1945 and given to other owners, then donated to the collective by those new owners only to be allocated to yet a third person for a house. In Vlaicu, approximately thirty houses sit on such land.

The problem of house-lots and gardens has proved a jural nightmare, in part because of the point raised in the preceding: the jural status of the collective's allocations of land is now open to legal challenge. Moreover, householders who have been using a garden plot for many years have the legal right to claim it on the basis of long-standing use.[41] Some judges generally support the claims of householders against the original owners as a matter of equity; others decide on a case-by-case basis. But the judges with whom I spoke said that lawsuits over ownership rights to household gardens are among the two or three most numerous and problematic of those relating to property restitution.

Land must stretch to accommodate extra amounts not only for those whose land went to others as house-lots but also for those with land the CAP withdrew from cultivation for infrastructural improvements. The buildings of collective farms occupy land that can no longer be used. On a larger scale are levies built around villages along the Mureş. The levy in Vlaicu occupies about thirty-five hectares of land that cannot be restored to its original owners; the law states that they must receive compensatory land elsewhere. Once again, Vlaicu's perimeter must be elastic.

Exchanges of Land

If CAP-allocated house-lots generate one set of problems, another comes from land exchanges that took place during collectivization. These were of three kinds: between CAPs and individuals, between CAPs and state farms, and among CAPs. Decree 151 (1950) enabled collectives-in-formation to work contiguous parcels by exchanging land with individuals. If villagers had joined the collective (or its precursor, the association [întovărăşire]) but their lands did not form contiguous blocks, officials had the right to exchange the lands of nonmembers situated in the middle of collective lands for parcels at its edge. State farms seeking to consolidate their fields had the same prerogative. Individuals could not refuse these exchanges,[42] by which many found themselves owners of parcels much inferior to those they had been compelled to turn over. Indeed, the decree stated that the contracts for such exchanges were valid even without signatures of the owners thus displaced, as long as the local authorities invoked decree 151 in their records.[43]

These exchanges of land create difficulties for restitution because many of those compelled to make them refuse to accept anything but their original parcel, even though the holding entered in CAP records—and which they should thus receive back—is not their original parcel but the one they were given in exchange. Some have brought legal challenges based on the widespread failure of local authorities to draw up the contracts stipulated in decree 151. Thus where local officials were cavalier in their treatment of property during collectivization, people now have room to challenge the jural status of such actions. One result, of course, is further tension within local communities, for the attempt to recover one's original land means taking it away from the early-collective member for whose parcel it was exchanged. Because the land amalgamated into CAPs was generally of higher quality than that given in exchange, conflict has reappeared between richer and poorer villagers having superior and inferior land.[44]

In the same spirit of rational cultivation, CAPs and state farms often exchanged the donated or confiscated lands that comprised them. Such exchanges were especially likely in cases (frequent enough) where a villager had land in another settlement: for example, a woman who had migrated or married into village A might have kept dowry lands in her home village B. If, conversely, someone from A had moved into village B, A's CAP and B's state farm could easily exchange their two "alien" parcels. Because CAPs and state farms held the property rights to the land, they could dispose of it as necessary to pursue their objectives; the wishes of the former owners had no place in such exchanges. The difficulty, however, is that only the collectives are being disbanded, while the state farms remain intact. Thus a person whose land was given to a CAP and was exchanged for land in a state farm might not receive the original land but only the (inferior) dividends paid to shareholders in the state farm corporation.[45] This was the case of the person quoted earlier, whose family land was in the village but who now finds himself entitled to dividends from land fifty kilometers away. Many in this situation have challenged the rulings of their land commissions, refusing to receive dividends and suing for return of their original parcel. Again, their suit comes at the expense of the current occupant of that parcel, who would be forced into becoming a shareholder instead of an owner and who, as a result, drags out the inevitable court case as long as possible.

Collectives also consolidated their fields by exchanging land with neighboring collectives or uncollectivized villages. Earlier patterns of marriage make neighboring settlements especially likely to have within their borders land owned by people in the adjacent villages; collectives rationalized cultivation by exchanging such pieces, in some cases even shifting the borders of villages or CAPs as a result. This has posed several problems for land restitution. First, people's land is listed in the village whose collective they entered, not in the one where their land is actually located. A commission may therefore think it has resolved all claims within village boundaries only to meet unexpected claims from outsiders. The land must therefore become even more elastic, since commissions would have established the reduction coefficient for creating extra land as a function of the surface area that villagers had requested in the first round; they are unprepared to come up with even more. From this kind of exigency came the "land-stretching" episode I described earlier.

Second, previous exchanges of land between neighboring collectives or villages complicate the matter of assessing how much land a village commission has at its disposal. In Vlaicu, the boundary with neighboring Gelmar is now quite indeterminate, having shifted back and forth. Ownership in this interstitial area is in a chaotic state: property belonging to people from four different villages (Vlaicu, Gelmar, Geoagiu, and uncollectivized Homorod) is all mixed up here; the "migrations" of the Mureş diminished the total surface area of the collectives; and a large estate, expropriated in 1945, straddles the border such that its size is almost impossible for anyone but the local authorities to discover (and they are not interested in revealing it).[46] The administrative decision to return some border fields to Vlaicu increases the total hectarage its land commission controls; if unclaimed, that land will augment the surplus available for other claimants (such as those owed for house-lots). When Vlaicu's fields came "home" to Vlaicu from Gelmar, then, Vlaicu's land was stretched.

Special problems stem from exchanges between collectivized and uncollectivized villages. Because land in the plains is much better than that in the hills, hill people have long sought to buy land in villages like Vlaicu. Some of them received it in other ways, such as the hill villagers of Homorod who acquired land in Vlaicu's perimeter through the 1921 land reform. Collectives exchanged land with these hill people as with anyone else, taking their lowland parcels in exchange either for other lowland parcels, unworkable by the CAP, or for upland parcels owned by hill people who had moved downhill and joined the CAP, giving it their upland plots. Since 1991, even residents of hill villages that were never collectivized are recovering lost land— and in some cases also refusing to relinquish the "unworkable" plots they received, which they claim by virtue of thirty years' undisturbed use.

Indeed, it is precisely these uplanders who seem to have pushed Geoagiu's land commission to restore property on its former (pre-1959) sites— something Law 18 did not require but left optional. A member of the commission explained to me that as soon as decollectivization was broached, people from the uncollectivized hill village of Boiu began entering into and forcibly occupying their former lands in collectivized lowland Cigmău (both settlements are in Geoagiu, related to one another like Homorod and Vlaicu). With the help of a local son who had become a lawyer, Boieni threatened to sue the commune commission unless they received precisely those lowland parcels they had owned before 1959. They flatly refused to keep the parcels forced on them in exchange during Cigmău's collectivization. Perhaps they defended their rights so promptly and vigorously because, while memories of property were fading from the minds of collectivists, hill villagers had retained a strong sense of private ownership.[47]

Still another consequence of how the collectives treated land has pitted inmigrants against locals. Admirably demonstrating that land is not fixed, collectives accepted as members inmigrants who had contributed land situated in their home villages. Their names are on the list of petitions to enter Vlaicu's collective (one of the sources for determining property restitution) with a hectare or two, but these hectares are not in Vlaicu. In one case, the hectare is nowhere at all, having been invented so its "owner" would look as if he were contributing something to his new home. Nonetheless, because their names are on the list, such people theoretically have the right to claim land. In the first year of the restitution process most of them received parcels, which they lost later when it became clear that in Vlaicu, elasticity notwithstanding, there was not enough land to go around. The result is a new class struggle in the village, for the locals' seemingly insatiable claims have deprived the inmigrants of land by pushing Vlaicu's elasticity to its limits.[48]

Thus perhaps the most important source of the elasticity of land is that the Communists treated it as a movable rather than an immovable good, as aggregate quantities rather than concrete qualities. Abstracting ownership from particular clods of earth into figures on paper, they shuffled those figures insouciantly among social actors. Land under socialism became a matter of totals manipulated in the interest of "the whole," irrespective of the particularities of prior ownership rights (not to mention those of plan-resistant local soils). Law 18 empowers villagers to reassert those particularities as they struggle to fix land in place, causing it to writhe and stretch under the weight of so many conflicting claims.

Problems in Property Restitution

The Local Commissions and Their Work

The disarray accompanying property restitution takes many forms besides those already suggested. I will describe a number of the problems I observed in Vlaicu, some of them specific to that place and most of them more widely found in Transylvania and even Romania as a whole. First, the composition and activities of the Vlaicu land commission. Its three members were supposed to have been elected by the village, but those on the 1993–1994 commission were in fact chosen by commune officials to replace the three men elected at the outset. Those first three had proven (by their account) unwilling to play along with the mayor and his cronies' desires to give excess land to friends and too little to others.[49] Many villagers see all three 1993–94 members as socially problematic: they claim that one is drunk most of the time (which does not prevent him from asserting with conviction his views about whose land should be where); another has at best middling prestige; and the third is a renowned troublemaker who often changes his mind about "the truth" of any matter under discussion. These three, then, judge the fates of Vlaiceni in quest of land. They agree on almost nothing and regularly undercut one another in private. My impression, in listening to them argue over various cases, was that the knowledge they collectively produced was as flexible and shifting as the surfaces to which they applied it.

Also open to improvement is the commission's modus operandi. The three assemble in the office of the postcollective agricultural association, there to be joined by the topographer and an agronomist from the commune center. On rare occasions the mayor, president of the commission, might also appear. Given where they meet, there are usually two additional people: the agronomist and accountant of the association, who have strong interests in the outcome of disputes involving the land of association members and who are eager to argue their views. The commission meets irregularly, sometimes not constituting itself for months on end, then appearing three or four days a week for a while, then disappearing again. When it meets, villagers hear by word of mouth and come to the office with their complaints.

The commission has no procedure for handling one case at a time. Three or four people might come in, one makes a complaint, the commission members begin to discuss it, then someone else launches a different problem, everyone's attention turns to the new plaintiff, then a third interrupts in the same way. The topographer or commune agronomist might go outside with one or another person, possibly to reach an understanding "among four eyes," as the Romanian saying has it.[50] The whole procedure resembles a juggling act, as one, then another, then another ball goes up into the air, none falling out into some sort of resolution. Often the outcome is, "We'll have to measure there again, but we can't do that until next fall, after the crops have been harvested."[51] In this way cases drag on, unresolved for several seasons.

Complaints to the commission frequently center on problems of measurement. People solicit remeasurement of parcels that were measured already, complaining that neighbors have removed the markers and encroached on their land. Given the flimsiness of most markers, this is a plausible scenario, but the topographer has grown ever more exasperated at the waste of time that remeasuring entails. Other measurement problems arise because the commission does not always do its initial measuring properly. For example, they might measure a parcel's front end but not its far end. When the new owner goes out to plow, he discovers that at the far end his parcel has vanished into nothing, since neighboring furrows are not straight. This means that the entire section has to be remeasured; with fields already plowed and sown, however, no one but the aggrieved party wants to revise the boundaries. In such circumstances, one solution is to sign the land over to the association and let its officers argue for remeasuring. In fact, giving land to the association for a season or two seems to be a common strategy for resolving disputes between persons who want to avoid friction. The association, for its part, wants to control as much land as possible so as to maximize possibilities for rational cultivation and income. It has thus become a prime force for clarity in the reassertion of Vlaicu's property grid.

Additional problems arise from competing claims to land on the border between villages; they occur because different topographers have been in charge of measuring and giving out land in different places. Thus one case involved a complaint by person X to topographer A that person Y had been given rights to X's land, while Y claimed he had gotten these rights from topographer B (a man known for taking bribes), assigned to the neighboring village. The topographer assigned to Vlaicu might perform his work conscientiously but find himself giving out areas already given out by someone else. And because people coming from neighboring villages to claim land in Vlaicu do not always bring documentation, the topographer cannot be as conscientious as he might like. I witnessed one case in which a couple came from some distance away to claim three hectares in Vlaicu but had not brought their property affidavit. Even had they brought it, the topographer would not know whether their land was in the territory of the former CAP or in that of the state farm, because the affidavits give only the amount of land awarded, not its location. Lacking proper evidence, he could only take the couple's word for it, trying to confirm this by going through the mammoth 1930s cadastre on which he bases his work (and which is far from up-to-date with the 1959 land situation).

Then there are problems emerging from the village or commune land commission's failure to apply the law properly—in other words, from abuse of power. The mayor, vice-mayor, and others often suppress information about property in prime fields, which they work for their own benefit. This usurpation of course diminishes the area available for distribution to villagers rightfully owed land. People whose complicated claims the land commission might resolve by giving them land in these prime fields will have to receive something else instead. In Vlaicu, some have been given rights to work one or another piece of land in the state farm. But the farm itself is supposed to be working that piece, along with others, for profits to pay rightful shareholders. So the authorities are trying to make a single surface area count twice: someone actually works it, withdrawing it from the state farm's use, while the mayor orders the state farm director to pay dividends to the original owner, whose claim has been doubled without being annulled.

But in many cases, not even the commission members know what is going on. Traipsing around in the fields one day with the mayor, topographer, agronomist, and a village land commission member, I was startled to hear them asking one another, "Who's working this piece?" "Who gave out this piece to these guys?" "Whose is this?"—and not knowing most of the answers. One or another of them would ask the question of someone working in a field and receive the answer, "I don't know." Finally someone commented, "We could spend all our time just trying to figure out who's occupied these lands. We'd have to camp out every night as well as sit all day watching who comes where." It was clear that in this highly confusing part of the village perimeter (its border with Gelmar), no one is fully in control.

The Mechanics of Restitution

There are also confusions stemming from the sources used to determine people's allotments. Claims were to rest on two recorded amounts: that dating from enrollment in the collective, and that in the 1959 Agricultural Register. Both had been based on self-declaration, not on official property records; it often happens that neither amount conforms with the others or with entries in the 1930s cadastre that the topographer uses to distribute land. As I explained earlier, people had reasons to underdeclare the land recorded in the Agricultural Register. Similarly unreliable are the amounts that people declared when joining the collective, after an often-lengthy process of coercion and intimidation. In the words of a friend, "By the time they finally wore you down so you joined, you didn't give a fat damn what amounts you wrote on that paper." The two sources for making claims therefore do not necessarily reflect what a family owned in the past—and if the persons who offered those declarations have died, their heirs may not even know what they had. A woman who helped draw up Vlaicu's list of property allotments clarified for me the magnitude of the problem. Asked what she found most difficult about the job, she replied, "Adding up all the claims and discovering an enormous gap between that figure and the area we had available."

Three possibilities are open to villagers wishing to contest the amounts awarded them. Two witnesses may declare under oath that they had a different amount. Or the claimant may present documents of past sale or donation, made with witnesses, if they are still alive to verify their assertions. Because many people threw away such documents, the latter is an option available to few. Or people can present evidence from the Land Register to contradict figures in other sources. But to get evidence from the Land Registry office, one must have the topographic numbers of all the parcels in question, and many people lost these numbers, thinking they would never be needed again. A person for whom none of these three options is viable need not give up: imposing oneself by force is a common enough alternative.

Problems arise too from villagers' failure to comprehend the legal niceties of the process of impropriation. Many cannot fathom why their right to land no longer exists just because they did not register their claim within the prescribed time limit in spring 1991. The law set thirty days as the initial period for registering claims, then extended it to forty-five. Anyone wishing to claim property was obliged to act within that limit; if they did not, their rights automatically became invalid at the end of it. Villagers are understandably befuddled that a right valid yesterday is invalid today, and they continue to pester the commission with their claims.

Myriad difficulties result from the fact that Law 18 reconstitutes holdings as they existed in 1959. The members of the land commission state plainly that their job is to re-create the grid of property as of collectivization, not to resolve inheritance disputes, which have to be handled through the courts. But one cannot go to court without a property deed, and those are being given out with much delay. As of June 1994, 24 percent of the expected landowners in Romania had received their property deeds.[52] Somewhere around a half-million court cases over land are already pending, and more can be expected with each increment in the percentage of deeds given out.[53] Other complications lie in divergences between customary and official law—for example, the custom that old people might give their land to those who took care of them rather than to kin whom the law would recognize as heirs. Compounding the problem, as I discovered by sitting in court and in the notary's office, is that from 1959 on, many people did not bother to legalize succession after a death, seeing no reason to do so once there was no land to inherit. Thus one now encounters quarrels among siblings and cousins over an estate that has been transmitted through up to two intervening generations without its division being legalized. Customary understandings among heirs may well clash with provisions of the law, yet those whose preferences would have clarified the matter have died intestate.

Meanwhile, kinsmen squabble with one another over division of the holding to which they have inherited rights. They might reach a provisional agreement out of court but then be unable to enforce it among themselves, turning to the commission for a verdict. These discussions, like so many others, are filled with shouting—"It's *mine*," "No, it's *mine*"—and threats of violence—"If I go and plow where I think I belong, my uncle will bash my head in." Most villagers I spoke with do not comprehend that the commission has no power to settle inheritance disputes but can only reconstitute 1959 holdings. When the commission refers people to the courts, they assume that "the commission doesn't want to help us; they're corrupt and are using the land for themselves," or "if you don't pay them off you can't get anywhere."

The principle that "as a rule," people should receive exactly the parcels they had owned prior to 1959 is yet another source of problems and delays in distributing land. It precludes consolidating parcels and decreasing the number of them to be both measured and worked. It also prevents the commission from creating viable new parcels by means of the reduction coefficient. In Vlaicu, initial calculations indicated that a 9 percent diminution of all reconstituted properties would yield enough land for everyone. But in the first provisional measurements, the commission did not subtract this percentage, because (they say) people would then complain about not being on their former sites. Since farms are composed of multiple parcels of .07 to 3.65 hectares in size, most of them less than a hectare, the commission's proposal to apply the nine-percent reduction at this point will yield tiny fragments to redistribute. Had the commission consolidated village holdings at the outset, the 9 percent reduction would have made viable parcels for many more people.

Further difficulties come from the absence of preexisting physical markers. I heard countless arguments of the following sort. X and Y are arguing where Y's land should be: "It was in Big Floodplain Field." "No, it was in Small Floodplain."[54] "It was two hectares." "No, it wasn't hectares, we didn't use hectares back then: it was two *yokes*."[55] "At the end of the parcel were some trees." "No, there were two paths there, the trees were over here, you were over there." "Your father's land came down from the Vinerea Road right to . . ." "Which road? Not that one but another. But where were the trees?" "You didn't have land there! Ion's Maria was there, and Avram's son Lazăr, and Lame Ştefan, but not you guys." "Well, but we bought it by a secret agreement." "The mistake is that you used the *new* road as your point of reference, but the topographer used the *old* one [now plowed over] when he measured for you the first time." In this fashion people might dredge up, manufacture, and contest knowledge for hours and months at a stretch.

From the collective's effacement of the land's individuality, then, comes decollectivization as a war of knowledge and memory. An anecdote from a village elsewhere in Transylvania reveals this starkly. In that village, at the time of collectivization villagers got together and buried large rocks deep beneath the surface at the boundaries between fields—deep enough to be out of reach of the collective's large tractors. Property restitution there is now simplified, as people have only to dig for the stones where they think the boundary should be. The materiality and ease of this uncommon practice confirm that the ghosts of an earlier property regime flutter above the landscape, haunting the recollections of those who strive to recover their rights.

Superimposed Ownership

As it turns out, no amount of elasticity could have stretched Vlaicu's land enough to satisfy all claims. The reason is Vlaicu's ethnic Germans, whose ancestors had settled in Vlaicu in the 1890s. They formed 15–20 percent of the village population until the 1970s; by 1993, however, they constituted a mere 3 percent—twenty-five resident individuals in twelve households.[56] Once the richest group in the village,[57] the Germans were expropriated of nearly all their land in the 1945 land reform, which awarded it to poor Romanian villagers and war veterans. It was those Romanian proprietors who gave the land to the collective, and it is they who in 1991 received it back. The Germans, in turn, received not land but shares in the state farm. But since they had had no land in what is now the state farm, they challenged the decision in court—and won. The commune commission awoke to a court order awarding the Germans seventy hectares; as they had requested, the land was given in a single block so they could work it in common.[58] With most of the village land already distributed, the commission had now to come up with seventy additional hectares. No matter how elastic the surface, it cannot stretch that far. Problems involving such double proprietorship— and the expectation that commissions will somehow resolve them with double the surface area in question—are not common in Transylvania, but where they exist they show clearly the lengths to which local commissions have to go in treating land as not a fixed but a flexible good.

Vlaicu's "German problem" has augmented the already numerous sources of social tension and conflict. It fans the resentment of inmigrant Vlaiceni, whose chances at land receded with the effort to unearth seventy more hectares for Germans. Moreover, the commission was dilatory in finding alternative parcels for the Romanians thrown off these seventy hectares. Many were angry, and some even broke into those fields by force, resulting in a court case and much ill will. The issue did not generate a full-blown ethnic conflict only because Romanian Vlaiceni were divided on who should rightfully have the land. Although the lines of cleavage are complex, they tend to divide those who formerly had little land in the village (one reason for their receiving some in the reform of 1945) from those who had more—that is, they reanimate an earlier class division, as well as exacerbating a new one.

From this discussion, it is easy to see why final property deeds might be slow in coming. If one adds the government's suspected foot dragging, the delays are even more understandable. President Iliescu has made no secret of his disdain for inefficient, private smallholding. His views doubtless influence those local officials charged with implementing Law 18, especially if they are of his party. Moreover, if Cornea is correct, the power of the "directocracy" that has run Romania up to 1996 rests on preserving the juxtaposition of private and state property by keeping private property rights uncertain.[59] This enables entrepratchiks to siphon state resources into their new private firms as they continue to obfuscate ownership claims of all kinds, including those to land. Against this sort of interest, villagers hoping to gain full property rights must engage not only in local wars of knowledge and local power struggles from which a new property grid will be forged, but also in higher-level battles over who will define Romania's future.

The Politics of Elasticity

Amid all the uncertainty, some (mostly vigorous men) seek to impose their rights by force: they simply plow into their neighbor's land. Neighbors appeal in vain to the commission, for it almost never exercises the limited sanctioning power it has (fining the usurper and threatening to sue him). One reason is that the commission's village members are reluctant to harm their relations with fellow villagers. Indeed, that commission activity is often indecisive stems from these members' unwillingness to resolve problem cases, which would inevitably alienate some people with whom they have to live. Commission members from outside generally lack the knowledge to resolve local cases, and the local members do not wish to apply the knowledge they have—if indeed they can agree on what it is. And so, as the agronomist from Geoagiu explained to me, the role of the outside members is to invoke abstract notions like "the rule of law" as a basis for decisions, hoping thereby to blunt the enmity of villagers toward the commission's local members. The outsiders also serve as scapegoats: the local members, as well as other villagers, routinely accuse the outside members of abuse of power and of corrupting or retarding the process of property restitution.

It is the local and commune commissions that enact most of the politics of elasticity—that look for hidden land, hide land themselves and stuff claimants into the rubber sack of the state farm corporation, adjudicate among competing claims from past exchanges, profit from ambiguities in the distinctions between remnant state property and the property of disbanded collectives, and have to cope somehow when the limits of elasticity are reached, as with Vlaicu's Germans. It is commission members who can take advantage of the skewed distribution of knowledge about past property. They can influence a decision by suddenly "remembering" that X never had land in the field whose ownership Y is contesting with him, and they can occupy lands (rather than pool them for redistribution) because they know where there are fields that no one (or no one important) is claiming. If it is they whom irate villagers most often accuse of corrupting the process of decollectivization, the reason is that they have the best chance to do so. The transformation of land in Romania parallels the transformation of Soviet-style socialism overall in that the most valuable asset is political capital: a position of authority and accompanying connections that can be used to acquire economic resources. Few people in such a position would fail to take advantage of it.

Local-Level "Abuse of Power"

Precisely because of who its perpetrators are, stories about local-level abuse of power are difficult if not impossible to verify. Abuse occurs on a sufficiently wide scale to prompt the Hunedoara county prefect, for instance, to call meetings of all the commune mayors to discuss the problem. Newspapers are also full of stories about officials who deprive others of property rights. I offer the following examples from my conversations and from TV mainly to illustrate what might be going on; I cannot verify the events. One concerns a certain commune secretary, a man who had for years controlled the commune archive. As of spring 1994 he was on seemingly permanent sick leave, the result of someone's having discovered a false entry in the commune land records that gave his family more land than they had owned, in a better location. He was reputed to have done this for friends and kin, and the evidence was sufficient to get him "pensioned" (but not punished otherwise, thanks to his cozy relations with influential people—a pattern familiar from before).

A second example involves a vice-mayor. A villager whose old aunt had asked him to plow her land with his tractor wanted her to show him where it was. When they reached the place—of which she was absolutely certain—they found it already plowed and planted. Inquiring of others in the vicinity, they learned that this was the work of the vice-mayor (a man who, not being born locally, would have no right to land anywhere in that commune). The nephew's requests that the land commission clarify things by measuring his aunt's parcel fell on deaf ears for three successive agricultural seasons; he was finally given to understand that in this area of the village, things would not be clarified.

The third example comes from an inspector called into a village to investigate a complaint against the mayor and the state farm director. Villagers wanting their lands back had sued this IAS (which stood on lands earlier exchanged with the CAP), had received a judicial sentence ordering the IAS to move back to its initial location, and had then plowed and planted their fields. No sooner had new shoots sprouted than the IAS plowed them under, planting its own crops instead. When villagers objected, police beat them up and arrested them—even though their protest stood on a legal decision. The inspector concluded his account by noting that the IAS director could only have been in league with the mayor (neither had shown up for the hearing), for only local authorities can summon the police against local citizens. He also observed that while villagers were being thus abused, the IAS director had just built a large villa with the proceeds from their land.[60]

It is not just people like mayors and their deputies who are thought to abuse their offices: villagers most frequently accuse the village members of land commissions. In their role as arbiters of property restitution, these members can use inside knowledge to acquire for themselves inheritances to which less knowledgeable others might have a better claim. They can favor their own kin in any dispute—indeed, Vlaiceni ousted one of their members from the commission because he was doing this so blatantly. In order to get more land, village commission members can collude among themselves or with others from the commune commission. Even without any overt wrongdoing, they can promote their interests simply by pressing the topographer, mayor and other non-village members to resolve their situation, and in a specific way. Outside members depend on village members too much to be indifferent to these requests. Although membership in a commission does not guarantee that one will resolve all problems to one's advantage, it is certainly no hindrance.

"Corruption" and abuse of power are nothing new in Romania. Talk about local officials abusing their power occurs in a political context that should make us pause, however, in assessing the stories' veracity. The fall of the Communist Party destroyed the hierarchical chain that had connected the political center with the lowest levels of the system. Whereas the governing party or coalition appoints county prefects and can count on their political loyalty, town and commune mayors are elected by their constituents; many of them, especially in Transylvania, are not of the governing party. Their autonomy thwarts government attempts to recentralize and to obstruct local-level control. Underlying talk about "local-level abuse of power," then, may be a struggle over political (re)centralization and local autonomy. If local-level abuses can be made to appear sufficiently rampant, they might justify the center's re-creating hierarchy and surveillance. That abuses undeniably do occur openly, in any case, indicates either the center's collusion or its ineffectual control over its subordinates—or both. It colludes because it cannot control them, precisely because it can no longer offer them protection and benefits adequate to securing their allegiance.[61] If local officials abuse their positions of power, the reason is that they can line their pockets only through their own actions, not through collaborating in the hierarchical system of privilege that served them before.

Talk about local-level abuse of power in implementing Law 18 therefore reflects, in my opinion, both a political struggle to reconstitute central control and the realities of life in the countryside. Abuse does occur, but not necessarily on the scale of the allegations. Moreover, most people cheated of their property rights have no idea whatsoever how to defend themselves. An acquaintance of mine, a woman with long political experience, described the extraordinary lengths to which she had gone to prove her ownership of a piece of land. Without the influence afforded her by past political connections, she said, she would never have managed to get what was rightfully hers—and even so, she had to give some of it away to obtain the rest. Backdoor access to the Land Registers, friendly advice from lawyers and state prosecutors, a relative on the land commission who told her confidentially what she would need in order to prove her case—most villagers do not have these resources, or the time or cash to make countless trips to the county capital in pursuit of proofs. Officials who defraud others of property thus have a good chance of turning their usurpation into ownership.

Who Loses and Who Gains?

At whose expense, one might ask, do excessive claims and forcible or fraudulent occupation shrink the available land? In addition to the village poor and the inmigrants already mentioned, two other groups are worth singling out for comment: widows and urbanites. When a land commission has to resolve a dispute or when a (male) villager wants to expand the field he is plowing, the most likely victims are widows. Presumed to be defenseless against these usurpations, widows are—and perceive themselves to be—a favorite target. In my second example above, it is no coincidence that the land the vice-mayor has reportedly occupied belongs to an old widow. I saw good evidence that widows feel it useless to resist these usurpations because they will never prevail. One widow, discussing how a relative had usurped a field belonging to her widowed aunt, said, "Where there's no man, people who are stronger or have sons will shove themselves on you by force, and you can't do anything about it." Another said, even more revealingly, as she explained how her neighbor had occupied a large chunk of her garden: "My son kept telling me not to give up, but I gave up. I used to have proof of ownership, but I threw it in the fire—never thought I'd need it again. I'm a woman! I gave up. I should be more manly—some women are more manly. But I always place my hopes in someone else."[62]

The other particularly vulnerable group comprises people who have acquired rights to land in villages where they no longer live. Nearly every urban intellectual in my circle of friends had long stories to tell of how they had been excluded from rights to land or been paid a pittance for its use if they gave it to their village association. Many urbanites live far from their places of birth; they have neither time nor money for frequent trips back home to defend their claims before the commission or in court. It is easy for local officials to tell them that their land falls, say, in the "fishpond" (a state farm that pays almost no dividends because it is bankrupt), while the same officials work the land themselves and pocket the proceeds.[63] It is equally easy for people who run the associations to underpay long-distance members. The travails of city people show us, then, that in deciding to accept all property claims regardless of the owner's place of residence, the Romanian parliament delivered to local authorities the means of considerable enrichment.[64]

In sum, my evidence suggests that the chief losers in decollectivization are widows, people in cities, inmigrants, and some of the former village poor. In each of these groups some people stand out for their determination to fight—something not all villagers do—for what they see as their rights. The people who tend to gain are local politicians, others associated with implementing the return of property and some of the old village elite. Because the situations of current losers had improved under socialism while the village elite had suffered, property restitution would seem to be restoring an earlier set of inequalities. This is not so, however, for the chief beneficiaries of the present conjuncture are the holders of political capital—many of whom also held it during the socialist period. In the unfolding class reconfiguration, their advantages not only afford them resources for high position at others' expense but also feed conflicts and resentments among those less favored, who confront the limits of elasticity and strive to escape them.

Strategies of Justification

When land no longer stretches to accommodate people, how do they defend their claims? What are villagers' strategies of justification in asserting their rights? In other words, what ideologies of ownership are (re)emerging? Because my data on this question are too extensive to present here, I will only summarize my conclusions from them.[65] First, for nearly all Vlaiceni, the criteria that matter in validating landownership are entitlement and desert (rather than some criterion such as efficiency). There are varying definitions, however, as to what makes people entitled. Some—chiefly those who had no land before—emphasize equity and fairness; others emphasize past suffering. Especially with respect to the claims of other ethnic groups, villagers legitimize their own claims by invoking the law, state authority, or patriotic values as grounds for desert.

By far the most common vehicles for legitimating possession, however, are kinship (or blood) and work: people deserve land because it belonged to their ancestors, because they or their parents worked it, because even if their parents had no land they worked in the collective, or because they are better able than others to work land now and in the future. They fight for their land, many of them say, because they owe this to their parents, who worked so hard for the land and lost it all. Although it might seem that ideas about labor derive from socialism's emphases on work and production, I believe they have an additional source in pre-1959 notions about personhood as something constructed through labor and possession. (Martha Lampland illustrates these notions beautifully in her book on Hungarian peasants,[66] and I believe they make good sense for the Transylvanian peasantry as well.) An important corollary of this justification through labor is that it posits social persons defined by their effort, persons who gain identity as possessors because they act. Tying this to kinship extends their "person-hood" backward in time (to the labor of ancestors) as well as outward in social space, thus producing significantly different bases for social identity from those available under socialism.

Depending on one's interlocutor, one might invoke either kinship or work situationally—that is, these justifications are not tied to specific social groups. They are, rather, ideological premises available to all. The partisans of kinship (mostly people whose parents owned land) are also sometimes partisans of work (their parents deserved land because they worked for it). If the inmigrants who labored in the CAP tend to be partisans of work more than of kinship, it is because they rarely have a claim they might justify by blood—but when they can, they do. Otherwise, they bolster work arguments with arguments of equity. Whether kinship and work are combined or in tension, all recognize them as significant grounds for a claim. Finally, although Germans tend somewhat more than others to legitimate by reference to law and state authority, kinship and work are as important to them as to their Romanian neighbors. They claim to deserve their seventy hectares because they had the land from their ancestors, who had sweated to obtain it. And many of the Romanians agree.

These findings warrant three comments regarding the ideological processes they imply. First, as collectivization aimed to delegitimate family-based owning and laboring units, decollectivization now relegitimates them—even if the "family" invoked is spatially dispersed across villages and towns. Thus property restitution entails reinforcing a kinship ideology, promoted by those whose kin had property. This is an ideology honored less in the observance than in the breach, as is clear from the many quarrels among kin; but it is a potent addition to the new (renewed) class struggle emerging in Transylvania's villages. Second, an ideology of kinship and ancestry necessarily invokes the past. Against socialism's relentless orientation to the future, many people now define themselves by where they have come from: they are possessors because their ancestors were. To the extent that Romanian socialism honored the past, it was a past dominated not by kinship but by the nation and its march toward Communism. Those who insist on the importance of ancestry are therefore broadening the legitimate forms of historical consciousness to include pasts and solidarities that are other than national. And third, the recrudescence of kinship provides an ideological counterweight to the atomizations of both the socialist period and the conflict-ridden present. It promotes ideas of personhood that extend the individual and his or her work both socially and temporally. Although these expanded self-definitions will not be available to everyone, they diversify the social landscape with potential foci of action and resistance larger than the individual farming household.

Conclusions

Because property restitution has been proceeding for only a few years, to draw conclusions about its effects at this point would be rash. I can at best open a few windows onto its possible significance. Let me suggest three areas for which it has implications, both for social processes and for any comparison with other times and places: postsocialist rationalization, an ideology of rights tied to individuation, and changes in state power.

To restore private landed property across the former socialist bloc means to (re)construct a rationalized landscape different from that of the socialist period, a more individuated, more particularized grid. Although socialism did not completely demolish such a grid, the one it created had different dimensions and was based on different sociogeographic distinctions from what is taking shape now. The significant categories of the socialist landscape were state vs. collective lands, and socialist vs. private farming; villages were no longer treated as the strongly bounded entities of before but saw their edges violated by border-defying state farms and exchanges of land. Rationalizing a landscape from this base is not the same as the modernizing rationalizations of early capitalism. It creates different balances of power, different resources for influencing this balance, different political subjectivities, different forms of justifying enclosure and proprietorship, and different trajectories for social ideology.

The agents of Transylvania's new grid operate in odd intersections of political force. They are, first, those individual village owners who insist—in land commission meetings, in public speech, and if necessary in court—on respect for their property rights. To insist on the return of their original parcel has become for these people a way of opposing the usurpation of their rights, by other villagers and especially by commune officials and others based in the state agricultural sector, who all want land but might have difficulty mustering the necessary proofs except through fraud. Even those officials who hoard knowledge and exclude measurement from fields they have selected as their own do not reject a grid of ownership: their abuse can be transformed into a right only if a property grid is firmly established. Additional agents of rationalization are the village associations, pressing for certainty so as to proceed with their work. A rationalizing impulse that began, then, in the prison cells of members of the historical parties and spread across Romania through political activity in the national arena is being pushed to conclusion by local struggles and localized wars of knowledge. The specificity of these processes should inform any comparison with the rationalizations of capitalist modernity.

Similarly comparable yet different is the discourse of rights underpinning these local struggles. As people fight their battles, defending their claims against one another and against local officials, they reinforce an ideology of rights. Over and over I heard people say, "Defend your rights!" "Why are you giving up? Don't give up; don't let them walk all over you!" Lest we too hastily find here liberalism triumphant, however, we might note that this ideology of rights has its origins in socialism, which encouraged subjects to see themselves as entitled to things.[67] Their sense of entitlement is now in the service of a demand for rights. Socialism too guaranteed rights, though not to property. One might say that socialism had made villagers rights-bearing subjects of a certain type, but by complaining repeatedly to the land commission, going to court, and plowing over their neighbor's furrow, villagers may now be actively *making themselves* into the bearers of rights. Whether they are doing so in some relation to legal procedures and guarantees is less certain. For some, the right they seek derives from might, for others from ancestry or labor, for still others from past deprivation. These may not have been exactly what the architects of liberalism had in mind.

In defending their rights to land, Transylvanians participate in a process of individuation (not to say atomization) that erodes the solidarities—such as they were—of socialism's "us" vs. "them." People who formerly cooperated have been pitted against one another; conflict divides cousins and siblings; neighbors who have gotten on well for decades no longer speak, owing to conflicts over the borders of their gardens. Through their arguments individual parcels will materialize from an unindividuated landscape, parcels bounded by newly planted saplings and by the whimsical markers people have contrived—a beer can on a stake, a blue plastic bag tied to a tree. The process of obtaining property deeds for these parcels will further individuate, for siblings who figure as joint heirs to a given set of holdings must seek a legal division in order to get permanent title. (Along with these separately owned parcels may come impediments to the collectivism that still pervades the consciousness of even those who think themselves thoroughly anti-Communist.) Nonetheless, if the emerging ideology of kinship gains purchase, the "atoms" of this process may be not individuals per se but families and networks of kin, howsoever constricted by quarrels over land.

Finally, as I will show at greater length in chapter 8, the struggles of property restitution contribute to transforming Romanian politics and state power.[68] The events of 1989 dealt a severe blow to the centralized Romanian party-state, an effect that extensive privatization should only enhance. Will those now in power succeed in reversing this trend? Will the conditions they create in agriculture favor collective actors—state farms, *Agromecs* (successors to the old machinery parks), and associations—at the expense of individuals struggling for land? And will those collective actors find themselves beholden to the state rather than independent of it? Will the legal battles of would-be owners prove a means of reconstructing the state's power through an ideology of "the rule of law"? If the governing coalition continues to obstruct the separation of powers (as it has to date), we can expect precisely this outcome: the struggle for individual possession will fortify the political center via its control of the courts. Local-level management of property restitution has comparable significance. If local authorities manage to resolve land conflicts and to avoid the center's intervention, this would promote local autonomy. Should they fail to do this, however, calling on the state to assist, they will rebuild state power. The implications of local struggles over land thus ramify far beyond the villages: they affect not only villagers' self-conceptions and social relations but the state's very capacity to dominate them in the future.

"Property reconstitution," a topographer said to me, "is like trying to reproduce an entire painting when you have only half of it." He might have added that the task is even more difficult if the canvas will not stay still. Property restitution in Transylvania involves pushing and pulling the canvas and much argument as to what the painting is supposed to look like. Not all those entitled to property join the fray, but those who do are affecting the most basic conditions of their lives as they strive to twist the canvas to their advantage and then tack it in place. Whether Transylvania's landscapes will gradually cease to stretch, accepting the girdle of private possession, the forms in which landed property will come to be both thought and worked, the people who will work it, and the fields of power in which they do so—these hang in the balance.

7

FAITH, HOPE, AND CARITAS IN THE LAND OF

THE PYRAMIDS, ROMANIA, 1990–1994

> Caritas has become not just an obsession but indeed emblematic
> of the profound crisis of the times in which we live. In such times,
> marked by social and political upheaval and by shortages of all
> kinds, prophets and quacks arise to heal everything, the coming
> end of the world gets a precise date, and every day a miracle or
> two happens. People crushed by hardship and without hope can
> hardly wait to believe in these things. The Caritas
> phenomenon is such a miracle.
> *(Constanţa Corpade, "Fenomenul Caritas:*
> *între iluzie şi îngrijorare")*

> To everyone who has will more be given, . . . but from him
> who has not, even what he has will be taken away.
> *(Matthew 25.29)*

EVEN BEFORE ENTERING Romania in September 1993 for a
year's research, I had begun hearing about Caritas.[1] As I lunched
one day that summer with a Romanian friend visiting Washington,
I learned that she had just bought an apartment in an expensive quarter of
Bucharest. "How did you manage that?" I asked, and she replied, "I bought
it with the money I got from Caritas." That same day, an official at the Romanian Embassy told me that deposits in Caritas were rivaling those in the
Romanian National Bank.

In early September when I stopped to visit Romanian friends living in
Germany, Caritas was all they wanted to talk about. The hitchhikers I picked

My fieldwork in 1993–94 on property restitution included sporadic interviewing on the sub-
ject of this chapter; data also came from Romanian newspapers for July 1993–September 1994.
The chapter was written in September 1994 and was presented at the Graduate Center of the
City University of New York and at the University of Michigan, whose audiences offered much
helpful comment. I am also grateful for the advice of Pamela Ballinger, Eytan Bercovitch,
Elizabeth Dunn, Ashraf Ghani, Christopher Hann, Robert Hayden, Claude Karnoouh, David
Kideckel, Gail Kligman, Kirstie McClure, and Jane Schneider.

This chapter was published in *Comparative Studies in Society and History* 37 (October 1995)
and is reprinted by permission of the Society for the Comparative Study of Society and History.

up after I crossed the Romanian border had the same preoccupation, as did my closest friends in the community to which I was returning for my research.[2] When I told friends I was driving to Cluj, their immediate reaction was "To put money in Caritas?" A prime respondent from earlier visits greeted my arrival with the words, "We have money in Caritas! I have a lot to tell you." Before I was properly unpacked, friends were urging me to let them deposit money for me on their next trip to Cluj. I gave them $350[3]— and suddenly found myself as obsessed with the subject as everyone else.

For the next several months, talk about Caritas was the thread that joined my encounters with hitchhikers, people in the village, and friends and new acquaintances in all the towns and cities I visited, as well as tying these with my daily assault on the mountain of newspapers to which I subscribed. It also dominated conversations I overheard. If I passed animated talk on city streets, Caritas was likely to be the subject. Shopkeepers would discuss it with their customers, bus drivers with passengers, people standing in line with others near them, judges with their plaintiffs in court. Caritas was the common coin of all social relations in Romania for that year. Its ubiquity makes it an excellent medium through which to examine Romania's transition from socialism: the anxieties and challenges people faced, the pressure exerted on their conceptions of money and value, and the alteration of their ambient social and political structures.

What Was Caritas?

Caritas was the largest and most far-flung of many pyramid schemes that sprang up in Romania during 1990–94. Far outstripping similar schemes that appeared in other East European countries (such as the Czech Republic, Slovakia, Bulgaria, and Yugoslavia), it equaled or even surpassed the mammoth MMM scheme in much-larger Russia.[4] Concerning its founder, Ioan Stoica, reliable information is sparse. Before 1989 he is said to have worked variously as an accountant,[5] a fixer for the Communist Party apparatus,[6] and a black-market currency trader;[7] it seems he had also done time for embezzlement.[8] Stoica opened Caritas in April 1992 as a limited liability company with assets of 100,000 lei,[9] moving its first headquarters from the Transylvanian city of Braşov to Cluj two months later. Billed as a "mutual-aid game" designed to help needy Romanians weather the transition, the scheme promised to multiply depositors' funds eightfold in three months. At first deposits were fairly small: people put in 2,000, 4,000, or perhaps 10,000 lei (maybe a month's pension[10]). Later, initial deposits were set at a minimum of 20,000 and a maximum of 160,000,[11] but there was no limit to the amount one could subsequently deposit or retrieve. People who had begun with 10,000 and were on their fourth round by the summer of 1993 might be picking up and redepositing forty million lei (over thirty times a professor's annual salary) or even more. While at first only residents of Cluj could make deposits—they became financial agents for their friends and relatives from elsewhere—during the summer of 1993 this restriction was lifted. To make a deposit, one had only to be a citizen of Romania—or have a Romanian friend, as I did, or some other link directly to the source.

Like all things Romanian, Caritas soon developed two parallel tracks: one for people with inside connections, and one for everybody else. People in the latter group would go and stand in line to make their deposit, and then stand in line again to receive their earnings three months later. Despite a stunning degree of organization, by the fall of 1993 these lines could take whole days. The delay came partly from an odd feature of the system: no matter how big one's deposit or withdrawal, one got a separate receipt for each 20,000 lei increment. For a person turning over a payout of twenty million lei, this meant getting money for one thousand receipts and waiting for that many again at the deposit window. Caritas thus became like all those other items of value for which people had queued interminably under social-ism.[12] Because it was not possible to turn over one's earnings without physi-cally moving mountains of bills from one cash register to another, many people had the novel tactile experience of handling large sums—their size reflected in the time needed to process them—whose disposition was theirs to determine.

People with connections, however, did not have to stand in line: they gave their money to whatever friend they had among the employees, or to Stoica himself or one of his associates, and would get their receipts sometime later. An entire subindustry for making connections—a sort of parallel banking system—came into being, with informal branches run by people having in-side connections who would deposit other people's money for a commission, usually 10 percent.[13] It was rumored that some of the people with inside connections received their eightfold payout faster than the rest. Indeed, an allegation in one of the many lawsuits pending against Caritas by June 1994 was that certain members of parliament had been sending their money to Cluj on Fridays and getting their payout not in three months but in three days, while others who helped Caritas become established were paid almost on the spot.[14]

This hidden dimension of Caritas endows all information about it with uncertainty. Friends told me that the people who put money in first were working-class families and pensioners, but the hidden participation of for-mer apparatchiks, current politicians, and the nouveaux riches is certain, if difficult to prove.[15] Although formally speaking it was only people from Cluj who deposited at first, the tentacles of Caritas spread not only to their rela-tives and friends elsewhere in Transylvania and beyond but doubtless to the corridors of power in Bucharest as well.[16] The fact that so much about Caritas was hidden from view inevitably makes my analysis here tentative and exploratory.

Although Caritas's "inside track" obscures its true magnitude, some indication of its size is necessary to show its significance.[17] Estimates of the numbers of depositors in Caritas range from two to as many as eight million—the latter figure (used by some of Stoica's supporters) is surely exaggerated.[18] The number that appears most often in Romanian newspapers is four million.[19] Estimates by foreign papers tended to be more conservative—generally two million (about 10 percent of the population).[20] If one takes the names published in the *Transylvanian Messenger*, a newspaper listing all those to be paid on a given day, then for the three dates of 24 September and 1 and 18 October (that is, payouts to people who deposited around 24 June and 1 and 18 July—June through September 1993 marking the scheme's maximal expansion), there are over 66,000 entries. This would suggest 660,000 depositors a month.[21] A report attributed to the secret service claimed that 1.2 million people had deposited in the first five months of 1993—thus *before* the scheme really took off.[22] The most startling estimate comes from Dan Pascariu, then head of the Romanian Development Bank, who put the number of Romanian households involved in the scheme at three to four in eight, or 35–50 percent of all Romanian households.[23] But even the lowest plausible figure—a total of two million depositors—is still a very large number of people.

Other estimates assess the amounts of money passing through the scheme. The same secret service report gave the amounts deposited between January and 1 June 1993 as 43 billion lei, or somewhere around $80 million.[24] One paper declared that Caritas had managed 1.4 trillion lei altogether (compare government expenditures for 1993, which totaled 6.6 trillion).[25] A November 1993 *New York Times* story quoted economists' estimate that the scheme had pulled in altogether $1–5 billion; the *Economist* had earlier stated that payouts totaled about 75 million lei a week and at that rate would overtake Romania's Gross Domestic Product within three months.[26] In autumn 1993 the president of the Romanian National Bank estimated that Caritas held a full third of the country's banknotes—a sizeable portion of its liquid reserves (which amounted then to over 2.5 trillion lei).[27] From a different angle, the Romanian government reportedly received 41 billion lei in taxes from Caritas for 1993.[28] Similarly substantial participation shows in some anecdotal evidence too, such as figures for auto registration in Cluj— the city with the largest number of "winners"—which placed it fifth among European cities in cars per capita. Beggars on that city's streets were said to take home 300,000 lei per day (a worker's *monthly* take-home pay being about 50,000 lei).[29] Vastly increased traffic spurred travel agencies to mount special bus trips, while trains got longer.[30] In the second half of September, whole new trains were added to handle the traffic into Transylvania, specifically from Iaşi (in Moldavia) and Craiova (in Oltenia). The former of these was named "the Caritas train," the latter "the train of hope."

Why such mass enthusiasm? Among the reasons were inflation running at 300 percent in 1993, a 40 percent drop in real income as compared with 1989, negative interest rates, and problematic access to credit and loans, especially for small producers.[31] Most people I spoke with said that Caritas was the only investment they could make to keep up with inflation: savings deposits at 50 percent interest lost value rather than gaining it, thus wiping out people's lifetime accumulations.[32] Large gaps between the official and black-market rates for hard currency, and the fact that hard-currency deposits totaled as much as 30 percent of all bank deposits,[33] show clearly that Romanians were fleeing from domestic assets. Moreover, people wanting loans to buy a tractor, say, discovered that the Agricultural Bank's much-touted special 15 percent credits were somehow unavailable and that they would have to pay 60 percent, 75 percent, or over 100 percent interest for their purchases.[34] These circumstances, breeding panic and desperation, have historically driven speculative schemes in many parts of the world (including the U.S. during the 1930s); Romania was no exception.[35]

By the summer of 1993, then, Caritas was a mass phenomenon. A television interview with Stoica that spring had shown pictures of people walking out with armloads and bagloads of 5,000 lei bills; Stoica had come across as a sober, compassionate, God-fearing man who wanted to help Romanians in need. His charitable intent was evident not only in the name he chose (cleverly invoking an international Catholic charity[36]) but also in the urns placed at the exit from the payout lines, labeled "for the poor," "for the homeless," "for street repair," and so on. According to rumor, Stoica took almost no profits from Caritas;[37] his aim was to help the poor, and he had sworn to kill himself if it fell. Reports sometimes compared him—competitively—with millionaire Hungarian émigré and philanthropist George Soros, whose support for culture and democratization in the Soviet bloc is legendary. The *Messenger* periodically listed the amounts Caritas had given to various charitable causes; for September 1993, the total was 112.5 million lei.[38]

Doubtless drawn in by these positive images, people entrusted their savings to Stoica. Some sold houses and apartments, moving in with relatives so they could deposit the proceeds with Caritas, get enough to buy their houses back, and also set themselves up in business.[39] Organizations sought to fund their activities by putting money into Caritas. Among them were reportedly associations of apartment-house residents, needing money to repair their buildings; high-school classes, wanting to fund their end-of-year festivities and class gift; the Cluj mayor's office; the Society for Help to Children; the Cluj University Chorus; consumers' cooperatives trying to cover their debts; village agricultural associations wanting to buy tractors or other farm equipment; church parishes; and the heating fund of the Miners' Union.[40] Employers in Bucharest paid their company chauffeurs to drive to Cluj to deposit the money of employees and even of their entire firms. Trains and highways were packed. People came from Hungary, Germany, Ukraine, and beyond to deposit money through their friends or else sent money to friends and relatives to encourage participation.

Testimony to its significance, Caritas now became a nationwide cultural symbol and entered common parlance. The expression "I'm not selling with Caritas money" became something to say if you thought you were giving someone a good price. The scheme was immortalized in the rhymed couplets of traditional Romanian folk verse (for instance, "From Sibiu to Făgăraş / There's no son of Romania / Who isn't in Caritas") and in other poetic forms as well ("A man has appeared / Who has saved us all / Make Stoica Emperor").[41] A national newspaper published the first song composed for Stoica: "Train, what are you carrying, / So much bad and so much good. / You stop and pick up in every station / The pain of the whole country. /[Refrain] To Caritas, to Caritas, / We still have hope left, / Our pain and our hope /That can change our life," and so on.[42] In addition, Caritas cropped up in homilies in all sorts of contexts. I overheard an inspector from the county capital admonish a villager who was trying to claim more land than he deserved: "Only Caritas can make eight hectares out of one!" In court, I heard a judge reprimand the parties with the words, "For an apartment and seven million lei that you could get from Caritas,[43] it's a shame to destroy your precious sibling relations!" And in the spring of 1994, when no work had yet been started on laying the gas main for which my co-villagers and I had paid large sums of money, several said to me, "I hope this gas thing isn't going to turn out like Caritas: you pay a lot of dough into it and get nothing back."

Ominous signs began to appear in autumn 1993. Several Western newspapers published stories about Caritas, asserting that its fall was only a matter of time.[44] Certain Romanian papers printed increasing numbers of critical and derisive stories about it.[45] In a late-September press conference, Romanian president Ion Iliescu said that as anyone with an elementary education ought to know, nothing that gives an eightfold return in three months can last; he predicted its imminent demise. There was talk that parliament would pass a law to ban all these so-called mutual aid games.[46] That something was politically up seemed clear on 7 October, when the government-controlled television aired a lengthy interview with Stoica, criticizing him mercilessly and giving him almost no chance to speak. This coincided with his first failure to make scheduled payouts, a two-day hiatus explained as a computer error. Operations resumed only to slacken shortly thereafter, explained this time by the need to help with payouts in some smaller towns. We now began to hear that people going to collect their money received only half of what they expected.

Maintaining the appearance of healthy activity, in September Stoica had opened a huge supermarket. Its christening was attended by several local luminaries, including the prefect of Cluj county and Cluj's mayor, Gheorghe Funar, who was head of the influential Party for Romanian National Unity.[47] Thereafter, Stoica dotted the landscape with new Caritas branches in more and more cities, ostensibly to ease travel constraints for old and new depositors and to reduce the pandemonium in Cluj. Despite this, Caritas seemed stuck on payouts for people who had deposited on 5 July; these stretched out interminably into November and December, as the lists of names in the *Messenger* dwindled from sixteen to twenty pages down to one-fourth of a page, with many of the names duplicated. In yet another TV interview in early February 1994, Stoica insisted that Caritas was not dead but was reorganizing itself and lengthening the payout period. Soon thereafter, he announced a temporary cessation of Caritas activity, blaming this on the authorities—especially those in Bucharest, who had refused him permission to open a new branch. (The ban aroused a large demonstration protesting his exclusion and demanding the new branch, as well as a hunger strike by Stoica, who sued city hall.) Further rumors spread that Cluj headquarters had been robbed and that this explained the problems with payouts; papers and the TV news carried pictures of the supposed culprits, who had reportedly stolen 95 million lei. By March 1994, even though city and county governments across Romania were banning all pyramid schemes, many people with whom I spoke still refused to believe it was ending. To my gloomy predictions, they would object, "But Stoica promised it would last three years, and it's been only one and a half!"[48]

Nonetheless, it was obvious that the public had lost faith in Caritas, and without new deposits payouts became impossible. Accompanied as always by rumors flying around it like buzzards over stumbling prey, Caritas was on its last legs. After months of asserting that it was merely reorganizing on a healthier basis, on 19 May 1994, Stoica officially announced its end. His staff began work on a formula to return some of the money, if only for first-time depositors who had not yet received anything.[49] Lawsuits and hunger strikes by groups of angry and disappointed depositors followed. In August 1994, Stoica was arrested and charged with fraud, false representation, and fraudulent bankruptcy.[50] To his credit, however, his delaying tactics and steadfast refusal to admit defeat had prevented the tremendous crash and accompanying social upheaval and ethnic violence that many had feared. Caritas ended "not with a bang but a whimper."

Caritas and Economic Transformation

A phenomenon of extraordinary magnitude, Caritas touched at least one-fifth of all Romanian households[51] and involved sums that on paper approached Romania's entire Gross Domestic Product. This means that it had many diverse consequences and performed varied social and cultural "work." To list a fraction of its effects: it temporarily depressed the market for unskilled labor in Cluj, if not elsewhere;[52] by mobilizing and bringing into circulation savings that had been kept in socks and under mattresses at home, it soaked up the monetary overhang,[53] and it facilitated capital formation in the absence of stable credit institutions and low interest rates;[54] it effected a massive redistribution of wealth;[55] it compelled people to begin thinking in new ways about money; and it focused their anxieties about the larger processes of Romania's transformation from socialism. Leaving aside most of these, in what follows I will treat Caritas as a window onto problems of the transition, from which we can see something of the troubles various Romanians were perceiving in the early 1990s, the challenges they felt to their conception of money, and the processes of class formation underway in the new encounter between "socialism" and "capitalism" to which the former Soviet bloc is host. My discussion moves from the speculations and hypotheses of those I spoke with concerning what Caritas means and how it works, to my own speculations about what it was accomplishing in Romania's emergent political economy. I conclude with a hypothesis about its place in the rise of a new class of entrepratchiks from the Party apparatus of before.

Folk Explanations of Caritas

How did ordinary Romanians understand Caritas? What does talk about it reveal concerning Romania's ostensible exit from socialism into a market economy? Caritas presented people with the reality—unknown to most of them for forty-five years—that money can proliferate with no visible effort. What did they make of this? Answers to such questions require noting briefly the forms of accumulation with which Romanians were already familiar from the socialist period.

Prior to 1989 there were several ways of mobilizing sizable sums of money (aside from illegal and "mafia"-based enrichment, not available to most people on any scale). Savings accounts were not one of them: for decades savings deposits earned 3 to 3.5 percent annual interest, providing (in a nearly inflation-free system) only modest increments in wealth. More promising for a tiny handful of people were the various forms of state-sponsored gambling—lotteries for which one bought a ticket or submitted an entry, and periodic drawings that brought the occasional lucky person an automobile or a sum of cash.[56] A third means, especially common in rural areas, was weddings: by hosting a huge party in the village hall and inviting hundreds of guests, each of whom gave the young couple a sum of money, newly allied families might clear enough (after not-inconsiderable expenses) for a car, an urban apartment, or a handsome bribe that would improve the couple's job prospects.[57]

Finally, there were various kinds of interest-free loans that operated in most workplaces, taking two forms in particular. One was a fund provided by the firm, from which its employees could borrow significant amounts from time to time, repaying at no (or very low) interest over a lengthy period. This was known as C.A.R. (from the Romanian for "mutual aid fund"), its three initials interestingly echoed in the first three letters of "Caritas" and its meaning resonant with Caritas as a "mutual aid game." The second was a fund created by small employee contributions, each employee having the right to harvest the entire fund on occasion for major purchases. Crucial to both forms was that they were closed circuits, used only by workers of the firm and rotating a fixed sum whose limits were set by member contributions or by the firm itself. Many who later deposited in Caritas, believing it paralleled these workplace forms, did not see the critical difference: unlike those forms, Caritas was not a closed circuit with fixed amounts but an open one with theoretically unlimited participation. Perhaps it was Romanians' long experience with these two workplace funds that disposed them to embrace Caritas so readily, and so innocently.

In each of these forms of accumulation, the mechanism by which money proliferated was easily apparent—funds provided by state or firm, contributions of guests or employees. With Caritas, however, the mechanism was more obscure. People who sought to explain how it worked—either on their own or to my questions—offered a veritable panorama of the sources of confusion they were facing in their changing society. When I asked how Caritas could pay an eightfold return in three months, many had no idea whatsoever; Stoica had a "secret," they said, and left it at that. Others, however, had a variety of explanations. A few grasped the basic pyramid principle, but most reached for something more intricate. For example, one person assured me that the money came from short-term loans Stoica made at 300 percent interest, probably for armaments being smuggled into Serbia. "Proof" of this was that the first interruption in payouts coincided with the much-publicized arrest of a barge on the Danube that had been caught running guns to the Serbs. A number of people argued instead that Stoica was taking the money deposited, investing it locally in some form of production, selling the product in the West, converting the hard currency back into lei, and making enough money on all this to octuple the funds deposited. The product mentioned most often was furniture, sold in Germany for Deutschmarks that were converted to lei at the black-market rate.[58] This theory, which sees foreign trade as capital raising, was by far the most common explanation I heard.

The theory has several significant elements and unifies people's puzzlement about a number of aspects of Romania's transition. One such puzzle concerned the skyrocketing exchange rate, which kept going up and up for reasons no one could fathom. I frequently heard people ask one another (or me) why the dollar, which had exchanged for between 12 and 20 lei for decades on end, should rise from 600 to 1,900 lei in the space of a few months. Given how baffling this was, might it logically be tied with the equally baffling Caritas payout rate? Second was the basic conundrum of Caritas itself: how could money make so much more money with no visible effort? It must have some connection with capitalist countries, where the streets are paved with gold and everyone is rich. A third puzzle this "foreign-trade" theory addressed was the relative roles of commerce and production as sources of earnings or value. In Communist propaganda, commerce always took a back seat to production; income from trade was presented as unearned and therefore stolen (hence the opprobrium cast on Roma, or Gypsies, who were very active in trade and were widely seen as thieves).[59] Yet with the new market emphasis, people are being asked to see commerce as a source of value, and income from it as legitimate. (Note, however, that the "foreign-trade theory" has Stoica beginning with a *productive* investment.)

The theory addressed all these enigmas in a single reasonable frame. It did so by attributing value to commerce but only as mediated by the West— that is, Romanian production is valorized only through foreign trade, combined with unofficial currency exchange. These ideas remind one of people's earlier rejection of socialist goods and of state-based economic policy. For decades, Romanians saw the production of value as centered outside their own society, which many consider incapable of generating value independently even now.

A great many explanations of Caritas took an additional form familiar from socialist times: suspicions of a conspiracy or plot. Possible agents of Caritas plots were Hungarians, the Catholic Church, the International Monetary Fund and World Bank, the Romanian government, the Securitate (Ceauşescu's Secret Police), and other Ceauşescuite groups. All the theories share a certainty that someone or some group is actively shaping Caritas, even producing the money for it. Most of the explanations were more elaborate than I have space to describe here, so I will summarize just a few of them briefly.

The "Transylvanian autonomy" scenario posited a plot to dismember Romania. It had certain unnamed groups (probably Hungarians, maybe with others) backing Caritas to increase the wealth of Transylvanians over that of Romanians from the capital and the other provinces; in consequence, the government would ban the game, causing Transylvanians to riot and demand independence from the rest of the country. This scenario has deep roots in Romanians' apprehension over the integrity of their multiethnic state, and I believe it expresses Transylvanian displeasure at policies and parties largely run by "those Balkan types" in Bucharest.[60] In contrast to this destruction-of-Romania plot was a salvation-of-Romania scenario: through Caritas, unknown patriots were returning to the Romanian people the money Ceauşescu had stashed in secret bank accounts abroad. A more cynical version of this dovetailed with the very elaborate conspiracy theory that Caritas was a laundromat for either the unspent bank accounts of the Communist Party or the illicit earnings of Securitate- and Party-operated underground firms, funds accumulated both before and after 1989 through activities like drug smuggling or gun running to Serbia.[61] A connection of some sort with the Securitate was widely suspected and fairly probable, for Caritas had close ties with the Party of Romanian National Unity (PUNR)—a party with strong Securitate backing, as we will see.

All these accounts invoke one or another shadowy group that might plausibly have an interest in promoting (or wrecking) a scheme such as Caritas. They all assume that Caritas is not part of an abstract circulation of money-making money but is under somebody's control, just as so many complicated events of the socialist period had been seen as the work of sinister forces, perhaps unidentifiable but undeniably concrete. The theories reflect long-standing paranoia about the dismemberment of Romania or the unseen actions of the presumably ubiquitous Securitate, and they project onto Caritas shady dealings like those reported daily in the press and once perpetrated by the Communist Party.

Also positing an active agent, crooked deals, and considerable distrust of the authorities were explanations involving the Romanian government. That the government could be backing Caritas had several possible justifications: the authorities wanted 1) to make all the country's money easily available for confiscation and monetary reform (of the kind that had happened in 1952); 2) to create an illusion of prosperity so the governing party would be reelected; 3) to foster inflation and thereby hold down unemployment; or 4) to feed into the economy banknotes not covered by gold reserves, so as to a) foil IMF austerity measures and foster inflation (see 3), or b) meet IMF and World Bank conditions for allowing the leu to float. (Caritas would accomplish this last goal by giving people so much money that they would willingly pay higher and higher prices to buy hard currency.[62]) Some people noted, too, that the government had received huge tax revenues from Caritas, enough to finance the unfinished rebuilding of Bucharest. Partisans of the "government plot" theory argued that Caritas would never have gotten so large if the government did not somehow support it.[63] All these explanations assume that just like their predecessors, current political leaders are engaged in shady business and have full power to shape economic life behind the scenes. The accounts also speculate about some of the same puzzles as the foreign-trade theory—inflation, exchange rates, Romania's interface with Western institutions. And they assume, further, that prosperity without work rests on an illusion, conspiratorially produced.

Plots thickened once Caritas began to fail—owing variously (it was said) to the Romanian National Bank, other Romanian banks, the government, the

World Bank and IMF, a Jewish-Hungarian international financial cabal, Romanian newspapers, and Stoica's own employees, said to be robbing him blind. This last theory (the most benign—and probably true) posited sums ranging from the 95 million lei reported on Romanian TV to 60 billion or more. More elaborate conspiracy theories explained Caritas's problems by an international campaign against it, particularly on the part of Jewish-Hungarian financial interests. Personified in Hungarian philanthropist Soros, these interests were thought to be bent on keeping Romanians from enrichment, from aspiring to a better life, and from challenging Jewish-Hungarian financial success. This account is redolent with the views of the Romanian nationalist parties (which tend also to be antireformist), in playing upon the well-developed anti-Semitic and anti-Hungarian sentiments of many Romanians. The scenario reflects the nationalists' open hostility to the democratizing and reformist activities that Soros has sponsored in Romania and that nationalist politicians have denounced in the Romanian parliament.

Other collapse-scenarios again blamed the government. It was said to be destroying Caritas because 1) Iliescu's party wanted to undercut the potential competition from one or another political rival tied to the scheme, 2) they were worried about the prospect of chaos if Caritas got any bigger and then fell, 3) all the parliamentarians had gotten rich and now they could kill it, 4) leaders were upset that the banking system was so weak owing to people's putting all their money in Caritas, or 5) the International Monetary Fund, disturbed by reports that projected Caritas payouts bigger than the total state budget, had put pressure on the government to kill Caritas as a condition for according Romania's next standby loan. In these scenarios we again see a specific agent undermining Caritas, rather than the working out of some mathematical or market principle.

In a similar vein, many blamed Caritas's troubles on Romanian banks, suspected of hoarding Stoica's deposits to prevent his making payouts. Stoica himself fed this explanation with hints that he would start his own bank so he would have fewer problems; he reportedly circulated a petition addressed to Mugur Isărescu, head of the Romanian National Bank, in which depositors demanded that Isărescu order the other banks to give Stoica his money. The bank theory highlights two bewildering aspects of the activity of banks in Romanian society. The first was their role in the incomprehensible devaluation of the leu and in raising interest rates to astronomical levels, with which even loan-starved villagers were familiar. Given this, it would only be in character for banks to deprive needy depositors of their Caritas earnings, as well. Second, the theory highlights yet another baffling thing about life in early-1990s Romania (and other postsocialist systems also): the so-called financial blockage. Immense sums of money were immobilized because firms were not paying their creditors, producing a chain reaction in which no one could pay anyone else because no one was being paid. One estimate put the amount of money thus immobilized at four trillion lei.[64] Owing to the financial blockage, many employees received no salaries for months on end but without understanding why—unless banks were simply hoarding the money. To see Stoica as the prisoner, like themselves, of banks that would not pay people what they were owed was a way of linking a widespread and confusing problem with Caritas's difficulties.

Most of these theories are plausible; some of them may also be right, although it is hard to know which.[65] I draw only two firm conclusions from the proliferation of theories about Caritas: it is effectively impossible—both for outsiders and for most Romanians—to know what was really happening; and proponents of these explanations tended to see economic processes as under someone's control. Many people had no theory at all, but for most of those who did, economic phenomena are subordinate to the political sphere and directed by it, just as was true under socialism. The party-state had convinced citizens of its potency and their impotence; its successors still benefit from that conviction, even if many citizens also attribute effective agency not just to political leaders but also to international capital and other forces external to themselves.

In addition to hosting the sorts of conspiracy theories familiar from before, however, Caritas was also paradoxically a site for thinking in new ways about economic processes, money, and its place in people's lives.

Rethinking Money

After four decades in which Romanians had not had to worry about inflation or struggle to find investments that would outpace it, suddenly these questions have become urgent for them. Likewise, it had made little sense to plan their financial futures expansively or seek profitable activities, but now it does. Caritas was a godsend in these respects. It permitted undreamed-of accumulation and savings; one could either roll over one's take for another eightfold increase or withdraw it for purchases or investment in business— or to change into hard currency, whose value (unlike that of the leu) was stable and high. With Caritas, people could plan an economic future different from the past. They could buy consumer goods not otherwise affordable, obtain tractors and plows for working newly acquired land or trucks for transporting goods to make extra money—or at least contemplate doing these things. For not only the elite but also average Romanians, then, Caritas promised capital accumulation. Unlike other ways of getting ahead, it required no political connections but only the nerve to risk one's money. And this both called for and enabled thinking about money differently. Caritas was thus part of the cultural reorganization necessary to any departure from socialism.

As a once-socialist economy increases the play of market forces, it opens up spaces for radically new conceptions of the economy and the place of money in people's lives. In saying this, I do not assume that the former Soviet bloc is moving inexorably from socialism to capitalism (which I doubt); I wish merely to signal critical sites at which we might look for change. Market-based systems regulate the flow of wealth very differently from the planned economy of socialism. The reason is not that plans unfolded as planned but that they obstructed the flow of money and goods in certain characteristic ways, different from the obstructions characteristic of market systems. For one thing, in socialism most prices were determined not by "supply and demand" but politically. Adjustments might come from bribery, gifts, shadow production, and barter, but these occurred within constraints set visibly by the Party—constraints of which people were generally very aware. In my experience, any Romanian asked to explain some aspect of the workings of the economy could readily generate an answer based in something the Party was up to, usually some nasty plot against common folk. People presumed (as I indicated earlier) that economic events had an agent: the political system and those who ran it.

Markets in advanced economies, however, work differently. Their secret lies in their being invisible, taken for granted, abstracted from the actions of concrete agents. Precisely here is the ongoing usefulness of Marx's insights about commodity fetishism: market exchange obscures the social relations surrounding production and distribution. Socialist systems too had a form of fetishism—plan fetishism, which produced the illusion of agency and obscured the anarchy and chaos that actually went on behind the scenes.[66] That is, socialist plans generated the illusion that everything is under social control. The illusion of market exchange, however, is exactly the opposite. If markets come to achieve greater significance in postsocialist society, then, we should look for transformations in social visibility, as the famed invisible hand begins replacing the all-too-visible one of the Party.[67] Things that were personal come to seem impersonal; "the economy" becomes a separate domain and a force of nature, for which no one in particular is responsible. Caritas was a critical locus for the recoding of money and the economy that such a shift might entail. Stoica himself stated this as his goal, in aiming to help form a middle class of Romanian businesspeople and investors: "From now on, people will differ as a function of how they think about money and about capital, how they get it, and what they know to do with it."[68] How might Caritas effect changes of this kind?

At the simplest level, by participating in it people began to think differently about money. It enabled them to manipulate in their minds sums they had never imagined, to think about what they might do with such sums—to *plan* their expenditures—and to grow accustomed to thinking about larger and larger sums in a gradual way. First they would have amounts that could go toward consumer goods, then the amounts would get so large that more ambitious possibilities suggested themselves: buying a tractor or a combine, opening a restaurant, founding a newspaper or publishing house. It created in people's imaginations a sphere in which money circulated and they themselves participated without really understanding its principles. But the change to a market economy also involves shifts that are more subtle. Socialist propaganda had taught that the only acceptable source of money and gain was work in the productive process; money from "commerce" and from "speculation" was polluting, unacceptable, tainted with capitalist traces. Now, however, with increased trade of all kinds and major efforts to increase the circulation of money through the financial system, these habits of mind are being challenged. Caritas was a prime site for challenging them.

We can see how this worked by exploring a distinction made by nearly everyone I spoke with, between "my money" and "their (or Stoica's) money." "My money" was the amount people first deposited. Most who received a payout withdrew that amount before turning over the rest: at this point, they would say, they were playing not with their own money but with Stoica's money, and it was no longer possible to lose. One woman in an overheard conversation in a train put it this way: "You put in 100,000, get 800,000 back, take 500,000 of it to buy things you need, and keep playing the game with 300,000—*their* money. Am I playing with *my* money then? No. If it gets lost, have I lost *my* money? No. YOU CAN'T LOSE in this game."[69]

Here is how another woman elaborated the same distinction:

> I got all my money back, so if it falls I can't complain. [Isn't the payout money also yours?] No, it's not quite the same, though I'm not sure why—I never really thought about it. When they pay it to me in cash, it's my money, but when it's not in my hand, it's not like my money.[70] If the thing collapsed, I wouldn't feel I'd lost my money. Even when you get it in hand you spend it differently from other money—you spend it more easily. I had *three million lei*—an unimaginable sum!—in my hands and I took it right over to the next window to deposit it. [Didn't that bother you?] No!

Changes in this woman's thoughts about money had gone unobserved until I drew her attention to them. Another couple who also made the distinction talked about it as follows, as they advised me how to dispose of my first payout:

> You should take out *your* money and play further with *theirs*. [If I put in 100,000 and get back 800,000, bring it home, and put it here on the table, is this my money?] No! [Why not? I'm not talking about money I rolled over but money I've brought home with me.] We have no idea. [But why did you say it isn't my money?] Well . . . because it's been in there only three months. It can't be yours. In a savings account, you leave money for a whole year and get 50 percent interest. Then it's more like your money. But eightfold in only three months. . . .

(In saying this they imply, interestingly, that something isn't one's property, an extension of oneself —"mine"— unless there is some sort of effort or sacrifice somewhere.[71]) Almost no one gave me the answer I got from a peasant woman who told me that she had a lot of money in Caritas. [But it's not *your* money, is it? You've rolled it over.] "It's still my money, isn't it? If I'd taken it out, it would have been my money." This woman was rare in not distinguishing "my money" from "theirs."

Alongside these ruminations on "my money" and "their money," other features of talk about Caritas help to illuminate the scheme's effects. I have already described some of the theories I heard when I asked how Caritas worked—how could people possibly get eight times their deposit in only three months? But many did not need to understand it at all: they had seen people on TV taking out huge piles of bills, or they knew of someone who had done so, and this was all the explanation they needed. Caritas works, for whatever reason. They had faith in it and required no further account. When I asked how they could entrust such large sums to something they didn't understand, they shrugged: the whole thing was incomprehensible. Some appear to have seen the money as a sort of free gift.[72] For them, it was just the logical result of the end of socialism and the much-touted transition to a market economy, which were finally bringing what Romanians had long seen as the main features of life in the West: unlimited riches, consumption, and abundance. Caritas thus epitomized the West; what need was there to understand it further?

From this I conclude that one of Caritas's most important effects was that it was producing an abstract sphere in which money circulates and multiplies without clear agency. Through it, "the economy" was beginning to become an impersonal, unregulated social fact, something to be taken for granted because it worked. A young sociologist expressed this nicely, in explaining what he thought were the consequences of his own participation in Caritas (on an "inside track"): "I noticed that it made money seem more distant, as if it were happening elsewhere, to someone else. It had become an abstraction, rather than *my money.*" Effects this man could articulate may also have been at work less consciously with others.

We might thus see Caritas as a "technology," in Foucault's sense, for new economic conceptions, one that fostered change in people's ideas about the economy toward a market sensibility.[73] Through Caritas, economic activity was being *made into* something one could call "the economy." It was not the only such instrument, but it was an especially widespread one. Although the scheme's collapse doubtless altered or even aborted its contribution to that process, the experience it afforded its participants was something new. Particularly for those who received and made use of a payout, the experience was significant. Nonetheless, whatever effects it realized were won against very strong habit, as my previous discussion of Caritas conspiracy theories has made amply clear. Those theories assumed that Caritas was not part of an abstract circulation of money-making money but was being actively managed. For this reason, we should be cautious in assuming that the scheme was producing an environment for capitalism and see it instead as a site for debating the extent to which the economy is an abstract, impersonal sphere.

Questioning the Moral Order

"My money" vs. "their money" was more than just a question of whether or not the economy is impersonal: it led directly into questions perhaps even more basic, about a changing economic morality and a new moral order. In pursuing these questions I am not arguing that socialism and capitalism have different moralities but rather that discourses about morality are crucial loci for defining the social order. They do this by positing distinctions between what is "good" and "bad," "right" and "wrong," oppositions that usually engage other kinds of distinctions, such as those between natural and artificial, normal and perverse, dirty and clean, and so on. Because such matters are so often associated with fundamental domains of existence, debate over them may point to basic shifts in a society's organization.[74] For example, given the negative value and dubious morality socialist systems assigned to trade and markets, we might expect increased marketization there to entail moral questioning, for the market in advanced economies is generally viewed as *a*moral, guided by rational interests and abstract economic principles rather than moral ones. This makes it useful to examine people's talk about Caritas for evidence of the moral questions they were reconsidering through it.

As I pursued "my money" and "their money" further, asking people if the money they got from Caritas was the same as the money they put in, it became clear that for the large majority what defined "my money" was that it was earned, whereas "their money" is unearned (*nemuncit*—from *munci*, to work). For most, "my money" embodies my work and is its concrete expression, whereas "their money" has none of me in it. "If you lose money you earned, you feel bad about it," said one woman, "but if you lose after that— money you didn't work for—you don't feel bad." Another: "In any case, money you've sweated for is different from this money." A Bucharest cab driver who had not yet received a payout greeted with these words my news that Caritas had stopped paying: "If we don't get anything, I'll string him up! I'll run a stake through him! That's *my hard-earned money*!" That many readers might think the same is beside the point; more important is that Caritas was making people ask such unaccustomed questions and arrive at new distinctions, understood as pertaining to morality.

The distinction between earned and unearned money was precisely this: a moral issue, as the following comments indicate. "We aren't used to living off unearned money. It seems somehow dishonest to us." "I'm not used to having money gotten for nothing; it seems somehow unnatural." "Something's wrong with it, it can't be honest, someone's going to lose." "I was raised to think that you never get anything except by hard work, you can't get something for nothing. There must be some trickery at the bottom of it. I won't put my money in something like that, I've worked too hard for it." Some people moralized the relationship between Caritas and work even more explicitly. "With Caritas, people lose interest in working." "People won't work any more, they'll just sit around and live off interest." "Earnings should come from productive investments, not from some crazy miraculous scheme."[75] "Caritas is dreadful! It encourages a beggar's mentality, it undermines people's interest in work. I've heard of people who simply quit their jobs and went home, expecting that it will go on forever. It's based on greed, and it creates inflation." These views show strong moral reservations about Caritas earnings, censured because they are based on greed, do not come from production, and make people stop working. It is striking that in a time of privatization-induced unemployment and concerns about Romanians' productivity, what we see people fearing is unemployment and laziness that are voluntary, brought on by Caritas.

Not everyone, however, is critical of Caritas money. A woman I know mused with me in this way: "Some say the money's bad because it's dirty, unearned, but at the hairdresser the other day someone was saying that not *all* money comes from work. Some is from services, some is interest on savings; so that's not a valid objection." Again, here are two agronomists who have bought a tractor with Caritas money and are embarked on an "entrepreneurial" trajectory: "Some people object to it because it's unearned money. This is an idea left over from before, that earned money is money you actually earn by producing something. Unearned money was from speculation, and it was condemned, along with anything that didn't have to do with producing. People who complain about its being unearned money are those who like to sit around, who have no enterprising spirit to risk something." This couple's opinion was informed by their success with Caritas— something that, I found, seemed to predispose one to a more positive assessment. They and others like them engaged in vigorous argument with other people concerning the morality of earnings from Caritas. Indeed, even those who were critical were likely to have mixed feelings; they too had money in Caritas, and perhaps their minds would change once the earnings started to roll in.[76] And so, as they waited for that to happen, people were debating the morality of Caritas money. That is, Caritas focused their genuine ambivalence about money's morality and became a space in which they sought to convince themselves and others that their old ideas about money were or were not outmoded, by arguing about just why Caritas money might not be so immoral after all.

Here are some examples. The first two see Caritas as a kind of moral compensation. To a friend in Cluj, I say that a lot of people seem upset that Caritas money is unearned and comes from greed. She replies, "Well, but

I've heard people saying, 'Isn't the West stealing from us with all this cheap labor?' And I know some pensioners who object to those criticisms of Caritas. They say, 'We pensioners worked our whole life, we put our money in savings, and now the money in those accounts is worth absolutely nothing. Who stole it from us? Is *that* moral? Stoica offers me a chance to eat better, have a TV—is this morally bad? Is it morally worse than the fact that the Communist Party reduced us to paupers? No!'" Second, a woman has been telling me how she plans to use her Caritas money. Then she volunteers, "Lots of people say it's immoral to live on unearned money, but I say, For all these years people worked unpaid, now we get a kind of compensation, don't you think?" (Note that in the first quotation the woman expresses her opinion through the words of someone else, and the second solicits my agreement; neither is really sure she likes what she is saying.)

Others puzzle over how much enrichment is acceptable, natural, or otherwise justifiable. Many people said, uncomfortably, that what motivates people to roll their money over is greed. As one fellow remarked of his stint in line, "People are so greedy! The guy right in front of me took out 120 million lei, went over to the next register, and deposited 100 million of it. I asked him, 'Why are you doing it *again*? Isn't what you already have enough?' And he replied, 'I can do what I want with it. It's my money.' But I said to him, 'It's *not* your money. It's mine and the other people's who've just deposited it. Leave some for the rest of us!'" This statement epitomizes the very common negative reaction to those who want to get rich—part of socialism's deeply internalized disapproval of disparities in wealth—as well as showing genuine puzzlement over whose resource Caritas money really is: some individual's, or ours collectively. A similar concern shows in the comment, "If Caritas money is immoral, it's because Stoica lets [some] people get so incredibly rich with it and others can't get in at all." The speaker added, however, "But we can't make ends meet with our work, so it's good to have Caritas money." Thus she finds enrichment acceptable after all because everyone is so needy.

It seems, then, that people are deeply divided as to whether it is acceptable to have money for which one has not worked. After years of hearing that commerce, high-interest loans, interest from capital, and the other forms of gain in the capitalist system were evil, Romanians are having to revalorize those forms as they struggle to make do in uncertain and inflationary times. Many (but far from all) see Caritas in terms of "greed," with clear disapproval—yet they too are getting or awaiting money from it. Some use words like "crookery" to describe it, see it as "unnatural," as a form of theft. The notion of theft recurs often—what is theft, after all? Who is stealing from whom? In other words, which forms of gain are licit, socially acceptable, and which are not? Under socialism certain forms of theft were acceptable, but how about now? If Caritas is a form of theft, can we justify it by our need?

Does or doesn't money have something to do with work? If money comes from nonwork, is that natural? Is greed natural? How should we feel about people who want to get rich? How should we feel about *ourselves* if we want to get rich? Romania's putative marketization breeds such questioning in all its citizens.

There were other forms of questioning the morality of Caritas money besides the distinction between earned and unearned money, though this was the most common. Another was a distinction anthropologists have encountered often, between "dirty" money and "clean."[77] That Caritas money might be dirty underlay most of the public criticisms of the scheme. Any of several sources might soil it: arms smuggling, drug trafficking, prostitution, the Italian mafia, roots in the Securitate, and so on—anything illegal. All these would require "cleaning," for which Caritas was an instrument, and all would make Caritas morally reprehensible for laundering money of this kind. In my experience, the concern with "dirty money" was a preoccupation of journalists, intellectuals, and politicians[78] rather than of average folks, who did not seem to care about the wider social provenance of Caritas funds. As one village friend said, when asked if she would take her money out if she found out it was from illegal sources, "No. If Stoica is doing something wrong, it's between him and God. It doesn't affect us. Besides, we're too poor. We need every possible source of income these days, never mind where it comes from. For so long we had no possibilities, we have to try to make ends meet with so little, prices keep going up, people lose their jobs. . . . We're just too needy to worry about whether it's dirty money." Questions of morality are central for her too, but they have to do with the immorality of want rather than that of illicit gain.

Debate over the morality of Caritas involved even Stoica himself, together with his supporters. He responded directly to the criticism of Caritas money as unearned, replying that it was not in fact unearned: he himself had done the work of seeing that it multiplied enough to pay people back eightfold, something that did not simply happen but required initiative and know-how.[79] In other words *he* had earned the money for other people. He and his allies marshaled a number of other arguments in defense of the scheme's morality—such as that in promoting privatization and decentralization of financial control, it was anti-Communist (an unquestionably "moral" quality, in post-1989 Romania!) and that it was no less moral than many other things in Romanian society and more moral than some. To the extent that Caritas is immoral, said one of his disciples, its immorality is that of all market economies: "In the Gospels it says that to him who has will more be given, but from him who has not it will be taken away. If there is a dose of immorality in Caritas, then this same dose of immorality exists also in life in general and even in the Gospel."[80] Making Caritas biblical was yet another way of allying it with a new post-Communist, anti-atheist moral order.[81]

I will pass over these arguments, however, to concentrate on a third, which links Caritas with Romanian nationalist political parties. The most energetic form of this argument came not from Stoica but from two of his defenders, authors of a booklet called *The Caritas Phenomenon; or, the Salvation of Romanians through Themselves.*[82] Its authors—an aide of Cluj mayor Funar and a chief acolyte of Romanian nationalism under Ceauşescu—make two central "moral" points: that Caritas is moral because it is the product of social solidarity (rather than of egotistical striving for gain) born of years of oppression, and that the beneficiary of this solidarity is the Romanian nation. Caritas is good, they proclaim, because it is the revolt of the united Romanian nation against the dictatorship of foreign money and foreign plans for "reform." It is "**a response, a solution, a reaction, a manifestation of national energy in the face of a fantastically well organized process of demolishing Romania and bringing the Romanian people to its knees through poverty and demoralization**"; the authors decry "so-called 'reform' and 'shock therapy' that were in essence nothing but a vast project of economic, spiritual, and biological **extermination** of an entire people."[83] They go on to describe in detail the international plot involving privatization and market competition through which foreigners will conquer all key positions in the economy, thus gaining control over Romania's political life. Why, these writers ask, do so many people proclaim Caritas a swindle, ignoring the real (and much bigger) swindle—"the veritable collapse of Romania under the burden of a program of 'reform' that has proved everywhere an economic catastrophe for the countries obliged to accept it."[84] To be sure they have made their point, they declare in large letters, "THE BATTLE FOR OR AGAINST CARITAS HAS BECOME PART OF THE BATTLE FOR OR AGAINST THE ROMANIAN PEOPLE'S RIGHT TO EXIST."[85]

Here, then, is a third kind of immoral money: not unearned or dirty money but *foreign* money. Against this kind of immorality Caritas becomes a patriotic institution that will produce an indigenous middle class, bearing good, moral money rather than the immoral money of foreigners. It is moral because unlike many other things going on in Romania (including, of course, criticism of Stoica and Caritas), it is pro-Romanian. It is more than this: it is a crusade by Romanians for their own salvation, "the salvation of Romanians, by the will and the grace of God, through themselves."[86] From the form of this argument it is clear, once again, that Caritas is by no means unambiguous in its relation to the spread of market forces or capitalism in Romanian society. Here, Stoica's nationalist allies do not invite capitalism in but seek to contain it, to deny it entry into their country except on very limited terms, which they themselves will set in accord with Romanian national values. Caritas, for them, is the seed of a homegrown capitalism vastly preferable to that of the West.

What these Romanian nationalist authors offer, then, is a new, Caritas-based morality that unifies religious faith, nationalism, and specific forms of legitimate money making. They quote with admiration the Romanian Ortho-dox vicar in the United States: asking who will buy the industries bank-rupted by government policy, he replies, "Foreigners will. But Caritas has not only come as a divine phenomenon bringing money and happiness; it is the salvation of the Romanian people. Now true Romanians will have mil-lions, maybe billions, so as to buy this economy and not have it in foreign hands."[87] Given that such views are common among nationalists, who con-trol 15 percent or more of parliamentary voting strength, they should not be simply brushed aside. And the failure of the quick fix that Caritas promised has enlarged the field upon which these sentiments might be cultivated.

Faith and Hope, God and the Devil

In the hands of allies like these, Caritas has ceased to be just a pyramid scheme; it has become a kind of social movement, one having millenarian overtones. Like other such movements, Caritas offered cargo cult–like vi-sions of an earthly paradise, the ushering in of a new life of plenty in which people would no longer have to work, and an imaginary world full of mate-rial goods; it posited new rules of morality suited to a new cosmic order.[88] From the way people spoke of Caritas, many seemed to view it as a means of imminent salvation (just as its critics foresaw, in suitably apocalyptic lan-guage, imminent disaster). Also like other millenarian movements, Caritas emerged from a clash between fundamentally different notions of time.[89] In the best-known Melanesian instances, the clash is between linear Western notions of time and local conceptions of it as cyclical, while in the case of Caritas, linear time confronts the peculiarly convulsive, messianic time char-acteristic of life under Romanian socialism. I have described elsewhere the kind of time implicit in the policies and discourse of the Romanian Commu-nist Party—a time that was at once spastic, arhythmic, and unpredictable and also flattened, motionless, teleological-immanent.[90] Because neither as-pect conforms well with capitalism's linear, progressive time, the encounter between these kinds of time will be awkward. Heightening their awkward-ness is a temporal shift within global capitalism itself, its own velocities ac-celerating in what Harvey has called "time-space compression."[91]

Lacking the traditional element of dead ancestors laden with goods tri-umphantly returning for the world's end, however, the millenarianism of Caritas was decidedly modern.[92] We see in this its descent through that "most dazzling of modern political eschatologies," as Mircea Eliade put it, the (millenarian) Marxist myth of the radiant Communist future.[93] We might view Caritas, then, as Marxism's antithesis, a millenarian social movement ushering in a radiant counterfuture. This movement came to be suffused with Christian imagery, as popular opinion gradually transformed Caritas into a religious cult and Stoica into a quasi-divine mythical hero.[94]

For his hopeful depositors, Stoica was "a saint," "the pope," "a messiah," "the prophet."[95] The folklore surrounding Caritas was full of "good Stoica" stories, such as one I heard in which an elderly man went to headquarters and asked to see "Mr. Caritas," offering a deposit of 2,000 lei so he could have a decent burial. Stoica took him to the cash register and gave him 20,000 lei on the spot. My informant concluded, "I don't know why but I have faith in what he says. He just isn't capable of taking our money and running." Her cousin chimed in, "It's said that God sent him to take care of us." I heard others state that he's a good man who's had a hard life, that he's not in this to make money for himself but gets satisfaction from seeing other people get some, that he's very religious and gives lots to churches, that he has the morality of a saint.

Stoica's repeated references to his faith and his use of religious expressions doubtless fed such beliefs. In an interview he observed, "The Bible says to help our fellow man. . . . That's how Caritas was born."[96] Reflecting the widespread reverence for Stoica, publications presented him as "the savior of the people" and "a god of the Romanians"; his supporters as prophets and apostles; Caritas as "the miracle of Cluj," "a divine phenomenon," and "the Mecca of thousands"; and depositors' journeys to Cluj as like "pilgrimages."[97] (Critics, in turn, viewed it as the "swindle of Cluj," "a demonic game," and "a perilous disease." They dismissed the salvational and moral imagery, and they refused to see in Stoica a new sacred leader.[98]) People's readiness to replace the quasi-religious personality cult that had surrounded Ceaușescu with worship of yet another "divine genius of the Carpathians" hints at the attitude of dependency socialism had cultivated.

Thus saturated with sacred symbolism, Stoica and Caritas became matters of faith, of belief—in Romanian, *încredere*. More than any other word, this was the one people used in speaking of them. I heard over and over the following rationale for putting money in Caritas: "I didn't have faith [*n-am avut încredere*] in it at first, but when I saw everyone else getting money, I decided to have faith too." As with similar movements, "faith" came partly through the social effects of others' behavior, a kind of conversion accompanying knowledge that others were in it too, and winning. Participants also proselytized actively: one woman told me she was fed up with the many friends and people in her workplace who kept trying to get her into Caritas, and I heard several stories about people who had gotten in because someone else deposited money for them as a "starter." (I myself was proselytized into depositing the money I lost.) Faith was what enabled people to accept for months all manner of excuses as to why payouts were stagnating or stopped, and it was on this that Stoica banked, in an October interview, when he urged people not to lose faith despite all the negative press. Faith did not apply to Caritas alone: ads for other pyramid schemes emphasized it too.

This faith was fragile, however. One reason offered for Stoica's moving Caritas to Cluj was that in Braşov, where he had started, earlier pyramid schemes had failed, so people there "didn't have faith," whereas those in Cluj (having had no such reality check) did.[99] In gaining and shoring up this faith a crucial role was played by Gheorghe Funar, the mayor of Cluj and head of the Party of Romanian National Unity (PUNR). It was he who gave Caritas its first headquarters—in city hall, thereby lending it authority. A number of my associates said they had faith that Caritas couldn't be a scam since it was right there in city hall. One woman, telling me about a pyramid in another town, said she didn't have faith in it "because there's no well organized party behind it." A newspaper article clarified the connection: although Caritas could expand its deposits by opening more branches, "the transfer of faith from Cluj to the branches is by no means simple" because "only in Cluj did the game enjoy the full support of local authorities."[100] Somehow a political presence (especially that of the populist and "pro-Romanian" PUNR) fortified Romanians to take the leap of faith into Caritas.

With faith came also hope. People referred to Caritas money as their "hope money" (*bani de nădejde*), without which they would have absolutely nothing. They spoke of the "train of hope" and declared that their only hope was Caritas, one of the few things to look forward to in otherwise anxious times. Through Caritas, hope could at last be institutionalized. Newspapers that insisted on predicting its fall were deluged with letters demanding why they were destroying miserable people's hope.[101] Even after it was clear that Caritas was indeed crumbling, other pyramid schemes kept springing up and finding depositors; as a friend explained it, "Every Romanian keeps hoping. If Caritas doesn't work, we go to some other game, always hoping *this* one will work." (As gloom over Caritas deepened during the winter of 1994, more people put their hope in a hard-currency scheme based in Vienna, arguing that at least these things ought to work properly in the West. This shows yet again how fragile was the faith in things Romanian.) Finally, a journalist drew a parallel between Caritas and the relics of St. Dimitrie, visited in Bucharest in October 1993 by thousands of despairing souls "in the hope that a miracle will happen in their daily lives." Both there and in the lines for Caritas, he saw people from the whole of Romania, with "the same terror that their turn [to see the relics] won't come, but above all the same terrible faith in the possibility of a miracle."[102] For most of these faithful souls, sadly, their hope would prove misplaced.

"Faith," "trust," and "hope": these were not words people had used to talk about life under socialism except, perhaps, for their most intimate family relations. Caritas was serving, then, to create and redistribute faith and hope, moving them from the inner sanctum of the family out into a market economy in which money and wealth would flow unobstructed, like trust. The moral-religious imagery was crucial to this process of making the circulation of money impersonal. Anyone who could not (or felt no need to) explain how it worked could assign it to the sphere of the divine.

The discourse of sacrality invited, however, its opposite and brought into play a very specific, malevolent agent: the devil. Did Caritas give out money from heaven, or money from hell? Some people unsure of the moral ground explored it in these cosmic terms. In research among a population of Transylvanian shepherds, Michael Stewart found a lively sense of the devil's intervention in Caritas. He reports that a family who had used their Caritas money to buy furniture later had it carted away, for the rattling of the devil in it had caused them too many sleepless nights.[103] Newspapers told comparable stories:

> The Antichrist is acting through Caritas. Lately, people returning from Cluj tell of extraordinary things. It is said that a woman by the name of Maria Badiu from Maramureş, who had deposited a certain sum of money in Caritas, had a dream in which an angel told her, 'Do not touch this money, for it is of the Antichrist! Go and tell them that you renounce it.' . . ."
>
> Another happening concerns Maria Pantea from Panticeu. She seems to have bought with Caritas money a new house, new furniture, and chandeliers for each room. The first night all the chandeliers in all the rooms fell, shattered into a thousand pieces, the furniture moved from its place, and the foundations of the house cracked.[104]

Among my own more urbanized village informants such views were rare, but even so a retired bus driver gave me this account of why his family had a new tractor but no plow. They had taken money out of Caritas to buy the plow, he said, but before they could do so, their son-in-law wrecked the car in an accident and they had to spend all the money repairing it. "The money was no good," he concluded, "it came too easily. We thought Caritas was okay, but look what happened." More concisely, a woman told me, "Caritas must be the work of the devil: money can't give birth!"[105]

Reminiscent of Taussig's Colombian peasants and other groups being drawn into a capitalist economy, these stories reveal yet other ways in which Romanians were struggling to moralize money and Caritas and to understand money's capacity to multiply without effort.[106] They were deeply suspicious of this capacity but at the same time desirous of it. The often apocalyptic imagery they used testifies to the urgent matters being addressed: What is money? Where does it come from? How should we use it? Is it acceptable to have money we haven't earned? What is the place of money in a moral universe? In looking for divine or diabolical intervention, people were giving the economy agents, yet these were nonetheless more abstract than the Party cadres who had controlled the system before. And in placing their revalorization of money in a divine context, they were helping to construct a new post-Communist moral cosmology. Surprisingly, then, we see that the process of learning forms of economic or market rationality—a process to which Caritas was central—has been occurring in part through the "irrational" means of faith and hope, God and the devil.[107] This suggests that Caritas was teaching people not market rationality but its mystification.

Caritas and the Reconfiguration of Power and Wealth

I have been exploring the place of Caritas in new cultural conceptions of money and morality. This far from exhausts its significance, however, for Caritas also provides a window onto changing social structures and the behavior of Romanian elites: it served as a means of accumulating political capital in the national political arena and was implicated, I believe, in new configurations of wealth and power. Necessary to describing these processes are concepts that label two kinds of groupings: political parties, and what I will call "unruly coalitions."[108]

Romanian political parties are not quite the platform-bound, disciplined organizations thought to characterize Western parliamentary democracies. Instead, they are formally institutionalized networks of friends, relatives, and other associates who engage corporately in the electoral and legislative process. Although some may have a primarily regional base, all are of national scope—that is, their referent is not chiefly territorial. Only some of them have a distinctive party ideology or program,[109] and different parties may share similar ideologies. People move in and out of these parties as they quarrel or aspire to positions of greater influence in Romanian politics; alliances among the parties have not been notable for their durability. As of 1995 neither the boundaries nor the identities of Romanian parties had stabilized. Not even the names were constant from one year to the next.

With the concept of "unruly coalitions," I am groping toward a label for certain collective actors that have emerged in several postsocialist contexts—some scholars call them "clans," others "mafia."[110] I see unruly coalitions as loose clusterings of elites, neither institutionalized nor otherwise formally recognized, who cooperate to pursue or control wealth and other resources. Their unions are unstable and their organization informal; their methods may include violence, influence peddling, collusion, and other mafia-like methods alongside more straightforward business and electoral deals. Like scholars who use terms such as "mafia,"[111] I see the skeleton of these unruly coalitions as the former Communist Party apparatus. I believe them to be territorially concentrated, although the territories may lie at several overlapping levels of inclusiveness, some more far-flung than others. Humphrey, writing about Russia, calls the territories "suzerainties" (see chapter 8)[112] For Romania, I suspect that their base is counties, owing to a quasi-feudalization of the Romanian Communist Party down to the county level during the later Ceauşescu years.[113] Thus although Romania's unruly coalitions exist at all levels, ranging from Bucharest to villages, the ones that count most for my discussion are those based in counties. The counties do not wholly contain them, however, for groups of them may cooperate across a wider sphere, and most are doubtless connected clientelistically with powerful figures in Bucharest.

Any major locale might have one dominant or more than one competing unruly coalition. Most coalitions will include members of Romania's county judiciary, police and Securitate, elected officials, directors and managers of local firms—many of them members of the old Communist nomenclatura. Their relations to specific parties will vary across time and space.[114] While parties may help individuals among them to create a platform for their operation, members of a coalition can be scattered across several parties—especially, I believe, those whose political base is former apparatchiks: the Socialist Labor Party, the governing Party of Romanian Social Democracy (PDSR), the Democratic Agrarian Party, and the nationalist parties PUNR and Greater Romania.

In short, what defines unruly coalitions in contrast to political parties is that they are less institutionalized, less visible, less legitimate, and less stable than parties, and their territorial base is primarily regional or local rather than national. Both sorts of groupings were implicated in Caritas. I begin by describing the place of Caritas in the party-based competition involving the party of government, led by President Iliescu,[115] and the largest nationalist party, led by Cluj mayor and Caritas-supporter Gheorghe Funar. I then suggest how unruly coalitions, pyramid schemes, and certain parties may have been interconnected in the pursuit of new wealth.

Political Capital for an Emerging Bourgeoiscracy

In the September 1992 elections, the Party of Romanian Social Democracy (PDSR), led by President Iliescu, won the presidency and 34 percent of the seats in parliament; the opposition umbrella party Democratic Convention and allied Hungarian party won 33 percent; another oppositional party, the Democratic Party, won 12.5 percent; the Party of Romanian National Unity (PUNR) won 9.6 percent and its presidential candidate, Cluj's mayor Funar, came in third in the presidential contest; three other parties won less than 5 percent each.[116] The PDSR was able to carry most parliamentary votes together with these three small parties and the nationalist PUNR, but clearly the latter was pivotal: if it defected, the PDSR was in trouble. Through the spring and summer of 1993, PUNR leader Funar took increasing advantage of the ruling PDSR's vulnerable position to press aggressively for more power for his party, including control of certain ministries. He also made no secret of his future presidential ambitions.

Funar's principal weapon in this power struggle was Caritas, with which he openly allied himself soon after his election in February 1992. He gave Stoica space in the Cluj city hall, appeared together with him at public functions and on television, and defended Caritas against the ever-more-strident attacks. At the inauguration of Stoica's new department store, Funar announced that he had already set aside space (which was at a premium in Cluj) for Stoica's projected bank.[117] Funar also hinted broadly to an enthusiastic public that his political wisdom lay behind the Caritas-induced prosperity of Cluj and that with their votes he could extend that prosperity to all of Romania. (Some of the villagers I talked with indeed expressed their intention to vote for Funar as president next time around, since he was "the only politician who seemed to be doing anything for Romanians.") Because three-fourths of the depositors in Caritas were PUNR members, he bragged, it was "a very rich party."[118] In addition, the PUNR and Funar drew substantial funds from Caritas in taxes and donations.[119] This Caritas-based political advantage gave the PUNR an edge with respect to not only the government but also the political opposition, which was thrown onto the defensive by the PUNR's get-rich-quick prescription for Romania's future.[120]

By mid-1993, then, as Romanians flocked in ever-greater numbers to it, Caritas was functioning as a means of accumulating not only economic but also political capital. Caritas-based political leverage included threats by PUNR leaders to reveal the names (and thus end the careers) of parliamentarians who were proposing to ban Caritas along with other pyramid schemes, and Stoica's threat to reveal the names (and thus end the sales) of journalists who had received money from Caritas and then written against it. An additional weapon in Funar's arsenal was the alarmist prediction that if Caritas collapsed or—more important—if the government put a stop to it, terrible violence and social upheaval would ensue. (President Iliescu himself commented that although the government would like to ban the game, he feared they would be ousted by an enraged populace if they did so.) This possibility and the scheme's (PUNR-backed) persistence worked against the government in another way, by making international lenders hesitant to give loans the Romanian government badly wanted.

By late September 1993, Funar was publicly ridiculing Iliescu, inviting him to put money in Caritas so he could buy a bicycle since he was so clearly bad at managing money on his own. Iliescu retorted that anyone could foresee the inevitable demise of Caritas when the curve of deposits intersected with the curve of payouts. Not only did this shrewd move expose the vulnerability of the PUNR as well as the government to Caritas's fate; it also was instrumental in diminishing public confidence in Caritas and thus contributed directly to the game's final collapse. Joining Iliescu's criticism were opposition parties, who saw Caritas as the PUNR's Achilles heel and attacked it in hopes of disrupting that party's alliance with the PDSR. Word spread that no city with an opposition mayor would accept new branches of the scheme. The two newspapers specifically tied to opposition parties stepped up their attacks on Caritas. Whereas Funar had emphasized the peril to the government if Caritas collapsed, the tables were now turned: his enemies knew that if it fell, the one who would lose votes was Funar.

Hoist with his own petard, Funar and other PUNR leaders began to signal distance from Stoica and sought to detach the PUNR from his fate. The proliferation of suspiciously PUNR-sounding conspiracy theories discussed earlier (explaining Caritas's troubles as caused by the government, by the Jewish-Hungarian/Soros plot, by banks and the IMF) may have been attempts at self-exculpation. The PUNR also sought to link Caritas with the Democratic Party, which was now (rumor had it) courting Iliescu to replace the PUNR in the government coalition. The two parties struggled to throw each other into Stoica's arms; internecine conflicts within the PUNR itself reveal the same tactic.[121] Even when Caritas ceased to be an asset in one's own accumulated political capital, then, it could be made a liability in that of one's opponents.[122] Following the scheme's collapse in May 1994, the PUNR was polling only 2 percent in public opinion polls, indicating that it had made a bad investment.[123]

Caritas, Pyramids, and Accumulation

Caritas's role in building political capital was part of an even wider process involving a reconfigured class system and new accumulations of wealth. All across the former Soviet bloc, entrepratchiks have consolidated their advantage by using Communist Party–based political connections and political office to gain control of wealth and other resources. This process, which Staniszkis labels "political capitalism,"[124] creates what I will call a "bourgeoiscracy." They are a natural outgrowth of socialism's political economy, in which the directorship of an enterprise was first of all a political and bureaucratic office entailing access to political resources and valuable contacts. Although after 1989 the Communist Party lost its institutional monopoly all across the region, many enterprise directors kept their jobs, and former Party activists joined new recruits in parliament (the latter quickly learning how to profit from their offices to accumulate wealth by various means). A common pattern has been for directors and their politician-allies to ensure the survival of certain state firms with subsidies and then create parasitic private firms, into which they drain these subsidies and other resources of the state firm. Political capital is thus converted into economic capital and means of future enrichment.

All these processes are particularly evident in 1990s Romania, and I believe Caritas and other pyramid schemes—numbering perhaps hundreds,[125] between 1990 and 1994—were part of them. This proposition builds on Romanian journalistic writings; proof of it must await more extensive research. Romania's "pyramid builders," I suggest, were the unruly coalitions described earlier, consisting of officials of the Communist Party, one or another fraction of the old/new Secret Police, members of the local police and judiciary, newly elected political officials, and the henchmen of all these—people like Stoica. The precise composition of the coalitions would vary from one place to another. Here is a list of the people who reportedly showed up for the opening of Caritas competitor "Gerald" in the city of Focşani: the vice-mayor, the county subprefect, the adjunct head of the county police, representatives of the secret service and the Financial Guard, the head of the economic police, military commanders from the region, directors of the county's large firms, as well as the several directors of the post office, state gasoline company, Vinexport, Agricultural Bank, National Bank, Commercial Bank, and so on.[126] Lacking only prosecutors and judges (who appear in other papers' reports), this is a Who's Who of the county elite, all out to support their local pyramid scheme.

Variants of this proposition appear in Romanian newspapers. The most thoughtful of them, by Romulus Brâncoveanu, argues the connection with Caritas as follows.[127] Because the government took action against the pyramid schemes so late (they had been bilking Romanians as early as 1990), some connection between power and these schemes is likely. Its locus was the point of interface between the official and parallel economies, the space that hosts the transfer of the public capital accumulated under socialism into the hands of private "entrepreneurs." While most of this public capital rested in state firms, there were also great masses of wealth dispersed across Romania in the pockets, socks, mattresses, and savings accounts of average citizens, who had had little to spend their money on in the last years of Ceauşescu's rule. Pyramid schemes, Brâncoveanu proposes, concentrated this highly dispersed capital and delivered it to people on the "inside track," even tossing an occasional coin or two to more lowly folk. This inside track would include the scheme's organizers, their friends, and their political allies—the scheme's unruly coalition. It was these people who, having "invested" earliest in the schemes, or having been lured expressly with the promise of handsome early returns to those who deposited large sums, were sure to collect in the first round of payouts.[128]

I would further specify Brâncoveanu's account in two respects. First, it seems likely that the people most active in enriching themselves via the pyramid schemes were second- or third-echelon entrepratchiks, not the most powerful members of the economic bureaucracy. Those most powerful individuals—government ministers and heads of the largest state firms—had direct access to the massive accumulations of wealth in the state-owned and subsidized enterprises, as well as to huge bribes and kickbacks, as part of their jobs. Disdainful of the dispersed sock-and-mattress savings of the broader populace (does Donald Trump stoop to retrieve a penny on the sidewalk?), they would leave those for their less well placed brethren. The latter might, of course, augment the circulating funds with launderable cash from illicit enterprise or local Party coffers (perhaps they helped to launder, as well, the illicit earnings of the more powerful).

Second, the fate of the Securitate after the 1989 revolution suggests that its former members might have played a significant part in the pyramid schemes. At the time of Ceauşescu's overthrow the Securitate was riven with fissures. The revolution left one faction (the "liberal" one, renamed the Romanian Information Service, or SRI) in power as allies of Iliescu and the winning apparatchiks, while at least two other factions were forced into the shade.[129] We cannot know what they did there, but forming nationalist parties and building pyramids are reasonable possibilities. Both Romanian and outside commentators assume a close link between the Securitate and the PUNR (with its precursor, Vatra Românească)—a link openly acknowledged by an early Vatra/PUNR leader[130]—and certain Romanian newspapers reported that founders of one or another pyramid scheme had past or present connections with the Securitate, PUNR, and Communist Party apparatus.[131] A Securitate-nomenclatura coloring of pyramid builders is further implied in the political connections and knowledge necessary to having a scheme registered and authorized by the courts, renting prime space, and forming links to other people whom one would have to pay off with favors or preferential access. That Stoica was fond of quoting *securist*-turned-novelist Pavel Coruţ[132] adds spice to the idea of a PUNR/Securitate/pyramid entente.

Pyramid builders were in a certain sense very much like the public whom they conned: both were looking for ways to make a quick buck, the one group by establishing pyramid schemes, the other by depositing in them. They differed chiefly in the social vantage point from which they attempted their killing, the take they might anticipate, and the kind of protection they might enjoy if their plans failed. It was not even essential that one have significant liquid assets to set up business (though one needed connections). If one happened not to have much capital, the depositors would provide that. Those lucky enough to pad initial deposits with illicit funds had an extra cushion and perhaps greater longevity for their firm.

A scheme did not have to last long to bring its organizers substantial revenues. Having collected funds for two or three months, placed them at high interest, or spent them, the organizers could declare bankruptcy. To give only two examples: "Impuls" took in 682 million lei and paid out 313 million (much of that going to politicians and influential people) before it crashed, leaving 369 million unaccounted for; "Philadelphia," which had around 600,000 depositors, took in 25 billion lei and paid out 23 billion; this left 2 billion for the scheme's boss.[133] Organizers therefore could easily emerge with over a billion-lei profit from a few months of running a pyramid, investing the deposits, then suspending operations.[134] Even if they returned to depositors 70–80 percent of their take, they might remain with a sizable profit (as one paper put it, "reward for the exertion of plundering thousands of people"[135]). Here, perhaps, is the significance of the crucial detail that several pyramid organizers were reported to have used deposits to purchase large quantities of property certificates (the basis for shareholding in privatized firms).[136] Many seem also to have used deposits to launch their own business ventures, treating depositors' money just as Caritas depositors treated their winnings—as a kind of windfall—the difference being the higher status that enabled pyramid builders to generate the windfall rather than merely await it. These activities, too, suggest "small fry" entrepratchiks, for the large fry had simpler routes into lucrative enterprise management.

The Field of Pyramids and the Demise of Caritas

We are unlikely to know for certain why Caritas fell when it did. All pyramid schemes collapse, but their demise can also be hastened. Hastening it in this case were statements by the newspapers and President Iliescu, as well as competition from other pyramid schemes offering even more tempting returns. Iliescu's criticisms doubtless stemmed from his jockeying with Funar, and perhaps also from the informal pressure of international lending institutions (see n. 65). Can we say anything more, howsoever tentatively, about the competition among pyramid schemes?

Even as Caritas began to falter in the autumn of 1993, producing ever more alarmed publicity and predictions of its fall, new pyramid schemes continued to appear all over the country alongside the older ones—and to attract swarms of depositors. Why should this be?[137] One journalist's interpretation was that the government had decided Caritas must be brought down, but given the overwhelming public support, authorities could not simply ban it without risking their necks. Instead, they resorted to a less visible solution: ordering the secret service to launch competing schemes. These would aim "to attract those who might [otherwise] prolong the life of Cluj-Caritas by depositing money there, and then . . . to bring [the competing schemes] down noisily with much damage to many depositors, thus undermining people's confidence and even creating a current of opinion in favor of banning all such games"—as indeed happened. The article offered proofs of the secret-service connections of people involved in one such spectacular failure, "Procent."[138]

This intriguing scenario has two shortcomings: first, it ignores the many pyramid schemes that were already operating long before Caritas gained notoriety; and second, it assumes a degree of central control that I find improbable. I prefer an alternative, truer to what I see as an anarchic, fragmented Romanian political field. In my view, individual pyramid schemes that localized second-tier elites started up as means of enriching themselves mushroomed into a nationwide field of pyramids, jointly constituting a space in which different coalitions competed to harvest the sock-and-mattress portion of Romania's wealth. Together they formed a "pyramid empire," collectively built up by entrepratchiks struggling for advantage. Each pyramid began in the large cities or capitals of specific counties. "Gerald" (which crashed spectacularly, soon after Caritas) was based in Focşani (Vrancea county); "Procent" and "Philadelphia" in Piteşti (Argeş county); "Mimi" in Galaţi (later spreading to Hunedoara at just the time when that county's residents began swarming to Cluj); "El Dorado Gold" in Oradea; "Adison" in Brăila; "Saba" in Arad; "Diomar" in Buzău; "Alecs" in Braşov; Caritas in Cluj; and so on. The county base conforms with the "feudal" structure of Romanian politics that the fall of the Communist Party had only exacerbated. Each county's strongmen would organize a scheme—perhaps several schemes (see n. 125), either associated with rival local coalitions or collusively pooling the capital resources each county's inhabitants could muster. The bigger, more successful schemes might later extend their reach by planting colonies in other cities and counties, as Stoica did, seeking to increase their collecting capacity in Romania's low-tech environment and thus poaching on the turf of other unruly coalitions.

But in 1992, within this dynamic field of competitive spoliation one scheme began to outstrip the others: Caritas. Perhaps it did so because unlike its competitors, with their serendipitous ties to political parties, Caritas established a secure—and novel—alliance with a party, the PUNR. As a well organized regional party, the PUNR was manageably small but still large enough to recruit a substantial capital base throughout Transylvania; its clientele soon spread far beyond the Securitate and PUNRists who had probably set it up. The scheme's initial advantage nevertheless proved a long-term handicap, I believe, precisely *because* its alliance with the PUNR "nationalized" its appeal, securing it a potentially nationwide catchment area that threatened other pyramid schemes and even the Romanian government. At this point, unruly coalitions sponsoring the other schemes—alarmed at the prospect that Caritas might devour the savings of the entire country, thus enriching that unruly coalition most closely tied to it and impoverishing all the others—mobilized in defense.

I believe they did so both by enhancing those schemes they were already managing and also by setting up new ones with even bigger stakes, to seduce clients away from Caritas. Whether these high-stakes schemes could survive was less important than that they reduce the supplies of money to Caritas in the short term, thus bringing down their formidable competitor. Consider the following thirteen examples; all appeared after Caritas was well established, and each garnered millions and billions of lei from many thousands of people. If Caritas repaid eightfold in ninety days, "Garant" promised tenfold in ninety days; "El Dorado Gold," tenfold in eighty days; "Gerald," tenfold in seventy-five days; "Novo-Caritas," tenfold in sixty days; "Tresor" and "American Trading," twelvefold in seventy-five days; "Proactiv," 12.4-fold in sixty days; "Ferati," elevenfold in fifty days and fifteenfold on the second round; "ALD Pitești," fifteenfold in sixty-five days; "Combat," sixteenfold in sixty days; "Philadelphia," seventeenfold in seventy-five days; "Mimi," fivefold in forty-five days or twenty-five–fold in ninety days; and "Procent-Caritas," an astonishing twentyfold in sixty days. From such variations in their bait it seems clear that they were striving mightily to outdo each other—and Caritas, above all.[139] Headlines about "Gerald" that announced "Moldavia Fights Transylvania in 'Caritas' War" and "El Dorado Gold from Arad Aims to Dethrone Caritas" enhance this impression.[140]

Perhaps the scenario I am proposing illuminates the wider proliferation of pyramid schemes throughout the former socialist bloc. Such schemes arose in each of these countries, some more than others. This may reflect a constant in post-Soviet societies: the fall of Communist Parties (which had more or less unified the political field), alongside the weakening of the state apparatus through programs of privatization and the intervention of international lending institutions, launched a free-for-all among lower-level authorities, former and present. Each lower-level fief hosts power struggles among those who would rule it and would consolidate their rule through alliances beyond. The units in these struggles have many names—"mafias," "clans," "suzerainties," "unruly coalitions," and so forth. One means in their war, I have suggested, is pyramid schemes that scoop up dispersed resources and concentrate these in the group.

From one country to another these units enjoy varying relations with the central authority, although an enfeebled center is probably a condition of their flourishing. In Slovakia and Bulgaria, for example, the government banned pyramid schemes as soon as they appeared, whereas in Romania and Russia interdiction was hesitant and late; these differences perhaps reflect differences in the center's power or in its ties to members of one or another unruly coalition. A measure of the schemes' success, if Russia's huge MMM scheme that fell in July 1994 is any indication, is that the defrauded public perceives them as its ally and the interdicting state as its enemy. Indeed, arrested MMM owner Mavrodi was elected to the Russian Duma from his jail cell, his defiant supporters insisting that MMM's crash was the government's fault.[141] An additional variable determining the pyramids' vigor may have been the presence of foreign capital and its internal location, or (even more likely) the relative strength or weakness of Party structures prior to 1989, insofar as these were the backbone of coalition activity.

Conclusion

It is too soon to assess the long-term consequences of the rise and fall of Caritas; one can only recapitulate hypotheses and raise questions. I have emphasized here the opportunity it provided for people to reconceptualize money, to see "the economy" as an abstraction not governed by human agents, and to reorder their moral universe in accord with the pursuit of gain in hitherto disapproved forms. I have indicated that these possibilities posed true dilemmas for people, who then argued with others and themselves about what kind of gain is worthy. What will the collapse of Caritas do to their conclusions? Did the shattering of so many dreams convince depositors that unearned money indeed comes from the devil? Are they now looking for internal and international plots, repersonalizing "the economy" as they do so? Among the villagers I knew, what seemed to prevail as I left Romania was a resigned feeling of victimization, but it was unclear to me whether they saw their loss as a divine reproof, the result of a plot, or a bit of bad luck. Will people be more inclined, or less so, to flock to other chance-based "miracles," such as the U.S. Department of State's "diversity lottery," in which 3,850 lucky Romanians were to get visas for permanent settlement in America by having their names drawn out of a hat?[142]

Other consequences of the fall of Caritas will be played out in people's personal and family relations for a long time to come. Those who sold houses and apartments so as to invest in Caritas will live in crowded conditions with in-laws, their domestic relations strained; reports indicate that the number of such cases is not small.[143] For some, the consequences will be an end to thoughts of starting a business or buying one's apartment from the state. As such planning is aborted, does that crush a person's fledgling sense of independence and initiative? Many people lost the financial cushion they hoped for against future catastrophe, as well as the cushion their own Caritas-devoured savings will no longer provide. People who took out high-interest bank loans they expected to repay with Caritas money had to tighten their belts and plead with relatives to help them cover their debts; a few had heart attacks or committed suicide.[144]

Finally, I have sketched another possible consequence of Caritas for Romania's social structure: it nourished segments of the rising bourgeoiscracy that feeds off the primitive accumulation realized under socialism in both public and private domains. Caritas, and other schemes like it across the formerly socialist world, helped to produce two opposing social groups: one whose new wealth enables them to make money and dominate politics, and one, increasingly impoverished and disenfranchised, who will see riches as immoral and risk as unrewarded. This makes Caritases crucial instruments of new class formation and of producing inner "Third Worlds" in post-Soviet societies. Will they also be spurs to civic and political organization, as the despoiled create associations to pursue redress through the courts?[145] Will people's experiences there confirm their influence, or break it? Will Stoica do time, and will the state confiscate his riches for his angry depositors; or will the resources he commands and the propensity of the Iliescu government for corrupt practices deprive his victims of the justice they seek?[146]

Summarizing an argument that pyramid schemes are an unconventional and unfortunately dynamic element of the "transition," Brâncoveanu writes:

> The dream of making a killing, the sentiment of participating in the great race for a stable position in the new society, and the need for economic security have pushed people toward the mutual-aid games. Scrimping and saving to deposit tens or hundreds of thousands of lei, they have the feeling that they *are doing something*, that they haven't been left out, that they aren't defeated, that they can withstand competition—a competition, alas, of the excluded. The bosses of the mutual-aid games have intuited and speculate upon this inclination of the masses to risk in the name of a better future.[147]

These bosses, like the pharaohs of old, built their pyramids with the faith, hope, and sacrifice of the multitudes below them. The parallel may end there, however, for we see little sign that the pyramids of Romania's ruthless entrepratchiks will become their tombs.

8

A TRANSITION FROM SOCIALISM TO FEUDALISM?

THOUGHTS ON THE POSTSOCIALIST STATE

We're going backward! We're not just going back to 1917,
we're going back to feudalism!
(Russian farmer)

A MONG the contributions of postmodernism to contemporary thought
is a heightened awareness of how objects of knowledge come to be
constituted, and of the generative force of images and metaphors in that process. What we can understand of something depends on
how we think our way into it in the first place; the questions we pose of it
flow in part from the image we have of it and the associations that suggests.
If we imagine society as like a clock, a mechanism, we ask different questions from those we ask if it is like an organism, and what we know in consequence differs also. An arresting example is Emily Martin's demonstration
that if we imagine conception—in the way medical textbooks do—as a dam-
sel in distress (the egg) being rescued by a knight in shining armor (the
sperm), then we miss the crucial detail that the egg, not the sperm, is the
active partner in their union.[1]

A number of the stories of postsocialism have the knights of Western
know-how rushing to rescue the distressed of Eastern Europe.[2] These stories present socialism—quite contrary to its own evolutionist pretensions—
as not the endpoint of human social development but a dead end on the far
more progressive road to capitalism, to which they must now be recalled.

An early version of this chapter was delivered in February 1992 as the last in my Lewis Henry
Morgan Lectures, University of Rochester. The discussion is based on secondary literature as
well as on ethnographic data from field trips in the summers of 1990 and 1991 and the academic
year 1993–94. Many persons assisted me in writing it, particularly József Böröcz, Michael
Burawoy, Gerald Creed, Elizabeth Dunn, Ashraf Ghani, Jane Guyer, Christopher Hann, Caroline Humphrey, Melvin Kohn, Jane Schneider, and Michel-Rolph Trouillot. My thanks to them
all. In addition, I am indebted to personnel of the Hunedoara County Court in Deva for facilitating my research there. The fieldwork reported in this chapter was funded by IREX.

Parts of this chapter appeared under the title "Notes Toward an Ethnography of a Transforming State, Romania 1991," in *Articulating Hidden Histories: Exploring the Influence of Eric R.
Wolf,* ed. Jane Schneider and Rayna Rapp (copyright © 1995 by the Regents of the University
of California); reprinted by permission of the University of California Press.

The rescue scenario has two common variants: "shock therapy," and "big bang." The first compares the former socialist bloc with a person suffering from mental illness—that is, socialism drove them crazy, and our job is to restore their sanity. The second implies that (*pace* Fukuyama) history is only now beginning, that prior to 1989 the area was without form and void.[3] While the image of "shock therapy" represents Western advisers as doctors, the "big bang" figures them as God.

With images like these guiding our approach to the transition, it would be surprising if we learned very much about what is happening in the former socialist world. I prefer an image that denies the notion of a progress (from sickness toward health, from nothingness to being, from backwardness into development) and purposely mocks the very idea of evolutionary stages. What if we were to think, then, of a transition from socialism not to capitalism but to feudalism? What, if any, evidence can be marshaled for such a view, and to what does it draw our attention, what associations does it mobilize, that other images of postsocialist processes might not? I explore these questions in three sections—privatization, mafia, and emerging state forms—prefaced by a brief discussion of what feudalism might mean.

Feudalism

Among the earliest hints that "feudalism" as an image might not be too farfetched was a remarkable paper published in 1991 by Cambridge University anthropologist Caroline Humphrey, "'Icebergs,' Barter, and the Mafia in Provincial Russia."[4] In it, Humphrey described what was happening as of 1990, as republics of the USSR and regions within them declared autonomy from the center; the result was great uncertainty about where government and law actually resided. In consequence, "organizations and enterprises in the regions, run in a personal way almost as 'suzerainties' by local bosses, have strengthened themselves and increased their social functions in order to protect their members. . . . It is not possible to rely on the law, or even to know what it is these days; and at the same time government, which used to regulate flows of goods and allocation of labour . . . has ceased to be universally or even generally obeyed."[5] Although some might view this as an inevitable part of market reforms, Humphrey saw it as leading to precisely the opposite of a free market, for business in the "suzerainties" was being conducted by quite nonmarket methods: coupons, food cards and "orders," barter, and various forms of influence peddling generally referred to as "mafia."[6]

Western media often mistook these methods for rationing. But the coupons and food cards were not imposed by the Soviet government with an eye to equalizing people's access to scarce basic necessities; rather, it was regional, local, and even workplace organizations that were giving them out, so as to limit access to particular goods by restricting those goods to persons having coupons. As of 1 December 1990, only people with residence permits could get coupons for certain products; outsiders could not buy those things at all. In the words of a Soviet economist, coupons "divide the market into 'apanage princedoms' and protect resources . . . from 'aliens.'"[7] Organizations and workplaces would procure shipments of goods straight from the factory and distribute them directly—and only—to those of their members who had signed up in advance. This arrangement was effectively binding people to their region of residence or their workplace for the procurement possibilities to be thereby gained.

A corollary of consolidating these suzerainties, however, as Humphrey showed in another paper, was the expulsion of various categories of people—the unemployed, economic migrants, people lacking stable connections with a local boss, vagrants and homeless people, and so forth.[8] Such people would roam the countryside in hopes of finding work or something to eat. It was partly against them that the local suzerainties were tightening their borders.[9] This phase of the transition in Russia was leading not to the spread of market forces, then, but (as a Soviet legal specialist put it) to "towns, [administrative divisions], republics fencing themselves off with palisades of rationing in defence against 'migratory demand,'" dividing up the market through increasingly aggressive particularism.[10]

These emerging patterns of encystment and transience were a logical outcome of certain features of work organization in socialist firms—which, as Simon Clarke suggests, had a certain affinity with feudalism. "The soviet enterprise is almost as different from the capitalist enterprise as was a feudal estate from a capitalist farm. Like the feudal estate, the socialist enterprise is not simply an economic institution but is the primary unit of soviet society, and the ultimate base of social and political power."[11] This unit provided all manner of services and facilities for its labor force (housing, kindergartens, sporting and cultural facilities, clinics, pensions, etc.). The collapse of the party-state reinforced the tendencies to personalism and patronage inherent in such arrangements, making many people dependent on their locality, their workplace, or their boss for access to food, housing, and loans. Belonging to a suzerainty, by either having a regular job or enjoying some other tie to a powerful and successful patron, meant dependence, but as in feudal times it also meant at least minimal security.

The period Humphrey discusses saw not only these forms of localized resource protection but signs of a reversion toward a "natural economy." Marked shortages of money, for example, led to demonetization. In some enterprises and collective farms, bosses were even printing their own money—one thinks of the "money of account" on the feudal manor, which was good there and nowhere else. This might happen at the level of entire republics, as well, such as Ukraine, where even before full independence a new currency was launched to keep Russian buyers out. Demonetization had other sources also, chief among them the tremendous inflation accompanying price reform. In Romania, for example, during 1991–92 price and wage inflation was so rapid that the mints could not produce enough new money to keep up. And as in Russia, in Bulgaria too a scarcity of money was pressing people backward toward a natural economy, with many cash-poor peasants living almost exclusively off their private plots.[12] Another aspect of demonetization was widespread barter.[13] Barter is nothing new: under socialism, firms and individuals exchanged goods widely on a nonmonetary basis, even to some degree in international trade. But for a variety of reasons, barter reached epic proportions after the collapse of the Soviet state. Its spread was related to the demise of the bloc's ruble-based trade, the disintegration of each country's centrally controlled distribution system, the virtual absence of commercial banks, and the unenforceability of contracts.[14] People would therefore make their own direct arrangements to procure what they needed, in kind. For example, Russian urbanites would help to harvest potatoes on a collective farm, receiving several sacks of them in exchange.[15]

Suzerainties resembling fiefdoms, personalistic ties binding people to the domains of local "lords," demonetized "natural" economies with endemic barter—and added to these, pervasive violence and a localized protection against it, furthering the parallel with feudalism. As with the other features, this last one was at its height in the collapsing Soviet Union, where confusion over who defined and enforced laws led to rampant lawlessness and scorn for central directives. With the progressive weakening and final disintegration of the Soviet Communist Party, each local lord could determine for himself what would go on in his suzerainty; he could even choose either wholehearted acceptance or flat rejection of perestroika's market reforms, for there was no longer an effective central discipline to enforce the reforms.[16] An exasperated Gorbachev finally issued a decree—to little avail— that central decrees must be obeyed. Thus even as collective farms dissolved in one region they might flourish in another, despite reformist orders emanating from Moscow.[17] Local autonomy extended even to managing violence, as bosses maintained order independently of the center's monopoly on coercion. "Protection" against vigilante actions, Humphrey says, was an important job of the local bosses (who, if my experience in Romania is any guide, often perpetrated those actions themselves).[18] A burgeoning literature on Russia's "mafia" confirms the center's loss of control over the means of violence,[19] with a corresponding rise in localized defense.

In a program on public television in late February 1992 about the changes in Russia, a farmer confirmed from the "native's point of view" what I am proposing here when he told the reporter, "We're going backward! We're not just going back to 1917, we're going back to feudalism!"[20] How might this unexpected image illuminate our understanding of the transition from socialism?

It is the nature of metaphors to contain many possible meanings, subject to numerous interpretations. Because feudalism—as both metaphor and social system—signifies many things, I should specify the meaning I wish to emphasize. Leaving aside such features of the feudal order as the lord-vassal relation, coerced labor, and an estate-based organization of power, I center my discussion around Perry Anderson's observation (following Marc Bloch) that "constitutive of the whole feudal mode of production" was the "parcellization of sovereignty." "The functions of the State were disintegrated in a vertical allocation downwards," he says, with sovereignties divided "into particularist zones with overlapping boundaries, . . . and no universal centre of competence."[21] Similarly Georges Duby: "The hierarchy of powers [was] replaced by a crisscrossing pattern of competing networks of clients."[22] "Hence," observes Gianfranco Poggi, "there developed acute problems of coordination, crises of order, and recurrent and apparently anarchic violence."[23] The initial cause of the process was the "barbarian" invasions and its consequence the collapse of an articulating center, epitomized in the sack of Rome.

With the collapse of socialism's party-state we see a disarticulation comparable to the end of the ancient slave-based polity, and, I suggest, a comparable "parcellization of sovereignty," to which Humphrey has called our attention. Perhaps the words of a World Bank economist who visited the Soviet Union in September 1991 make the point: "I expected to find the national government somewhat weakened, but I didn't expect to find no central government at all. I expected to find some sort of republican government, but there wasn't any. There's no government over there whatsoever!"[24] The effects of central collapse have been starkest where a preexisting federal authority crumbled and republics declared sovereignty, as in the Soviet Union and Yugoslavia (and, differently, Czechoslovakia). In such cases, the center's destructuration was both sudden and complete, and its effects have included persistent violence and instability. Similar effects— if less visible, and maybe more transient—have accompanied the decomposition of the party-state in other countries of the region also.[25] Some areas of the former Soviet empire—Hungary and perhaps the Czech Republic— may partially escape the "feudal" reversion, just as in the ancient world the fall of Rome did not produce feudalism everywhere (not, for example, in its Middle Eastern part). But I think it is illuminating to pursue the feudal metaphor a while, for it has the merit of startling the automatic presumption that what is happening in the former socialist bloc is a transition to markets and capitalism.

To round out my discussion and my metaphor I note one more point from Anderson's analysis of feudalism. No less important than the "parcellization of sovereignty," he argues, were processes that prevented sovereignty from fragmenting altogether and bringing anarchy, for that would have disrupted the organization of privilege sustaining feudal nobles as a class. "There was thus an inbuilt contradiction within feudalism, between its own rigorous tendency to a decomposition of sovereignty and the absolute exigencies of a final centre of authority in which a practical recomposition could occur"[26]— that is, contradictory tendencies breaking down the center and shoring it up.[27] In pursuing parallels with feudalism, I will be asking what ensues when the overarching party-state collapses and its power is "parcellized," and what processes we can identify that reconstitute a political center—a state of a potentially new kind, compared with the past. Although I recognize that "sovereignty" is more than simply the state, I will focus my discussion by speaking of the latter, and I will call the processes breaking down and shoring up a center "destatizing" and "restatizing" tendencies.[28]

Investigating the "feudal" aspects of the transition from socialism contributes to what we might call an ethnography of the state. Anthropologists have not examined the state much—they have chiefly invoked it, as a frame for other topics. Theorists from other disciplines (sociology, history, and political science), on the other hand, rarely investigate the state ethnographically, by which I mean at close range from within its daily routines and practices. But with worldwide changes in the nature of state administrations, it is high time for ethnographies of the state, and the former socialist world is an excellent site for them. Such ethnography should treat states not as things but as sets of social processes and relations. Examples of ethnographic approaches to the state can be found in the work of people such as Ann Anagnost on the "socialist imaginary" and the Chinese state, John Borneman on nationness in the two Germanys, Ashraf Ghani on state making in Afghanistan, and Gail Kligman on women and the state in Romania.[29] This exploratory chapter augments that literature while suggesting some new approaches to the end of Party rule.

Although one might investigate the parcelization and reconstitution of sovereignty in any number of areas, a central arena for them is privatization. This term generally refers to the legal redefinition of property rights as pertaining to jural individuals, conferring exclusive ownership upon them so as to rationalize the economy (on the assumption that owners will take an active managerial role in "their" firms as socialist managers did not).[30] Because such a redefinition decomposes the corporate property managed by the Party apparatus and lower-level collective entities, it very evidently parcelizes sovereignty, for collective property ownership was the foundation of socialism's bureaucratic apparatus and sustained its power.[31] Beyond this specific link between property forms and the socialist state, states have been understood more broadly as designating and enforcing property-rights structures and setting rules for them so as to maximize rents to the ruler.[32]

It therefore makes sense to look at changes in property rights in examining transformations of the state. I speak here of privatization in terms of not only the redistribution of property rights but also what I call the privatization of power, meaning the arrogation of formerly central instruments of rule— especially coercion—by lower-level actors; this parcelizes sovereignty even further.

Privatization

A good working definition of privatization comes from Janusz Lewandowski, Poland's former Minister of Property Transformation, who commented: "Privatization is when someone who doesn't know who the real owner is and doesn't know what it's really worth sells something to someone who doesn't have any money."[33] We might guess from this that "privatization," like "democracy," "civil society," "markets," and other features of postsocialist politics, is partly a symbol. As a symbol, and again like those other symbols, one of its functions has been to generate external and internal support by signifying the end of socialism. After 1989, any government or party that talked convincingly of privatization increased its likely access to aid, credits, and investment, especially from international organizations like the World Bank and International Monetary Fund. At least initially (that is, before the 1993– 94 elections that returned socialists to power in several countries), "privatization" was also vital to legitimating new governments, for it symbolized revolution and helped to delegitimate the former regime. As Appel has shown for the Czech Republic, privatization's legitimating role was so crucial that it forced compromises potentially injurious to the new government's fiscal capacity, concerns about justice outweighing concerns for revenue.[34]

Aside from its symbolism, privatization is a multifarious set of processes filling that symbol with meanings. They range from altered laws to changes in pricing policy to a complete resocialization of economic actors. Within five years of the 1989 revolutions, a huge interdisciplinary literature had arisen to monitor these changes.[35] I will not engage this literature from a juridical or economic point of view but will instead discuss privatization as an arena of state formation, in which one can look for contradictory destatizing and restatizing processes.

State property has entered into private hands in very different ways in each East European country; in each, it has encountered tremendous obstacles and been the subject of extended, often bitter, political debate.[36] The debate gained momentum fast, after 1989, for covert privatization had already been occurring for several years. Polish sociologist Jadwiga Staniszkis places its beginnings in about 1987 for Poland; David Stark as early as 1984 for Hungary.[37] Romanian friends, too, suggested to me that the "transition" was merely furthering processes already apparent two to three years before. Indeed, a major impetus behind perestroika was growing pressure from socialist bureaucrats (nomenclatura) to become owners rather than mere managers of state property. Among the main forms these preprivatizations took were incursions by managers of firms into the ownership prerogatives of the state, and expansions of the so-called second economy—those informal activities operating in integral relationship to the formal state-run production system but in its interstices. Both were especially advanced in Hungary, where legalization of the second economy through "subcontracting" became so prevalent in the late 1980s[38] as to produce the joke, "What is the quickest way to build socialism? Contract it out." I will offer examples from both privatizations of state firms and expanded second economy, showing for each how "privatization" itself has been produced—and a new state along with it—through a struggle between forces promoting divestiture of state property and other forces promoting the accrual of paternalist and oversight functions in the state.[39]

For several reasons, such as difficulties in establishing a suitable purchase price for firms and abuses that gave the former elite an edge in acquiring property, privatization rapidly proved a nightmare. Because the socialist economy was not run according to market-based principles of valuation and profitability, it was almost impossible to assess the book value of state firms so as to sell them. Thus any estimate of their value was shot through with politics. Evidence points to a systematic devaluation of state assets, in part through controlled bankruptcies; this enabled would-be manager-owners or foreign buyers to pay far less than the potential value of the holding acquired.[40] Since most firms found it impossible to do without state subsidies, and since the supply of raw materials was more uncertain than ever because economic ministries no longer guaranteed them, it took no effort at all to bankrupt a firm. Properties might be sold at auctions having only one bidder. In Hungary, Poland, Romania, and doubtless elsewhere, newspapers reported scandals in which a piece of valuable property had been sold at a derisory price, leading to accusations that public assets were being squandered and to calls for state regulation of the process.[41]

Beyond this, many former apparatchiks and managers of firms took advantage of uncertainties in the status of property law, thereby gaining possession of properties before their acquisition could be legally regulated. All over the former Soviet bloc, major factories and department stores quickly went from being state property to being joint-stock companies, "owned" collectively by groups of former apparatchiks and managerial or engineering personnel. Likewise, ownership of state farms and parts of some collectives passed into the hands of those who had managed them before. The bureaucratic positions of these entrepratchiks gave them an edge in becoming owner-entrepreneurs.

Privileged and differential access to property came not only from legal ambiguities but also from the extraordinary complexity of the arrangements for privatizing. David Stark's account of how Hungarian firms developed institutional cross-ownership, with managers of several firms acquiring interests in one another's companies, makes it clear that only people with extensive inside information and contacts had the knowledge to participate in such schemes.[42] Published descriptions of Romania's proposed voucher privatization plan, which gave the public certificates amounting to 30 percent of the value of newly created joint-stock companies while the other 70 percent was held in state management firms, were so complicated as to be impenetrable.[43] From correspondence columns in the Romanian press during the early 1990s, it was clear that average citizens suspected they were being hoodwinked by these schemes and that what was presented as a windfall for them would prove yet another swindle, in the time-honored tradition of Romanian political life. In 1995, the government quickened these fears by proposing significant alterations in the voucher program, revaluing the certificates and setting limits on their use.

In each country the groups acquiring control over former state enterprises had slightly different compositions and different intermixtures of foreign capital, but in all, those who benefited the most were the former bureaucratic and managerial apparatus of the party-state. Profiting from their access to administrative positions in state firms, they could create parasitic companies on the side, draining into these the state firm's assets as well as ongoing state subsidies, and could use their political influence to secure monopolies on state orders and preferential access to foreign contracts.[44] Their privileged relations with foreign firms and management consultants also bring them more intimate knowledge of Western business practices—a kind of symbolic capital that further reinforces their advantage.[45]

Several scholars offer interpretations of these processes. Stark, for example, in a vivid phrasing, speaks of a transformation not from plan to market but from "plan to clan," and he identifies the resulting property forms in Hungary as neither private nor collective but "recombinant" property. He sees the capitalization of preexisting networks as the only possible route to economic transformation, noting that just such networks underlay the economic success of Japan.[46] Romanian scholar Andrei Cornea writes of the "directocracy" that profits from its dual status as managers and entrepreneurs to siphon off state assets.[47] According to Cornea, the possibilities for gain put a premium on continued confusion in the system of property rights, reducing incentives for the well-placed to define and closely enforce the boundaries separating private, collective, and state property. Thus bureaucratic parasitism on state property means stalled privatization, unclear title, uncertainty as to who may exercise property rights, and incomplete, overlapping ownership claims. As I have already noted, Staniszkis speaks of "political capitalism," with its partial disaggregation of central control as homogeneous state ownership gives way to dual ownership of fixed assets, treated sometimes as if they are still state property and at other times as if specific groups had come to own them. She too points to the nonexclusive ownership rights that result, reminiscent of the fuzzy property rights of feudalism.[48]

Although these scholars differ in the end point they anticipate for the processes they describe, each of them reveals powerful interests in favor of retaining a state presence. Such analyses show that even as entrepratchiks drain the state's assets, thus debilitating the state and changing both its capacities and its nature, they also support its continuing existence for the resources and subsidies it provides. Because the allocative state of socialism is too valuable to be dispensed with, these groups retard privatization, preserving ambiguity and instability of ownership. By resisting full-scale privatization, then, they also resist the fuller parcelization of sovereignty that would accompany it, preferring a partial concentration at the center.

A number of other forces besides these favor restatization. One is political pressure, stemming both from popular outrage at the speed with which old managers became new elites and from machinations by those among the old elites who did not move fast enough and found themselves left out. Michael Burawoy and János Lukács, as well as Stark, describe how privatization in Hungary led to "bringing the state back in" so as to regulate illegalities in the process of property transfers.[49] Owing to public outcry against the tremendous profits that Hungary's former elites had amassed so quickly, in January 1990 Hungary's parliament passed the Law for the Defense of State Property that created the State Property Agency; its aim was to prevent further abuses by decelerating privatization and thereby to calm public resentment.

Aside from these responses to public pressure, restatizing tendencies arose from logistical difficulties and the unexpectedly slow pace of privatization. It began to seem that emerging markets were inadequate to solve the problems of decreased production and living standards, endemic corruption, labor unrest, and so on, and that "shock therapy" would so neuter the state as to eliminate vital levers of control over the transition process.[50] Thus emerged a neostatist position within political debates across the region, arguing that socialism's centralized political economy could be dismantled only by further strengthening the state so it could manage the process of its own dissolution. That is, as David Stark and László Bruszt put it, "The solution to weak and inadequately functioning markets was not more markets but a stronger, more effective, state."[51] This, say some, may even require expressly *re*nationalizing property so as to *de*nationalize it. The problem is worst in Hungary, where preprivatization so diffused property rights as to preclude their easy distribution without renationalizing them first.[52]

In addition to these sources of restatization, the heads of newly privatizing firms and other state employees have themselves also helped to re-create a central authority. For example, a high government official in Bucharest observed to me in June 1991 that his economic program had eliminated central planning, but firms kept coming to him to ask for planning and regulation. Speaking with doctors irate at the government's failure to provide adequate supplies for health, Romania's Minister of Health asked why they did not consider private practice. One replied to him bluntly, "Why should I pay to rent space and to get insurance, material stocks, and all that expensive equipment when the state can do it for me? And besides, where would I get the money?"[53] Comparable demands for state intervention came from all quarters but were especially vociferous in the domain of culture. Romania's Minister of Culture described to me how editors of publishing houses had resisted his plan to privatize the publishing business and begged him instead for subsidies. As he put it, "Everyone shouts, 'Down with Communism!' and with their next breath, 'Up with the State!'" Following a visit to New York's Metropolitan Museum, where he learned how the museum raises funds by such gambits as selling earrings like the ones in a famous Rubens painting, this minister proposed that the directors of his own cash-strapped museums do likewise. The reaction: "That is a debasement of art! Museums should not have to become commercial operations; the state should subsidize them!" Archeologists sought state protection against privatization of land, because peasants no longer wanted them digging up old ruins on soil that could produce marketable crops. Literary magazines ran stories with dire predictions that Romanian culture would die unless the state controlled the price of paper, thus subsidizing the publication of books and journals.[54] In the most dramatic such case, numerous literary magazines appeared in mid-December 1991 with their front page blackened; one headline blared, "Romanian culture at an impasse! Journals of the Writers' Union suspend publication . . . until the government assumes its necessary responsibility to support the national culture."[55] Everywhere, in asking for subsidies people were reaching out for the familiar allocative state of before, and in so doing they re-created a role for it. Or, looked at from the other side, whatever "the state" is, it does not relinquish domains easily.[56]

Results similar to these in the official, state sector of the economy can also be seen in the growth of "private enterprise" through an expanded second economy. By second economy, I mean all those income-generating activities that workers in socialism carried on outside their formal job—often using equipment or time or even the physical premises of their formal job, in many cases unofficially and sometimes illegally. Workers who drove black-market taxis in their off hours, construction crews that borrowed tools and supplies from their work site to build houses for themselves and their friends, clerks in stores who held goods under the counter to sell to someone who had given them a gift or bribe or who was a friend or relative, and peasants cultivating the plot of land allotted them by the collective farm—all were engaged in socialism's second economy. It is important to note that these activities were not a suppressed form of entrepreneurship struggling valiantly to survive: their success depended upon their integration with the state sector. Hence, for such entrepreneurs the state's demise would be far from good news.

An example from Romania makes the point. Between 1991 and 1994, the most visible form of this kind of enterprise to my traveler's eye was that the former black-market taxi business had now been transformed into private taxis competing with the state taxi company. As a result, one could, for a change, find a taxi almost whenever one wanted it. Interviewing private taxi drivers taught me a good deal about privatization, most of it irrelevant to my concerns here. One finding, however, pertains directly to the place of the state in a postsocialist economy. Although every cab driver I spoke with in the summers of 1991 and 1992 said he made more money with his cab than with his regular job and could earn even more if he drove the taxi full-time, only one of them had left or would leave his state-sector job to become a fully "private entrepreneur." The same was true two and three years later, except that more had lost their state-sector jobs. Thus nearly all these drivers who had not been forced out of their official jobs were driving the cab outside regular working hours. They preferred to retain a state sector to which they could adhere so as to siphon off resources from it, even at the cost of tremendously lengthening their working day. In some cases, the official job was directly tied to taxi work: an employee of an auto service firm would borrow tools and supplies, in the best tradition of the socialist "second economy," in order to keep his private taxi in good repair. More often, people clung to the state sector job for its anticipated security, benefits, and pensions, which they did not want to or know how to provide on their own. If scattered anecdotes are any indication, the attitudes of these taxi drivers are replicated throughout the Romanian work force. One consequence is that many Romanians have not one occupation but two or three, at least one of which—that in the state sector—serves as a platform for pursuing the others, just as was true in the socialist period.

One could find countless other loci for illustrating privatization's destatizing and restatizing effects.[57] Sometimes the restatization comes from public demands for the state to regulate the reform process more tightly. Sometimes it comes, rather, from people's pursuit of new opportunities, in which they see an ongoing state presence as useful.[58] Such instances show how Romanians accustomed to the presence, subsidies, and interventions of socialism's paternalistic state have responded to its seeming disintegration by reconstituting a center to which they can continue to appeal. Although the state's power has been deeply compromised, they have continued to anticipate it in their plans. Any ethnography of the postsocialist state must take account of the ways in which such behavior will reconstitute a form of state power, and must ask how the state being re-created differs from the one supposedly overthrown. I return to this question later.

Mafia

So far I have been concerned primarily with the question of property rights. I turn now to a closely related aspect of privatization: the privatization of power. By looking at how local bosses arrogate central coercion and evade the center's sanctions (often to protect their new entrepreneurial activities),[59] we discover additional parallels with feudalism's "parcellization of sovereignty." A suitable starting point is the idea of "mafia," central to Humphrey's discussion of "suzerainties" with which I began this chapter. I have presented some ideas relevant to "mafia" in chapter 7 under the label "unruly coalitions," but here I will speak of "mafia," because that is the word people themselves employ.

Talk of mafia has been especially common in the former Soviet Union, with its rash of highly publicized murders during 1992–95, attributed to mafia gangs involved in privatization. Sources have estimated the number of such gangs in Russia as anywhere from 150 to two or three thousand.[60] But mafia was not confined to Russia. One heard about it all across Eastern Europe—in Hungary, in Bulgaria, in Poland—though not always in reference to precisely the same groups in each place. In Romania during my research between 1991 and 1994, people spoke of mafia often, usually to explain why Romania was not moving swiftly on the anticipated course to a better future. Friends complained that too many of the same old boys were still running things, that connections were still displacing merit and quality as criteria for advancement, that the average citizen could not hope to get space for a small restaurant or a permit for a small shop without connections or bribes well beyond the means of any but the most highly placed. Typesetters, said one friend who had set up his own publishing house, are a real mafia: if you don't pay them off, they won't typeset your books. An acquaintance who is a concert pianist complained that if there were really a market in Romania, she might get a recording contract, but instead the Party-based mafia that controls the record business still goes by connections rather than talent. The level of corruption, people insisted, was infinitely worse than under Ceauşescu, when it was already pretty bad. There was talk of death threats and beatings. "In place of the old Communist Party structures, we now have rule by the mafia." "The provinces are no longer fully subordinate to the center; the whole system now rests on local mafias, systems of relations not controlled by the center, often making use of their own vigilantes." "We're in a transition from socialism to constitutional mafia." Comments such as these could be quoted from any part of the former socialist bloc.

What is being captured in this image? People typically invoked the expected features—payoffs and bribes, personalistic ties, influence peddling and the corruption of justice, money laundering, and violence. I could give examples of them all, but I will concentrate here on two from Romania: localized violence by bosses usurping the center's former monopoly on force, and a generalized recourse to horizontal and localized networks, in place of the former vertical allegiance to the center.

Romania during the early 1990s was almost as propitious a site as Russia for localized usurpation of violence formerly under state control. Because Ceauşescu was deposed only with the help of factions in the army and Secret Police (Securitate), it was impossible to purge these groups from the new order, as happened in countries like East Germany and the Czech Republic. It was equally impossible, however, to incorporate all their members. I believe (but cannot prove) that much of the violence of Romania's first three or four postsocialist years came not from central directives but from self-organizing groups of ex-Securitate who had lost out in the power scuffle and hoped to improve their place by preserving a climate of political instability. Members of the Securitate, exiled from their former omnipotent position, had every reason to worry about joblessness in a new, "democratic" Romania. They would not need central directives (though they may sometimes have received these) to telephone death threats to active leaders of the political opposition and successful entrepreneurs who are not part of the old-boy network; to beat up demonstrators or political opponents; to smash the windows of newly formed private shops; and so forth.

Securitate members might also be working with local bosses. One story of vigilante violence that I received firsthand seemed clearly a local job, ordered up by local entrepratchiks. This spectacular story—unfortunately too long to be recounted here—tells how a collection of county politicos, businessmen, judges, and offspring of former Party bureaucrats drained into their pockets the immense financial assets of the county's former Communist Youth League, along with some hotel and tourist properties. The journalist who uncovered the story soon began to receive telephoned threats, and his girlfriend was savagely beaten in broad daylight on two occasions, once with attempted rape, by men who escaped in a car with brown paper pasted over its license plate. When I last saw him, he was planning to emigrate to France, convinced that he was no longer safe in his city. Comparable stories appeared often in the Romanian media during my research in 1993–94—for example, a TV report of how local police had set upon and beaten a group of villagers trying to occupy the lands they had formerly owned, which the village mayor and state farm director were now working (see chapter 6).

Such episodes reveal the tenuousness of the center's control over local processes throughout the former socialist bloc, as local bosses build up power by exploiting local networks and informally "privatizing" both the Party's funds and its monopoly on coercion. This has furthered the rampant bureaucratic anarchy resulting from the collapse of a central authority and from "a crisis of obedience and control appearing at all levels of the administrative and economic hierarchy"; the crisis is rooted in the inability of bureaucratic superiors to ensure those beneath them a strategy for survival.[61] In earlier times, socialism's bureaucracy operated through networks of reciprocity, both vertical and horizontal, that were built up over the decades and enabled production to take place despite severe shortages. With the collapse of the party-state, the vertical ties became less valuable, as superiors could no longer guarantee deliveries and investments; subordinates therefore abandoned their vertical loyalties so as to cement local, horizontal relations that might serve them better.[62] These horizontal ties of reciprocity, sometimes culminating in violence, are what constitute "mafia." Its seeming pervasiveness during the 1990s stems from the removal of the Party's controlling hand, which left the horizontal links unsupervised and uncapped the possibilities for extortion.

Talk of mafia not only aptly renders this privatization of power but also points to useful interpretations, such as Jane and Peter Schneider's account of mafia in Sicily.[63] The Schneiders see mafia as part of what they call "broker capitalism," in which petty entrepreneurs having minimal capacity to accumulate capital (compared with the capacity of merchants, industrialists, or financiers) capitalize instead on the only significant resources they command: networks of personal contacts. Mafia flourishes, say the Schneiders, where the center does not effectively administer local-level activities involving production and marketing. Such conditions promote short-term speculative investments rather than long-term productive ones, since one cannot oneself control one's markets, which are often in the hands of foreigners.[64] These ideas are clearly relevant to the postsocialist situation in Romania, the former Soviet Union, and elsewhere. For the rising class of entrepratchiks who aim to acquire state property, their most capitalizable asset to start with was, precisely, their political positions and the personal connections that were so well developed and so vital to managing production in an economy of shortage. Once central control ceased to be effective, local and regional bosses—relying on these ties more than ever—formed mafias in the sense to which we are accustomed. Their situation, shaped by disintegration at the center, indeed parallels that of nineteenth-century Sicilian broker capitalists. Whether these mafias will have only pernicious effects or serve, instead, to foster capitalism (as Stark suggests, pointing to Japan's mafia-like networks of trust, cross-ownership, and subcontracting) remains to be seen.[65]

Mafia is more, however, than a real phenomenon, a group of people privatizing power along with state assets. It is also an active symbol, one that has spread because it symbolically expresses many of people's difficulties in the transition. That is, we must distinguish between "real mafia" and "conceptual mafia," or mafia-as-symbol. To grasp mafia's symbolic meaning fully, one would need to know more about who is talking about it and under what circumstances, but we might start with the following ideas.

First, mafia-as-symbol implies considerable anxiety about something that is integral to a market economy. Mafia, like markets, rests on a system of invisible horizontal linkages. Indeed, Hann reports that in Hungary, some people equate the market with mafia,[66] as well as with Gypsies, or (as in Romania) with former criminals, Securitate, and other unsavory characters. Talk of mafia is one way of saying that exchange and enterprise are still suspect, if not in fact condemned, as they were under socialism—that they bring unmerited riches and rely on questionable practices. Talk of mafia, then, may reveal people's ambivalence about the effects of the deepening marketization of their countries.

This is related to a second possible meaning of mafia as symbol: it marks off a space within which certain fundamental distinctions are being reconfigured, such as distinctions between "criminal" and "legal," "exploiter" and "exploited." The socialist regime defined certain kinds of activities as criminal—speculation, use of state property for private gain, and so forth. With the supposed departure from that system come redefinitions as to what is acceptable or prohibited. "Mafia" talk plots the trajectory of this redefinition. Something similar occurs around ideas about exploitation. From a system of production in which the state was clearly the exploiter of labor—and workers were fully conscious of this fact, as I showed in chapter 1—there has emerged a chaotic system in which it is completely unclear who owns what, who is exploiting whom, why there suddenly seems to be not enough money to go around, and why nothing is as it was expected to be in the first flush of postrevolutionary enthusiasm. Mafia is a symbol for what happens when the visible hand of the state is being replaced by the invisible hand of the market. The image suggests that there is still a hand, but it has disappeared into the shadows. (For some people, the earlier situation may seem preferable: as a villager said to anthropologist David Kideckel in the spring of 1990, "It's better to be exploited by the state than by other persons."[67]) Reading the literature on mafia, one suspects that this image even substitutes for the old image of the socialist state itself: just as the party-state was seen as all-powerful, pervasive, and coercive, with violence against the citizen always a possibility, so too is mafia.[68] In this sense, the image of mafia perhaps gives voice to an anxiety about statelessness, alongside other forms of insecurity.

Similar ideas about mafia as symbol appeared in Russia's *Independent Gazette*, which described the idea of the "invisible hand of the mafia" as something used to scare the Soviet public.[69] Alternatively, talk of mafia is like talk of witchcraft: a way of attributing difficult social problems to malevolent and unseen forces. And like witchcraft, mafia can become an accusation: with it one points the finger at a certain person or group—the opposing faction in the village leadership, a coalition of business interests competing with one's own—and accuses them of being agents of malevolent forces. The prevalence of mafia as an image during the 1990s suggests how general were the social problems and dislocations, with their accompanying feelings of anxiety. That there are also real mafias, producing the privatization of power from which "local suzerainties" and "parcellized sovereignty" result, merely makes the witchcraft imagery of mafia more compelling.

Emerging State Forms

I have been speaking of the contradictory tendencies that on the one hand erode state power and on the other reconstitute it, and I have suggested that an ethnography of the postsocialist state should document these contradictory processes. The task is more than simply descriptive, however; it should also engage the larger project of understanding better what "the state" actually "is" and what forms "it" takes. Just as the various absolutist states that feudalism incubated differed from the political forms that preceded it, so the various forms of state power being re-created in the former socialist bloc will differ both from those of before and from one another. In other words, to speak (as I have) simply of "restatizing" tendencies is misleading, for the states being reconstituted are not expected to be of the same kind as socialism's party-state. For many people in the region, the hope is precisely to build something else—something more closely resembling a "liberal-democratic" state, for instance.

Comprehensive treatment of the theme of state transformation requires an understanding of the state forms peculiar to socialism. Among those who have approached this problem are Jan Gross, István Rév, and Stark and Bruszt, all of whom emphasize the fundamental weakness of the apparently all-powerful socialist state—that is, its incapacity to accomplish objectives and (in Stark and Bruszt's happy phrasing) to "orchestrate concertation."[70] To explore state forming after socialism we might also employ a less immediately performative and more cultural approach, emphasizing the different concepts of power and rule that underlie different state forms, or pursuing the particulars of the cultural relationship generally known as "legitimacy." Humphrey illustrates the first of these in her analysis of Russian ideas about power, according to which order is the product of a central personification of power rather than of the exercise of law, the observation of certain principles, or a robust civil society.[71] I wish to use the second possibility—concepts of legitimacy—so as to show how an ethnographic strategy might proceed in analyzing departures from the socialist state. This requires abandoning the generalizing style I have employed so far and focusing on particulars. In other words, the structure of my discussion replicates what I see as the task of an ethnography of the state: to move between large comparative questions and very localized data.

A common feature of post-1989 political rhetoric is invocation of the "law-governed state." In each country of the region there is a specific expression that has this meaning, best rendered with the German *Rechtsstaat* (*statul de drept* in Romanian, *jogállam* in Hungarian, *pravo gosudarstvenno* in Russian, etc.). The term shows up constantly in political discourse and the press, in the form either of complaints that a law-governed state clearly does not yet exist or of arguments that a given behavior would help to construct one. The idea of the law-governed state, like so many other aspects of the transition, is a political symbol: it sets up a contrast with the form of government under socialism, seen as based in terror, fiat, arbitrariness, and deceit; it also sets up a contrast with the mafiotic forms discussed earlier. Anyone using the image of the law-governed state in political contest, then, wishes to be understood as promoting a departure from those kinds of political processes to postsocialist ones based in accountability to one's constituents and universal acceptance of legal mediation.

Beyond symbolizing an alternative to socialism, the image of the law-governed state indicates a set of practices that might build a new legitimation to distinguish the emerging state from the one of before. It indicates, that is, certain places to examine in order to see new state-forming processes at work. To take this approach is to forsake an image of the state as a reified entity or set of institutions in favor of attending to the practices of government, or power's microphysics. One could look for these practices and techniques of rule not just in the corridors of power but wherever rule is present, legitimacy perceived, subjection accomplished. I will briefly illustrate the possibilities with material on decollectivization, for which chapter 6 provides the background. What can we learn from inspecting the state's procedures and practices around decollectivizing that might clarify whether new forms of legitimation—new cultural relations of state and subjects—are taking shape?

Chapter 6 described a number of the conflicts arising for people in my Transylvanian research community, Aurel Vlaicu, as a consequence of decollectivization. Some people tried to resolve these conflicts by force and others by complaining to the local commissions. Still others had recourse to the law. This is not because they see the law as a neutral arbiter of last resort: my discussions with villagers revealed widespread skepticism about the very idea of "law." In the words of a judge I interviewed, there are two Romanian views of law: those who win a case in court say justice was done and the law is impartial, whereas those who lose say justice is corrupt and the judge was bribed. My discussions amply confirmed this judge's opinion. Most Vlaicu villagers do not believe that the law is neutral and impartial, and this shapes their relation to both law and supposedly law-governed state. Those who lost cases that I followed were convinced from the start that their opponents had bribed the relevant officials, or that because the evident interest of "those in power" was to have them lose the case, the judge would be so instructed.[72] At the same time, even people who won a case often had trouble enforcing the judgment, owing to resistance by local authorities. These attitudes and experiences suggest that legitimation through the "rule of law" is problematic, and that people view their defense of their rights as something taking place as often *against* the political system as facilitated by it through reliable legal procedures.

For those who pursue their rights in court, what is this experience like? What sorts of dispositions are likely to result from meeting the postsocialist Romanian state in its guise as dispenser of justice? First, going to court involves often costly and time-consuming trips, since cases are not prepared in advance by legal counsel and then brought to trial but are created *in situ*, through repeated court appearances to hear yet another witness, yet another piece of testimony, yet another expert evaluation. This aspect of legal practice discourages many would-be participants at the outset. Second, because cases do not come up in the order posted, parties coming to court on the appointed day may sit for hours awaiting their moment. During this time, people spectate the law: they hear the judge speak over and over about the need for proofs and documentation, argue as to what judicial level has or does not have competence, admonish participants for their posture or their attitude, dismiss or postpone cases because the parties do not have full property title or lack even the preliminary title from the local commissions, throw cases back to the local authorities or to the county commission, advise parties to get a lawyer because they are not competent to defend themselves, and complain frequently about the failure of local officials to comply with court orders to produce documents. Among the things court spectators learn are that the court does not have power to resolve many of the cases brought before it, particularly against local officials' resistance; that much of the court's work is carried on in arcane, specialist language to which ordinary people do not have access; that they can be tripped up by numerous procedures and rules; and that the practices of participation in defense of one's rights eat up large amounts of time and money.

Third, from my attendance at court I saw in the experience of bringing suit subtle forms of domination that participants will come to associate with their experience of the law. An example is the way their words enter into the court record. Instead of being taken down verbatim by a stenographer, the proceedings enter the record only when the judge periodically dictates a summary to the secretary. This practice leaves no doubt that ordinary citizens' words have legal effect only if translated (and thus authorized) by state officials. I read postural and behavioral signs as suggesting that many parties to a suit had not come there confident of their rights but, rather, as supplicants. The same attitude appeared in the behavior of those coming to legalize inheritances at the state notary. These orientations to law continue those of the socialist period, when the governors perceived the governed as "children to be corrected and educated" rather than as legal subjects with certain rights.[73]

It is nonetheless this latter view that underpins not only the concept of the law-governed state but also the actions of all those who bring suit. Even among those who do not, there is evidence of self-conceptions that resist "correction" as people strive to create themselves as effective agents against the state. I detected in some of my village encounters signs of self-conceptions premised on a state having diminished capacities, one far less intrusive than the party-state had been concerning their household activities, their use of their time,[74] the crops they could plant on their so-called private plots,[75] and even their sex lives.[76] With decollectivization, such people have begun to insist on their right to make plans independent of those a state might make for them. As one villager said to me about her land, "Even if I just turn it over to the association, it's still *my land*, as it wasn't before. If I don't like how they're running the thing, or if I think I'm not getting a big enough share, I can withdraw my land from the association and sell it or give it out in sharecropping." Others made similarly clear that what was at stake in decollectivization was their sense of themselves not just as owners but as people worthy of respect. Several people protesting to local authorities about allotments they considered unjust told me, "We want them to know they *can't treat us like this!*" One village friend who had won a lengthy court case against local officials only to give her land over to the village association explained to me why she had sued for her land even though she could not work it: "The important thing is *not to let those people rip me off again!*"

We see, then, encounters that discourage people from perceiving the state as lawful, as well as behavior by which they assert themselves against the state. Both of these indicate that a legitimating cultural relationship through a "law-governed state" is not very robust in parts of rural Romania. Under these circumstances, the fact that privatization—which has its own legitimating effects, independent of the legal encounters that sometimes accompany it—is proceeding so slowly further shapes rural people's dispositions toward the state as either resigned or defiant. Whether they will be discouraged and give up defending themselves or will persist, and whether their persistence will result in positive or negative dispositions toward the law, is not yet clear. It would be useful to compare the outcome in Romania, where many structures of the party-state survived the "revolution," with cases in which those structures were more deeply compromised, such as Poland and the Czech Republic. Perhaps in the latter cases quotidian encounters with the law provide a more effective state legitimation than seems to be true for Romanians.

Decollectivization as a vehicle for transforming the state operates not just through practices related to law-based legitimation but through other practices as well, such as the actions of local authorities. Far from being insignificant in reconfiguring state power, local-level management of property restitution has very high stakes for it, inasmuch as the Law on Agricultural Land Resources (Law 18) gave commune authorities and their topographers sufficient independence to foster local autonomy. Their ability to contain and resolve localized conflicts over land and to create some form of order without intervention from the center would impede recentralization of the state and would further local self-government. But if, instead, they become embroiled in infighting and corruption, squandering their independence and enabling or inviting the center to step back in, reconstituted central power will be the result. My evidence shows a tendency for local commissions not to resolve cases on their own but instead to toss them up to the county commission and the courts; both of these were beholden to a national governing coalition (through 1995) whose aims were patently state-expanding and clientelistic. Even the county-level organs lacked adequate means for final resolution of property cases, first of all because no legal suit could be brought without a property title, and local land commissions have been dilatory in producing them. The delay caused President Iliescu to break a parliamentary deadlock concerning agricultural taxation, in the spring of 1994, by proposing that the state resolve the problem, through an executive decree that the preliminary titling papers (*adeverințe*) would automatically become permanent. In other words, delays and disorder in local and county management of property restitution were effectively "bringing the state back in."[77]

At the same time, the political center was itself contributing to these delays, thereby obstructing the decisive implementation of the property law and preventing villagers from becoming full owners. Not only did the government fail to train enough topographers to carry out the measuring but it neither solicited nor accepted offers of trained topographers from elsewhere. Moreover, it postponed for nearly two years a USAID project for satellite mapping, which would have facilitated property restitution: the relevant ministry refused to supply the project with the five to seven key coordinates essential to starting the work.[78] That detail suggests a ministry—perhaps even the government as a whole—with minimal interest in resolving ownership questions, which in turn suggests a field of power in which the center faces almost no autonomous propertied individuals capable of articulating an independent interest or exerting certain pressures on the state. This kind of stalling and resistance makes the experience of property restitution a disheartening one for many villagers, as they seek to participate in shaping their futures but find themselves thwarted much of the time. With respect to both legitimation and the field of power constituted around the state, that is a more telling experience than any participation in "free" elections.

I have been suggesting that by examining decollectivization we see something of how state power is being reconfigured in Romania. To what extent is it different from the state power of before? Hints as to the nature of the newly emerging state lie in certain bureaucratic practices that relate to land. For example, decollectivization provided an opportunity to reinstitute the sort of rule-by-records that characterized the Habsburg period in Transylvania; the post-1989 state might have proposed a machinery for re-creating this form of rule, making records a predictable basis for resolving conflicts and then guaranteeing ownership based on them.[79] So far, however, this does not seem to be the outcome. Instead, the procedures for implementing Law 18 have muddied such records and practices as already existed. An entirely new system of topographic numbers was instituted, for instance, in the absence of legislation to link them to the older set. Thus even a villager with a property title cannot use it effectively in court, for the property numbers on it bear no resemblance to anything else on record.

Together with what I have already said, this suggests that instead of a power institutionalized and exercised through predictable procedures (which many see as the hallmark of liberal-democratic states),[80] what we see reemerging in mid-1990s Romania are ruling practices similar to those of socialism's predatory "spoiler state," consolidated by preventing other actors from acting effectively.[81] "Government" in this context rests on maintaining an environment of uncertainty, one in which would-be owners can readily doubt legal guarantees to their possession (these are, after all, the same people who lost their supposedly law-guaranteed property after World War II). "Law" in this context becomes not only a space for actively pursuing one's rights but an occasion to experience inefficacy, as cases drag on for months only to be thrown elsewhere, unresolved. "Local self-government" in this context means struggling to assert oneself against powerful local authorities whose failure to resolve problems creates an expanded role for those at the center. During 1994–95, that center moved to consolidate its advantage, as

Romania's ruling coalition dismissed on grounds of corruption more and more local mayors belonging to opposition parties. This would ensure the government's local-level control over the 1996 elections. Accountability therefore began to migrate up the hierarchy rather than down—to superiors, rather than to constituents—reminiscent of accountability under the party-state. Adding to this my earlier examples of practices and requests that reinforced not just a state presence but one resting (like that of socialism) on allocation, it seems that state-forming processes in Romania involve less transformation than reconstitution.

It would be inadvisable, however, to generalize this picture to other countries of the region. Staniszkis, for example, finds that Poland is best understood in terms not of a re-created socialist state but of something akin to the medieval *Ständesstaat* (or "estates' state").[82] In this postfeudal, preabsolutist state, the center has lost control over political and economic processes, and the structures of domination are segmented. Constituting the segments, which are of variable origin and function, are collective actors distinguished not by their economic interests (as would be true in a corporatist state) but by group ethoses resting on different genealogies and traditions; they work out their mutual interrelations not by a law that is the same for all but rather by ad hoc political agreements. The *Ständesstaat* that Staniszkis depicts is a hybrid form, each segment reflecting different organizational principles and different sources of social power. Because no group has a clear social base, parties do not compete for support by claiming to represent specific interests; instead, they offer and promise to realize particular visions of the social order. Prominent among these visions, I suggested in chapter 4, are those that favor nationalist politics. For Poland, at least, Staniszkis foresees a gradual evolution of the *Ständesstaat* into a corporatist state, rather than into a liberal-democratic, "law-governed" state of West European type. The prognosis differs for Romania, and probably for other countries of the region as well.

An ethnography of the postsocialist state might proceed in this way, then: looking at privatization as it relates to "statizing" tendencies; noting the points at which one or another actor appeals to the once-paternalist state to intervene; inspecting the terms of those appeals and their acceptance or rejection; examining the legal processes through which citizens may come to experience domination as legitimate or not; investigating actors' self-conceptions for signs of recoil from a state-saturated subjectivity; and exploring the state-enhancing behavior of local authorities and government ministries. This research procedure would inquire into the implications that state tasks such as regulating property acquisition, enforcing contracts, subsidizing culture and medical care, and so on might have for emergent political and cultural relationships and institutions—elements of potentially new state forms. It would focus on events in which forms of violence the state is supposed to monopolize are wielded instead by groups—miners, Secret Police, wealthy businessmen—whose very action makes manifest and simultaneously reproduces the state's incapacity. From these and other practices we may better discern the fields of force emerging in postsocialist contexts and the new forms of domination taking place through them.

Conclusion

This chapter has treated three themes—privatization, mafia, and state—as simultaneously symbols and social processes. Each indicates a set of developments: those pertaining to property rights, to active social networks that employ coercion, and to the transformation of state power. Each also provides symbols and images that enter into postsocialist politics. In similar fashion, my suggestion of a "transition from socialism to feudalism" has entailed both processual analysis and metaphor. As analysis, the chapter has indicated some processes by which sovereignty has been de- and recomposed in Eastern Europe. As metaphor, it participates in a politics of knowledge construction, in which the images that represent and name an object of knowledge crucially shape how that object will be thought. My skepticism about whether the former socialist countries are undergoing a transition to democracy and market economy has led me to propose instead the apparently absurd image of a "transition to feudalism."

In doing so, I have had two things in mind. The first is to bring a fresh set of associations into play, associations not mobilized by concepts relating to liberal capitalism. From the array of ideas "feudalism" mobilizes I have emphasized the disintegration of socialism's centralized, paternalist state and its consequences for state re-forming throughout the region. The feudal metaphor also contains a reminder about variation: as the Roman Empire collapsed, feudalism developed in only some of its domains, while in others there arose a variety of prebendal and tributary forms. *Ständesstaten* and absolutist states grew out of some but not all of these. I submit that thinking about feudalism points us in directions at least as fruitful for gaining knowledge of what is happening in the former Soviet bloc as do images of a transition to capitalism, with its big bangs, markets, democracy, shock therapy, and private property. All these highlight not current developments but an expectation, a telos.

This relates to my second purpose in using the metaphor of feudalism. Teleological thinking has plagued the region for decades; perhaps we should abandon it.[83] Socialist regimes saw themselves as ushering in the radiant future, the final stage of human happiness. They classified all human history into a gigantic sequence with themselves at its apex. Precisely because of that teleological orientation, they became vulnerable to the terrible disappointment of their wards. So too with Western leftists: had they not been convinced of socialism's evolutionary teleology, they might have felt less betrayed by the system's shortcomings. Observers who likewise expect from the present transition progress toward a specific end expose themselves to comparable risk. Attending to what is happening rather than looking for what ought to happen might be fairer, humbler, and more prudent.

As is so often the case in Eastern Europe, the most telling summary of my point is a joke.[84] The Roman emperor is luxuriating in his bath one day. Suddenly three of his councilors rush in, breathless and barely able to speak. "Sire! You must come immediately to the balcony! The slaves are in revolt! Speak to them and calm them down!" The emperor hastily dries himself and puts on his clothes. Emerging onto the balcony, he beholds a sea of placards. They read, "Long live feudalism, the bright future of mankind!"

AFTERWORD

And *Theory*? How are we to proceed without *Theory*? Is it
enough to reject the past, is it wise to move forward in this
blind fashion, without the Cold Brilliant Light of Theory to
guide the way? What have these reformers to offer in the way
of Theory? . . . Market incentives? Watered-down Bukharinite
stopgap makeshift capitalism? NEPmen! Pygmy children of a
gigantic race! . . . Change? Yes, we must change, only show
me the Theory, and I will be at the barricades. . . .
The snake sheds its skin only when a new skin is ready; if he
gives up the only membrane he has before he can replace it,
naked he will be in the world, prey to the forces of chaos:
without his skin he will be dismantled, lose coherence
and die. Have you, my little serpents, a new skin?
Then we dare not, we cannot move ahead.
(*Tony Kushner*, Slavs!)

S O SPOKE Aleksii Antediluvianovich Prelapsarianov, Tony Kushner's
imaginary Oldest Living Bolshevik, in his last address to the reformist
faction in the Soviet Chamber of Deputies, 1985. Prelapsarianov notwithstanding, however, socialism did shed its skin before a new one was
ready, and it did so with no real theory of how to proceed. In this book I have
described some early stages in the process of growing a new skin. That process has been guided in a few countries by the "Theory" of shock therapy;
other theories—together with outright improvisation—have prevailed elsewhere. The war of theory in Eastern Europe's transformation makes the
former Soviet bloc resemble those military battles in which the superpowers
fought by proxy, as client-combatants tested out their arsenals (one thinks of
the various Arab-Israeli conflicts and Desert Storm). The arsenals being
tested on this occasion include not just theoretical blueprints for a new future but theories to account for how the future is unfolding.

This is not the first time that the region has been vexed by inopportune
nakedness and ill-fitting theory: the entire Bolshevik experiment can be
seen as another such example, in which a theory created for conditions that
did not obtain broke down existing structures and produced more chaos
than order. Theory is not necessarily the best route to social change. This is

Elizabeth Dunn, Gail Kligman, Gale Stokes, and Brackette Williams improved this section
markedly over its initial version; I am in their debt.

particularly true when the very concepts embedded in the theory are themselves in need of rejuvenation, having grown crusty and stiff. In other words, the former socialist world is not the only thing that needs a new skin; so, too, does Western social science.

As I suggested at the end of chapter 1, the collapse of socialism was more than just the disappearance of a regime type. The year 1989 was the sign of a thoroughgoing change in the contemporary world, one that affects both the former Soviet bloc and foundational Western concepts and ways of life as well. At its heart is a change in the global economy, sometimes called a shift to "flexible accumulation"; its implications flow well beyond "the economy" into political organization, all manner of social institutions, and systems of meaning. Among the many things around which struggle is newly developing in this moment of change are notions of ownership and property,[1] the content of political forms such as democracy and the durable party structures through which it has been sustained,[2] the nature and role of the state,[3] and the meaning of citizenship and nation.[4] All those themes appear in this book about rethinking Eastern Europe, but rethinking them with regard to Western contexts and theories is just as necessary. The two rethinkings should proceed together.

This is clear from the picture that begins to take shape from this book as a whole. First, we see among Romania's Caritas investors persistent evidence of nonlinear notions of time—just as postmodernism is calling temporal linearity into question more broadly.[5] It is not only among Romanians that one can detect eschatological thinking: one finds it both among certain American fundamentalists, who anticipate Armageddon in the year 2000, and also among neoconservatives proclaiming "the end of history." Second, all across Eastern Europe we see struggles over property rights, not yet resolved in favor of individual ownership but suspended, rather, in a state of ambiguity; this is happening as new questions about property rights appear in numerous arenas elsewhere, concerning (for example) the Internet and surrogate parenthood. It may be that in the era of flexible accumulation, the fuzzy boundaries of postsocialist property rights—a liability, in Western property-rights theory—will prove an advantage.[6] Third, we see not stable political parties in Romania but changeable, shifting political coalitions (is this type of party suited to flexible accumulation too?) just as party identities in countries like Italy and the United States are coming unstuck. Fourth, we see struggles around social homogeneity, individuation, and inequality all across the formerly socialist world. While some politicians promote pluralism, individualism, and social differentiation as part of a developed and civilized European future, other—nationalist—politicians voice resistance to these same things. In the U.S., Canada, and the United Kingdom, similar questions inform the very different discourses around multiculturalism and diversity.

Fifth, we see major battles concerning the inviolability of borders. Will Romania be invaded by foreign capital, or can nationalists prevent that? Will Hungarians gain autonomy within a Romanian state? Will there develop a system of overlapping sovereignties, as minority rights are guaranteed from without? These questions are compounded by the transnationalization of identities like that of Hungarians or Slovenes, such that Hungarianness or Sloveneness is less confined within territorial borders than ever before. Similar transnationalizations—and similar concerns with border permeability— appear all over the world, manifest in the developed countries through political struggles over immigration.[7] In Romania, questions about transnational identities are further advanced among Hungarians than Romanians (probably because of the size of the Hungarian diaspora) but are visible among the latter as well, as Romania's government tries to determine who is "in" and "out" for purposes of property restitution. Thus questions of nation and property overlap and complicate each other, as nonterritorial nations have to be somehow aligned with localized property rights. What kind of being, then, will the ultimate "possessor" of property be: individuals? or some collectivity, perhaps the collective individual known as "nation"?

In addition, throughout the bloc the (re-)creation of new states, such as in the Baltic region and former Yugoslavia, raises questions of citizenship. Who is "in" and "out," without respect to the territory they happen to inhabit? Are Slovaks or Croats in America "in" as Slovak and Croatian citizens, while "others" living in the territory of Slovakia or Croatia are defined as "out"? Who is entitled to vote: those who inhabit the territory of a nation-state, or only some of them—perhaps along with others having the "right" ethnicity and living abroad? These issues now arise in all states of the world in which large populations of "outsiders" have come to dwell, not only in the former states of the Soviet bloc. Questions concerning state, territory, nation, property, and democracy seem to have become completely entangled.

As the meanings of citizenship, individuality, time, homogeneity, states, inequality, nations, property, and territory are newly contested everywhere, it becomes ever more apparent that present theory cannot encompass postsocialism without reconsidering its own foundations—without growing, that is, its own new skin. This means attempting to think differently. For such an effort, anthropology might prove an interesting companion. To begin with, it has long concerned itself with conditions of "liminality"—that is, states of transition, such as the process of shedding a skin or the rites that mark the passage from youth to maturity. This discipline's perspective would see as vital elements of transitions certain ritual forms: elections, for instance, which ritually consecrate new polities as "democratic" well before a full multiparty infrastructure is in place. Second, transitions (like shed skins) are about death and new birth. Of the various social sciences now feasting on socialism's corpse, only anthropology has much to say about these elemental themes. Revolutionary moments often bring talk of death and new birth—talk aimed at extinguishing the old order and justifying what comes next. We might begin to see these processes from an anthropological angle by thinking about the political lives of dead bodies.

Dead bodies, of both flesh and bronze, were essential to symbolizing (and thus helping to produce) the end of socialism. The dismantling of the statues of socialism's founders—Lenin, Stalin, Dzherzhinsky—in Moscow, Warsaw, Bucharest, and elsewhere resembled the spectacle of public execution treated so vividly by Foucault.[8] Some of these newly fallen heroes received public burials, as well. In Erevan, Armenia, when Lenin's statue was taken down from its pedestal it was placed on a truck and, like the body of a deceased person, driven round and round the central square as if in an open coffin, while bystanders threw upon it pine branches and coins, as they would for the dead. In Mongolia, where an immense statue of Stalin was belatedly felled in 1990, peasants sprinkled milk on the spot where the statue had stood. Mongolians believe that by this practice they will prevent the angry evil spirit from returning to haunt them.[9] (Precisely such haunting is explored in the 1984 Georgian film *Repentance*.) By these "deaths" their perpetrators thought to kill and bury socialism itself.

The *cortèges* of bronze corpses had their counterpart in fleshly ones, as all over the region, the collapse of socialism produced veritable parades of dead bodies: exhumed, shuttled from New York to Budapest, from Washington to Warsaw, from Paris to Bucharest, dug up and turned over, exiled from the Kremlin Wall to more lowly sites.[10] For those bodies already "at home," the process was relatively simple. For those abroad, it required resolving uncommon forms of overlapping sovereignty (someone else has "our" body) through novel diplomacy, to extradite bodily substances that had now become precious. Entire battalions of dead bodies fought to secede from Yugoslavia, as rival groups exhumed hundreds of corpses from karstic caves and claimed them as their opponents' victims of genocide.[11] By such actions, people seized and revalorized the past in the service of a new future by seizing and revalorizing the dead bodies of persons once and now newly significant. The revalorizations could be startling: the former First Party Secretary Imre Nagy, for example, leader of the 1956 Hungarian uprising, was dug up and reburied in such a way that somehow he was made to seem an *anti*-Communist hero.[12] The treatment of bodies can signify not just a revalorization of persons but changes in the political winds. Anyone interested in the Communist "restoration" so feared by Romania's political opposition should keep a hawk's eye on Ceauşescu's grave in Bucharest.

Following the revolutions, East Europeans seemed overcome with necrophilia. In 1989 a rich Hungarian entrepreneur spent huge sums on an expedition to Siberia, where he was convinced he had found the skeleton of famous nineteenth-century revolutionary poet and national martyr Sándor Petőfi (it turned out to be a young Jewish woman).[13] Crowds numbering in the thousands gathered in Bucharest in 1993 to view the relics of St. Dimi-trie.[14] Cluj mayor Gheorghe Funar produced an international incident in 1994 when he announced his plan to move the statue of Hungary's fifteenth-century king Mátyás from its central location in Cluj, in order to excavate for ancestral bones in the Roman ruins thought to lie beneath it. Medieval and present-day reliquaries seem suddenly cognate.

How is social memory shaped and reshaped by the treatment of corpses? What kind of consciousness is this, in which entire political orders are resig-nified by moving dead bodies around and reburying them? Are corpses an odd form of investment, whose value is realized by taking them from the vault and putting them back again?[15] How is one to understand the political relation of the living to the dead—a problem central to anthropology?[16] As these examples proliferate, it begins to seem that the science best suited to understanding postsocialism is necromancy, and anthropologists will be its scribes.

Death and rebirth are conjoined not only through the politics of corpses but also through two major systems of meaning: kinship and nationalism. Beliefs and rituals around kinship link the living to one another and to future generations through ties to the dead. So, too, do ideas about the nation. Nations, like kin groups, thrive on their ancestors—indeed, it is national sentiment that insists on the question of which dead to honor, retrieving them from the silence of unmarked or foreign graves into the noisy celebra-tions of a revivified national being. Again like kin groups, nations also insist on the importance of their heirs, on continuing the national line. Controver-sies around the status of abortion in nearly every East European country testify eloquently to an obsession with "extinction" and the births that will prevent it.[17] As Salecl observes, "When members of the former Croatian opposition write that 'a foetus is also a Croat' they clearly demonstrate that an opinion about abortion is also an opinion about the future of the nation."[18] Such nationalist pro-natalism ties the dreaded extinction with images of so-cialist policy now seen as having threatened the nation's very existence. Thus socialism equals death, and burying it demands a national rebirth in the name of the future.

Anthropological work on nationalism is revealing it to be quintessentially about kinship, something that is organized around ideas of youth and age, male and female, shared substance, blood and bone, and exclusion.[19] If na-tionalism is kinship, then these same axes will organize nationalism as well. We might therefore expect national ideas to bury the socialist past and reshape the postsocialist future in part through notions of gender and sub-stance. Gendered images of kin—images of "brotherhood," "forefathers," and "mother-" or "fatherland"—are at the very heart of nationalist imagery. Thus, students of postsocialist citizenship rights and democracy should at-tend closely to the almost-invisible theories of procreation underlying such images, theories that privilege men as genitors of the nation's eternal spirit while women provide merely its vessel.[20] The nationalist insistence on fertilizing this vessel and keeping it "clean" deeply affects the prospects for postsocialist politics, for it asserts the rights and needs of the collectivity over the desires of individuals to give or not give birth to the nation's heirs. Nationalist pro-natalism stigmatizes small families, career-oriented women, and prolific "aliens" (such as Roma) as enemies of the nation, pollutants of the body politic. Looking, then, at the symbolism of death and procreation and at the gendering of national imagery will help to reveal how the past political order is being buried and what sort of new one is being born.

Finally, if nationalism, like kinship, involves shared substance, then we should look for representations of the national soil as the body, bones, or congealed blood of the ancestors, or for notions similar to the old climatological theories that rooted a nation's character quite literally in the climate and soil.[21] To uncover such meanings would cast decollectivization in an unexpected light, tying property with national ideas. Property owners would thus become not only the emanations of the nation's soul but the very particular guardians of its body, for its soil is their ancestor's substance and the molder of their own national being. Moreover, nations are thought to have "heritages," often called "patrimonies" (a term widely used to refer to property, particularly social property, in Romania), of which the soil is an important constituent. By this logic, property becomes an extension of a kin-ordered relation to the world, and the territorial nation-state a giant patrilineage. The process of decollectivization, given that possibility, may turn out to be a struggle over competing notions as to who, or what social entity— "private" individuals? the national collectivity as embodied in the state?—is the best custodian of the nation's body that is our ancestral soil. As I noted above, questions concerning state, territory, nation, property, and democracy have once again become completely entangled, but this time by an unanticipated detour, a kind of thinking very different from that of the usual theories. Is this a path to theory with a new skin?

I have been discussing death and rebirth from the perspective of the skin; we might take for a moment the perspective of the serpent. Was Prelapsarianov right to liken the transformation of the Soviet bloc to serpents shedding their skins? A serpent with a new skin is still, after all, a serpent; it has changed its exterior, but the inner being remains largely the same. This is surely not an optimistic image for postsocialism. Should we think instead of caterpillars, which die as one thing and spring forth from their casings as something else?[22] Perhaps, on the other hand, that metaphor inaptly shares the unfortunate telos of Bolshevism and shock therapy: a certainty that the end result is known. Better not to label these transforming creatures and instead watch closely to see what they will become. Perhaps their very nakedness and indeterminacy make them the vanguard of the future.

NOTES

INTRODUCTION

1. The exact figure for the numbers who died during the 1930s is contested. Robert Conquest gives 14.5 million for deaths resulting from collectivization and the famine in the Ukraine, and 13 million from Stalin's purges. (His figures are generally thought to be high.) See Robert Conquest, *The Harvest of Sorrow: Soviet Collectivization and the Terror-Famine* (New York: Oxford University Press, 1986), p. 306, and *The Great Terror: Stalin's Purge of the Thirties* (New York: Macmillan, 1968), appendix 1. For a discussion of contrasting opinions on numbers in the gulag, see Edwin Bacon, *The Gulag at War: Stalin's Forced Labour System in the Light of the Archives* (London: Macmillan, 1994), pp. 1–41.

2. I prefer this term to the word *Communism*, which none of the Soviet-bloc countries claimed to exemplify. All were governed by Communist Parties but identified themselves as *socialist* republics, on the path to true Communism.

3. For example, the resignations from various Western Communist Parties in the wake of the Soviet invasions of Hungary in 1956 and Czechoslovakia in 1968 (not to mention the people in Eastern Europe who either abandoned Party work or refused to join as a result of these actions).

4. Cf. Rudolph Bahro's term "actually existing socialism," in his *The Alternative in Eastern Europe* (London: Verso, 1978).

5. I owe this formulation to Michael Kennedy and David William Cohen, of the University of Michigan's International Institute, and I thank them for providing me with an opportunity to think about my own work in the context of the Cold War. A related discussion is to be found in Stephen Cohen, *Rethinking the Soviet Experience: Politics and History since 1917* (Oxford: Oxford University Press, 1985), chapter 1.

6. For a useful discussion of some properties of American anti-Communism, see M. G. Heale, *American Anticommunism: Combating the Enemy Within, 1830–1970* (Baltimore: Johns Hopkins University Press, 1990).

7. As chapter 1 suggests, I understand *détente* as a symptom of the growing systemic crisis in both world capitalism and socialism.

8. Other organizations include the Kennan Institute and East European Program, both of the Woodrow Wilson Center, and the ACLS/SSRC Joint Committees on Eastern Europe and Soviet Studies. All these benefited from at least partial funding through the Congressional Act known as Title VIII, passed in 1984. Most of my own research was supported by IREX.

9. The only ethnographic fieldwork done prior to détente was in Serbia, resulting in Eugene Hammel's *Alternative Social Structures and Ritual Relations in the Balkans* (Englewood Cliffs, N.J.: Prentice-Hall, 1968) and Joel Halpern's *A Serbian Village* (New York: Columbia University Press, 1958). (The research for sociologist Irwin Sanders's *Balkan Village* [Lexington: University of Kentucky Press, 1949], about Bulgaria, was completed before the Cold War.)

10. Succession anxieties in Yugoslavia, together with some scandals in the late

1960s over anthropologists' alleged involvement in intelligence, precluded research in that country; the strongly philo-Soviet Bulgarian government was even less receptive.

11. In retrospect, it is possible that the "anthropology" Romania thought it was welcoming was physical anthropology, rather than sociocultural, for the former had a certain importance in Romania, whereas the latter in its North American variant was unknown. As soon as a few U.S. sociocultural anthropologists (Andreas Argyres, myself, John Cole, Steven Sampson, Sam Beck, David Kideckel, Marilyn MacArthur, and Steven Randall, all of whom worked in Romania between 1972 and 1975) began requesting permission to live and work for twelve to eighteen months in rural settlements, the government may have begun to rethink its position; some of us who had worked without extensive surveillance during the 1970s found the climate much more tense by the early 1980s.

12. These constraints did not preclude sound and independent research, however. See the exchange on that question in the Social Science Research Council's newsletter *Items* for June–September 1994 and March 1995.

13. Not to mention the agenda of the government, as Stephen Cohen (for example) has argued in *Rethinking the Soviet Experience*.

14. Following either 1989 or the emigration of friends prior to that year, I learned of several cases in which people I knew had been urged to collaborate with the police, having been assured that I was a treacherous spy.

15. Surveillance was stepped up in part owing to the regime's austerity program. During the 1980s, the Romanian government decided to repay the foreign debt ahead of schedule so as to escape the possibilities for foreign leverage that Poland's debt crisis had made all too apparent. Squeezing the population to the wall by reducing supplies of fuel and food, the regime hoped to generate enough hard currency to pay off the debt. But under these circumstances, which might lead to rebellion, an American at large was extremely dangerous and had to be closely watched. Adding to this was the suspicion that I was not only a spy but a closet Hungarian (see n. 17).

16. Berkeley and Los Angeles: University of California Press, 1991.

17. Nor would I say that the matters I discuss here are all there is to say about personal identity in relation to research in Eastern Europe. In my own case, for example, at least as important were problems having to do with my implication in Romanian-Hungarian national conflicts. I became an unwitting party to these because of the ethnic jokes in my first book (*Transylvanian Villagers*), as well as the form of my name, with its Magyar-like first-syllable accent and -*y* ending. For many years, as a result, Romanians unhappy with one or another aspect of my work have labeled me Hungarian. (My ancestry is French.) It is likely that this imputed identity caused me far more problems than did the climate of the Cold War.

18. That winter was an unusually cold one, with energy shortages in Western Europe that gave the Ceauşescu regime a new idea for securing hard currency with which to pay off their debts: heat was cut back in all apartment buildings, electricity was likewise curtailed, and no one was allowed to drive private automobiles, all the energy savings from these measures being exported to Italy and West Germany for hard currency. Added to the already reduced availability of food (much of it was being exported, giving rise to countless jokes as well as considerable difficulty in procuring a balanced diet), these policies made life in Romania fairly nasty.

19. I believe that the emphasis in constructions of "Communism" shifted between the 1950s and the 1970s–80s, coming to focus more on matters of Communism's failures in the sphere of consumption (long lines in stores, shoddy goods, etc.) rather than on the earlier obsession with "too much state power." In the earlier period, "Communism" was useful in discussing whether the expanded state of the New Deal was too much government. Later, the more pertinent topics came to be the problematic balance between consumption and accumulation—related, I believe, to capitalism's systemic crisis—which socialist economies aptly symbolized.

20. The department of anthropology at Johns Hopkins, where I was fortunate to work beginning in 1977, had been intellectually formed in the early 1970s by Sidney Mintz. Together with Eric Wolf (University of Michigan, then CUNY), he produced the most consistent body of outstanding anthropological work of Marxist inspiration.

21. See Gerald Creed, "The Politics of Agriculture: Sustaining Socialist Sentiment in Rural Bulgaria", forthcoming in *Slavic Review* 54 (1995).

22. See the superb ethnographic work by nonanthropologists such as Joseph Berliner, Michael Burawoy, Mária Csanádi, István Rév, and Michael Urban.

23. I think especially of scholars such as Michael Burawoy, Caroline Humphrey, David Kideckel, Sam Beck, Gail Kligman, John Cole, and Steven Sampson (in addition to myself).

24. See also my "Theorizing Socialism: A Prologue to the 'Transition,'" *American Ethnologist* 18 (1991): 419–39; and chapter 2 of *National Ideology under Socialism: Identity and Cultural Politics in Ceauşescu's Romania* (Berkeley and Los Angeles: University of California Press, 1991).

25. See, for example, Michael Burawoy and Pavel Krotov, "The Soviet Transition from Socialism to Capitalism: Worker Control and Economic Bargaining in the Wood Industry," *American Sociological Review* 57 (1992): 16–38.

26. See Caroline Humphrey, "Creating a Culture of Suspicion: Consumers in Moscow, A Chronicle of Changing Times," in *Worlds Apart*, ed. Daniel Miller (London: Routledge, 1995), pp. 43–68.

27. Thanks to Elizabeth Dunn for raising this question, which emerges from the juxtaposition of material such as that in chapters 6 and 7 of this book.

28. Among the works exploring this kind of question are Michael Kennedy and Pauline Gianoplus, "Entrepreneurs and Expertise: A Cultural Encounter in the Making of Post-Communist Capitalism in Poland," *East European Politics and Societies* 8 (1994): 58–94; and Elizabeth Dunn, "Managed Selves: Privatization and the Creation of a New Managerial Class" (typescript, 1993).

29. E. P. Thompson, "Time, Work-Discipline, and Industrial Capitalism," *Past and Present* 38 (1967): 56–97.

30. A further account of the significance of the national idea, for Romania in particular, can be found in my *National Ideology*, chapters 1, 3, and 6.

31. See, for example, Yuri Slezkine, "The USSR as a Communal Apartment, or How a Socialist State Promoted Ethnic Particularism," *Slavic Review* 53 (1994): 414–52; and Veljko Vujacic and Victor Zaslavsky, "The Causes of Disintegration in the USSR and Yugoslavia," *Telos* 88 (1991): 120–40.

32. For discussion of this point, see C. M. Hann and Elizabeth Dunn, *Political Society and Civil Anthropology* (London: Routledge, 1996).

33. See Louis Dumont, "Religion, Politics, and Society in the Individualistic Uni-

verse," *Proceedings of the Royal Anthropological Institute* (1970), pp. 31–41; and Richard Handler, *Nationalism and the Politics of Culture in Quebec* (Madison: University of Wisconsin Press, 1988).

34. David Stark, "Recombinant Property in East European Capitalism" a paper presented at the conference on Bureaucratic Capitalism in China and Russia, University of Wisconsin, 1993; and Michael Burawoy, "Industrial Involution: The Russian Road to Capitalism," Havens Lecture I, January 1995. See also Valerie Bunce and Mária Csanádi, "Uncertainty in the Transition: Post-Communism in Hungary," *East European Politics and Societies* 7 (1993): 266–67.

CHAPTER 1

1. Cf. Bahro's "actually existing socialism." Rudolph Bahro, *The Alternative in Eastern Europe* (London: Verso, 1978).

2. János Kornai, *The Socialist System: The Political Economy of Communism* (Princeton: Princeton University Press, 1992).

3. See especially Elemér Hankiss, *East European Alternatives* (New York: Oxford University Press, 1990); Ágnes Horváth and Árpád Szakolczai, *The Dissolution of Communist Power: The Case of Hungary* (New York: Routledge, 1992); and Jadwiga Staniszkis, *The Dynamics of the Breakthrough in Eastern Europe: The Polish Experience* (Berkeley and Los Angeles: University of California Press, 1991) and *The Ontology of Socialism* (New York: Oxford University Press, 1992).

4. In particular: Pavel Campeanu, *The Origins of Stalinism: From Leninist Revolution to Stalinist Society* (Armonk, N.Y.: M. E. Sharpe, 1986) and *The Genesis of the Stalinist Social Order* (Armonk, N.Y.: M. E. Sharpe, 1988); Ferenc Fehér, Agnes Heller, and György Márkus, *Dictatorship over Needs: An Analysis of Soviet Societies* (New York: Blackwell, 1983); George Konrád and Ivan Szelényi, *The Intellectuals on the Road to Class Power: A Sociological Study of the Role of the Intelligentsia in Socialism* (New York: Harcourt, Brace, Jovanovich, 1979); and János Kornai, *The Socialist System*, and *Economics of Shortage* (Amsterdam: North-Holland Publishing, 1980).

5. See also my "Theorizing Socialism: A Prologue to the 'Transition,'" *American Ethnologist* 18 (1991): 419–39.

6. Jan Gross has argued the weakness of socialist states from a somewhat different vantage point. See his discussion of the "spoiler state" in *Revolution from Abroad: The Soviet Conquest of Poland's Western Ukraine and Western Belorussia* (Princeton: Princeton University Press, 1988). See also my "Theorizing Socialism," pp. 426–28.

7. This section draws upon Michael Burawoy's discussion in *The Politics of Production* (London: Verso, 1985), as well as the sources listed in n. 4.

8. See Kornai, *Economics of Shortage* and *The Socialist System*.

9. See Burawoy, *The Politics of Production*, chapter 4.

10. Michael Burawoy and János Lukács, *The Radiant Past: Ideology and Reality in Hungary's Road to Capitalism* (Chicago: University of Chicago Press, 1992), chapter 5.

11. Cf. Burawoy, *The Politics of Production*.

12. Andrei Şerbulescu (Belu Zilber), *Monarhia de drept dialectic* (Bucharest: Humanitas, 1991), pp. 136–38.

13. These observations show how fraught is the use of files in assessing fitness for political office (as in the Czech practice of "lustration").

14. Campeanu, *The Genesis of the Stalinist Social Order*, pp. 117–18.

15. Horváth and Szakolczai, *The Dissolution of Communist Power*, pp. 77–78.

16. See, e.g., István Gábor, "The Second (Secondary) Economy," *Acta Oeconomica* 3–4 (1979): 291–311; and Steven Sampson, "The Second Economy in Eastern Europe and the Soviet Union," *Annals of the American Association of Political and Social Science* 493 (1986): 120–36.

17. Fehér et al., *Dictatorship over Needs*.

18. John Borneman, *After the Wall* (New York: Basic Books, 1990), pp. 17–18.

19. Jadwiga Staniszkis, "Patterns of Change in Eastern Europe," *East European Politics and Societies* 4 (1990): 77–97; Burawoy and Lukács, *The Radiant Past*, pp. 90–92, 96–100; Campeanu, *The Genesis of the Stalinist Social Order*, pp. 143–57; Konrád and Szelényi, *The Intellectuals on the Road to Class Power*, p. 153; Horváth and Szakolczai, *The Dissolution of Communist Power*, pp. 204–5. See also Leslie Benson, "Partynomialism, Bureaucratism, and Economic Reform in the Soviet Power System," *Theory and Society* 19 (1990): 92.

20. Campeanu, *The Genesis of the Stalinist Social Order*, pp. 143–57; and Horváth and Szakolczai, *The Dissolution of Communist Power*, pp. 204–5.

21. Horváth and Szakolczai, *The Dissolution of Communist Power*, pp. 48–49.

22. Analyses that attempt something like this include Terry Boswell and Ralph Peters, "State Socialism and the Industrial Divide in the World Economy," *Critical Sociology* 17 (1990): 3–34; and Valerie Bunce, "The Empire Strikes Back: The Evolution of the Eastern Bloc from a Soviet Asset to a Soviet Liability," *International Organization* 39 (1985): 1–46. See also Daniel Chirot, "After Socialism, What?" *Contention* 1 (1991): 29–49.

23. Paul Hare, "Industrial Development of Hungary since World War II," *Eastern European Politics and Societies* 2 (1988): 115–51.

24. David Harvey, *The Condition of Postmodernity* (Oxford: Blackwell, 1989), p. 184.

25. Ken Jowitt, "The Leninist Extinction," in Daniel Chirot, ed., *The Crisis of Leninism and the Decline of the Left* (Seattle: University of Washington Press, 1991), p. 78.

26. Jadwiga Staniszkis, "'Political Capitalism' in Poland," *East European Politics and Societies* 5 (1991): 129–30.

27. Staniszkis, "Patterns of Change in Eastern Europe," pp. 79–83.

28. David Stark, "Privatization in Hungary: From Plan to Market or from Plan to Clan?" *East European Politics and Societies* 4 (1990): 364–65.

29. Staniszkis, "Patterns of Change in Eastern Europe," pp. 77–78.

30. Staniszkis, "'Political Capitalism' in Poland," p. 131.

31. Staniszkis, *The Dynamics of the Breakthrough in Eastern Europe*, p. 164.

32. See Harvey, *The Condition of Postmodernity*, pp. 156, 164, 340–41.

33. Ibid., pp. 340–41.

34. E.g., Eric Hobsbawm, *Nations and Nationalism since 1780* (Cambridge: Cambridge University Press, 1990), pp. 181–83; and Charles Tilly, "Prisoners of the State," *International Social Science Journal* 44 (1992): 329–42, and *Coercion, Capital, and European States*, A.D. 990–1990 (Oxford: Blackwell, 1990).

35. Harvey, *The Condition of Postmodernity*, pp. 164–65.

36. Thanks to Jane Guyer for this observation.

37. Peter Murrell, "Privatization Complicates the Fresh Start," *Orbis* 36 (1992): 325.

38. Harvey, *The Condition of Postmodernity*, p. 147.

39. See chapter 2 of this volume.

40. Mikhail Gorbachev, *Perestroika: New Thinking for Our Country and the World* (New York: Harper and Row, 1987), pp. 5, 6.

41. Bunce, "The Empire Strikes Back," p. 39.

42. Jowitt, "The Leninist Extinction," pp. 80–81.

43. Ibid., pp. 81–82.

CHAPTER 2

1. E. E. Evans-Pritchard, *The Nuer* (Oxford: Clarendon Press, 1940); E. R. Leach, "Two Essays Concerning the Symbolic Representation of Time," in *Rethinking Anthropology* (London: Athlone Press, 1961), pp. 114–36.

2. E.g., Irving Hallowell, "Temporal Orientation in Western Civilization," *American Anthropologist* 39 (1937): 647–70; Christine Hugh-Jones, *From the Milk River: Spatial and Temporal Processes in Northwest Amazonia* (Cambridge: Cambridge University Press, 1979); Nancy Munn, *The Fame of Gawa* (New York: Cambridge University Press, 1986); R. Burman, "Time and Socioeconomic Change in Simbu," *Man* 16 (1981): 251–67; and Michael French Smith, "Bloody Time and Bloody Scarcity: Capitalism, Authority, and the Transformation of Temporal Experience in a Papua New Guinea Village," *American Ethnologist* 9 (1982): 503–18.

3. Because this chapter is about time and because in "real" time Romania is now a rather different society from the one described here, I will use not the "ethnographic present" but the past tense.

4. Norman Manea, "România în trei fraze (cu comentariu)" (unpublished typescript, 1989). (Published in English as "Romania: Three Lines with Commentary," in *Without Force or Lies: Voices from the Revolution of Central Europe in 1989–90*, ed. William M. Brinton and Alan Rinzler [San Francisco: Mercury House, 1990], pp. 305–34.)

5. There is no room in this chapter for extended definitions of terms. I would nonetheless distinguish between the concept that invokes those organizational structures which administer a polity, defend its territory, and maintain order (the "state," monopolized in the Romanian case by the Communist Party organization until early 1990) from the concept that refers to its ideal inhabitant, the "nation." Both are ideologically constructed "entities," but the discourses, activities, and personnel that construct and lead them are not identical. A "nation" often aspires to control its own "state" (particularly when it is subject to rule by persons of "other nations"); yet achieving that condition does not mean that the two are permanently fused. Trouillot also makes an argument that separates the two notions (Michel-Rolph Trouillot, *Haiti, State against Nation: The Origins and Legacy of Duvalierism* [New York: Monthly Review Press, 1990]).

6. The examples offered here come from several different sites and time periods. In 1984–85 I conducted a year's field research that took me to the Transylvanian city of Cluj and to two villages in south-central Transylvania; in 1987 and 1988 I returned

for two summers, visiting both urban and rural locations and adding two other cities (Iaşi and Bucharest). All the examples I give here came from overheard conversations (rather than from interviewing expressly on these themes) in one or another of these times and places. Some examples draw as well on earlier fieldwork in 1973–74 and 1979–80 (see my *Transylvanian Villagers: Three Centuries of Political, Economic, and Ethnic Change* [Berkeley and Los Angeles: University of California Press, 1983]).

7. A more detailed discussion of the points summarized here can be found in my *National Ideology under Socialism: Identity and Cultural Politics in Ceauşescu's Romania* (Berkeley and Los Angeles: University of California Press, 1991), chapter 2, and in chapter 1 of this volume.

8. Cf. James C. Scott, *Weapons of the Weak: Everyday Forms of Peasant Resistance* (New Haven: Yale University Press, 1985).

9. See Verdery, *National Ideology under Socialism*, chapter 3, for clarification of this point.

10. János Kornai, *Economics of Shortage* (Amsterdam: North-Holland Publishing, 1980).

11. Kornai's own country led the departure from the model described here, with China and the Soviet Union later following Hungary's lead. Romania continued to be the classic example of a centralized economy of shortage, until the 1989 overthrow of Ceauşescu; hence, despite changes within particular socialist economies, the model I employ continued to be applicable there.

12. The dynamics outlined in these paragraphs explain why Schwartz and others are wrong to speak of the "wasted" labor of all those Soviet citizens standing in lines by the hour. Schwartz, citing a Soviet émigré, comments that the time Soviet citizens wasted annually in shopping for food in the late 1960s was thirty billion hours, or the equivalent of a year's work for fifteen million people (Barry Schwartz, *Queuing and Waiting: Studies in the Social Organization of Access and Delay* [Chicago: University of Chicago Press, 1975], p. 13). Many of those wasted hours would have been spent in idleness at factories, underutilized because of shortages of supply. In a capitalist economy, much of that same labor would be "wasted" in unemployment.

13. Eviatar Zerubavel, "Time Tables and Scheduling," *Sociological Inquiry* 46 (1976): 91.

14. Eric R. Wolf, *Europe and the People without History* (Berkeley and Los Angeles: University of California Press, 1982), pp. 96–98.

15. Ferencz Fehér, Agnes Heller, and György Márkus, *Dictatorship over Needs: An Analysis of Soviet Societies* (New York: Blackwell, 1985), p. 65.

16. Pavel Campeanu, *The Genesis of the Stalinist Social Order* (Armonk, N.Y.: M. E. Sharpe, 1988), pp. 116–17.

17. David Stark, "La valeur du travail et sa rétribution," *Actes de la recherche en sciences sociales* 85 (1990): 17.

18. Jan T. Gross, *Revolution from Abroad: The Soviet Conquest of Poland's Western Ukraine and Western Byelorussia* (Princeton: Princeton University Press, 1988), p. 234.

19. Pavel Campeanu, *A Sociology of Queues* (unpublished typescript, 1987). This manuscript was not available to me for page references. I offer a summary from a brief prospectus of its argument. The work was later published as *România: Coada pentru hrană, un mod de viaţă* (Bucharest: Ed. Litera, 1994).

20. Cf. Schwartz, *Queuing and Waiting*, p. 102.

21. See George Konrád and Ivan Szelényi, *The Intellectuals on the Road to Class Power: A Sociological Study of the Role of the Intelligentsia in Socialism* (New York: Harcourt, Brace, Jovanovich), p. 48.

22. Ceauşescu referred to these "new" forms in agriculture, improbably enough, as the "new agricultural revolution." Apropos the apparent reversal of technological progress in Romania, note the following joke. Q: What did we have before the candle? A: Electricity.

23. *Flacăra Iaşului*, 20 August 1988, p. 2.

24. Zygmunt Bauman sees the arrogation of the right to initiative and control over time as an element of the new structure of domination that marks the "modern world" more broadly; he would thus see in these socialist examples merely an intensification of processes at work everywhere, through the forms of the modern state. See Bauman, *Legislators and Interpreters: On Modernity, Post-Modernity, and Intellectuals* (Ithaca: Cornell University Press, 1987), pp. 64–67.

25. See Verdery, *National Ideology under Socialism*, chapter 6.

26. "Expropriated" is, I think, a better word than something like "wasted," for people did not often report their experience of such immobilizations as a "waste of time." Sometimes they used the expression "*loss* of time," suggesting an experience of time as finite but not necessarily commodifiable or wastable. Those whose reaction was most likely to resemble my own (that time had been wasted) were some urban intellectuals.

27. Schwartz, *Queuing and Waiting*, pp. 39–41.

28. This useful phrasing was suggested by a participant in the discussion following oral delivery of this chapter as a paper at the 1989 American Ethnological Society meeting.

29. The question of why there was less overt resistance in Romania than in other Eastern European countries prior to December 1989 is one on which area specialists disagree. Some invoke "cowardice," some "Balkan traditions," and some a variety of structural variables. I side with the third of these. The degree of surveillance and repression, the successful squelching of opposition, the leadership's purging of disagreement within its own circles, and the destruction of independent organizational forms (church, voluntary organizations not tied to the Party, etc.) all gave no leverage to those who might have formed dissident movements from which other Romanians would have drawn encouragement. Also important was that Western governments—particularly that of the U.S.—failed to take an interest in opposition to the rule of the applauded "maverick" Ceauşescu. All these factors enabled the Romanian Party leadership to act with an extreme arbitrariness that facilitated control over the population and kept it constantly off balance, to a greater degree than elsewhere. To observe that there was little overt resistance in Romania is not, of course, to say that the state under Ceauşescu was omnipotent. Covert resistance, sabotage, and withdrawal of effort and loyalty undermined regime projects throughout his rule.

30. See, e.g., János Kenedi, *Do It Yourself: Hungary's Hidden Economy* (London: Pluto Press, 1982).

31. I borrow this term from political scientist Kenneth Jowitt (personal communication).

32. Michael Burawoy, *The Politics of Production: Factory Regimes under Capitalism and Socialism* (London: Verso, 1985), p. 193.

33. See Ashraf Ghani, "Consciousness of Conjuncture: Struggle over Seizure of Time, Afghanistan 1978–1988," a paper delivered at the Spring 1989 meeting of the American Ethnological Society, Santa Fe.

34. Ibid.

35. Eviatar Zerubavel, *Hidden Rhythms: Schedules and Calendars in Social Life* (Chicago: University of Chicago Press, 1981), pp. 70–80.

36. Although Sunday remained the "day of rest" in most factories, during the 1980s there were repeated incursions into this. Workers would be assigned a different day in the week as their "Sunday," making it impossible for them to attend church (for those who still wanted to) or, more subtly, to punctuate their week in identification with Christian norms.

37. See also C.A.P. Binns, "The Changing Face of Power: Revolution and Accommodation in the Development of the Soviet Ceremonial System," *Man* 14 (1979): 585–606, and vol 15 (1980): 170–87.

38. Zerubavel, *Hidden Rhythms*, pp. 12–30.

39. Hospitality may be an important component of Hungarian ethnic identity in Romania, as well, though my experience of this group is limited. One example in what follows comes from a family of Hungarians, behaving in this respect like my Romanian friends.

40. See Verdery, *Transylvanian Villagers*, pp. 64–65.

41. I owe this observation to Ashraf Ghani.

42. The observation noted in this paragraph is better called an impression, but I think it is a significant one.

43. Cf. E. P. Thompson, "Time, Work Discipline, and Industrial Capitalism," *Past and Present* 38 (1967): 56–97; and Smith, "Bloody Time and Bloody Scarcity."

44. Thom offers a fascinating discussion of linguistic aspects of this flattening of time. She observes that the prose style of Soviet-type socialism (called "Newspeak," in the book's English translation of the original *la langue de bois*) regularly sacrificed verbs to nouns. This fate befell, above all, those verbs that contain temporal referents or suggest temporal sequence. "Whenever possible, Newspeak avoids the precision of the verb and opts for a vague timelessness, carefully evading narrative while stressing the movement that is immanent in all things." See Françoise Thom, *Newspeak: The Language of Soviet Communism (La Langue de Bois)* (London: Claridge Press, 1989), p. 22. Additional aspects of the flattening of time, such as in Romanian historiography, are found in Verdery, *National Ideology under Socialism*, chapter 6.

45. Pavel Campeanu, *The Origins of Stalinism: From Leninist Revolution to Stalinist Society* (Armonk, N.Y.: M. E. Sharpe, 1986), p. 22.

46. David Harvey, *The Urbanization of Capital* (Baltimore: Johns Hopkins University Press, 1985), p. 37.

CHAPTER 3

1. For my use of the word "socialism," see chapter 1, n. 2.

2. I am indebted to Mary Poovey for this phrasing.

3. R. W. Connell, "The State, Gender, and Sexual Politics," *Theory and Society* 19 (1990): 523–26.

4. I owe this point to Mary Poovey. See also Eve Kosowsky Sedgwick, "Nation-

alisms and Sexualities in the Age of Wilde," in *Nationalisms and Sexualities*, ed. Andrew Parker, Mary Russo, Doris Sommer, and Patricia Yaeger (New York: Routledge, 1992), p. 239.

5. Eric R. Hobsbawm, *Nations and Nationalism since 1780* (Cambridge: Cambridge University Press, 1990), pp. 18–20.

6. Consider the following: "Workers of Romanian, Hungarian, German, and other nationalities together constitute the great family of socialist Romania" (from an article significantly entitled "The Socialist Nation" [*Naţiunea socialistă*], in *Documente ale Partidului Comunist Român: Culegere sintetică* (Bucharest: Ed. Politică, 1972), p. 106. I am grateful to Gail Kligman for this reference.

7. See, e.g., the introduction to Nira Yuval-Davis and Floya Anthias, *Woman—Nation—State* (New York: St. Martin's, 1989).

8. This is nicely illustrated in George Mosse, *Nationalism and Sexuality: Middle-Class Morality and Sexual Norms in Modern Europe* (Madison: University of Wisconsin Press, 1985). See also John Higham, "Indian Princess and Roman Goddess: The First Female Symbols of America," *Proceedings of the American Antiquarian Society* 100 (1990): 45–79.

9. See, e.g., Ann L. Stoler, "Making Empire Respectable: The Politics of Race and Sexual Morality in 20th-Century Colonial Cultures," *American Ethnologist* 16 (1989): 634–60; and Partha Chatterjee, "Colonialism, Nationalism, and Colonialized Women: The Contest in India," *American Ethnologist* 16 (1989): 622–33. A wonderful example of this point is E. M. Forster's celebrated novel *A Passage to India*.

10. See also Katherine Verdery, "Theorizing Socialism: A Prologue to the 'Transition,'" *American Ethnologist* 18 (1991): 419–39, and *National Ideology under Socialism: Identity and Cultural Politics in Ceauşescu's Romania* (Berkeley and Los Angeles: University of California Press, 1991).

11. See, inter alia, Irene Dölling, "'We Now Live from Day to Day, Because Nothing Is Certain Anymore': On Changes in the Daily Lives of Women in the New 'Länder'" (unpublished typescript, 1991); Joanna Goven, "Gender Politics in Hungary: Autonomy and Anti-Feminism," in *Gender Politics and Post-Communism: Reflections from Eastern Europe and the Former Soviet Union*, ed. Nanette Funk and Magda Mueller (New York: Routledge, 1993), pp. 224–40, and *The Gendered Foundations of Hungarian Socialism: State, Society, and the Anti-Politics of Anti-Feminism, 1949–1990* (Ph.D. dissertation, University of California, Berkeley, 1993); A. Heitlinger, *Women and State Socialism: Sex Inequality in the Soviet Union and Czechoslovakia* (London: Macmillan, 1979); Gail Kligman, *The Wedding of the Dead: Ritual, Poetics, and Popular Culture in Transylvania* (Berkeley and Los Angeles: University of California Press, 1988), "Women and the State: Ceauşescu's Pro-Natalist Policies," a paper prepared for a Wenner-Gren Symposium on the politics of reproduction, Brazil, 1991, and "The Politics of Reproduction in Ceauşescu's Romania: A Case Study in Political Culture," *East European Politics and Societies* 6 (1992): 364–418; Maxine Molyneux, "The 'Woman Question' in the Age of Perestroika," in *After the Fall*, ed. Robin Blackburn (London: Verso, 1991), pp. 47–77; and Dorothy Rosenberg, "Shock Therapy: GDR Women in Transition from a Socialist Welfare State to a Social Market Economy," *Signs* 17 (1991): 129–51.

12. See George Konrád and Ivan Szelényi, *The Intellectuals on the Road to Class Power* (New York: Harcourt, Brace, Jovanovich, 1979), pp. 47–52.

13. Cited in Mikhail Geller and A. M. Nekrich, *Utopia in Power: The History of the Soviet Union from 1917 to the Present* (New York: Summit Books, 1986).

14. This is the term used to refer to large patrilineally extended family forms in the Balkans, containing not only at least three generations but also several brothers with their families. (For discussion of whether these forms ever actually existed, see Maria Todorova, *Balkan Family Structure and the European Pattern: Demographic Developments in Ottoman Bulgaria* [Washington, D.C.: American University Press, 1993].)

15. Discussion with Lauren Sobel, who pointed out that there seemed to be a curious "doubling" of family in my argument, helped me to reach this formulation.

16. This chapter suffers from the unavailability of a good historical account of family/gender configurations from one or another Eastern European society prior to 1945 (except for Martha Lampland, "Family Portraits: Gendered Images of the Nation in Nineteenth-Century Hungary," *East European Politics and Societies* 8 [1994]: 287–316). Therefore I cannot say to what extent the patterns of the socialist period continue or depart from something earlier, and I must fall back on generalizations about "bourgeois" family forms.

17. These provisions did not, however, include much access to other forms of contraception. In Romania, widespread access to abortion prevailed until a pro-natalist campaign began in 1966. The cost of an abortion had been 30 lei, at a time when the monthly wage of a skilled worker might be about 2,500 lei. For details, see Kligman, "The Politics of Reproduction in Ceauşescu's Romania," the best source on Romanian pro-natalism and gender questions in Romania more broadly.

18. Ibid., p. 374, n. 24. Kligman also reports a joke that the elderly came to be called "falcons of the market" (*şoimii pieţii*), in a wonderful pun on the name of the Communist children's organization "falcons of the homeland," *şoimii patriei*).

19. Decision of the plenary session of the Central Committee of the Romanian Communist Party, 18–19 June 1973 (brochure).

20. Kligman, "The Politics of Reproduction in Ceauşescu's Romania," pp. 386–95, discusses at length how doctors were enlisted in policing natality.

21. Quoted in Charlotte Hord, Henry P. David, France Donnay, and Merrill Wolf, "Reproductive Health in Romania: Reversing the Ceauşescu Legacy," *IPAS Reports* 22 (July–August 1991): 232. The quotation continues, "Giving birth is a patriotic duty. . . . Those who refuse to have children are deserters."

22. Rosenberg, "Shock Therapy," p. 147.

23. Julia Szalai, "Some Aspects of the Changing Situation of Women in Hungary," *Signs* 17 (1991): 161.

24. For an excellent description of gender "homogenization," see Joanna Goven, *The Gendered Foundations of Hungarian Socialism*, chapter 2. See also Kligman, "The Politics of Reproduction in Ceauşescu's Romania," pp. 366–69. For a discussion of homogenization in relation to ethnic groups, see, e.g., Michael Stewart, "Gypsies, the Work Ethic, and Hungarian Socialism," in *Socialism: Ideals, Ideologies, and Local Practice*, ed. C. M. Hann (London: Routledge, 1993), pp. 187–203.

25. Especially the unsocializable core of the labor of childbearing. Kligman, "The Politics of Reproduction in Ceauşescu's Romania," discusses this feature in detail; she also describes (p. 377) the various official honors accorded women who bore and raised many children (Heroine of Socialist Labor, etc.).

26. See *Scînteia*, 8 March 1986, articles on p. 3.

27. See, e.g., articles on p. 2 of *Scînteia*, 8 March 1986.

28. Ágnes Horváth and Árpád Szakolczai, *The Dissolution of Communist Power: The Case of Hungary* (New York: Routledge, 1992), esp. pp. 54–56, 137–38.

29. Kligman, "Women and the State," p. 5.

30. Nicolae Ceaușescu, speech at the National Women's Conference, 7–8 March 1985, *Femeia* 38 (1985): 5–7.

31. A particularly striking example of this is Andrzej Wajda's film *Man of Marble*.

32. Susan Gal, "Gender in the Post-Socialist Transition: The Abortion Debate in Hungary," *East European Politics and Societies* 8 (1994): 266–67. More extended information is found in Goven, *The Gendered Foundations of Hungarian Socialism*, chapter 5.

33. Szalai, "Some Aspects of the Changing Situation of Women in Hungary," p. 155.

34. Among the reasons for this policy orientation were Ceaușescu's desire to rule over a large country and the necessities of a capital-poor economy compelled to labor-intensive strategies. From 1966 to 1989 Romania was the only Eastern European country where abortion was *not* readily available.

35. Victor Crăciun, "Chipul luminos al mamei, un mare model al literaturii române," *Scînteia*, 20 February 1986. (This is being said in the main Party daily.)

36. Decision of the plenary session of the Central Committee of the Romanian Communist Party, 18–19 June 1973 (brochure), pp. 27–30.

37. See, e.g., telegram addressed to Nicolae Ceaușescu by participants in the National Women's Conference, 7–8 March 1985, in *Femeia* 38 (1985): 8–9.

38. The article was signed by Silviu Achim. *Scînteia*, 18 September 1986: 4.

39. The observation about patriarchy is Gail Kligman's. I note, however, that this historian is in good company: Hegel is reported to have said, "He who is not a father is not a man" (cited in Victoria de Grazia, *How Fascism Ruled Women: Italy, 1922–1945* [Berkeley and Los Angeles: University of California Press, 1992], p. 43).

40. Romania's territorial claims to Transylvania often rest on showing continuous settlement since the time of the Dacians (the indigenous group conquered by the Roman emperor Trajan in the early second century A.D.).

41. I have discussed some reasons for this in *National Ideology*, chapter 3.

42. Transylvania was conquered and settled by ancestors of today's Hungarians during the eleventh and twelfth centuries. It held a special quasi-autonomous status within the Hungarian kingdom, gaining even greater autonomy after Turkish troops occupied most of lowland Hungary after 1526. Since as long as population statistics have been collected, however, the majority of the region's people have been Romanian. Following World War I, Transylvania was removed from Hungary by plebiscite and absorbed into Romania. Its population is about three-fourths Romanian, one-fourth Hungarian.

43. It was sometimes joked that Romanians were the only people eager to claim descent from Neanderthal man, remains of whom were found on "Romanian" soil.

44. The emperor Trajan's defeat of the Dacians was memorialized in an immense bas-relief, wound around a column forty meters tall. The costume worn by the Dacians on the column resembles that worn until recently in parts of Transylvania.

45. Kligman, *The Wedding of the Dead*.

46. The low level of industrial investment in Maramureș may have been partly

motivated by the desire to retain this stronghold of peasant "tradition" as a historical argument. The agricultural base being insufficient to support its population, many men from the region migrated as agricultural laborers or for other kinds of work, leaving their women to farm and to reproduce the local culture.

47. Kligman, *The Wedding of the Dead*, p. 257.

48. This outcome is similar to that analyzed by Jane Collier for contemporary Andalusia, but the mechanisms producing it are somewhat different. See her "Bullfights and Sevillanas: Gendered 'Traditions' Engendering Nationalism," a paper presented at the 1991 meeting of the American Ethnological Society in Charleston, S.C.

49. The most important part of the national history concerns proofs of continuity from the time of the Dacians (see n. 44). I do not take up those arguments here.

50. This text (in English in the original) was part of a huge eight-page special advertising supplement taken out in the *London Times* (and paid for at what cost?) by the Romanian government in 1972. It opened with an immense photo of Ceauşescu and a quotation from him. Other articles treated social and economic change in Romania, Romanian humanism, Romanian cultural values and achievements, education, folk poetry, and Romania's participation "in the world exchange of cultural assets." The extract I present was therefore part of a concerted attempt at self-definition for outsiders. It is nonetheless very similar in its emphases to any number of Ceauşescu's speeches for internal consumption (see, e.g., Nicolae Ceauşescu, *Istoria poporului român: culegere de texte* [Bucharest: Ed. Militară, 1983]), even though the person listed as author is a literary critic who considered himself an opponent of the regime. (He denies having written the text.) I have excised substantial portions, marked with ellipses.

51. Adrian Marino, "Great Figures in the History of Romanian Genius," *London Times*, special advertising supplement, 29 December 1972.

52. I take this expression from Richard Handler, *Nationalism and the Politics of Culture in Quebec* (Madison: University of Wisconsin Press, 1988).

53. Cf. ibid. I would like to raise parenthetically a question I do not have space or material to take up properly: whether the "collective individualism" of Western national ideologies differs significantly in other contexts where individualism has been less thoroughly developed. The first paragraph of excerpt 1 suggests that this author thinks there is something importantly different in the exemplary biographies of Romanians, as compared with Western "great men."

54. For example, at his speech to the 1985 National Women's Conference, Ceauşescu referred to the "best sons and daughters of the homeland." Usually he referred only to "sons." As pro-natalism intensified during the 1980s (a decade after Marino's article was written), it occasionally became necessary, perhaps, to bring women into history—and then usually through examples of women with many children. See, e.g., *Scînteia*, 18 September 1986, p. 4.

55. Mosse, *Nationalism and Sexuality*.

56. I am grateful to Emily Martin for pointing out the significance of death and eternal life as the products of these heroic Romanian men.

57. See Carole Pateman, "The Fraternal Social Contract," in *Civil Society and the State*, ed. John Keane (London: Verso, 1988), p. 114. Original emphasis.

58. Connell, "The State, Gender, and Sexual Politics," p. 526.

59. Scholars of nationalism have not (with the possible exception of social psy-

chologists) devoted the kind of attention to how subjects' identity is created *as national* that feminists (such as Chodorow and others) have devoted to how subjects' identity is created *as gendered*. One especially interesting attempt is found in John Borneman's work on nationness in the two Germanys, which I do not have space to discuss fully. He suggests that basic to the "practice of national belonging" is a parallelism in the narrative structures of and the external parameters shaping the lives lived by individuals, as compared with the "life" of the nation presented in textbooks about the national history. A national history, then, presents a narrative with which people identify more or less fully, according to the lives they have been able to live. See John Borneman, *Belonging in the Two Berlins: Kin, State, Nation* (Cambridge: Cambridge University Press, 1992).

60. The translation is my own. I have preserved the exceedingly long sentences of the original and have added a few commas to increase readability. I should note that Romanian is a language with grammatical gender, almost always visible in the form of the noun (most feminine nouns end in *a* or *e*, masculine and neuter nouns in something else), with obligatory adjectival agreement. The country's name, "România," is also feminine, as are all adjectives modifying it. This contributes an even more "feminine" flavor to the original than I can give to the translation.

Other words referring to Romania or to the "nation" include the two feminine nouns *ţara* (from Latin *terra*, "land"), and *patria* (cf. French *patrie*; often translated "fatherland," but I think "homeland" is a better rendering. Romanians often use the expression "patria-mumă," meaning literally "Mummy-*patrie*"). The two most common words for "people" in the ethnic sense are *poporul* (from Latin *populus*) and *neam*, from a Finno-Ugrian or Turkic root meaning "family/tribe/clan"—hence, a basic kinship term. Both are neuter nouns. The words *naţie* or *naţiune* (both feminine) are also used, though less often than *neam*.

As in English, collective or generic nouns and pronouns in Romanian take the masculine form. Thus an appeal to all Romanians will be addressed to *românii* (masculine plural), a discussion of the national character of "the Romanian" will speak of *românul* (masculine singular), as in "The Romanian [masculine singular] is adaptable, gregarious, cheerful, and brave [unlike the Hungarian, who is rigid and bellicose, etc.]." I once observed to two historians, one male and one female, that all the literature I had been reading that defined the "national character" rendered for me a grammatically masculine Romanian; my male interlocutor saw nothing to remark in this, and the female was stunned by it.

61. See, e.g., E. M. Simmonds-Duke [Katherine Verdery], "Was the Peasant Uprising a Revolution? The Meanings of a Struggle over the Past," *Eastern European Politics and Societies* 1 (1987): 187–224.

62. That the Hungarian side was not immune to such themes is evident in the vigorous reply made to Lăncrănjan's book by György Szaraz, a "court poet" of the Hungarian minister of culture, Aczel.

63. The word used here (*dragoste*) has carnal as well as spiritual connotations.

64. Meaning both group of kin and people or nation in the ethnic sense.

65. Nineteenth-century Romanian Romantic poet, whose early death cut short a brilliant career.

66. Three important figures of Romanian history, one a revolutionary, one a politician and historian, the third a writer.

67. All these were famous figures, most of them princes and rulers.

68. From Ion Lăncrănjan, *Cuvînt despre Transilvania* (Bucharest: Ed. Sport-Turism, 1982), pp. 69–71, 81–84.

69. See Mosse, *Nationalism and Sexuality*, chapter 6. In the nineteenth century, "Romania" was often visually portrayed as a sleeping woman being awakened (the image of Romanians' efforts to free themselves from Hungarian and Turkish overlords).

70. See my discussion of nation and gender in the first section of this chapter.

71. Perhaps these observations cast additional light on the rapes of women on the contested territories of former Yugoslavia.

72. Eva Huseby-Darvas, "'Feminism, the Murderer of Mothers': Neo-Natalist Reconstruction of Gender in Hungary," a paper presented at the 1991 annual meeting of the American Anthropological Association, Chicago, pp. 3–4 (forthcoming in *Women out of Place: The Gender of Agency, the Race of Nationality*, ed. Brackette F. Williams [New York: Routledge, 1996]).

73. I am not well enough informed about the Czech and Slovak cases to know whether they form an exception to this statement.

74. Kligman, "The Politics of Reproduction in Ceauşescu's Romania," p. 400. As of this writing (May 1993), the Romanian parliament was considering a law that would reintroduce the celibacy tax on childless persons and reduce the length of maternity leaves.

75. See Gal, "Gender in the Post-Socialist Transition," Goven, "Gender Politics in Hungary," and Huseby-Darvas, "Feminism, the Murderer of Mothers" on Hungary; Ewa Hauser, Barbara Heyns, and Jane Mansbridge, "Feminism in the Interstices of Politics and Culture: Poland in Transition," in Funk and Mueller, *Gender Politics and Post-Communism*, pp. 257–73, on Poland; and Olga Supek, "The Unborn Are Also Croats," a paper presented at the 1991 annual meeting of the American Anthropological Association, Chicago, on Croatia.

76. Huseby-Darvas, "Feminism, the Murderer of Mothers," p. 1.

77. Supek, "The Unborn Are Also Croats," and Hauser et al., "Feminism in the Interstices of Politics and Culture" (which also reports Polish feminists' counter-slogan: "Onanism is genocide," p. 259).

78. Hauser et al., "Feminism in the Interstices of Politics and Culture," p. 4; and Huseby-Darvas, "Feminism, the Murderer of Mothers," pp. 4–5.

79. Supek, "The Unborn Are Also Croats," pp. 2–4.

80. Gal, "Gender in the Post-Socialist Tradition," p. 7; and Huseby-Darvas, "Feminism, the Murderer of Mothers," p. 5.

81. Huseby-Darvas, "Feminism, the Murderer of Mothers," p. 6.

82. Goven, "Gender Politics in Hungary."

83. Goven (ibid., p. 232) quotes the following statement from a magazine article: "Society [i.e., socialism] liberates the woman from family shackles, gives her economic independence, spares her many of the burdens of child-rearing, and in exchange asks for an alliance in crushing male obstinacy. The women take on their part in the alliance with their usual violent moods and aggressiveness."

84. Ibid., p. 230.

85. Gal, "Gender in the Post-Socialist Transition," p. 270.

86. Goven, "Gender Politics in Hungary," p. 234.

87. Ibid., pp. 227–28, 230–31, 236–37.

88. Goven interprets the backlash against aggressive women as related to pecu-liarities in Hungarian divorce laws. While I have no reason to question her analysis, I would see divorce laws as the place in which these problematic reactions to re-configured gender roles happen to have settled in that country, but I would then look for different places, elsewhere, in which the same thing is happening. I was not listening for talk about women's "aggressiveness" in Romania but would not be sur-prised to find it, precisely as a way of opposing socialism's "unnatural" intervention into the appropriate familial roles.

89. Cited in Goven, "Gender Politics in Hungary," p. 229.

90. See, e.g., Fran Markowitz, "Striving for Femininity: Soviet Unfeminism," a paper presented at the 1991 annual meeting of the American Anthropological As-sociation, Chicago, p. 7.

91. Rosenberg observes that in the March 1990 elections, 46 percent of East Ger-man women voted for a party that opposed abortion, day care, and the equivalent of affirmative action ("Shock Therapy," p. 146).

92. See, e.g., Immanuel Wallerstein, "Household Structures and Labour-Force Formation in the Capitalist World-Economy," in Etienne Balibar and Immanuel Wallerstein, *Race, Nation, Class: Ambiguous Identities* (New York: Verso, 1991), pp. 107–12. As Folbre shows, the "unproductive" character of housework was a nineteenth-century development (Nancy Folbre, "The Unproductive Housewife: Her Evolution in Nineteenth-Century Economic Thought," *Signs* 16 [1991]: 463–84).

93. In the former GDR, the impetus came strictly from unification with a West Germany where the level of social welfare was lower and laws concerning abortion more stringent. In Poland and Croatia the impetus has come largely from a resurgent Catholic Church and from the necessity (in Poland) of paying the Church back for its earlier support of Solidarity. In Hungary the active forces are harder to identify, though it is undeniable that Hungary is farther than anyone else on the road to capitalism.

94. I owe this observation to Brackette Williams.

CHAPTER 4

1. Because none of the countries ruled by Communist Parties described them-selves as "Communist," I prefer not to use this term; I speak instead of "socialism" and "postsocialist" Romania.

2. Eminent Yale historian Ivo Banac discovered as much when an initial invitation to appear on a national news program foundered on his refusal to defend this expla-nation (Ivo Banac, personal communication).

3. See Johannes Fabian, *Time and the Other: How Anthropology Makes Its Object* (New York: Columbia University Press, 1983).

4. It may serve nationalist East European politicians as a way of justifying their actions and Western policy-makers as a justification for their *in*action.

5. I am grateful to Ashraf Ghani for suggesting this phrasing, in another context.

6. Eric Hobsbawm, *Nations and Nationalism since 1780* (Cambridge: Cambridge University Press, 1991), pp. 18–20.

7. In many cases, issues that had engaged much passionate debate in the 1920s

and 1930s began to recur in political discussions of the 1970s and 1980s. For example, in Poland and Romania, interwar arguments reappeared as to whether or not the Polish or Romanian soul is quintessentially peasant, as opposed to urban and cosmopolitan. See Katherine Verdery, *National Ideology under Socialism: Identity and Cultural Politics in Ceaușescu's Romania* (Berkeley and Los Angeles: University of California Press, 1991), chapter 5; and essays in Ivo Banac and Katherine Verdery, eds., *National Ideology and National Character in Interwar Eastern Europe* (New Haven: Yale Center for Area Studies, Russian and East European Publications no. 13, 1995).

8. Although not phrased in exactly these terms, Hélène Carrère d'Encausse's analysis was perhaps the first to signal the significance of this fact for the Soviet Union. See her *Decline of an Empire: The Soviet Socialist Republics in Revolt* (New York: Newsweek, 1979). For further discussion of the significance of reified nationality in the Soviet context, see Victor Zaslavsky, "Nationalism and Democratization in Post-Communist Societies," *Daedalus* 121 (Spring 1992): 97–121; and Philip G. Roeder, "Soviet Federalism and Ethnic Mobilization," *World Politics* 43 (1991): 196–232.

9. Valery Tishkov, "Fire in the Brain: Inventions and Manifestations of Soviet Ethnonationalism," a paper presented at the annual meeting of the American Anthropological Association, Chicago, 1991. See also the works cited in n. 8.

10. The Romanian Communist Party claimed, for instance, to represent the national minorities proportionately in its membership and governing bodies. This sort of "affirmative action" program necessitates, of course, a prior reification of group identities.

11. The analysis of socialism and shortage was least applicable to Yugoslavia, yet the disparities among regions produced a consciousness of *relative* shortage that was perhaps of similar consequence.

12. For an expanded version of the argument summarized here, see Verdery, "Ethnic Relations, Economies of Shortage, and the Transition in Eastern Europe," in *Socialism: Ideals, Ideologies, and Local Practice*, ed. C. M. Hann (London: Routledge, 1993), pp. 172–86.

13. See my *Transylvanian Villagers: Three Centuries of Political, Economic, and Ethnic Change* (Berkeley and Los Angeles: University of California Press, 1983) chapter 5.

14. See chapter 6 for further discussion.

15. See Sergei Arutiunov, "Ethnic Conflicts in the Caucasus," a paper presented at Johns Hopkins University, 18 February 1993.

16. Ibid.

17. Robert M. Hayden, "Constitutional Nationalism in the Formerly Yugoslav Republics," *Slavic Review* 51 (1992): 654–73. See especially his discussion on pp. 657–58, concerning how the Croatian constitution systematically excludes Serbs.

18. Hungarians with whom I spoke generally viewed the resulting constitution as discriminating against them; Romanians saw it as giving Hungarians suitable rights but not the "privileges" they claim Hungarians were demanding.

19. In the runoff elections for President, these parties urged their members to vote for President Ion Iliescu. Their programs, like his, were skeptical of "Europe" and reform, preferring policies that would preserve the institutions and privileges of

the former Communist Party (which institutionally no longer exists, although several organizations can be seen as its heirs).

The influence of these parties was extended by publications such as the weekly paper of the Greater Romania Party, which had a very large circulation. In the summer of 1991 *Greater Romania* apparently had a print run of about six hundred thousand—that is, almost one for every ten members of the Romanian labor force. (It fell to about two hundred thousand by the following summer.)

20. See e.g., Ion Cristoiu, "Un document care nu rezolvă nimic," *Expres magazin*, 17–23 July 1991, p. 16; also Nicolae Manolescu, "Ideologie extremistă şi joc politic," *România literară*, 15 August 1991, p. 2; "Sub cizma Securităţii," *Românul liber* 7 (1991): 8; and Dennis Deletant, "Convergence vs. Divergence in Romania: The Role of the Vatra Românească Movement in Transylvania " (an unpublished typescript).

21. See the report in "Revista revistelor," *România literară*, 12 December 1992, p. 24. For changing party names and acronyms, see chapter 5, n. 12, and accompanying text.

22. My sources are, for Hungary, József Böröcz, personal communication; for Poland, Adam Michnik, "The Two Faces of Europe," *New York Review of Books*, 19 July 1990, p. 7; and for Slovakia, Andrew Lass, personal communication. My argument holds for some of the Soviet nationalisms as well, where a move from Communist boss to nationalist leader similarly afforded a new lease on power.

23. An excellent account of the link between anti-Communism, old elites, and nationalism is to be found in Adam Michnik, "The Two Faces of Europe."

24. It has long been rumored that at least a wing of the Romanian Securitate was funded by the KGB, and that this support continued after the December 1989 "events."

25. This is not a necessary association, for in other countries former Communists have found it possible to take up the banner of reform. I suspect it is partly Romania's lesser likelihood of rapid economic growth and partly the positions already occupied by other political forces in Romania that relegated the ex-Communists to the nationalist option.

26. Officially, 79 parties presented candidates, but a total of 144 considered themselves to be participants. See Petre Datculescu, "How Romania Voted: An Analysis of the Parliamentary and Presidential Elections of September 27, 1992," an unpublished typescript (1992).

27. For the Romanian case, see Dennis Deletant, "Convergence vs. Divergence in Romania"; for Bulgaria, see Gerald Creed, "The Bases of Bulgaria's Ethnic Policies," *Anthropology of East Europe Review* 9 (1990): 11–17.

28. Many Romanians believe that the Hungarian party was organized from Budapest, hence its capacity to organize so rapidly and well. This view is lent some credence by a Hungarian journalist in Bucharest, who explained to me that the day after the revolution, he had been given the text of a declaration of principle for a Hungarian party, to print in his newspaper, and then a day later had been given a "revised version," which to his eyes was not of local origin: it was typed in a typeface not generally found on typewriters available in Romania. This journalist suspects that Hungarian émigrés from Transylvania, now living in Budapest, were responsible for the party's rapid organization.

29. For details on this process, see Jadwiga Staniszkis, *The Dynamics of the Break-*

through in Eastern Europe (Berkeley and Los Angeles: University of California Press, 1991); and David Stark, "Privatization in Hungary: From Plan to Market or from Plan to Clan?" *East European Politics and Societies* 4 (1990): 351–92. The term "entre-pratchiks" is my own.

30. The historians are especially important, for, as Eric Hobsbawm put it, "Historians are to nationalism as poppy growers in Pakistan are to heroin-addicts: we supply the essential raw material for the market" (E. J. Hobsbawm, "Ethnicity and Nationalism in Europe Today," *Anthropology Today* 8 [1992]: 3).

31. In Romania, it happens that those most likely to take this line also served as Ceauşescu's court intellectuals. In the confusion surrounding the dictator's fall, they lost influential positions (as heads of institutes, university professors, or editors of important publications) to intellectuals from the opposition. Thus in that country the humanist-intellectual nationalists coalesce with nationalists privileged by the former regime.

32. These comments accord well with Steven Sampson's observation that many of the ethnic conflicts in the region are the direct consequence of the transition to democracy and markets, just as African "tribalism" was the consequence of the formation of new states. See his "Is There an Anthropology of Socialism?" *Anthropology Today* 7 (1991): 19.

33. Andrew Lass, personal communication.

34. See, e.g., Michael Stewart, "Gypsies, the Work Ethic, and Hungarian Socialism," in *Socialism: Ideals, Ideologies, and Local Practice*, ed. C. M. Hann (London and New York: Routledge, 1993), pp. 187–90.

35. See Mira Marody, "The Political Attitudes of Polish Society in the Period of Systematic Transitions," *Praxis International* 11 (2): 227–39; and David Ost, "Interests and Politics in Post-Communist Society: Problems in the Transition in Eastern Europe," *Anthropology of East Europe Review* 10 (1991): 7.

36. Claude Lefort, "The Image of the Body and Totalitarianism," in *The Political Forms of Modern Society: Bureaucracy, Democracy, Totalitarianism* (Cambridge: MIT Press, 1986), p. 297.

37. I borrow this phrasing from John Borneman. See also Ken Jowitt, "Moscow 'Centre,'" *Eastern European Politics and Societies* 1 (1987): 296–348.

38. See Lefort, "The Image of the Body and Totalitarianism," p. 298.

39. The idea of representing the social whole entered into many of the opposition parties, after the changes of 1989. Leaders of Poland's Solidarity, for example—before it broke apart—saw themselves as *successfully* representing the whole, unlike the Communist Party. (See Marody, "The Political Attitudes of Polish Society in the Period of Systematic Transitions"; and Jerzy Szacki, "Polish Democracy: Dreams and Reality," *Social Research* [Winter 1991]: 718.) Anthropological observers of electoral politicking in Romania and Hungary have noted the same thing. Gail Kligman and I attended the founding congress of a new Romanian political party in the summer of 1991, at which it was clear that the party saw itself as representing all of Romanian society rather than a selected group of interests within it; the governing National Salvation Front employed the same rhetoric (see chapter 5 of this volume). Susan Gal likewise observed a local electoral campaign in Hungary in which the most common claim was to represent the *whole* interest, the *community* interest (see Gal, "Local Politics in Post-Socialist Hungary," an unpublished typescript).

40. Jan Urban, "Nationalism as a Totalitarian Ideology," *Social Research* 58 (1991): 776.

41. See also Marody, "The Political Attitudes of Polish Society in the Period of Systematic Transitions," p. 237.

42. I am grateful for a lecture by Czech psychotherapist Helena Klímova, which made the significance of this point apparent to me.

43. I have this story from psychologist Jerrold Post of George Washington University.

44. A similar suggestion is made by Sampson, "Is There an Anthropology of Socialism?" p. 19.

45. Fredrik Barth, *Ethnic Groups and Boundaries* (Boston: Little, Brown, 1969).

46. See also Szacki, "Polish Democracy," pp. 717–18.

47. See Steven Sampson, "Towards an Anthropology of Collaboration in Eastern Europe," *Culture and History* 8 (1991): 116.

48. Communists have not been "othered" in precisely this way everywhere. Andrew Lass notes that in 1991 Czechoslovakia, the Communists were represented not as *ethnic* aliens but as pariahs, lepers, sick or diseased people (Lass, personal communication).

49. My thanks to Melvin Kohn, who posed both the problem and part of the solution I offer here.

50. We see the same mixing of registers—Communist others and ethnic ones—in the vexed question of who should be blamed for the disaster everyone is now facing. After the "revolutions," establishing blame was an obsession all across the bloc, perhaps least marked in Hungary and particularly virulent in Romania and the former Soviet Union. Russian sociologist Igor Kon argues (personal communication) that Russians think it more important to establish *who is guilty* than to decide *what to do*. The obsession with blaming facilitates substituting the ethnic dichotomy for the Communist one—precisely, as Czech president Václav Havel explains, because *everyone* was complicitous with the Communist authorities, who therefore cannot be uniquely blamed.

51. The closest attempt I know of is Edmund Wnuk-Lipinski's paper on social schizophrenia, "Dimorphism of Values and Social Schizophrenia: A Tentative Description," *Sisyphus* 3 (1982): 81–89. See also Ilie Bădescu, *Sincronism european şi cultura critică românească* (Bucharest: Ed. Ştiinţifică, 1984), which has a number of interesting observations linking "social schizophrenia" with the articulation of modes of production.

52. I thank Susan Gal for this observation.

53. From "Destinul culturii româneşti," cited in Alexandru George, "Onesti bibere," *România literară*, 15 August 1991, p. 4.

54. Florin Toma, "De veghe în elanul de ocară," *România literară*, 19 September 1991, p. 3.

55. See also Vamik D. Volkan, *The Need to Have Allies and Enemies: From Clinical Practice to International Relationships* (Northvale, N.J.: Jason Aronson, 1988), p. ix.

56. In taking this line, I follow Alexander Hertz's views on anti-Semitism: "It is not the few Jews . . . who are the source of the anti-Semitism but certain . . . wide-ranging diseases that eat away at the society in which [they] live. Jews become only

a convenient means to facilitate the polarization of certain feelings and reactions" (*The Jews in Polish Culture* [Evanston, Ill.: Northwestern University Press, 1988], p. 1).

57. See Nicolae Gheorghe, "Roma-Gypsy Ethnicity," *Social Research* 48 (1991): 832, 833.

58. See Hertz, *The Jews in Polish Culture*.

59. Jews and Gypsies share an important feature, related to their being "non-European" groups: both (until the formation of Israel) are stateless peoples who defy national borders, in an area obsessed with statehood and borders. They are therefore particularly good symbols of the border-violating mobility of international capital.

60. The Soros Foundation is a philanthropic foundation set up by Hungarian émigré George Soros (living in the U.S.); the "stooges" named are the parties and newspapers of the political opposition. This quotation is by Greater Romania Party Senator Corneliu Vadim Tudor, from his paper *Greater Romania*. I have it from an issue of the opposition paper *22*, 4–10 February 1993, p. 12 (emphasis in original).

61. Raoul Şorban, *Fantasma imperiului ungar şi casa Europei* (Bucharest: Ed. Globus, 1990).

62. See the discussion of this in the next chapter.

63. I refer here to the Congress of Hungarian Émigrés and the World Conference on Transylvania, both held in Budapest during July 1992. Parts of them were shown on Romanian television.

64. See Brackette F. Williams, "A Class Act: Anthropology and the Race to Nation across Ethnic Terrain," *Annual Review of Anthropology* 18 (1989): 401–44.

65. See also my "Whither 'Nation' and 'Nationalism'?" *Daedalus* 122 (Summer 1993).

66. See Verdery, *National Ideology under Socialism*, conclusion. "Complementary schismogenesis" comes from Gregory Bateson, *Naven* (Cambridge: Cambridge University Press, 1936).

67. This final section is a rejoinder to Robert Hayden and owes much to his objections.

68. E. A. Hammel, "Demography and the Origins of the Yugoslav Civil War," *Anthropology Today* 9 (1993): 8.

CHAPTER 5

1. The first statement comes from the founding charter of the Civic Alliance Party, from speeches at its founding convention (see below); the second is from Senator Corneliu Vadim Tudor, *Politica*, 15 February 1992.

2. See my "Theorizing Socialism: A Prologue to the 'Transition,'" *American Ethnologist* 18 (1991): 426–28.

3. See George Konrád and Ivan Szelényi, *The Intellectuals on the Road to Class Power* (Brighton: Harvester Press, 1979), and other works by Szelényi.

4. See my *National Ideology under Socialism: Identity and Cultural Politics in Ceauşescu's Romania* (Berkeley and Los Angeles: University of California Press, 1991), pp. 15–19.

5. The most obvious exception to this way of phrasing things is Hungary, where the defeat of the Party in the 1956 Soviet invasion paved the way for the rise of a

counterelite defined in terms of technical competence—the architects of the New Economic Mechanism.

6. See, for example, the discussion in chapter 7 of *National Ideology under Socialism*.

7. We can see clearly the lengths to which this attitude might go in an example after 1989, the convention of a newly forming opposition party in Romania: after many speakers had proclaimed the new party's high moral standing, someone raised a tiny complaint that the party could not *just* be moral, it must also have a program! (From the Civic Alliance Party's founding convention; see n. 32.)

8. See, for example, Joanna Goven, "Gender Politics in Hungary: Autonomy and Antifeminism," in *Gender Politics and Post-Communism: Reflections from Eastern Europe and the Former Soviet Union*, ed. Nanette Funk and Magda Mueller (New York: Routledge, 1993), pp. 225–26.

9. See the papers in Zbigniew Rau, *The Reemergence of Civil Society in Eastern Europe and the Soviet Union* (Boulder: Westview, 1991), for illustration of these combinations.

10. See n. 32.

11. In political discourse in some East European countries, after 1989 the symbol "civil society" began to float free of the "nation" with which it had sometimes been intertwined earlier, while in other cases building or invoking the one was seen as essential to the health of the other. The separability of the two notions may have been a direct function of the extent to which quasi-autonomous organizations had developed in a given country prior to 1989. (This is a modified form of an idea in László Bruszt and David Stark, "Remaking the Political Field in Hungary: From the Politics of Confrontation to the Politics of Competition," in *Eastern Europe in Revolution*, ed. Ivo Banac [Ithaca: Cornell University Press, 1992], pp. 14–15.) I do not mean that everyone in Hungarian or Polish or Czech politics would now separate "civil society" from "nation" in contrast to Bulgarians and Romanians but, rather, that the *possibility* of separating them in effective political rhetoric became greater in the former countries than in the latter. Wałęsa's not-so-covert anti-Semitism in his presidential campaign shows nonetheless how the two symbols could be combined even in the country where a pre-1989 "civil society" was most fully developed.

12. The name of the original FSN, or National Salvation Front, went to the Petre Roman faction that split off from Iliescu's faction; the latter first called itself the *Democratic* National Salvation Front, subsequently becoming the Party of Romanian Social Democracy, while the Roman faction became the Democratic Party.

13. Among these opposition groups were the "civil society" movements Civic Alliance and Group for Social Dialogue and the National Peasant, Civic Alliance, and National Liberal parties. The most important nationalist parties were the Greater Romania Party (PRM) and Party of Romanian National Unity (PUNR).

14. See *National Ideology under Socialism*, chapters 4–7, for several examples.

15. See ibid., chapters 1 and 3.

16. See Bruszt and Stark, "Remaking the Political Field in Hungary," p. 16, where they suggest that the old elites in the later revolutions learned from the earlier ones how better to stay in power.

17. The report on her arraignment in the opposition paper *România liberă* used exactly the terms of my discussion here: "The power gathered in the hands of Ion Iliescu, the same person who, in December 1989, used the moral capital embodied

by the dissident Doina Cornea to his own benefit, accuses her today of undermining the state power" (international English edition, 12 February 1993, p. 2).

18. I mean by this that a "nationalist" strategy preserves the state structures that members of the old nomenclatura—the social base of the PDSR, PUNR, and PRM— know how to profit from, whereas an "internationalist" strategy would swamp the country with foreign investors and techniques, destroying the advantage of the former Party apparatus.

19. For excellent illustration of this advantage, see Gail Kligman, "Reclaiming the Public: A Reflection on Recreating Civil Society in Romania," *East European Politics and Societies* 4 (1990): 393–438.

20. This has sometimes occurred. See, e.g., Anton Uncu, "Anything Wrong with the Voting Machine? It Works According to Programme," *România liberă* (international English edition), 26 February 1993, p. 7.

21. My sources for these examples are two newspapers central to the political opposition: the daily *România liberă*—I use its weekly international English edition—and the weekly 22, put out by the Group for Social Dialogue.

22. Letter of Eugen Barbu and Corneliu Vadim Tudor to Prime Minister Petre Roman, 2 March 1990. Published in full in 22, 17–23 December 1992, p. 7.

23. See Florin Iaru, "Extremist Vadim Tudor Claims Communism Trial for 'Anti-Romanian Activities,'" *România liberă* (international English edition), 20 November 1993, p. 6.

24. Interview with Emil Constantinescu, summarized in *România liberă* (international English edition), 12 February 1992, p. 4.

25. See Ilie Şerbănescu, "Acestea ne sînt interesele naţionale?" 22, 11–17 February 1993, p. 5.

26. Tia Şerbănescu, "A reapărut 'Scînteia,'" 22, 11–17 February 1993, p. 7.

27. Ibid.

28. See *National Ideology under Socialism*, p. 1.

29. Vera Maria Neagu, "Iliescu Censures Roman Imperialism," *România liberă* (international English edition), 17 November 1992, p. 11.

30. The social composition of this group was varied—at its maximal extent, it included a fair number of working-class people alongside its primarily urban white-collar base. In the Civic Alliance Party, most of the leaders were intellectuals— university professors, journalists, researchers, teachers, and a handful of others (a trade union leader, a peasant, etc.).

31. These three quotations come from speeches made at the Party of Civic Alliance (henceforth PAC) convention, 5 July 1991. All quotations are approximate, inasmuch as I did not tape-record the proceedings but kept only an extended handwritten record of what was said. Translations are my own.

32. Fellow anthropologist Gail Kligman and I witnessed several instances of this at meetings of the civil-society group Civic Alliance in 1991. I am very grateful to Gail Kligman for suggesting that we attend these events and for securing our permission to participate, as well as for many hours of stimulating reflection on what we saw. I wish also to thank the organizers of the Civic Alliance conference for allowing us to attend.

33. Stelian Tănase, speech to the Civic Alliance convention, 7 July 1991. See previous note.

34. The Romanian word is *reîntregire*, which means "making *whole* again." This is

something more, it seems to me, than simple "reunification" (making *one* again), which might seem the more natural English translation. The issue of Moldova was fresh in people's minds because Romanian president Ion Iliescu had not long before signed with Gorbachev a treaty accepting the present borders between Romania and the Soviet Union; this treaty, regarded as a "betrayal of the nation" by many at the conference, guaranteed that at least over the short run, the government of Romania would not press for reintegration.

35. This episode was clear to Gail Kligman and me—though not for any others present except the organizers, who knew the proposed agenda. The fight went on entirely backstage; our (particularly Gail's) friendships with some of the leaders enabled us to witness what would otherwise have been completely invisible.

36. The Convention polled 19 percent of the vote and the PUNR 18 percent.

37. "Masa rotundă la GDS: Ultimele luări de poziție ale U.D.M.R. privitor la minorități și problema națională," 22, 12–18 November 1992, pp. 8–11.

38. Ibid., p. 9.

39. This comment referred particularly to the Party of Romanian National Unity, which had expressed certain attitudes favorable to the Convention and was being explicitly courted by the latter, in hopes of breaking the Front's lock on power in parliament.

40. "Masa rotundă la GDS," p. 11.

41. Ibid., p. 9.

42. This concern of the Romanians is deeply lodged in Transylvania's history. For many centuries a part of the kingdom of Hungary, the region's population has been well over half Romanian since at least the 1760s. Romanians struggled for over 150 years to gain civic rights in Hungary, finally succeeding when, in the wake of World War I, the region passed by plebiscite from the Hungarian to the Romanian state. During World War II, however, Hitler gave the northern part of Transylvania back to Hungary, an event many Romanians found personally traumatic. Most Romanians suspect Hungarians both in their country and in neighboring Hungary of incurable irredentism.

43. "Masa rotundă la GDS," pp. 9–10.

44. I say "rationales" because it is quite possible that the principled argument for decentralization as a way to reduce the Front's power was an ex post facto argument from Hungarians who mainly wanted autonomy for their own reasons.

45. "Masa rotundă la GDS," p. 10.

46. Romania's population is approximately 90 percent Romanian.

47. The immediate response to this comment was to bring in the example of the U.S., where group rights (for blacks, Asians, women, homosexuals, etc.) have gone so far that one is better off being a "minority"—clearly not an appealing prospect in Romania.

48. "Masa rotundă la GDS," p. 11.

49. Ibid., p. 9.

50. See chapter 4.

51. Ilie Neacșu, "Funar și Ardealul," *Europa*, 18–25 January 1993, pp. 1, 3.

52. The writers of these lines also describe the faculty of the University of Cluj (which had put up a fierce resistance to the Romanizing initiatives of Mayor Funar) as "Judaized internationalist freemasons" aiming to make Cluj a "powerful

center of Zionism" (although none of the persons their text names is Jewish). See Emil Ardeleanu, "Inima Transilvaniei, Cluj-Napoca, în vizorul francmasoneriei," *Europa*, 18–25 January 1993, p. 10.

53. Mircea M. Dabija, "Aşa vă vrem, domnule preşedinte!" *Europa*, 18–25 January 1993, p. 3.

54. See, for example, the report in *România liberă* (international English edition), 21 January 1993, p. 11: "Mr. Tudor . . . also reiterated an appeal that a number of purportedly anti-Romanian organizations and publications should be banned"— thus underscoring the appeal quoted in my text. Tudor does not hesitate to use the weapon of expulsion even upon his near associates: a report in the 12 February 1993 *România liberă* (international English edition, p. 11) reveals that he had expelled from his party a member of parliament who had criticized Tudor's dictatorial tendencies.

55. See n. 60 of chapter 4 for explanations. This quote from Tudor appears in an issue of the opposition paper 22, 4–10 February 1993, p. 12; it is from his paper *Greater Romania*, but further details about the source are not given. Emphasis in original.

56. This message was perhaps a reply to an open letter published in 22 by Hungarian Péter Banyai. Banyai had complained that the Civic Alliance's failure to invite Hungarians to speak at its conference in Cluj, following the Cluj Declaration, was having the effect of radicalizing the UDMR, delivering it into the hands of the populist Hungarian nationalists who claimed that Hungarians could not count on the Romanian opposition for support. See Péter Banyai, "Scrisoare deschisă congresului Alianţei Civice," 22 17–23 December 1992, p. 4. The publication locus of this letter guarantees that it was seen by the Civic Alliance and Convention leaders.

57. See Andrei Cornea, "UDMR—victoria moderaţilor," 22, 21–27 January 1993, pp. 8–10.

58. The words of Greater Romania Party leader C. V. Tudor. Cited in Radu Călin Cristea, "Ruleta rusească," 22, 4–10 February 1993, p. 4.

59. Ibid.

60. Horaţiu Pepine, "Viclenie balcanică," 22, 11–17 February 1993, p. 3. See also Cristea, "Ruleta rusească."

61. Andrei Cornea, "Cine sînt 'aliaţii noştri'?" 22, 4–10 February 1993, p. 7.

62. Cristea, "Ruleta rusească."

63. Interview with Nicolae Manolescu, 22, 11–17 February 1993, pp. 8–9.

64. Cristea, "Ruleta rusească."

65. See opinions from the nationalists' press cited in ibid.

66. Oana Armeanu, "Vrea într-adevăr F.D.S.N. integrarea României în Europa?" 22, 4–10 February 1993, p. 5.

67. See Pavel Câmpeanu, "După alegeri," 22, 19–25 November 1992, p. 11. As Câmpeanu shows, the Convention's electorate was also considerably more male than female.

68. Cf. Ladislav Holy, "The End of Socialism in Czechoslovakia," in *Socialism: Ideals, Ideologies, and Local Practice*, ed. C. M. Hann (London and New York: Routledge, 1993), pp. 204–17.

69. See, for example, Gerald Creed, "Civil Society and the Spirit of Capitalism: A Bulgarian Critique," a paper presented at the 1991 annual meeting of the American

Anthropological Association; Christopher Hann, "Property Relations in the New Eastern Europe: The Case of Specialist Cooperatives in Hungary," in *The Curtain Rises: Rethinking Culture, Ideology, and the State in Eastern Europe*, ed. Hermine G. De Soto and David G. Anderson (Atlantic Highlands: Humanities Press, 1993), pp. 99–119; David Kideckel, "Peasants and Authority in the New Romania," in *Romania after Tyranny*, ed. Daniel Nelson (Boulder: Westview, 1992), pp. 67–83; Peter Skalník, "'Socialism Is Dead' and Very Much Alive in Slovakia: Political Inertia in a Tatra Village," in *Socialism: Ideals, Ideologies, and Local Practice*, ed. C. M. Hann (London and New York: Routledge, 1993), pp. 218–26.

70. See Creed, "Civil Society and the Spirit of Capitalism," who makes this argument for Bulgaria.

71. See Elizabeth Dunn, "Rethinking Civil Society," unpublished typescript (1993), pp. 7–9.

72. See the concluding chapter of Verdery, *National Ideology under Socialism*, for a discussion of how socialism fortified national ideology.

73. Nicholas Dirks, "Subaltern Intellectuals and Postcolonial Politics: India," a paper presented at the annual meeting of the American Anthropological Association, 1992.

CHAPTER 6

1. Collectivization began in Romania as early as 1948, in the form of "associations" (*întovărăşiri*). The drive to collectivize fluctuated during the next several years and was pursued with vigor only from 1957. Collectivization was declared complete across the country in 1962 but had been concluded in many villages well before this date. In the text to follow I use the date 1959, when the collective farm in Aurel Vlaicu (the community of my research) was officially inaugurated.

2. State farms (IASs) were run as state enterprises with salaried labor and an appointed director; neither employees nor the director had any necessary relation to the land the farm worked. Much state farmland came from expropriating large landowners, political prisoners, or "war criminals." Collective farms (CAPs), by contrast, were formed from "voluntary" donations of land by villagers who thereby became their members and their labor force. Members were not paid a fixed salary but various forms of remuneration in cash and kind; the rates were determined variously at various points in time. Although a CAP might have members who had given no land to it, the bulk of its members—and quite possibly its president—would have close ties to the land they worked since it had once been theirs. IASs tended to be favored in the distribution of state resources and to specialize in capital- rather than labor-intensive farming; CAPs did both, the latter particularly in the form of members' "private plots."

As of 1980, 61 percent of Romania's agricultural land was in collective farms (including private plots), 30 percent in state institutions, and 9 percent in individual private farms. If we look at arable land rather than all agricultural land, the figures are 74 percent, 21 percent, and 5 percent (David Turnock, *The Romanian Economy in the Twentieth Century* [New York: St. Martin's Press, 1986], p. 184).

3. I thank M.-R. Trouillot for a stimulating discussion that informs my own here.

4. Information obtained from discussions with various specialists and citizens of

the respective countries. To date, there is little published literature on decollectivization. Frederic Pryor's *The Red and the Green: The Rise and Fall of Collectivized
Agriculture in Marxist Regimes* (Princeton: Princeton University Press, 1992) is
chiefly a history, not about postrevolutionary achievements. Papers by scholars such
as David Kideckel, Christopher Hann, and Gerald Creed helpfully discuss the earliest moments of decollectivization in Romania, Hungary, and Bulgaria, but in relatively brief compass; somewhat more detailed is Peter Agócs and Sándor Agócs,
"'The Change Was but an Unfulfilled Promise': Agriculture and the Rural Population in Post-Communist Hungary," *East European Politics and Societies* 8 (Winter
1994). See David Kideckel, "Once Again, the Land: Decollectivization and Social
Conflict in Rural Romania," and Christopher Hann, "Property Relations in the New
Eastern Europe: The Case of Specialist Cooperatives in Hungary," both in *The Curtain Rises: Rethinking Culture, Ideology, and the State in Eastern Europe*, ed. Hermine G. DeSoto and David G. Anderson (Atlantic Highlands: Humanities Press,
1993); Gerald Creed, "An Old Song in a New Voice: Decollectivization in Bulgaria,"
in *East-Central European Communities: The Struggle for Balance in Turbulent Times*,
ed. David Kideckel (Boulder: Westview, 1995), pp. 25–45; and Agócs and Agócs,
"The Change Was but an Unfulfilled Promise."

5. This provision was not included in Law 18 but was passed later. Because of it,
there has been much less argument in Romania than in neighboring Hungary over
how to ensure that people receive land of a quality comparable to their previous
holdings.

6. These qualifications apply to land distribution in Armenia and Albania, for instance.

7. Most conspicuously the head of the National Peasant Party, Corneliu Coposu.

8. Stelian Tănase, "Simple Note," *Sfera politicii* 11 (November 1993): 4.

9. The idea of property restitution was obviously important to the historical parties for not only its moral justice but also its potential to create a material base for the
parties' members. For some who advocated it, it may also have been motivated by
revenge—by the desire to destroy all that had happened under the Communists, who
had ruined these people's lives and fortunes.

10. According to the 1948 agricultural census, 6.6 percent of all farms exceeded
ten hectares, but the figures do not indicate how much land they contain (see Henry
L. Roberts, *Rumania: Political Problems of an Agrarian State* [New Haven: Yale University Press, 1951], p. 374). I am uncertain how the ten-hectare figure was chosen.
One participant in the process said it came from calculating how much land would
have to be made available so as to give something to landless village residents. There
may also have been other kinds of political calculation, however.

11. I am indebted to Sorin Antohi for this observation. Antohi is convinced that
this was indeed the aim of the ten-hectare limit; I believe its determination was more
complex.

12. As explained in chapter 5, n. 12, the names of Romania's main parties changed
several times, in confusing ways. For most villagers, the party's label mattered less
than Iliescu's candidacy.

13. I had spent several days in the village during each of the preceding three
summers as well. For a social history of this community, known before 1926 as
Binținți, see my *Transylvanian Villagers: Three Centuries of Political, Economic, and*

Ethnic Change (Berkeley and Los Angeles: University of California Press, 1983). The name of the village is pronounced "vlAiku," its inhabitants are Vlaiceni ("vlaich*E*ni"); the commune (Geoagiu) is "djo.Adju." According to commune statistics, Vlaicu's population in 1992 was 915, in approximately 270 households.

14. Other reasons why my discussion does not apply readily to all of Romania are Transylvania's higher population density, which means there is less arable land available to resolve conflicting claims, and the longer history of peasant ownership there than elsewhere—that is, Transylvanians' sense of private ownership was more highly developed. Elsewhere in the country, peasants became proprietors in large numbers only after the land reform of 1921 broke up *latifundia* and distributed them to villagers.

Vlaicu, for its part, is not wholly "typical" of Transylvanian villages—as an uneasy county official hastened to remind me. It is multiethnic and has a high percentage (about a third) of inmigrants, and its location subjected it to more than the normal number of border adjustments. Believing, however, that atypical cases are especially revealing of social processes, I am not daunted by these aberrations but find Vlaicu an excellent vantage point for examining property restitution.

15. A land-rental law passed in 1994 alters the situation, enabling people with land in IASs to repossess it after five years if they wish.

16. This was in 1993; in 1994 the figure was to be raised to 600 kilograms per share. The wheat prices used are those set by the state, not those of the free market.

17. See the discussion, in what follows, on the property regime of socialism.

18. Once people had submitted their petitions for land and been awarded an amount, the land commission measured this amount for them in the appropriate number of fields and gave them an affidavit stating how much they had received. This affidavit is a provisional document; unlike a property deed, it cannot be used as collateral with a bank or as the basis for selling one's land. The amounts on affidavits are subject to revision if others challenge allotments in court. Because the affidavit gives only a person's total land area and does not state where the land is or in how many pieces, people who do not realize that some of it may count as IAS dividends (rather than as actual workable surface) can be genuinely confused about what they are turning over to the association.

19. All across Romania, agricultural associations were formed following liquidation of the collective farms. Their raison d'être was that people who received land from the CAP did not also receive farm implements; hence most of them were unable to work their new acquisitions. The task of the associations is to arrange for the cultivation of its members' lands, paying the members a percentage of the yield for each season. Far from all households give their land to the association: those who have managed to buy tractors or who find themselves allergic to the idea of communal farming arrange to work it themselves. In Vlaicu, about half of all landowning families have at least some land in the association.

20. I heard rumors that some people in the governing council of the association were engaged in a comparable scam: they would tell the association that they were giving it their land, and would then assign the same piece to someone in a share-cropping arrangement and collect produce from both sources. This scam and the one discussed in my text could work only because of the chaotic state of property restitution at the time: because the association rarely knew with precision where fields were

that had been turned over to them, if they found someone working land they thought was theirs, they might simply move over a few meters and proceed.

21. For helpful discussions of this process in other socialist contexts, see István Rév, "The Advantages of Being Atomized," *Dissent* 34 (1987): 335–50; and Vivienne Shue, "Taxation, 'Hidden Land,' and the Chinese Peasant," *Peasant Studies Newsletter* 3 (1974): 1–12.

22. None of my informants could recall exactly the percentages taken, but all remembered that there was a big break around four hectares. For some figures on the magnitude of quotas in Hungary, see Martha Lampland, *The Object of Labor: The Commodification of Agrarian Labor in Socialist Hungary* (Chicago: University of Chicago Press, forthcoming).

23. Cf. Rév, "The Advantages of Being Atomized."

24. Gail Kligman, who has worked extensively with Romanian population statistics, finds a large number of similarly "elastic" categories there.

25. See, for example, my "Theorizing Socialism: A Prologue to the 'Transition,'" *American Ethnologist* 18 (1991): 419–39.

26. I use the word "yoke" to translate the Romanian *iugăr* (cf. *jug*, yoke). This form of measurement is widespread throughout the world, indicating the amount of land one can reasonably expect to plow in a day with a yoke of oxen.

27. C. Martinovici and N. Istrati, *Dicționarul Transilvaniei, Banatului și celorlate ținuturi alipite* (Cluj: Ardealul, 1921). Data in this work are based on the 1910 Hungarian and the 1920 Romanian censuses.

28. One was the nominal listing of individuals with their land, animals, and agricultural implements, known as the Borderoul Agricol de Producție, or BAP. I consulted this listing in the state archives in Bucharest (Institutul Central de Statistică, *Recensămîntul agricol și al populației din ianuarie 1948*). The second listing is in the state archive branch in Deva, Hunedoara county ("Recapitulația generală a tarlalelor din hotarul comunei Aurel Vlaicu." Fond Camera Agricolă Deva, dos. 49/1948, Aurel Vlaicu). It shows fields, rather than individuals; each field is listed with the persons who hold parcels in it and the cultigens planted on each parcel.

29. These figures appear in an unnamed file kept in the offices of the former CAP in Vlaicu.

30. From the 1988 cadastre for Vlaicu, kept in and used by the OCOTA office in the county capital (*Registrul cadastral al parcelelor, Aurel Vlaicu*, 1988).

31. This figure is from a file in the commune archives, dated 1 January 1990; the file is entitled "Situații Centralizate Rapoarte [*sic*] Fond Funciar: Documente în Sprijinul Aplicării Legii 18/1991." Various tables in this file give contradictory figures for the amounts of land brought into the collective. While I was copying these figures, a lively discussion went on around me as to how unreliable they were.

32. The figures 599 and 759 hectares are from the topographer in charge of measuring and redistributing the land in Vlaicu; the 631-hectare figure is from "Situații Centralizate Rapoarte Fond Funciar: Documente în Sprijinul Aplicării Legii 18/1991."

33. The motive for this "gift," I was told, had been Gelmar's inclusion in the collective of neighboring Geoagiu, a village with very little and very poor-quality land. In order to increase the prospects for its success, the fertile soils of Vlaicu's floodplain were included in the production plans for Gelmar.

34. "Situații Centralizate Rapoarte Fond Funciar: Documente în Sprijinul Aplicării Legii 18/1991."

35. "Se 'evaporă' hectarele?" *Expres*, 9–15 August 1994, p. 10.

36. See Daniela Păunescu, *Drept cooperatist* (Bucharest: Universitatea din București, Facultate de Drept, 1974), p. 46. This "volitional" character was in most cases, of course, a fiction: the coercion applied to get people into the collectives was a favorite topic of village discussion even before 1989. I note that in Romanian, collective farms are referred to as *cooperative* (cooperatives), not collectives; I prefer the latter since it is more commonly used in English.

37. Ibid., p. 161.

38. Ibid., pp. 56, 83. Local officials observed this difference in practice quite variably, but recognition of it was not wholly absent. For example, I asked one former mayor of Geoagiu whether he had observed any distinction between state and collective farms during his tenure as mayor; he replied that he had never considered that he could impose solutions on the collectives as he could on the state farms. Even if this answer does not conform with his actual behavior, it indicates his awareness of the distinction mentioned in my text.

39. Ibid., p. 127.

40. Indeed, when I discussed this problem with a member of the local land commission, he acknowledged that he had not realized the implications of the house-garden problem.

41. The law specifies that undisturbed use of a piece of land for a certain length of time entitles its user to claim it as owner. I am uncertain what that length of time is: the two judges with whom I discussed this matter gave me two different figures, twenty years and thirty years.

42. The decree specified that the exchanges were "obligatory for all owners whose lands are subject to commassation" (Republica Populară Romînia, *Legislația civilă uzuală II* [Bucharest: Ed. Științifică, 1956], p. 101).

43. Ibid., p. 102.

44. Those who joined the early associations and collectives were usually the poorer peasants rather than the better off.

45. The money paid by most state farms to their "shareholders" is much less than the income a person could receive by working the land, although the shareholding arrangement does have the advantage of getting one's land worked for one.

46. Despite considerable effort, I was unable to find out how big this property is—as was the woman who was trying to claim restitution of a part of it. A crucial file from the Vlaicu Land Register is missing; moreover, because the estate straddles the border with Gelmar, some of its area would be listed only in the Land Register for that village, to which I did not have access.

47. Their insistence on the former sites precluded rationalizing the property structure through a new commassation, however. In Cigmău, the topographer told me, the average size of newly established holdings is 3–4 hectares; but the average number of parcels per holding is 20–30 and the average parcel size thus no bigger than the old "private plot" of .15 hectares!

48. How can the claims be insatiable? Law 18 specified that land could be claimed by any relative up to the fourth degree. This means that cousins, aunts, and uncles, as well as the original owners plus their children, have the right to claim land. Many

of these people would not have received it had normal inheritance practices prevailed; their claims thus reduce the surface area that would have entered into a "reserve" for distribution to the landless.

49. Party considerations seem to have played no role in this. Geoagiu's mayor and vice-mayor as of 1993 were from the Democratic Agrarian Party, whose members are largely the managers and technical staff of state and collective farms, not village farmers.

50. I never witnessed bribe taking, but villagers allege that it occurs. See the discussion in what follows on local-level abuse of power, however, for arguments that might call this allegation into question.

51. In a neighboring village I found a much more rigorous procedure: the commission met in a room into which one person at a time would enter, the door would be locked to prevent others from coming in, and the complaint would be pursued to resolution. Clearly the modus operandi of commissions varies widely, a function of the probity and degree of organization of their members.

52. In Hunedoara county the figure was 28 percent. Figures by personal communication from the Romanian Ministry of Agriculture.

53. I was unable to determine exactly how many court cases involving land were pending in the courts. The leader of the main opposition group in Romanian politics, Emil Constantinescu, used the figure of four hundred thousand in a May 1994 speech on television, but the paper *Expres* published a lower figure of three hundred thousand (19–25 October 1994, p. 10).

54. The land of each village is divided into a number of named fields and subfields. As I was able to confirm from maps dating from the 1880s, many of these names are of at least a century's duration. For Vlaicu, most of them appear to be locative, rather than invoking personal names: thus "At the Pear Trees," "Behind the Church," "The Vinerea Road," "Where the Parcels are Long," "Where the Parcels are Short," etc. A few invoke persons: i.e., "At Barcsay" (*Bârceana*, from Barscay, a noble Hungarian family living in the village in the nineteenth century), or "At the Ford by the Priest's" (*Vadul popii*). For many of these names, no one I asked could explain the meaning.

55. Official measurement was usually taken in yokes until the Communist regime came to power and began to use measurements in hectares. Villagers are genuinely confused about what measure applies, having become accustomed to "hectares" and not realizing that a different measure applied when their parents were property owners. Since a yoke is slightly over half a hectare (.5757), the difference is considerable.

56. A few of these people spend the winters in town with relatives. Like urban Romanians, Germans who live in town also can claim land, and do.

57. See Verdery, *Transylvanian Villagers*, chapter 5.

58. In the early phase of property restitution, when many villages were forming associations to work the land received, it was common to give association members their land in a single block for ease and efficiency of cultivation. The Germans' request for a single block thus conformed with practice up that point. One need not suspect, as Vlaiceni do, that the mayor was bribed to give them this large field.

59. Andrei Cornea, "Directocraţia remaniază guvernul," 22, (16–22 March 1994), p. 7.

60. For these three cases, I know the party affiliations of only the second with

certainty (he is in the Democratic Agrarian Party). I did not note those of the other two.

61. See Jadwiga Staniszkis, *The Dynamics of the Breakthrough in Eastern Europe* (Berkeley and Los Angeles: University of California Press, 1993), for a discussion of how the inability of higher-level Party authorities to deliver the goods to those beneath them contributed to undermining Party rule.

62. Gail Kligman (personal communication) points out that in this respect, as in several others, the situation I report is not universal. In the northern Transylvanian region of Maramureş, for instance, long-term labor migration by men gave women almost complete responsibility for running family farms. Kligman doubts that Maramureş women would let themselves be pushed around as some of Vlaicu's widows do.

63. Another group likely to be cheated consists of people without social connections, or people who are not themselves valuable as connections. Those least likely to be cheated are powerful persons who could cause trouble for a local commission that trod on their rights. Even this is no guarantee, however, for a judge I know told me how she couldn't seem to get four hectares belonging to her family.

64. My term "local officials" here includes officers of village associations, who are among the chief beneficiaries of the land obtained by urbanites. Not all such officers will handle the land unscrupulously, but urbanites are the association members most easily cheated if one is bent on doing so. As is clear from my text, the most common form of abuse is to underpay the landowner for use of the land. Commune mayors are more likely to abuse the rights of urban-based proprietors by assigning the amount of their land to a state farm, which will pay them little or nothing, and working the actual land themselves.

65. The data concern three sorts of conflicts: between Germans and the Romanian farmers impropriated on their land, among Romanians who are all locally born and gave land to the CAP, and between locals and the inmigrants who worked in the CAP but gave it no land. My sources are my discussions with people and their responses to questions about whose ownership claim ought to prevail, volunteered opinions on this topic, and arguments that I overheard as I followed the land commission on its rounds.

66. Lampland, *The Object of Labor*.

67. For a further discussion of this sense of entitlement, see chapter 3 of this volume.

68. Special thanks to Ashraf Ghani for the ideas in this paragraph.

CHAPTER 7

1. That project, an inquiry into decollectivization, was supported by a grant from the International Research and Exchanges Board (IREX). Among IREX's funders are the National Endowment for the Humanities, the United States Information Agency, and the U.S. Department of State, which administers the Russian, Eurasian, and East European Research Program (Title VIII) set up by the U.S. Congress.

Because my research focused on a topic other than Caritas, I did not collect data on Caritas systematically. Far from being an "opportunistic" sample, mine is serendipitous; the newspapers from which I clipped Caritas stories (primarily *România liberă, Evenimentul zilei, Adevărul, Expres,* and *Cuvîntul liber—Free Romania, Event of the Day, The Truth, Express,* and the *Free Word)* tended to be critical of the scheme. I sought to compensate for these deficiencies with some pro-Caritas brochures and by talking with a wide variety of people—from various parts of Romania (though concentrated in Transylvania); Germans, Hungarians, and Romanians; farmers, industrial workers, and white-collar workers, in both urban and rural areas. Although I cannot present statistically sound results, I believe my data broadly capture the so-called "Caritas phenomenon."

2. The site of my research was the community of Aurel Vlaicu, in the county of Hunedoara, south-central Transylvania. For a social history of this community, see my *Transylvanian Villagers: Three Centuries of Political, Economic, and Ethnic Change* (Berkeley and Los Angeles: University of California Press, 1983).

3. This was worth 350,000 lei at the time, representing perhaps five months' salary for a professor (see n. 10).

4. The different schemes in these countries operated according to a variety of rules. For example, the largest ones in Yugoslavia (Serbia) were banks promising high interest; they worked only with hard currency and are thought to have been a mechanism by which the government aimed to seize the hard currency reserves of the populace (R. Hayden, personal communication). The best-known Czech schemes and the Russian MMM were complicated investment schemes that sold shares in themselves and promised excessive dividends, rather than turn over people's savings as Caritas did.

MMM was reported to have had one to two million investors as of August 1993 (its organizer, Sergei Mavrodi, claimed ten million) (*Financial Times,* 30–31 July 1993, p.9). Tax police following the scheme's closure estimated the worth of its shares at ten trillion rubles. Although these figures equal or exceed those for Caritas, the population of Russia is many times larger than Romania's twenty-three million. (For details on MMM, see the *Financial Times* for July through September 1994, as well as the Foreign Broadcast Information Service and RFE-RL reports for this same period.)

5. This is the most widespread of the rumors about his former occupation. See, e.g., *Business Central Europe,* October 1993, p. 55; and *Financial Times,* 18 October 1993, p. 3.

6. I have this from a member of the Hungarian parliament.

7. Michael Shafir, "The Caritas Affair: A Transylvanian Eldorado," *RFE-RL Reports* 2 (24 September 1993): 24.

8. This was confirmed by the prosecutor in charge of the case against him following his August 1994 arrest. See *România liberă* (international English edition), 3–9 September 1994, p. 12.

9. The Romanian currency unit is the *leu* (plural *lei*). It is difficult to give equivalents for figures in lei, owing to the 250–300 percent inflation and the discrepancy between official and black-market exchange rates. Stoica's 100,000 lei would have been worth about $300 (at the official rate) in the spring of 1992; by September 1993 it was worth $100; and by May 1994, when the scheme collapsed, $60.

10. Owing to ever-widening discrepancies in income after 1989 (as well as the factors in the preceding note), it is difficult to express in terms of average salaries the magnitude of monetary sums for Romanians who deposited in Caritas. In summer 1993, when many people were putting in 20,000–40,000 as a first deposit, some

Romanians were receiving collective-farm pensions of 5,000 lei per month, university professors were earning 60–80,000, industrial workers might have (on paper, at least) over 100,000, and miners (Romania's best-paid workers) over 250,000.

11. I obtained these figures from a cashier at one of the deposit centers in Cluj, in September 1993.

12. See chapter 2 in this volume; and Pavel Câmpeanu, *România: coada pentru hrană, un mod de viaţa* (Bucharest: Ed. Litera, 1994). Several publications noted that the "psychology of the queue" was an important part of Caritas's success (e.g., *România liberă*, 22 July 1993, p. 1).

13. Shafir, "The Caritas Affair," p. 24; and *Adevărul*, 10 August 1993, p. 3. There were different sorts of inside tracks, as well—those for regular depositors who found a way to circumvent the queue, and those for well-placed cronies of the organizer and his patron, for instance.

14. See *România liberă* (international English edition), 26 May–3 June 1994, p. 3, and 10–16 September 1994, p. 4. Cf. also *România liberă* (international English edition), 23–29 July 1994, p. 11, concerning hidden lists and premature reward in another "mutual-aid game."

15. See, e.g., stories in *Evenimentul zilei*, 9 October 1993, p. 4, and 16 October 1993, p. 8; *Adevărul*, 15 October 1993, p. 1, and 19–20 March 1994, p. 1; *România liberă*, 21 March 1994, p. 1, and 4 May 1994, p. 16.

16. One politician close to Caritas claimed that 260 parliamentarians had deposited in the scheme (*Adevărul*, 29 October 1993, p. 2).

17. Officials at the U.S. Department of State told me that reliable figures on the numbers of depositors cannot be had. The Department of State was sufficiently concerned about the possible effects of Caritas to have gotten regular reports on it, both classified and unclassified. The International Monetary Fund was at that time negotiating a new standby loan with Romania; given the scheme's apparent magnitude, IMF negotiators were doubtless concerned about its possible impact on Romania's finances, but the IMF was not able to provide me with reliable figures on its size. (My thanks to Mark Asquino and Brady Kiesling for discussion of this point.)

18. See Dan Zamfirescu and Dumitru Cerna, *Fenomenul Caritas sau mântuirea românilor prin ei înşişi* (Bucharest: Ed. Roza Vânturilor, 1993), p. 17. Cluj mayor Funar also used these large figures.

19. E.g., *Evenimentul zilei*, 27 October 1993, p. 3; *Adevărul*, 18 March 1994, p. 8; *Mesagerul*, 7 December 1993, p. 5.

20. For example: Adam Le Bor, "Pyramid Game Grips Romania," *London Times*, 19 November 1993, p. 11; "Ponzi, by Any Other Name," *Economist* 328 (18–24 September 1993): 87; Peter Maass, "Romanians Grasp a Straw," *Washington Post*, 17 October 1993, p. A25; Jane Perlez, "Pyramid Scheme a Trap for Many Romanians," *New York Times*, 13 November 1993, pp. 1, 47; Virginia Marsh, "Faith, Hope and Caritas," *Business Central Europe*, October 1993, p. 55; Hugo Dixon, "Pyramids with Giddy Heights," *Financial Times*, 18 October 1993, p. 3; and Charles Lane, "Ubi Caritas," *New Republic*, 8 November 1993, p. 9.

21. The chief editor of the *Transylvanian Messenger* said in an undated interview (but before 6 October 1993) that the paper was publishing sixteen thousand names daily; this would mean about half a million per month. (See Gheorghe Smeoreanu et al., *Caritas: radiografia unui miracol* [Rîmnicul Vîlcea: Ed. Antim Ivireanul, 1993], p.23.) There are problems with estimating the number of depositors by the num-

ber of names in the *Messenger*, since a given person might deposit several times in a single month; thus the figure of two million for three months could include many duplicates. But at the same time, a single person might deposit for many others under his or her own name; the friend who deposited my money was also depositing for at least six others, whose names appeared on no lists. Moreover, the names of people on the "inside track" might not be on the lists, either. For these reasons, the number of names in the *Messenger* may in fact underestimate the total number of people depositing.

22. *Evenimentul zilei*, 10 November 1993, p. 3.

23. *New York Times*, 13 November 1993, p. 1.

24. *Evenimentul zilei*, 10 November 1993, p. 3. For dollar equivalents, see n. 9.

25. *România liberă* (international English edition), 3–9 September 1994, p. 12, cites this as the state prosecutor's figure for the total amount circulated through Caritas. In August 1994, Stoica himself claimed to owe depositors $700 billion, which would be approximately 1.2 trillion lei (*România liberă* [international English edition], 6–12 August 1994, p. 5). I have the figure for government expenditures from the IMF.

26. *New York Times*, 13 November 1993; *Economist*, 18–25 September 1993.

27. My thanks to Mugur Isărescu for this information. The 2.5 trillion figure for liquid reserves is from the International Monetary Fund, for the month of June. A Romanian source gives the figure of 2.9 trillion lei for July and 3.1 trillion for August (*România liberă*, 20 October 1994, p. 4).

28. *România liberă* (international English edition), 3–9 September 1994, p. 12. Caritas paid taxes on profits (Stoica designated 10 percent of the proceeds as profit, used to pay employees, make donations, etc.), and a value-added tax was additionally withheld from the payouts to depositors, beginning in the summer of 1993.

29. *Adevărul*, 18 December 1993, p. 4; *Evenimentul zilei*, 14 October 1993, p. 2. Again, equivalents for these amounts are problematic. *România liberă*, 22 July 1993, p. 16, states that 100,000 lei is the mean salary for three months.

30. For instance, I saw signs in Deva, capital of Hunedoara county, saying "Tourist agency Coratrans organizes excursions to Cluj (for Caritas) leaving every Tuesday and Friday at 16:00, price 3,850 lei round trip." Deva is about three hours' drive from Cluj.

31. The newspaper *Expres*, 13–19 September 1994, p. 8, reported that the banking system was giving very little credit to the private sector, reserving its funds chiefly for state firms and joint ventures.

32. The bank interest on savings accounts eventually (winter 1994) rose to 100 percent or more (though not before many people's savings had vanished), successfully attracting funds from the pyramids.

33. The 30 percent figure is from June 1993, courtesy of the IMF.

34. Precisely this difficulty with bank interest rates was what drove two friends of mine to sell some farm animals and put the proceeds in Caritas, turning their investment over twice and buying a tractor, because exorbitant interest had foreclosed their making the purchase through "normal" banking channels.

35. Since the early 1980s there has been yet another spate of pyramid schemes in the U.S.; there has also been a proliferation of multilevel marketing programs, whose relation to pyramid schemes is sometimes very close. See, for example, stories in *American Heritage*, November 1994, pp. 18–20; *Atlantic*, October 1987, pp. 84–90;

Baltimore Sun, 10 December 1994, pp. 1B, 4B; *Business Week*, 3 September 1990, pp. 40–42; *Forbes*, 11 November 1991, pp. 139–48, and 15 March 1993, pp. 46–48; *Los Angeles Times*, 25 August 1991, p. D3; *New York Times*, 28 March 1993, section 13NJ, p. 1; and *Washington Post*, 12 October 1991, p. C1, and 11 April 1991, p. B11.

36. Indeed, the Roman Catholic diocese of Oradea protested the name, threatening to bring suit against Stoica for damage to the good name of their organization. See *România liberă*, 9 August 1993, p. 16.

37. This seems unlikely, for he was able to open a large supermarket with the proceeds.

38. This equaled about $112,500 at the time—a far larger sum in the Romanian context than it is in the American one.

39. See, e.g., *Evenimentul zilei*, 18 December 1993, p. 4; and *Adevărul*, 14 February 1994, p. 1.

40. My sources for these are the reports of friends who claimed to have certain knowledge of the organizations they were naming; Alexandru Stănescu, a researcher doing a project about Caritas; the head of one consumer co-op; the president of the Aurel Vlaicu village association; *Adevărul*, 19 November 1993, p. 1; and *România liberă*, 19 March 1994, p. 1.

41. In Romanian: "Din Sibiu în Făgăraş, Nu-i pui de românaş, Să nu joace Caritas"; "A apărut un om, Pe toţi ne-a salvat, Lăsaţi pe Domnul Stoica Împărat." I have the first from ethnographer Claude Karnoouh and the other from *România liberă*, 20 October 1993, p. 16.

42. In Romanian: "Trenule ce duci cu tine, Atîta rău şi-atîta bine, Opreşti şi iei din gară-n gară, Durerea din întreaga ţară. La Caritas, La Caritas, Speranţa noastră ne-a rămas, Durerea noastră şi speranţa, Ce poate să ne schimbe viaţa." See "Ţiganul Viorel Mărunţelu a compus primul cîntec dedicat patronului 'Caritas'-ului," *Evenimentul zilei*, 4 November 1993, p. 10.

43. The verb used by nearly everyone to describe the money they received from Caritas was *a cîştiga*, which translates as both "to win" and "to earn." It is appropriately used for the wage one receives at work, prizes awarded, the proceeds of games of chance, a victory in a competition, and the sympathy of one's fellows. Thus its root meaning is "to obtain, acquire, or get," without implying whether the thing gotten is *earned* or not. The verb most often used for participating, however, was *a juca*, "to play," as in a game: *am jucat la Caritas*, meaning "I played [at] Caritas." One might also say "I deposited" (*am depus*) or "I put" (*am băgat*) money in Caritas.

44. See n. 20.

45. Among the most critical were *România liberă*, *Evenimentul zilei*, and *Cotidianul*.

46. In fact, the Romanian Supreme Court had already issued a decision banning such "games," on 15 September 1992 (Decision 150). This may partly explain why Stoica regularly insisted that Caritas was not a "mutual-aid game" (*joc de întrajutorare*) but a "financial circuit" (*circuit financiar*).

47. *Mesagerul transilvan*, 24 September 1993, p. 1.

48. Sources for some of the points in this paragraph: *Adevărul*, 12 November 1993, p. 1; *Adevărul*, 2 November 1993, p. 1; *Evenimentul zilei*, 6 November 1993, p.1; *Evenimentul zilei*, 4 March 1994, p. 1; *Evenimentul zilei*, 5 March 1994, p. 8; *Adevărul*, 11 March 1994, p. 1; and *Adevărul*, 4 March 1994, p. 1.

49. *România liberă*, 20 May 1994, p. 1; *Adevărul*, 6 June 1994, p. 1. This unfortunately would not include the author of this paper, since my money was deposited under the name of someone who had already turned sums over twice.

50. According to the prosecutor in the case, these charges would carry a jail sentence of two to seven years (22, 31 August–6 September 1994, p. 3). As of this writing, Stoica had been convicted of fraud in the first of many lawsuits against him and sentenced to six years imprisonment. Whether he will serve out his sentence fully is an open question.

51. I reach this estimate—more conservative than that reported in the *New York Times*—in the following way. Households are a more meaningful unit than individuals for this calculation, given that 1) one-third or more of the population is under twenty years old and is unlikely to be participating seriously in the game, and 2) my experience suggests that although it did happen that spouses deposited individually, in many if not most cases the household deposited as a unit. If we divide Romania's population by 3.2 (the figure given in Romanian statistics for the number of persons per household), we get 7,187,500 households. Taking what I consider to be the lowest plausible figure for participation—two million depositors—and assuming, conservatively, that as many as half of these deposits would be made by entire households and the other half might be duplicated within a household, we have 1.5 million participating households, or 21 percent of all households.

52. I heard several stories about people who could no longer find babysitters, housekeepers, temporary construction workers, or care-givers for the elderly, since no one was willing to spend time doing this kind of work when they could sit at home and wait for their Caritas money to roll in. The household of some Bucharest friends was turned upside down because they had to bring their aging mother-in-law from Cluj, where nursing care was no longer available, and move her into their sons' bedroom (the sons moving out to various aunts and grandparents).

53. Comparable effects were achieved differently in other East European countries. For instance, in Poland domestic savings were soaked up by monetary policies, which pushed inflation so high that people had to change dollar savings into złoty just to make ends meet. See Jeffrey Sachs, *Poland's Jump to the Market Economy* (Cambridge: MIT Press, 1993), p. 53.

54. At least some of this potential was realized: I knew of cases in which Caritas earnings had bought trucks for transport and tractors or other instruments of agricultural production, funded small businesses, or enabled payment of bank debts on businesses already established. Caritas served as a source of "windfall profits" of a magnitude nothing else could produce.

55. This took at least two forms: a redistribution from the many to the few, and possibly another from the non-Transylvanian parts of Romania to Transylvania.

56. "Loto" was a classic lottery; one selected a set of numbers and waited to see if they would be drawn. "Loz-în-Plic" was simpler: one bought an envelope inside which was (or was not) an announcement of a prize. "Prono-Sport" involved betting on specific sports teams for particular games. Periodic drawings of names for autos were carried out by savings institutions, inter alia, using the numbers of savings accounts for a random draw. One pursued this kind of luck by opening a specific kind of savings account.

57. Thanks to David Kideckel for this point. Even though weddings cost a lot of

money to put on, most of those held during my 1970s field research made a substantial "profit." At that time, the sum usually given by guests was about 3,000 lei, or a month's average wage for factory work. Some weddings cleared 80–100,000—thus two and a half to three years' wage, or about the price of a new Romanian car. Weddings might therefore provide a major windfall. (Funerals, by contrast, might wipe out long-accumulated savings and were thus comparable, from the individual's point of view, to a stock-market crash.)

58. By the spring of 1994 the government's fiscal policies had brought the official and black-market rates for hard currency into alignment, but for the year prior, the discrepancy between the two rates was substantial.

Few could tell me why Stoica would pick furniture rather than something else; the only reason offered was that it had to be something valuable with a good market in the West, and furniture met these conditions (other items mentioned were mineral water, cement, and porcelain). During the Ceauşescu period, several industries had operated specifically for export, and furniture manufacture was one of them. Furniture also seemed to have disappeared from the internal market or else was selling at astronomical cost, a fact that may have predisposed people toward this explanation.

59. Herein may lie the significance of popular representations of Stoica as part Gypsy, as well as the increase in newspaper reports (after Caritas had stopped making payouts) of Gypsy participation in it. The link between Caritas and Gypsies—including threats against Stoica by the upstart emperor Iulian I, who was in revolt against the Gypsy king Cioaba and perhaps (like Funar) using Caritas for his own political ends—is a fascinating angle I cannot cover here. (See, e.g., *Adevărul*, 5–6 February 1994, p. 5.)

60. Cf. *Adevărul*, 17 November 1993, pp. 1–2.

61. This theory may well have something to it. It is widely believed both inside and outside Romania that 1989 opened a new drug-smuggling corridor through Eastern Europe; in addition, smuggling of armaments, oil, and other goods through Romania to Serbia is extremely likely. Anthropologist Claude Karnoouh learned from well-placed sources in Budapest and Warsaw the routes by which illegal accumulations and Party funds had been moved out of Hungary and Poland, through a series of transactions with local banks and transfers to Western ones. Probably the more rudimentary state of Romania's banking system and the later entry of Western finance capital into that country closed this option for disposing of the funds from Romania's Communist Party or illegal enterprise. Instead, they would have to be laundered internally, such as on inside tracks of Caritas. The hypothesis gains credence from Stoica's failure to put an upper limit on the size of withdrawals—a chief cause of the eventual collapse of the pyramid's base. If the point was to run huge sums through the first few cycles until all were "clean," an upper limit would only be an impediment.

62. It is true that once Caritas stopped paying out, the exchange rates for foreign currency stabilized and then dropped. At the height of its operation in Cluj, foreign currency was much more expensive in that city than elsewhere in Romania.

63. The "support" might also, of course, be indirect—either the absence of legislation to control such schemes (Russia's MMM scheme aroused much official reflection about the lack of legislation to protect citizens, for example), or the clear benefits to the government from letting the scheme persist: its absorbing the "mon-

etary overhang," and its providing people with a means other than strikes and protests for coping with inflation.

64. Andrei Cornea, "Se convertesc oare comuniştii la capitalism?" *22*, 16–22 February 1994, p. 6. This figure would constitute almost two-thirds of the level of state expenditures.

65. My personal inclinations favor a money-laundering scheme as part of Caritas's pool of funds (see also what follows), and international pressure on the government as contributing to its fall. Off-the-record discussions indicate that international lending agencies were indeed concerned about the fiscal and social instability—and especially the potential for ethnic violence—that would accompany Caritas's collapse; they expressed these concerns quite clearly to the Romanian government, without, however, making loans conditional on the government's bringing Caritas to an end. The timing of Iliescu's comments about the scheme's fragility and of changed National Bank fiscal policy makes it likely that this informal pressure indeed contributed to the scheme's collapse. (Significantly, the collapse of the MMM scheme in Russia preceded the arrival of an IMF team to negotiate a standby loan in that country as well. See *FBIS-SOV-94* no. 172, 6 September 1994, p. 38.) This note shows that my Romanian associates succeeded in teaching me to look for conspiracies.

66. See my "Theorizing Socialism: A Prologue to the 'Transition,'" *American Ethnologist* 18 (1991): 422–23.

67. Czech Finance Minister Václav Klaus put it in almost exactly these terms in 1990: "The aim is to let the invisible hand of the market act and to replace the hand of the central planner" (cited in Ladislav Holy, "Culture, Market Ideology and Economic Reform in Czechoslovakia," in Roy Dilley, ed., *Contesting Markets: Analyses of Ideology, Discourse and Practice* [Edinburgh: Edinburgh University Press, 1992], p. 236).

68. Smeoreanu et al., *Caritas*, p. 7. Random ethnographic details suggest that he was to some extent succeeding. One friend, asked whether Caritas money was like any other money, replied, "Only your attitude toward it is different, as you continue to risk it." "Now when someone sets a price," another told me, "Caritas intervenes in how they think about the values of money." Still another friend, just returned from six months abroad, said she noticed a tremendous change in the people around her: "Because of Caritas, they've started to behave as if they were independent, to take initiative rather than wait for things to happen, to have the courage to make a plan, and to take risks."

69. Aside from the fact that many people did lose, this comment betrays a certain naiveté about the loss of value in an inflationary period. Between the deposit of a certain sum and its retrieval eightfold three months later, inflation would have reduced the value of the initial deposit considerably.

70. This observation reminds one of the psychology behind credit-card spending in the U.S.

71. See what follows, and also chapter 6 of this volume.

72. See Enikő Magyari-Vincze and Margit Feischmidt, "The Caritas and the Romanian Transition," unpublished typescript (1994), p. 24.

73. I owe the ideas in this and the preceding paragraph to Kirstie McClure.

74. That money and market exchange require "moralizing" is an anthropological truism far beyond the East European context. See, e.g., Maurice Bloch and Jonathan

Parry, eds., *Money and the Morality of Exchange* (Cambridge: Cambridge University Press, 1989); Roy Dilley, *Contesting Markets*; and Emily Martin, *The Meaning of Money in the United States and China* (Lewis Henry Morgan Lectures, University of Rochester, 1986).

75. This opinion was offered by the managing director of the state-controlled Romanian TV in one of several editorials touching on Caritas (editorial for 2 October 1993). Other opinions given here come from my fieldwork.

76. By criticizing and participating simultaneously, people adopted the same relation to Caritas that they had to the former regime: a relation of "complicity." This sort of complicity creates complex dispositions and ambivalences, which we might expect to find as attitudes toward money evolve further. Complicity may have disposed people to relax their moral scruples about "unearned money," especially if they had already gotten sums and spent them.

77. See, e.g., essays in Bloch and Parry, *Money and the Morality of Exchange*; and Michael Taussig, "The Genesis of Capitalism amongst a South American Peasantry: Devil's Labor and the Baptism of Money," *Comparative Studies in Society and History* 19 (1977): 130–55.

78. See, e.g., Smeoreanu et al., *Caritas*, p. 51; and Zamfirescu and Cerna, *Fenomenul Caritas sau mântuirea românilor prin ei înşişi*, p. 14.

79. Smeoreanu et al., *Caritas*, pp. 91–92.

80. Ibid., pp. 48, 49.

81. Ibid., p. 40; *Adevărul*, 1 October 1993, p. 4; and *Expres*, 9–15 November 1993, p. 16.

82. Zamfirescu and Cerna, *Fenomenul Caritas sau mântuirea românilor prin ei înşişi*.

83. Ibid., p. 17. Boldface in original.

84. Ibid., p. 23.

85. Ibid., p. 24. Capitals in original.

86. Ibid., p. 17. (Written in capital letters.)

87. Cited on the back of Zamfirescu and Cerna, *Fenomenul Caritas sau mântuirea românilor prin ei înşişi*.

88. Cf. Mircea Eliade, *The Two and the One* (London: Harvill Press, 1965), pp. 126–50. David Lempert finds a "cargo cult" attitude in Russia also ("Changing Russian Political Culture in the 1990s: Parasites, Paradigms, and Perestroika," *Comparative Studies in Society and History* 35 [1993]: 643).

89. In a review of work on millenarian movements in Melanesia, Trompf cites as the one durable generalization about them Eliade's insight that they arise when different understandings of time come together. See G. W. Trompf, *Melanesian Religion* (Cambridge: Cambridge University Press, 1991), p. 192. See also Andrew Lattas, ed., "Alienating Mirrors: Christianity, Cargo Cults, and Colonialism in Melanesia," *Oceania* 63 (special issue, 1992). My thanks to Eytan Bercovitch for these references.

90. See chapters 1 and 2 of this volume, as well as my *National Ideology under Socialism: Identity and Cultural Politics in Ceauşescu's Romania* (Berkeley and Los Angeles: University of California Press, 1991), pp. 249–51.

91. David Harvey, *The Condition of Postmodernity* (Oxford: Blackwell, 1989). See also chapter 1 of this book, p. 35.

92. Owing to its nationalism, the Caritas "millenarian movement" is very different

from those of Oceania or other places where they have been found. Classic literature on those latter forms sees them as prepolitical, paving the way for more explicitly political and even national movements; whereas Caritas, with its associate, the PUNR, had already trodden this path. See Peter Lawrence, *Road Belong Cargo: A Study of the Cargo Movement in the Southern Madang District, New Guinea* (Manchester: University of Manchester Press, 1964); K.O.L. Burridge, *Mambu: A Melanesian Millennium* (London: Methuen, 1960); and Peter Worsley, *The Trumpet Shall Sound: A Study of "Cargo" Cults in Melanesia* (New York: Schocken, 1968).

93. Eliade, *The Two and the One*, p. 155.

94. Some argue that the religious imagery was manufactured by Stoica and his supporters (e.g., Shafir, "The Caritas Affair," p. 24). Although I think it possible that stooges placed in the long lines at Caritas may well have planted some of these ideas, more important (as my fieldwork convinced me) is that people took them up with gusto.

95. Smeoreanu et al., *Caritas*, p. 31; and *Adevărul*, 10 October 1993, p. 4, and 11 November 1993, p. 1.

96. Smeoreanu et al., *Caritas*, p. 37.

97. See ibid., p. 31; *Adevărul*, 6–7 November 1993, p. 1; *Evenimentul zilei*, 8 November 1993, p. 3; *Adevărul*, 11 November 1993, p. 1; and Magyari-Vincze and Feischmidt, "The Caritas and the Romanian Transition," p. 36.

98. These quotations are all from Magyari-Vincze and Feischmidt, "The Caritas and the Romanian Transition."

99. The schemes had not just failed but caused much social disturbance (see, e.g., *România liberă*, 25 June 1993, p. 5).

100. Marius Niţu, "Odată cu apropierea iernii Caritasul se 'răceşte,'" *Adevărul*, 22 October 1993, p. 1. The cities in which Caritas did best were those where local authorities were of the PUNR, such as Petroşani, whereas those having mayors of opposition parties (such as Bucharest) sought to exclude it. In this vein, perhaps a more important reason for the failure of Caritas in Braşov was that its mayor belonged not to the nationalist parties that gave Caritas such a boost in Cluj but to the political opposition.

101. *Evenimentul zilei*, 2–3 November 1993, p. 1.

102. Ioan Cristoiu, "De la 'Caritas' la moaştele Sfîntului Dimitrie cel Nou," *Evenimentul zilei*, 27 October 1993, p. 1.

103. Michael Stewart, personal communication.

104. Smeoreanu et al., *Caritas*, pp. 14–15.

105. *E lucrul dracului, că banii nu fată!* More common, however, was the expression, "leave your money in so it will hatch chicks" (*Lasă-i să facă pui*).

106. Taussig, "The Genesis of Capitalism amongst a South American Peasantry." See also Jacques M. Chevalier, *Civilization and the Stolen Gift; Capital, Kin, and Cult in Eastern Peru* (Toronto: University of Toronto Press, 1982); Olivia Harris, "The Earth and the State: The Sources and Meanings of Money in Northern Potosí, Bolivia," in Bloch and Parry, *Money and the Morality of Exchange*, pp. 232–68; and Michael Stewart, *The Time of the Gypsies: Poverty, Cultural Identity and Resistance to Proletarianisation in Socialist Hungary*, chapter 9.

107. Cf. John Davis, *Exchange* (Minneapolis: University of Minnesota Press, 1991), p. 20. My thanks to Elizabeth Dunn for the idea and the reference.

108. This is a modification of Bianchi's term "unruly corporations." See Robert

Bianchi, *Unruly Corporatism: Associational Life in Twentieth-Century Egypt* (New York: Oxford University Press, 1989). Thanks to Ashraf Ghani for this suggestion.

109. Cf. Jacek Kochanowicz, "The Disappearing State: Poland's Three Years of Transition," *Social Research* 60 (1993): 831.

110. See Caroline Humphrey, "'Icebergs,' Barter, and the Mafia in Provincial Russia," *Anthropology Today* 7 (April 1991): 8–13; David Stark, "Privatization in Hungary: From Plan to Market or from Plan to Clan?" *East European Politics and Societies* 4 (Fall 1990): 351–92; and Lev Timofeyev, *Russia's Secret Rulers* (New York: Knopf, 1992), p. 127. I reject both "mafia" (too Italian in its connotations) and "clan" (inaptly implying kinship).

111. For example, Louise Shelley, "Post-Soviet Organized Crime," *Demokrati-zatsiya* 2 (Summer 1994): 341–58; and Lev Timofeyev, *Russia's Secret Rulers* (New York: Knopf, 1992).

112. Humphrey, "'Icebergs,' Barter, and the Mafia in Provincial Russia."

113. Kenneth Jowitt, personal communication. See my *National Ideology under Socialism*, pp. 129–30.

114. For instance, where a city mayor is of the nationally governing party, this suggests a composition very different from that of an area where the mayor is of an opposition party. Local elections will produce shifts in the composition of unruly coalitions, as will scandals involving networks of persons central to them.

115. Iliescu is not, technically speaking, the head of his party, but for all practical purposes, he is.

116. I use the standard Romanian initials for these parties rather than their English equivalents; and for parties that changed their names I use the initials appropriate as of 1995. The percentages I give here are not those won by each party in the overall vote but the percentages they each gained in the parliament. Because no party was allowed parliamentary representation unless it received 3 percent of the votes (and there was a large number of parties), over 1.5 million votes were cast that did not elect parliamentarians. I use the voting figures given by the Foreign Broadcast Information Service (*FBIS-EEU-92-193*) for 9 October 1992, p. 27.

117. *Mesagerul transilvan*, 24 September 1993, p. 1.

118. *România liberă*, 3 November 1993, p. 3.

119. Ibid., 22 July 1993, p. 16, and 22 March 1994, p. 16; and Tom Gallagher, "The Rise of the Party of Romanian National Unity," *RFE-RL Reports* 3 (18 March 1994): 30. The first source gives a figure of $2,500 per month, the last as $5 million total, for the amount the PUNR got from taxes on Caritas.

120. See Tom Gallagher, "The Political Dimensions of the Caritas Affair in Romania," unpublished typescript (1993), pp. 20–21.

121. See, e.g., *România liberă*, 13 May 1994, p. 9.

122. See, e.g., *Evenimentul zilei*, 2 January 1994, p. 8, in which Cluj prefect Zanc seeks to undercut mayor Funar through Caritas.

123. See 22, 29 June–5 July 1994, p. 3. Its standing did not improve in subsequent months.

124. Jadwiga Staniszkis, "'Political capitalism' in Poland," *East European Politics and Societies* 5 (Winter 1991): 127–41.

125. Although several publications gave the number of Romanian pyramid schemes as around 100, I think this figure is low. Taking only numbers for the six

cities of Braşov (100 schemes), Oradea (36), Piteşti (30 in six months), Constanţa (25), Ploieşti (80 between 1991 and 1993), and Brăila (35), we have 306 such schemes— and they appeared in many other cities as well. Some of the localized schemes were branches of larger organizations, but because travel time was a significant ingredient in people's participation (not to mention in moving the money used for payouts, given the rudimentary state of Romania's banking system), it makes sense to see even these branches as quasi-separate instances of their parent scheme. Sources for the above figures: *România liberă*, 25 June 1993, p. 5; *Adevărul*, 20 January 1994, p. 1; *Adevărul*, 27 January 1994, p. 1; *Adevărul*, 21 March 1994, p. 3; *Adevărul*, 11 January 1994, p. 3; and *România liberă*, 23 July 1993, p. 5. (I note that the figures are not certain, since papers reported varying totals even for the same city.)

126. *Evenimentul zilei*, 16 October 1993, p. 8. Many other papers told comparable stories. In May 1994 the lines of Caritas-victims registering complaints was said to include "pensioners, the unemployed, peasants, workers, intellectuals, and . . . Gyp- sies. . . . It is interesting that in the line of people waiting to register complaints we do not find the former or present nomenclatura, Securitate members, and potentates of the present regime. It seems they pocketed tens and tens of millions of the money of those who have been swindled" (*România liberă*, 16 May 1994, p. 16).

127. See Romulus Brâncoveanu, "Fenomenul 'Caritas' şi escrocheria politică," *România liberă*, 8 March 1994, p. 2. Also see *România liberă*, 21 March 1994, p. 1; *România liberă*, 6 January 1994, p. 10.

128. Here is how "Gerald" reportedly got its start: when local officials gave it the green light, they received assurances that they would be at the top of the lists of depositors and would receive one million lei two months after depositing 100,000 each. See *Evenimentul zilei*, 15 October 1993, pp. 1–2.

129. See Katherine Verdery and Gail Kligman, "Romania after Ceauşescu: Post- Communist Communism?" in *Eastern Europe in Revolution*, ed. Ivo Banac (Ithaca: Cornell University Press, 1992), pp. 117–47.

130. Tom Gallagher, "Vatra Românească and Resurgent Nationalism in Romania," *Ethnic and Racial Studies* 15 (1992): 579. Here is some further anecdotal evidence for the connection. First, in my one visit to Caritas headquarters, I asked my guide what job he had held before starting to work for Caritas; he replied that he had been a chauffeur and had been in counterintelligence, joining the Romanian Information Service after the revolution. When I commented on how well organized Caritas was, he said, "No surprise! It's been planned for five years"—which would put its origin *before* the revolution. The friends to whom I reported this said they had heard that the Securitate had already had pyramid-like schemes underground before 1989. Fi- nally, friends in Cluj said that the first people in their workplaces to deposit in Caritas had long been suspected of being Securitate informers.

131. See Gallagher, "Vatra Românească and Resurgent Nationalism in Roma- nia," and "The Political Dimensions of the Caritas Affair in Romania"; Dennis De- letant, "Convergence vs. Divergence in Romania: The Role of the *Vatra româneas- că* Movement in Transylvania" (a paper presented at the School of Slavonic and East European Studies conference, 8–14 December 1990); and chapter 4 of this volume. For Romanian newspaper reports, see, e.g., *Adevărul*, 14 March 1994, p. 3; *România liberă*, 22 March 1994, p. 16; *Evenimentul zilei*, 9 October 1993, p. 4; and *România liberă*, 4 May 1994, p. 16. (I note that these papers are not always

credible.) For a disproportionate PUNR presence among Caritas depositors, see the lists of parliamentary Caritasians published in *Adevărul*, 12 November 1993, p. 1).

132. In his televised interview of 8 February 1994, for example.

133. *Adevărul*, 20 January 1994, p. 1, and 26 January 1994, pp. 1–2.

134. *România liberă*, 8 July 199, p. 2, published a detailed calculation as to how much money might be expected to come into a newly established pyramid scheme and how fast it would grow in six months, payouts included. Interest rates on bank savings deposits fluctuated greatly during the period under discussion; by autumn 1993, when many of the competitor schemes were being started, one could get 50 percent or more annually, and that figure rose during the winter (when schemes were still being founded despite the evident difficulties of Caritas). Thus for pyramid organizers to place deposits at high interest was indeed an option. Given how much money often came into a newly opened scheme—"Gerald," for instance, reportedly took in three hundred million lei in its first four days (*Adevărul*, 15 October 1993, p. 1)—their short-term profit from interest alone could be enormous.

135. *Adevărul*, 26 January 1994, p. 2

136. *Cronica română*, 28 September 1993, p. 3; *Evenimentul zilei*, 19 March 1994, p. 3, and 12 April 1994, p. 10. During summer 1994, there was a lengthy discussion in the Romanian press about the government's plan to count only one property certificate per citizen, so as to rectify the fact that many people had sold their certificates without understanding their potential value as stocks in profitable firms. It is possible that beneath this plan was a conflict among groups of entrepratchiks over who would control the wealth embodied in the certificates.

137. The part of this question that I do not try to answer—why depositors kept coming, despite overwhelming evidence that they would lose their money—points toward the most ethnographically significant aspect of this chapter: it reveals among Romanians a frame of mind most readers will find wholly unfathomable. That is what the "transition from socialism" is really about.

138. The article, published in the Constanța *Telegraf*, was excerpted without the author's name, in *Evenimentul zilei*, 2 February 1994, p. 3. I add that a very well placed source told me (for what it's worth) that the scheme had collapsed so quietly because the secret service had carefully managed it down.

139. These figures are from ads and articles in the Romanian newspapers *Evenimentul zilei*, *România liberă*, and *Adevărul* for November 1993 through February 1994. There were many more games, but these are the ones for which I know both the stakes and that they began after Caritas gained momentum.

140. *Evenimentul zilei*, 16 October 1993, p. 8, and 28 October 1993, p. 8.

141. See, e.g., *Financial Times*, 8 August 1994, pp. 1, 2. The shareholders' slogan was reportedly "Trust MMM, don't trust the bureaucrats." The story of Mavrodi's election comes from National Public Radio (31 October 1994).

142. These questions must be answered differently according to where people were in the cycle of earnings. Those who received and spent substantial amounts will probably have had their conceptions durably altered, whereas this is less likely for those who had yet to benefit.

143. *Evenimentul zilei*, 18 December 1993, p. 1, reported that some Cluj banks were repossessing fifty apartments that had been mortgaged so that their owners

could participate in Caritas. *Adevărul*, 14 February 1994, p. 1, reported, similarly, that every day Hunedoara banks were auctioning off the houses of people who had used them as collateral, to borrow for Caritas.

144. *România liberă*, 18 March 1994, p. 1, and 25 June 1993, p. 5; *Adevărul*, 3 March 1994, p. 2.

145. By early June, a number of such associations had been formed, with names like "National Association for Proving Abuses," "Action Committee for Recovering Money Deposited in Caritas," "Association for Recovery of Caritas-Type Deposits," "Association of Victims of Caritas," and "Association of People Deceived by Mutual-Aid Games." Certain lawyers offered their services free of charge. News reports during the summer of 1994, however, suggested political harassment of some of their activities. See, e.g., Virgil Lazăr, "Boss Stoica Gets Hysterical while Damaged Claim International Protection," *România liberă* (international English edition), 30 July–5 August 1994, p. 7. Similarly, in Russia following the collapse of MMM, shareholders organized rallies and a union, to defend depositors' rights nationwide. See *FBIS-SOV-94* no. 148 (2 August 1994), pp. 16–18; no. 157 (15 August 1994), p. 15; no. 162 (22 August 1994), p. 25; and no. 168 (30 August 1994), p. 14.

146. During the same period as Stoica's arrest (August 1994), the PUNR clinched a deal with the government and received the four cabinet portfolios it had long been seeking. That this occurred even as its standing in the polls plummeted casts an unexpected light on Stoica's arrest and his prospects. One possibility is that sacrificing Stoica and Caritas was the price the PUNR paid for its goal of entering the government. The new alliance in turn suggests, however, that Stoica will not be in jail for long—in other words, in exchange for managing Caritas's demise to prevent social chaos and consenting to be arrested (rather than fleeing, as so many other pyramid owners have done), Stoica will be quickly pardoned and allowed to keep his fortune. His fate would thus parallel that of the potentates of the Ceauşescu regime, who (it now seems) agreed to be sacrificed so their successors might take over and pardon them later.

147. Brâncoveanu, "Fenomenul 'Caritas' şi escrocheria politică."

CHAPTER 8

1. Emily Martin, "The Egg and the Sperm: How Science Has Constructed a Romance Based on Stereotypical Male-Female Roles," *Signs* 16 (1991): 485–501.

2. Elizabeth Dunn finds good evidence that the glossy business magazines read by aspiring Polish businessmen present these men as like women, wanting to learn how to please their (male) Western counterparts. See her "Managed Selves: Privatization and the Creation of a New Managerial Class," a paper presented at the annual meeting of the American Anthropological Association, 1993.

3. One could scarcely express better than this Westerners' nonchalance about the long, painful, varied, and formative histories of the region's inhabitants.

4. Caroline Humphrey, "'Icebergs,' Barter, and the Mafia in Provincial Russia," *Anthropology Today* 7 (1991): 8–13.

5. Ibid., p. 8.

6. Similarly, Michael Burawoy and Pavel Krotov, "The Soviet Transition from Socialism to Capitalism: Worker Control and Economic Bargaining in the Wood

Industry," *American Sociological Review* 57 (1992): 16–38, see the consequence of the reforms as heightened monopolies rather than as the formation of markets.

7. Cited in Humphrey, "'Icebergs,' Barter, and the Mafia in Provincial Russia," p. 9.

8. Caroline Humphrey, "Mythmaking, Narratives, and the Dispossessed in Russia," a paper presented at the annual meeting of the American Anthropological Association, 1993.

9. In the feudal period, also, it was against marauding bands of "nomads" and other warriors that encysted fiefdoms took shape.

10. Humphrey, "'Icebergs,' Barter, and the Mafia in Provincial Russia," p. 10.

11. Simon Clarke, "The Quagmire of Privatisation," *New Left Review* 196 (1992): 7.

12. Gerald Creed, "Civil Society and Spirit of Capitalism: A Bulgarian Critique," a paper presented at the annual meeting of the American Anthropological Association, Chicago, 1991.

13. I would not argue that barter and demonetization lie in an evolutionary progression toward capitalism, disappearing once that economic form develops. There is ample evidence of barter within even the most advanced capitalist economies. See Caroline Humphrey and Stephen Hugh-Jones, eds., *Barter, Exchange, and Value: An Anthropological Approach* (Cambridge: Cambridge University Press, 1992).

14. Humphrey, "'Icebergs,' Barter, and the Mafia in Provincial Russia," pp. 10–11.

15. Although the phenomena Humphrey describes were particularly common in Russia, they existed elsewhere too. Among the more unusual instances of barter was one I encountered in 1990 in Romania. It involved the procurement of recording tapes by the radio station in the city of Iaşi, near the then-Soviet border. The East German tapes Romania had obtained for years through intrabloc trade had become unavailable, and others of comparable quality could be had only for hard currency, which Iaşi Radio lacked. Its solution was to barter tapes from the French broadcasting system, in exchange for broadcasting one hour of French radio programs per day into the Soviet Union; the French liked the arrangement because it enabled them to compete with British and German cultural penetration of the East. Iaşi Radio was an excellent partner for this purpose, since Romania had propagandized for years in the predominantly Romanian-speaking republic of Soviet Moldavia and had therefore endowed Iaşi Radio with one of the most powerful radio signals in Eastern Europe.

16. Humphrey, "'Icebergs,' Barter, and the Mafia in Provincial Russia," p. 10.

17. Sergei Arutiunov, personal communication.

18. Humphrey, "'Icebergs,' Barter, and the Mafia in Provincial Russia," p. 13.

19. See, e.g., Stephen Handelman, "The Russian Mafia," *Foreign Affairs* 73 (1994): 83–96; Louise I. Shelley, "Post-Soviet Organized Crime: Implications for Economic, Social and Political Development," *Demokratizatsiya* 2 (1994): 341–58; Lev Timofeyev, *Russia's Secret Rulers* (New York: Knopf, 1992); Arkady Vaksberg, *The Soviet Mafia* (New York: St. Martin's, 1992); J. Michael Waller, "Organized Crime and the Russian State: Challenges to U.S.-Russian Cooperation," *Demokratizatsiya* 2 (1994): 364–84.

20. I do not have the details of this program, which was reported to me by a colleague. It was aired around 25 February 1992.

21. Perry Anderson, *Passages from Antiquity to Feudalism* (London: Verso, 1974); all portions quoted are found on p. 148.

22. Georges Duby, *La société aux XIe et XIIe siècles dans la region mâconnaise* (Paris: A. Colin, 1953), p. 171.

23. Gianfranco Poggi, *The Development of the Modern State: A Sociological Introduction* (Stanford: Stanford University Press, 1978), p. 31.

24. An employee of the World Bank quoted this remark to me secondhand. Cf. Richard Rose, "Getting By without Government: Everyday Life in Russia," *Daedalus* 123 (1994): 41–62.

25. See Jacek Kochanowicz, "The Disappearing State: Poland's Three Years of Transition," *Social Research* 60 (1993): 821–34.

26. Anderson, *Passages from Antiquity to Feudalism*, pp. 151–52.

27. Bloch makes a comparable argument but with different reasons from those I emphasize in what follows; see his "Natural Economy or Money Economy: A Pseudo-Dilemma," in *Land and Work in Medieval Europe: Selected Papers* (Berkeley and Los Angeles: University of California Press, 1967), pp. 230–43.

28. While pressures to restatize come from many quarters and have many justifications, here is a comment that links them with a recoil from "feudalization." The comment comes from an interview by anthropologist Thomas Wolfe with two Russian journalists: "We have to begin a process of accumulation which for you proceeded during the course of your entire history. We have no other path, except to collapse as a sovereign power. We'd have the Moscow principality, here, and there the Novgorod principality, see, a reversion to old principles. We can't let that happen." Thomas C. Wolfe, "The Most Invisible Hand: Russian Journalism and Media-Context," in *Late Editions 4: Cultural Studies for the End of the Century*, ed. George Marcus (Chicago: University of Chicago Press, forthcoming).

29. Ann Anagnost, *National Past-Times: Writing, Narrative, and History in Modern China* (Durham, N.C.: Duke University Press, forthcoming); John Borneman, *Belonging in the Two Berlins: Kin, State, Nation* (Cambridge: Cambridge University Press, 1992); Ashraf Ghani, *Production and Domination: Afghanistan, 1747–1901* (New York: Columbia University Press, forthcoming); and Gail Kligman, *The Politics of Complicity: Women, Abortion, and the State in Ceauşescu's Romania* (Berkeley and Los Angeles: University of California Press, forthcoming).

30. Unfortunately this assumption has proved erroneous. Some people sought to become owners of a firm only so as to raid it of its assets and leave it to go under. Several of the voucher schemes have prevented "owners" from exerting any influence on the firm, thus their presumed interest in it goes unasserted; and other schemes involve management by neither the stockholders nor professional managers, meaning that ownership and economic rationality are not joined in any management form. (Thanks to Elizabeth Dunn for these points.)

31. For the purposes of this chapter, I do not distinguish between small- and large-scale privatization or between allocating new rights and restoring old ones, although each of these differs in its implications for transforming the state.

32. See, e.g., Douglass North, "A Framework for Analyzing the State in Economic History," *Explorations in Economic History* 17 (1979): 250.

33. Cited in Jan Szomberg, "Poland's Privatization Strategy," a paper presented at

the conference on Transforming Economic Systems in East-Central Eastern Europe, Munich, June 1991.

34. Hilary Appel, "Justice and the Reformulation of Property Rights in the Czech Republic," *East European Politics and Societies* 9 (1995): 22–40.

35. A very partial listing would include Appel, "Justice and the Reformulation of Property Rights in the Czech Republic"; Michael Burawoy, "Industrial Involution: The Russian Road to Capitalism," Havens Lecture I, January 1995; Burawoy and Krotov, "The Soviet Transition from Socialism to Capitalism"; Michael Burawoy and János Lukács, *The Radiant Past: Ideology and Reality in Hungary's Road to Capitalism* (Chicago: University of Chicago Press, 1992); Roman Frydman and Andrzej Rapaczynski, *Privatization in Eastern Europe: Is the State Withering Away?* (Budapest: Central European University Press, 1994); Roman Frydman, Andrzej Rapaczynski, and John S. Earle, *The Privatization Process in Central Europe* (Budapest: Central European University Press, 1993); three essays by Christopher Hann: "Market Principle, Market-Place, and the Transition in Eastern Europe," in *Contesting Markets*, ed. Roy Dilley (Edinburgh: Edinburgh University Press), pp. 244–59, "From Production to Property: Decollectivization and the Family-Land Relationship in Contemporary Hungary," *Man* 28 (1993): 299–320, and "Property Relations in the New Eastern Europe: the Case of Specialist Cooperatives in Hungary," in *The Curtain Rises: Rethinking Culture, Ideology, and the State in Eastern Europe*, ed. Hermine G. DeSoto and David G. Anderson (Atlantic Highlands, N.J.: Humanities, 1993), pp. 99–121; Michael Kennedy and Pauline Gianoplus, "Entrepreneurs and Expertise: A Cultural Encounter in the Making of Post-Communist Capitalism in Poland," *East European Politics and Societies* 8 (1994): 58–94; Yudit Kiss, "Privatization Paradoxes in East Central Europe," *East European Politics and Societies* 8 (1994): 122–52; Kazimierz Poznanski, *Constructing Capitalism: The Reemergence of Civil Society and Liberal Economy in the Post-Communist World* (Boulder: Westview, 1992); Adam Przeworski, *Democracy and the Market: Political and Economic Reforms in Eastern Europe and Latin America* (Cambridge: Cambridge University Press, 1991); Jadwiga Staniszkis, *The Dynamics of the Breakthrough in Eastern Europe* (Berkeley and Los Angeles: University of California Press, 1991), and "'Political Capitalism' in Poland," *East European Politics and Societies* 5 (1991): 127–41; three essays by David Stark: "Privatization in Hungary: From Plan to Market or from Plan to Clan?" *East European Politics and Societies* 4 (1990): 351–92, "Path Dependence and Privatization Strategies in East Central Europe," *East European Politics and Societies* 6 (1992): 17–54, and "Recombinant Property in East European Capitalism," a paper presented at the conference on Bureaucratic Capitalism in China and Russia, University of Wisconsin, 1993; and David Stark and László Bruszt, "Restructuring Networks in the Transformation of Post-Socialist Economies," Cornell Working Papers on the Transition from State Socialism 95.4, Einaudi International Center, Cornell University (1995).

36. An excellent summary of these debates for Hungary is found in Stark, "Privatization in Hungary."

37. Staniszkis, "'Political Capitalism' in Poland," p. 128; Stark, "Privatization in Hungary," p. 364. Gerald Creed suggests 1987 as the comparable watershed year for Bulgaria, also. See his "Economic Development under Socialism: A Bulgarian Village on the Eve of Transition" (Ph.D. dissertation, City University of New York, 1992).

38. See, e.g., David Stark, "Coexisting Forms in Hungary's Emerging Mixed

Economy," in *Remaking the Economic Institutions of Socialism: China and Eastern Europe*, ed. Victor Nee and David Stark (Stanford: Stanford University Press), pp. 137–68.

39. See also Stark, "Recombinant Property in East European Capitalism," pp. 8–9.

40. Burawoy and Lukács, *The Radiant Past*, p. 154. See also Stark, "Privatization in Hungary," p. 360.

41. One such story had a major hotel in downtown Bucharest being sold to a foreign buyer for seven million dollars, which the columnist thought half the suitable asking price and decidedly to the disadvantage of Romanians. See Pia Rădulescu, "Din nou despre contractul 'Athenee Palace' și 'Marc Rich,'" *România liberă*, 12 July 1991, p. 5.

42. Stark, "Privatization in Hungary," p. 374; see also his "Recombinant Property in East European Capitalism."

43. This was my own reaction to them, and I was not alone. See Ioan Benedict, "Ce vor fondurile proprietăţii private?" *România liberă*, 12 July 1991, p. 3a, which sets forth the incredibly confusing procedures for getting stocks in companies and for buying and selling them.

44. Staniszkis, *The Dynamics of the Breakthrough in Eastern Europe*, p. 47.

45. This point comes from research by Elizabeth Dunn on management practices in Polish firms run jointly with American businesses. See her "Managed Selves."

46. Stark, "Privatization in Hungary" and "Recombinant Property in East European Capitalism," and Stark and Bruszt, "Restructuring Networks in the Transformation of Post-Socialist Economies."

47. Andrei Cornea, "Directocraţia remaniază guvernul," 22, 16–22 March 1994, p. 7.

48. Staniszkis, *The Dynamics of the Breakthrough in Eastern Europe*, pp. 8–9. Her argument differs from Cornea's in that she sees the eventual outcome as capitalism, as nomenclatura companies attached to the state sector throw their costs onto the state, using their dual assets as owner-managers and political cronies to increase their own profits and accelerate the formation of capital. Cornea, by contrast, sees the result as stagnation; in this he agrees with Burawoy ("Industrial Involution").

49. Burawoy and Lukács, *The Radiant Past*, p. 155; Stark, "Privatization in Hungary," pp. 366–69, 376. *Bringing the State Back In* is the title of a book edited by Peter D. Evans, Dietrich Rueschemeyer, and Theda Skocpol (Cambridge: Cambridge University Press, 1985).

50. See Kochanowicz, "The Disappearing State," and Burawoy, "Industrial Involution."

51. Stark and Bruszt, "Restructuring Networks in the Transformation of Post-Socialist Economies," p. 9.

52. See András Sajó, "Diffuse Rights in Search of an Agent: A Property Rights Analysis of the Firm in the Socialist Market Economy," *International Review of Law and Economics* 10 (1990): 41–59.

53. Personal communication from Andrei Pleşu.

54. See G. Dimisianu, "Dispar revistele literare," *România literară*, 8 August 1991, p. 1; and Cornel Moraru, "Agonia intelectualităţii," *România literară*, 6 December 1990, p. 7.

55. From *România literară* for 19 December 1991, p. 1.

56. This conclusion applies not only to attempts to downsize the postsocialist state but even to efforts by the U.S. Congress of the 1980s and 1990s to reduce government spending.

57. Valerie Bunce and Mária Csanádi likewise discuss restatizing pressures, for Hungary. See Bunce and Csanádi, "Uncertainty in the Transition: Post-Communism in Hungary," *East European Politics and Societies* 7 (1993): 255–57, 271. See also chapter 6 in this volume, on decollectivization.

58. The examples are not, of course, limited to privatization: here is one drawn from university teaching. An acquaintance told me of a discussion she had overheard late on New Year's Eve, at a party of high university personnel. They were talking about the need to restore surveillance of the students, to re-create dossiers with notes as to what political parties each student favored, what political attitudes they held, and especially what views they had of the ruling National Salvation Front (the political party that those present obviously supported). From the way they talked, it was quite clear to my friend that this was *their own* idea, not an order sent down from some higher authority. Thus the professors who had replaced discredited Marxist-Leninist hacks in university chairs were now reconstituting for themselves a position of omnipotence based on a hopeful alliance with a new, intrusive political center.

59. See Shelley, "Post-Soviet Organized Crime."

60. See n. 2 of Kathryn Lyon, "Crime and Punishment: Mafia and the Discourse of Power in Russia's Transition to a Market Economy," a paper presented at the annual convention of the American Association for the Advancement of Slavic Studies, 1994.

61. Staniszkis, *The Dynamics of the Breakthrough in Eastern Europe*, pp. 88, 164–67.

62. For a different area altogether, China, Jowitt quotes an article from the *New York Times* that says provinces are carving up the national market into vast protectionist fiefs, and restrictions on internal trade show evidence of centrifugal forces capable of fragmenting that country (Ken Jowitt, *New World Disorder: The Leninist Extinction* [Berkeley and Los Angeles: University of California Press, 1992], p. 315).

63. Jane and Peter Schneider, *Culture and Political Economy in Western Sicily* (New York: Academic Press, 1976).

64. The discussion in this paragraph draws upon ibid., pp. 11–13. For additional anthropological research on mafia, see also Anton Blok, *The Mafia of a Sicilian Village, 1860–1960: A Study of Violent Peasant Entrepreneurs* (New York: Harper and Row, 1974).

65. Stark, "Privatization in Hungary," p. 377.

66. Hann, "Market Principle, Market-Place, and the Transition in Eastern Europe," p. 249.

67. David Kideckel, "Peasants and Authority in the New Romania," in *Romania after Tyranny*, ed. Daniel N. Nelson (Boulder: Westview, 1992), p. 76.

68. See also Lyon, "Crime and Punishment."

69. Mikhail Leontiev, "The Invisible Hand of the Mafia: A Scarecrow for the Soviet Public," *Nezavisimaya Gazeta* (weekly English edition), 2 July 1991, p. 5.

70. Jan T. Gross, *Revolution from Abroad: The Soviet Conquest of Poland's Western Ukraine and Western Byelorussia* (Princeton: Princeton University Press, 1988); István Rév, "The Advantages of Being Atomized: How Hungarian Peasants Coped

with Collectivization," *Dissent* 34 (1987): 335–50; and Stark and Bruszt, "Restructuring Networks in the Transformation of Post-Socialist Economies." See also my "Theorizing Socialism: A Prologue to the 'Transition,'" *American Ethnologist* 18 (1991): 426–27.

71. Humphrey, "Mythmaking, Narratives, and the Dispossessed in Russia," pp.8–9.

72. In the most extended case I followed, the plaintiff boasted to other villagers that he was sure he would win because I was "friends" with the judge (and he was "friends" with me). When he lost, he considered an appeal because he has a relative at the court of appeals and could probably win there.

73. Graham Burchell, "Peculiar Interests: Civil Society and Governing 'the System of Natural Liberty,'" in *The Foucault Effect: Studies in Governmentality*, ed. Graham Burchell, Colin Gordon, and Peter Miller (Chicago: University of Chicago Press, 1991), p. 120.

74. See chapter 2 in this volume.

75. In Romania starting in 1984, villagers had been given a list of amounts and crops they were required to contract to the state from their private plots. This meant that their own plan for their household consumption had to be subordinated to this new drain from outside.

76. Peasant women, like all others, had to undergo gynecological exams to ensure that they had not had abortions. See Kligman, *The Politics of Complicity*.

77. Cf. Evans, Rueschemeyer, and Skocpol, *Bringing the State Back In*. I might add that for the commune in which I conducted research in 1993–94, local authorities were further diminishing their own prospects by not collecting some of the few sources of revenue to which they had access independent of the political center. For instance, they have the power to levy fines for failure to maintain cleanliness of village streets and ditches, but they did not do so, hoping thereby to maintain their electoral popularity in the village.

78. A USAID project was struggling to work around the obstacles to measuring but, according to the office director in Bucharest, not making much headway.

79. Thanks to Ashraf Ghani for this observation.

80. Bunce and Csanádi, "Uncertainty in the Transition," pp. 266–67.

81. Gross, *Revolution from Abroad*, pp. 234–36. See also chapter 2 in this volume.

82. The discussion in this paragraph is from Staniszkis, *The Dynamics of the Breakthrough in Eastern Europe*, pp. 171–75.

83. Thanks to Erik Mueggler for an enlightening discussion on this theme.

84. I heard this in Hungary in the mid-1980s.

AFTERWORD

1. For example, the battles around reproductive technologies and intellectual property rights (especially relating to electronic media) in the United States.

2. These have been placed in doubt in American politics, for example, as of the 1992 presidential campaign, as well as earlier with increasing discussion of the role of PACs in the American political process.

3. See, e.g., Charles Tilly, *Coercion, Capital, and European States, 990–1990* (Oxford: Blackwell, 1990), for only one of many discussions of the decline of the state.

4. See, e.g., the special Summer 1993 issue of *Daedalus*; Rogers Brubaker, "Rethinking Nationhood: Nation as Institutionalized Form, Practical Category, Contingent Event," *Contention* 4 (1994): 3–14; and Eric Hobsbawm, *Nations and Nationalism since 1780: Programme, Myth, Reality* (Cambridge: Cambridge University Press, 1990), chapter 6, for discussions of the changing meanings of nation and nationalism.

5. See, for instance, the film *Pulp Fiction*, as well as any of the films of David Lynch (not to mention hosts of others), and Martin Amis's novel *Time's Arrow* (to mention only one), for contemporary works calling into question the conventions of linear time. My comments on nonlinear time should not be taken to mean that questioning linearity is something new: to take only one example, Henri Bergson built an entire philosophy, in the early twentieth century, around this kind of questioning. (Significantly, Bergson wrote at a time like the present one, a moment of massive change in global processes of accumulation.)

6. See David Stark, "Recombinant Property in East European Capitalism," a paper presented at the conference on Bureaucratic Capitalism in China and Russia, University of Wisconsin, 1993, p. 19.

7. Examples are California's anti-immigrant Proposition 187, passed by the state's voters in November 1994, and the expected impact of that vote on the Republican Party platform for the 1996 U.S. presidential election. See Michael Kearney, "Borders and Boundaries of State and Self at the End of Empire," *Journal of Historical Sociology* 4 (1991): 52–73.

8. Michel Foucault, *Discipline and Punish: The Birth of the Prison* (New York: Pantheon Books, 1978), chapter 2. See, e.g., the film of the toppling of Felix Dzherzhinsky in Warsaw (*Eastern Europe: Breaking with the Past—the Polish Experience* [Washington, D.C.: Global View Productions, 1990]).

9. These two examples are by personal communication from Armenian ethnographer Levon Abrahamian.

10. See, for instance, Susan Gal, "Bartók's Funeral: Representations of Europe in Hungarian Political Rhetoric," *American Ethnologist* 18 (1991): 440–58, and "Nagy Imre's Funeral: Ritual and Public Discourse in Socialist Hungary," a paper presented at the annual meeting of the American Ethnological Society, 1990; István Rév, "Parallel Autopsies," working paper no. 10, Institute for International Studies, University of Michigan; and Ewa Hauser, "Traditions of Patriotism, Questions of Gender: The Case of Poland," *Genders* 22 (1995): 78–104, which discusses the reburial of Paderewski.

11. See Bette Denich, "Dismembering Yugoslavia: Nationalist Ideologies and the Symbolic Revival of Genocide," *American Ethnologist* 21 (1994): 367–90; Robert M. Hayden, "Recounting the Dead: The Discovery and Redefinition of Wartime Massacres in Late- and Post-Communist Yugoslavia," in *Memory, History, and Opposition under State Socialism*, ed. Rubie S. Watson (Santa Fe: School of American Research Press, 1994); and Pamela Ballinger, "The Politics of Submersion: History, Collective Memory, and Ethnic Group Boundaries in Trieste," an unpublished typescript (1993).

12. Rév, "Parallel Autopsies."

13. Ibid.

14. See chapter 7 in this volume.

15. I owe this analogy to Tamás Hofer.

16. See, e.g., Cécile Barraud, Daniel de Coppet, André Iteanu, and Raymond Jamous, *Of Relations and the Dead* (Oxford: Berg, 1994); Maurice Bloch, *Placing the Dead: Tombs, Ancestral Villages and Kinship Organization in Madagascar* (London: Seminar Press, 1971); Maurice Bloch and Jonathan Parry, eds., *Death and the Regeneration of Life* (Cambridge: Cambridge University Press, 1982); and Gillian Feeley-Harnik, *A Green Estate: Restoring Independence in Madagascar* (Washington, D.C.: Smithsonian Press, 1991).

17. As of 1995, Romania remains the exception to this statement, since Ceauşescu's pro-natalism was so unpopular that no political group has since dared to resuscitate it. On pro-natalism elsewhere, see the references in chapter 3.

18. Renata Salecl, "Nationalism, Anti-Semitism, and Anti-Feminism in Eastern Europe," *Journal of Area Studies* 2 (Autumn 1993): 84.

19. See, e.g., the collection edited by Sylvia Yanagisako and Carol Delaney, *Naturalizing Power: Essays in Feminist Cultural Analysis* (New York: Routledge, 1995), and that of Brackette Williams (*Women out of Place: The Gender of Agency, the Race of Nationality* (New York: Routledge, 1996).

20. Carol Delaney, "Father State, Motherland, and the Birth of Modern Turkey," in Sylvia Yanagisako and Carol Delaney, *Naturalizing Power*.

21. I hinted at this possibility in chapter 6. For climatological theories, see Jovan Cvijič, *La Péninsule Balkanique, géographie humaine* (Paris: A. Colin, 1918); and Charles de Secondat, Montesquieu, *The Spirit of the Laws* (New York: Appleton, 1900).

22. Thanks to Elizabeth Dunn for this image.

INDEX

Abkhazia, 88

abortion, 64; and nationalism, 69, 79, 81, 82, 233. *See also* Romania, pro-natalism in

AC. *See* Civic Alliance

accumulation, under socialism, 25–27, 29, 30, 45, 47. *See also* capital

"actually existing socialism." *See* socialism, actually existing

adeverință. See property affidavit

affidavit. *See* property affidavit

Agricultural Register (Romania, 1959), 143, 155

agriculture. *See* collective farm; collectivization; decollectivization; Law 18; state farm

Albania, 105, 135, 261n.6

Aluaş, Ioan (Romanian sociologist), 133, 144

Anagnost, Ann, 209

Anderson, Perry, 208

Antall, József (Hungarian prime minister), 100

anthropology: and Eastern Europe, 5–7, 10, 231, 235nn. 9 and 10, 236n.11

anti-Communism: in East bloc, 92, 108, 110, 111, 128; and postsocialist legitimation, 82, 90, 136, 137, 187, 232; in U. S./West, 8, 9, 108, 235n.7. *See also* Cold War; legitimation

antifeminism, 79, 80, 82. *See also* gender; gender regime

anti-Semitism, 83, 89, 90, 95, 97, 99, 179, 254n.56, 256n.11, 258n.52

arhythmia (of socialist temporality), 54, 57. *See also* time

Armenia, 135, 232, 261n.6

Arutiunov, Sergei, 88

association [*asociație*], agricultural (post-1989 Romania), 166, 172, 223, 262n.19, 265n.58; clarifies land titles, 142, 153, 154, 165; illicit enrichment, in 162, 262n.20, 266n.64. *See also* decollectivization

association [*întovărăşire*] (Romania), 149, 260n.1

Association of Former Political Prisoners (Romania), 108

atomization, 24, 52, 55, 164, 166

Aurel Vlaicu (Binţinţi) (Transylvanian village), 138–40, 148, 151, 157, 262n.13; collectivi-

zation in, 143, 260n.1, 263n.33; process of decollectivizing, 88, 138–64, 221; surface areas of, 144–45

austerity measures, 41, 43–45, 48, 50, 98, 178, 236nn. 15 and 18

autonomy: of Hungarians in Romania, 118–24, 231; of local governments 138, 161, 167, 207, 224, 226, 285n.77. *See also* decentralization; Hungarians; state

Baltic states, 15, 83, 91

bankruptcy, controlled, 211

banks (in East bloc), 207, 269nn. 31, 32, and 34; and Caritas, 135, 144, 178, 179, 197, 273n.65

bargaining (in socialist economy), 21–23

barter, 21–22, 181, 205, 207, 280nn. 13 and 15

Barth, Fredrik, 95

Bauman, Zygmunt, 48

BBC, 36

Berlin Wall, 31

Bessarabia, 78, 114. *See also* Moldavia; Moldova

bişniţa ("business"), 98

black market. *See* market, black

blockage, financial. *See* financial blockage

Boiu (Transylvanian village), 151

Borneman, John, 28, 209, 247n.59

Brâncoveanu, Romulus, 197, 203

Braşov (Romanian city), 169, 191, 275n.100

"broker capital," 218. *See also* mafia

Bruszt, László, 213, 220

Bucharest, 168, 170, 173, 174, 177, 178, 191, 194, 214, 232–33

Bucovina, 114

Bulgaria, 10, 110, 135, 207, 216, 235nn. 9 and 10; and pyramid schemes, 169, 201; civil society in, 105, 107, 256n.11; ethnonational issues in, 83, 86–87, 91, 96

Burawoy, Michael, 15, 16, 23, 213, 283n.49

Campeanu, Pavel, 46–47, 57

CAP. *See* collective farm

capital: accumulation of, 15, 33, 180, 193, 195, 196–99, 277n.128; international flows of, 31–34, 37, 42, 50, 237n.19, 272n.61; moral, 106, 108, 109, 121, 126, 256n.17; political,

capital (cont.)
15, 106, 108, 159, 163, 194–97; symbolic,
212. See also broker capital; capitalism; entrepratchiks; legitimation; political capital
capitalism, crisis in, 33, 34, 36, 237n.19. See
also flexible accumulation
C.A.R. (Romanian loan fund), 176
cargo cult, 189, 274n.88
Caritas (Romanian pyramid scheme), 13, 15,
168–203; and Bible, 187, 190, 192; and
changing social structure, 193, 196–99,
202; and reconceptualization of money,
180–93; and Romanian nationalism, 188–
89, 195, 200, 277n.130; as religious/social
movement, 188–92, 275n.91; collapse of,
173–74, 196, 199–202, 272n.61, 273n.65;
competitor schemes of, 201; effects of, 174,
181, 183, 185, 202–3, 271n. 52 and 54,
273n.68, 278n.143; established, 169; folk
explanations of, 175–80, 183; "inside track"
of, 170, 171, 183, 197, 268nn. 13 and 21,
272n.61; size of, 171, 269n.27. See also
market; money; Stoica; theft; "unruly coalitions"
Cartea Funciara. See Land Register
Caucasus, 88
CD. See Democratic Convention
Ceauşescu, Nicolae (Romanian dictator), 42,
49, 50, 144, 178, 190, 236n.18; and nationalism, 65, 73, 128, 144; foreign policy of 41,
242n.29; overthrow of, 53, 56, 198, 217
Cigmău (Transylvanian village), 151, 264n.47
citizenship, 119, 230, 231; and gender, 13, 63,
73, 79, 82, 233; and national questions, 63,
82, 84, 89. See also constitutions; democratization; gender; nationalism
Civic Alliance (AC) (Romania), 112, 115,
256n.13, 257n.30; and national questions,
116–22, 124
Civic Alliance Party (PAC) (Romania), 112,
123, 256n.13, 257n.30; and national questions, 116–19, 253n.39; founding convention of, 115–18, 256n.7, 257nn. 31 and 32
Civic Forum (Czech party), 93
civil society, 104, 107, 108, 120, 121, 221; and
gender, 73, 82
"civil society" (used as symbol), 10, 14, 89,
104, 105, 109–11, 114–16, 119–21, 123,
125, 126–29, 256n.11
Clarke, Simon, 206
clientelism, 22, 33, 218. See also connections;
socialism

Cluj, 86, 169, 171, 190, 191, 275n.100
Cluj Declaration, 118, 119
coalitions, unruly. See unruly coalitions
Cold War, 4–10, 37, 108. See also détente
collective farm (CAP, cooperativă agricolă de
producţie) (Romania), 134, 137, 150,
260n.2; dissolution of (see decollectivization); nature of property in, 142, 147, 159,
264n.36; operation of 27, 43, 48, 51–52,
141, 143, 146–47, 149. See also collectivization; decollectivization; private plot; socialism; theft; usufruct
"collective individual," 15, 73, 77, 78, 93, 231,
247n.53
collectivization (process of), 139, 140, 145,
147–49, 150, 155, 157, 260n.1, 264n.44.
See also socialism; uncollectivized (hill)
villages
"Communism" (as construct), 3, 8, 9, 20,
235n.2, 237n.19
Communist Parties (in East bloc), 10, 82, 92,
99, 102, 106–7, 136, 201; assets of, 178,
198, 217; factional divisions within (see factionalism); moral universe of, 66, 93, 97,
100, 107, 127, 253n.39; opposition to (see
opposition). See also Bulgaria; Czechoslovakia; East Germany; homogenization;
Hungary; legitimation; morality; new socialist man; Poland; Romania; Soviet
Union; "us" vs. "them"
competition (forms of), 22, 23, 26, 32, 86, 87,
102
connections, 22, 86, 140, 152, 153, 160–61,
218; in Romania, 48, 51, 52, 170, 194, 198,
285n.72. See also clientelism; mafia; second
economy
Connell, R. W., 62, 74
conspiracy theories, 97, 124, 177–80, 181,
184, 188, 196, 199
constitutions, and ethnonational conflict, 88–
89, 119, 251n.18. See also citizenship; nationalism
consumption: in socialism (general), 13, 20,
22, 25–29, 30, 32–34, 46–47, 181; and gender, 67, 70; and system crisis, 34, 50; in Romania, 43–47, 51–52, 55, 180–81. See also
Czechoslovakia; East Germany; Hungary;
Poland
contestations (of land allotments), 155, 158
Coposu, Corneliu (Romanian politician), 108,
261n.7
Cornea, Andrei, 158, 212, 283n.47

Cornea, Doina (Romanian dissident), 108–10, 256n.17

"corruption." *See* clientelism; connections; second economy

Coruţ, Pavel (Romanian writer), 198

Council of Europe, 115, 121, 124–26

Craiova (Romanian city), 172

Creed, Gerald, 91

Croatia, 79, 83, 86, 89, 231, 233, 250n.93

Czech Republic, 99, 208, 217, 224, 256n.11; aspects of privatization in, 91, 92, 135, 169, 211, 267n.4. *See also* Czechoslovakia

Czechoslovakia, 6, 27, 32, 87, 107, 110, 128; ethnonational issues in, 83, 86, 96, 208, 254n.48

dead bodies, politics of, 232–33

decentralization, 87, 187, 217; in socialist system, 30, 33–34; and local autonomy 85, 120–22, 161, 167, 258n.44. *See also* Hungarians; state; suzerainties

decollectivization, 14, 127, 166, 207, 214, 224, 234; and "law-governed state," 221–25; and national conflict, 87–88; and increased social conflict, 134, 148, 150, 152, 154, 156, 158, 159, 163, 164, 166, 265n.55; logistics of, in Romania, 134, 136–38, 142, 144, 148, 150–58, 159, 265n.52; political rationale for, 136, 261n.9; significance of, 135, 165–67, 223. *See also* association; land; Law 18; socialism; uncollectivized villages

Decree 151 (1950) (Romania), 149, 150

"democracy," varied meanings of, 94, 110, 112, 113, 120, 121, 123, 125, 128. *See also* original democracy; Iliescu; symbols

Democratic Agrarian Party (PDAR) (Romania), 194, 365n.49

Democratic Convention (CD) (Romanian party), 111–13, 115, 118–22, 123, 124, 126, 194

Democratic National Salvation Front (FDSN) (Romanian party), 90, 109, 256n.12, 276n.116

Democratic Party (DP) (Romania), 109, 194, 196, 256n.12, 261n.12

democratization, 120, 225, 233; and gender, 13–14, 82; and nationalism, 82, 84, 91–92, 99, 103, 111–12, 116–24, 128, 253n.32. *See also* citizenship; constitutions; democracy; nationalism

demonetization, 206, 280n.13. *See also* barter

denunciation, 24. *See also* spoiler state

Department of State (U.S.), 202, 268n.17

departments A and B (socialism's heavy and light industry), 26, 30. *See also* consumption

détente, 5, 31, 32, 235n.7. *See also* Cold War

devil (and Caritas), 189–93

Dinescu, Mircea (Romanian dissident), 109

"directocracy," 158, 212. *See also* entrepratchiks; political capitalism

Dirks, Nicholas, 128

dissidence, 8, 93, 104, 107–9, 242n.29. *See also* opposition; West

dividends (of state farms), 136, 142, 150, 154, 158, 262n.18, 264n.45. *See also* state farm

Dölling, Irene, 64

dossiers (files), 24, 239n.13. *See also* "lustration"; Secret Police; surveillance

"double burden" (women's), 65

Duby, Georges, 208

Duma (Russian Parliament), 201

Dunn, Elizabeth, 279n.2

Dzherzhinsky, Feliks (statue of), 232

East Germany, 24, 31, 50, 110, 217, 250nn. 91 and 93

economy of shortage, 20–23, 26–29, 30, 42–43, 86, 219. *See also* Kornai

Economist, The, 171

"economy, the" (as newly separate domain), 181, 183, 193, 202

elections (East bloc, general), 10, 11, 89, 210; in Romania, 90, 91, 100, 109, 110, 118, 126–27, 137, 194, 226–27, 251n.19, 252n.26, 276n.116. *See also* democratization; nationalist parties; Romania; Transylvania

Eliade, Mircea, 96, 189

elites: agrarian, 137, 160–62, 218, 266n.64; postsocialist, 193, 196, 197, 199, 213, 277n.128; of Communist period, 14, 29, 137, 170, 194, 198, 212, 217; "teleological," 106–7. *See also* directocracy; entrepratchiks; nationalism; nomenclatura; political capitalism; unruly coalitions

Embryo Memorial, 79

entitlement (sense of), 28, 163, 166

"entrepratchiks" (general), 33, 91, 196, 212–13, 278n.136; in Romania 137, 158, 175, 198–200, 203, 217–18. *See also* Caritas; directocracy; nomenclatura; political capitalism

Estonia, 86, 89

"etatization" (defined), 40
ethnic stereotypes, 97–100
ethnonational conflict. *See* nationalism
"Europe" (used as symbol), 104–5, 114–16, 120–21, 124–28
Everac, Paul, 114
exchange rates, 176, 267n.9, 272n.62
exchanges (of land). *See* land

factionalism (in Party bureaucracy), 13, 29–32, 37, 109, 198. *See also* Communist Parties; socialism; Soviet Union, collapse of
faith, 183, 189–91
family. *See* gender regime; kinship; zadruga
FDSN. *See* Democratic National Salvation Front
Fehér, Ferenc, 45
fetishism (of plan, in socialism), 181
feudalism, 205, 208–9, 213, 228; as metaphor, 208, 227, 228
files. *See* dossiers
financial blockage, 179–80
"first (or official) economy," 27. *See also* second economy; socialism, models of
flexible specialization/accumulation, 34–35, 230. *See also* capitalism
food lines. *See* consumption; queues
Fordism, 34
Foucault, Michel, 183, 232
fragmentation (of land), 157, 264n.47
France, 280n.15
FSN. *See* National Salvation Front
Funar, Gheorghe (nationalist politician, Romania), 122, 174, 188, 191–99, 232
funding (of research in Eastern Europe), 5, 9, 235n.8. *See also* Cold War

Gal, Susan, 67, 253n.39
GDS. *See* Group for Social Dialogue
Gelmar (Transylvanian village), 145, 151, 155, 263n.33
gender, 14, 80–81, 159, 162, 266n.62, 279n.2; and nationalism (general), 13, 61–64, 82, 247n.59; and nationalism, in socialist Romania, 68–79; and postsocialist nationalism, 14, 68, 79–82, 233–34; defined, 62
gender regime, 62, 74, 64–69, 80, 81
Geoagiu (Transylvanian commune), 151, 263n.33
Germans (in Aurel Vlaicu), 88, 157, 164, 265n.56
Germany, 173, 176

Ghani, Ashraf, 209
Gligorov, Kiro (Macedonian president), 92
Gorbachev, Mikhail, 3, 31, 32, 36, 116, 207, 257n.34
Goven, Joanna, 64, 79–80
Greater Romania Party (PRM), 89, 100, 110, 194, 251n.19, 256n.13
greed, 186
Gross, Jan T., 45, 220. *See also* spoiler state
Group for Social Dialogue (GDS) (Romania), 112, 115, 119, 122–23, 256n.13
Gypsies (Roma), 93, 95, 177, 219, 234, 255n.59, 272n.59; attitudes toward, 9, 83, 90, 97–99

Habsburg (Austro-Hungarian) Empire, 138, 139, 225
Hann, C. M., 219
Harvey, David, 34, 35, 57, 189
Havel, Václav, 108, 254n.50
Hayden, Robert, 89
Hegel, G.W.F., 254n.56
Heller, Agnes, 45
Herder, Johann Gottfried von, 102
Hertz, Alexander, 254–55n.56
hidden land. *See* land
historiography (national), 78, 96, 97
hoarding, 21–22, 33, 34, 42, 144
Hobsbawm, Eric, 63, 253n.30
homogenization: as socialist policy, 54, 61, 66, 67, 93, 94, 122, 127; in nation-states, 62, 101. *See also* gender regime; legitimation; nationalism; new socialist man
Homorod (Transylvanian village), 139, 140, 151
hope, 191
Horváth, Ágnes, 66
Humphrey, Caroline, 194, 205–7, 208, 216, 220
Hungarian Democratic Union of Romania (UDMR) (political party), 112, 115, 118–21, 123–24, 194, 259n.56
Hungarians (in Romania), 83, 86, 100, 177, 231; in Romanian politics, 91, 97, 112, 117, 118–21, 123–24, 128, 252n.28, 258n.42, 259n.56. *See also* autonomy; Hungarian Democratic Union of Romania; Hungary; nationalism
Hungary, 6, 23, 27, 31, 41, 74, 90–92, 110, 173, 209, 255n.5; and conflict over Transylvania, 69, 78, 90, 100, 177; aspects of privatization in, 16, 33, 91, 211–14, 216, 219;

civil society in, 107, 110, 128, 256n.11; ethnonational questions in, 83, 92, 96–100, 253n.39, 255n.63; gender issues in, 66–67, 79–81, 250n.88

IAS. *See* state farm
Iaşi (Romanian city), 172
Iaşi Radio, 280n.15
identity, national. *See* national identity
Iliescu, Ion (Romanian president), 108, 109–12, 116, 158, 194, 198, 256n.12, 258n.34; and Caritas, 173, 179, 195–96, 199, 273n.65; and relations with nationalist parties, 90, 114, 123–24, 194, 251n.19; and rural population, 137, 158, 224, 261n.12. *See also* elections; Party of Romanian Social Democracy; Romania
IMF. *See* International Monetary Fund
inflation, 98, 100, 172, 175, 177–78, 180, 207, 267nn. 9 and 10, 273n.69
inheritance (of land), 156, 161, 223, 264n.48
inmigrants (to Aurel Vlaicu), 148, 152, 158, 162–64, 265n.55. *See also* uncollectivized villages
International Monetary Fund (IMF), 35, 98, 177–79, 195–96, 199, 210, 268n.17, 269n.27, 273n.65, 278n.138
International Research and Exchanges Board (IREX), 5
"invisible hand," 30, 181, 219, 220, 273n.67. *See also* market economy
involution (industrial), 283n.48
IREX. *See* International Research and Exchanges Board
Iron Curtain, 5, 6, 9
Isărescu, Mugur (Romanian banker), 171, 179, 269n.27

Jews, 95, 97, 99, 254nn. 56 and 59. *See also* anti-Semitism; ethnic stereotypes
jokes, 57, 96, 211, 228, 242n.22, 245n.18, 246n.43
Jowitt, Ken, 32, 37–38
justification, forms of, 107, 108, 122, 163–64. *See also* legitimation; suffering

Karnoouh, Claude, 272n.61
KGB, 33. *See also* Secret Police; Securitate
Kideckel, David, 219
kinship, 163, 164, 166, 233–34, 264n.48. *See also* gender; legitimation; zadruga
Kligman, Gail, 64, 65, 69, 79, 266n.62

knowledge, politics of, 9–11, 154, 159–61, 165, 204, 227–28
Kon, Igor, 254n.50
Konrád, György (Hungarian dissident), 108
Kornai, János, 19
Kuron, Jacek (Polish dissident), 108

labor: as legitimation for landowning, 163, 164; situation of, in socialism, 22–23, 43, 47–48, 51, 215. *See also* gender regime; socialism
Lampland, Martha, 163
Lăncrănjan, Ion (Romanian poet), 74
land: conflicts over, 88, 135, 143, 146, 149–53, 156–60, 162, 165, 265n.55; exchanges of, 140, 149–52, 264n.42; hidden, 14–45, 159; measurement of, 141, 153, 154; overlapping claims to, 148, 154, 157–58; private vs. collective, 139, 140, 151; stretches, moves, 135, 139–43, 145, 148, 149, 151; usurpation of, 139, 154, 155, 159, 160–63. *See also* Aurel Vlaicu; decollectivization; Decree 151; land commission; land reform; Law 18; socialism
land commission (for decollectivization process), 138, 152, 156, 159, 222, 224; abuse of power by, 154, 159, 160–63, 266n.64; activities of, 141, 150, 153, 265n.51
land reform (Romania): of 1921, 140, 145, 151, 262n.14; of 1945, 88, 158
Land Register (Austrian) (*Cartea Funciară*), 146–47, 155, 161
law (in Romania): as experienced in court, 149–50, 156, 158, 222–24, 225, 265n.53; views of, 222
Law 18/1991. *See* Law on Agricultural Land Resources
Law for the Defense of State Property (Hungary), 213
Law on Agricultural Land Resources (Law 18/1991, *Legea Fondului Funciar*, Romania), 133–34, 135–38, 151–52, 156, 167, 224, 225, 264n.48
"law-governed state," 159, 166, 221–23, 226. *See also* decollectivization; legitimation; state
Lefort, Claude, 93
Legea Fondului Funciar. *See* Law on Agricultural Land Resources
legitimation (in East bloc, general), 94, 104, 106, 108, 210, 220–21; in postsocialist Romania, 90, 108, 110, 112–16, 126, 136, 163,

legitimation (*cont.*)
187, 193, 222–25; in socialist period, 20, 23,
24, 26, 56, 64, 107. *See also* Communist
Parties; Europe; justification; labor; law-
governed state; kinship; nationalism; natu-
ralization; symbols
Lenin (statue of), 232
"Leninist Extinction," 37
Lewandowski, Janusz, 210
Liberal Party. *See* National Liberal Party
Literary Romania (*România literară*) (Roma-
nian newspaper), 123
Lithuania, 86
lottery (forms of, in Romania), 271n.56
Lukács, János, 213
"lustration," 239n.13. *See also* dossiers

Macedonia, 92
"mafia" (East bloc forms of), 15, 193, 201, 205,
207, 210, 216–20
Manea, Norman, 40
maps, 139, 144, 145, 224
Maramureş (northern Transylvania), 69,
246n.41, 266n.62
"market" (used as symbol), 10, 16, 89–91, 210
market, black, 29, 51, 169, 172, 176, 214–15
market economy (introduced into East bloc):
aggravates nationalism, 84, 91–92, 98–101;
and increased social difference, 127–28;
causes cognitive reorganization, 177–83,
192–93, 219, 278n.137; effects of 196–203,
205–7, 212–16, 279–80n.6, 283n.48. *See
also* Caritas; markets; money; nationalism;
privatization
markets: in capitalism, 22, 30, 180, 184; in socialist countries, 6, 30–32, 46, 181, 211
Márkus, György, 45
Martin, Emily, 204
Marx, Karl, 181
Marxism (as theory), 9, 189, 237n.21
Mavrodi, Sergei (Russian businessman), 201,
267n.4, 278n.141. *See also* MMM
McClure, K. M., 61, 104, 168, 193–94,
273n.73
memory (concerning land ownership), 146,
151, 157, 159, 233. *See also* land
Michnik, Adam (Polish dissident), 108
millenarianism, 189, 274n.92
Mintz, Sidney W., 237n.20
MMM (Russian investment scheme), 169,
201, 267n.4, 272n.63, 273n.65, 278n.141,
279n.14. *See also* Caritas; Mavrodi

Moldavia (Soviet Republic of), 116, 280n.15.
See also Bessarabia
Moldova, 116–17, 257n.34
Molyneux, Maxine, 64
money, 175–76, 180, 192, 271n.57; and moral
order, 184–89; changed conceptions of,
180–86, 193, 273n.68; dirty vs. clean, 187;
foreign, 188, 189; laundering of, 178, 187,
198, 217, 272n.61, 273n.65; "my" vs.
"their," 182, 184, 186. *See also* Caritas;
Communist Parties; market economy
Mongolia, 232
morality, redefined, 184–87, 202, 219. *See
also* Communist Parties, moral universe of
Mosse, George, 73
Mureş River, 139–40, 149, 151
mutual aid games, 169, 173, 176, 270n.46. *See
also* Caritas; Stoica

Nagy, Imre, 232
nation (concept), 74–79, 82, 233, 247–48n.59,
248n.60; and patrilineality, 70–74, 77, 234;
as victim, 71–73, 75–77, 96, 97; defined,
62–63, 84, 240n.5; shifting meanings of, 63,
84, 94, 101; socialist, 63, 68, 69, 244n.6. *See
also* gender; nationalism; symbols
"nation" (used as symbol), 14, 103, 105, 107,
109–11, 113–15, 122, 123, 125, 128, 129,
256n.11
National Council for Soviet and East European Research (NCSEER), 5
national identity, 13, 14, 38, 62, 86, 105; in
Romania, 55, 69–79, 122, 236n.17; and socialist "self," 94, 97, 101. *See also* ethnic
stereotypes; nation; nationalism
National Liberal Party (Romania), 111, 136,
256n.13
National Peasant Party (Romania), 108, 112,
136, 256n.13
National Salvation Front (FSN) (Romania),
109–11, 137, 256n.12, 261n.12
"National-Communists," 90, 110, 125, 128
nationalism, 73, 85, 102, 107; and opposition
to market reforms, 90–92, 98, 99, 179, 188;
defined, 62, 84; furthered under socialism,
84, 85–87, 92–97, 101, 102, 251n.11; of
Ceauşescu regime, 42, 63, 68–79, 109, 122,
128, 164, 247n.50; of former Party elites,
14, 90–92, 100, 251n.19, 252n.25, 253n.31,
257n.18; rhetoric of (examples from Romania), 70–73, 74–77, 99, 100, 111, 112–15,
122–24, 188. *See also* constitutions; decol-

lectivization; democratization; ethnic stereotypes; gender; Gypsies; historiography; homogenization; Hungarians; kinship; legitimation; market economy; nationalist parties; privatization; self
nationalist parties (Romania), 89, 91, 100, 110, 112, 179, 188, 189, 191, 196, 251–52n.19, 256n.13, 275n.100. *See also* Greater Romania Party; PUNR
naturalization (as symbolic process), 68, 78, 80, 81, 101, 184. *See also* legitimation; symbols
Neanderthal man, 246n.43
New Economic Mechanism (Hungary), 255n.5
"new socialist man," 9, 42, 54
New York Times, 171
nomenclatura, 68, 194, 198, 211, 257n.18, 277n.126, 283n.48. *See also* directocracy; elites; entrepratchiks; nationalism; political capitalism

OPEC, 31
opposition (to Party rule), 22–24, 28, 78, 87, 96, 107, 128; in Romania, 8, 41, 42, 50, 53, 54, 56, 70, 143, 242n.29. *See also* dissidence; "us" vs. "them"; West
opposition parties (Romania), 90, 110–29, 195, 227, 275n.100. *See also* Civic Alliance Party; Democratic Convention; National Liberal Party; National Peasant Party; Romania
"original democracy," 112. *See also* democracy; Iliescu
ownership. *See* land; property rights

PAC. *See* Civic Alliance Party
parcelization of sovereignty, 208, 209, 214, 217
parties, nationalist. *See* nationalist parties
Party of Romanian National Unity (PUNR) (Romania), 89, 110, 118, 122, 127, 174, 178, 191, 194–96, 198, 200, 256n.13, 258n.39, 275n.100, 279n.146. *See also* Caritas; elections; Funar; nationalism; Romania
Party of Romanian Social Democracy (PDSR) (Romania), 109–13, 115, 118, 120, 124–28, 194–96, 256n.12, 261n.12, 276n.116. *See also* Iliescu; National Salvation Front
Party-state. *See* state
Pascariu, Dan (Romanian banker), 171
Pateman, Carole, 73

Patočka, Jan (Czech dissident philosopher), 108
PD. *See* Democratic Party
PDSR. *See* Party of Romanian Social Democracy
perestroika, 36, 207, 212
person (as social construct). *See* self
Petőfi, Sandor (Hungarian poet), 232
Petroşani (Romanian city), 275n.100
planning (centralized), 20, 48. *See also* bargaining; barter; hoarding; socialism
plot. *See* conspiracy theories
Poggi, Gianfranco, 208
Poland, 29, 91, 110, 226; civil society in, 105, 107, 256n.11; economic change in, 33, 212, 216, 271n.53; gender issues in, 79, 250n.93; in socialist period, 6, 27, 29, 32, 36, 50; ethnonational issues in, 83, 90, 95–96, 98, 99, 251n.7
"political capitalism," 33, 196, 213. *See also* directocracy; entrepratchiks; property rights; Staniszkis, Jadwiga
Prague Spring, 32
Prelapsarianov, Aleksii Antediluvianovich, 229
Preobrazhensky, Evgenii, 64
"private plot" (of collective farmers), 27, 43, 44, 147, 215, 223, 260n.2, 285n.75. *See also* collective farms; second economy; socialism
privatization, 10, 13, 209–10, 215, 281n.31; aggravates ethnic conflict, 87, 88, 98, 99, 157–58; and state strength, 35, 201, 209, 210–16, 220–27; of power, 210, 216–18; pre-1989, 33, 210; process of, 133–45, 152–67, 210–16, 217, 281nn. 30 and 31; retarded, 14, 153, 159, 213, 223–24. *See also* decollectivization; entrepratchiks; land; mafia; political capitalism
"privatization" (used as symbol), 210, 227
PRM. *See* Greater Romania Party
pro-natalism, 79, 233–34. *See also* Romania, pro-natalism in
profit, 25, 26, 30, 32, 33, 36, 47
property (forms of), 16, 140, 142, 147, 165, 212, 260nn. 1 and 2. *See also* property affidavit; property certificates; property rights
property affidavit [*adeverinţă*] (for reconstituted landholdings), 142, 154, 222, 224, 262n.18. *See also* property deed, property rights
property certificates, 199, 212, 278n.136

property deed (title), 156, 158, 166, 222, 224, 225, 262n.18

property rights, 155, 183, 209, 210–13, 214, 224, 230, 285n.1; ambiguity in, 15, 158, 159, 211, 212, 230. *See also* Decree 151; directocracy; entrepratchiks; Law 18; political capitalism; usufruct

PUNR. *See* Party of Romanian National Unity

purges, 3, 235n.1

pyramid schemes (general), 169, 172, 201, 203, 267n.4, 269n.35; in Romania, 174, 191, 195, 197–200, 272n.130, 276n.125, 278n.134. *See also* capital; Caritas; entrepratchiks; Mavrodi; MMM; Stoica

queues, 12, 46, 47, 51–52, 65, 51, 114, 170, 241n.12. *See also* consumption

Radio Free Europe, 36, 113

reciprocity ("corruption"). *See* connections

redistribution, 23–26, 30, 45, 64

reduction coefficient (in Romanian decollectivization), 136, 150, 157

Repentance (Soviet film), 232

restitution (of property). *See* decollectivization; privatization; Law 18

Rév, István, 220

rights: collective vs. individual, 118–22; discourse of, 126, 165. *See also* property rights; usufruct

Roman Catholic Church, 79, 177, 250n.93, 270n.36

Roman, Petre (Romanian politician), 109, 256n.12

Romania: changed state power in, 16, 214, 225; civil society in, 105, 107, 109, 111, 115–24, 126–29, 256nn. 11 and 13; compared with other East bloc countries, 27, 31, 41, 86, 110, 211, 216; ethnonational conflict in, 88, 89, 97, 100, 118–23, 128, 158; ethnographic research in, 6–8, 11, 235n.11; foreign debt of, 41, 47, 50; image of, 77, 96, 113, 125, 249n.69; mafia in, 216–18; nationalism in (postsocialist), 89–101, 112–15, 116–29; political parties in, 91, 109–11, 124, 126, 135, 193–94, 196, 256n.12, 261n.12, 270n.36, 276n.116; privatization in, 15, 133–67, 211, 215; pronatalism in 45, 65, 67, 68, 245nn. 17 and 25, 246n.34, 285n.76, 287n.17; revolution in, 109, 113. *See also* Caritas; Ceauşescu; connections; consumption; decollectivization;

democratization; elections; entrepratchiks; gender; Hungarians; land; law; Law 18; nationalism; nationalist parties; opposition; Securitate; time

"Romanian Hearth." *See* Vatra Românească

Romanian Information Service (SRI), 171, 198, 199, 277n.130, 278n.138

Romanian National Bank, 168, 178, 179, 273n.65

Romos (Transylvanian village), 143

Russia, 16, 99, 205–8, 216–20, 274n.88; market reforms in, 16, 135, 206–7; pyramid schemes in, 169, 201, 267n.4, 279n.145. *See also* barter; Humphrey; Mavrodi; MMM; perestroika; Soviet Union; suzerainties

scapegoating, 97

scavenging, 51

scheduling, control over, 44, 45

Schneider, Jane, 218

Schneider, Peter, 218

Schwartz, Barry, 49, 241n.12

"second (or informal) economy," 27, 29, 43, 87, 94, 214; and gender, 66, 67; and privatization, 211, 214, 215; in Romania, 51, 52, 214. *See also* connections; consumption; market, black; private plot

Secret Police (in East bloc), 24, 46, 91, 217, 227. *See also* Securitate

Securitate (Romanian Secret Police), 23–24, 42, 95, 217, 252n.24; and Caritas, 177, 197–98, 200, 277nn. 126 and 130; and "mafia," 194, 197, 217, 219; and nationalism, 90, 124, 178, 198; surveillance by, 7–8, 42, 236nn. 11, 15, and 18, 284n.58

self (as cultural construct), 37, 41, 53, 94, 223, 225; and land, 135, 163, 164, 223; and nationalism, 14, 73, 85, 87, 95–97, 101; under socialism, 29, 42, 55–56, 94–97

Serbia, 125, 176, 178, 187, 235n.9, 272n.61

"shock therapy," 188, 205, 213, 229

shortages, 21, 33, 49, 55. *See also* bargaining; economy of shortage; hoarding

Slovakia, 83, 87, 89–92, 99, 135, 169, 201

Slovenia, 83, 86, 89

"social schizophrenia," 94, 254n.51. *See also* self

socialism, 237n.2, 243n.1, 250n.1; "actually existing" or "real," 4, 11, 61, 235n.4, 238n.1; compared with capitalism, 21–23, 25–26, 28, 34–35, 47, 57, 181; crisis of, 6,

29, 30–37; models/theories of, 12–13, 20–30, 42, 45–46, 64; political economy of, 20–37, 42, 45–46, 64–68, 141–44, 161, 181, 196, 206–7, 215, 218; power in, 8, 20, 22, 24, 29, 46–49, 51, 56–57, 66, 219–20; treatment of land under, 134, 140–41, 143, 145, 146–52, 157; values learned under, 25, 93–94, 127, 148, 163, 166, 177, 180–83, 184–87, 190, 219, 222. *See also* accumulation; collectivization; collective farm; Communist Parties; consumption; fetishism; gender; labor; land; nationalism; queues; self; state; state farm; Secret Police; Securitate

Socialist Labor Party (Romania), 110, 194

socialist paternalism, 24, 25, 47, 63, 64, 66, 79, 80, 93, 190, 216. *See also* entitlement; gender; zadruga

soft budget constraints, 21, 42. *See also* economy of shortage

Solidarity (Poland), 36, 93, 105, 253n.39

Soros Foundation, 123

Soros, George (Hungarian philanthropist), 172, 179, 196

sovereignty, parcelization of. *See* parcelization of sovereignty

Soviet Union, 24, 85–87, 91, 257n.34, 280n.15; collapse of, 32, 205, 207, 208. *See also* Gorbachev; perestroika; Russia

space, 63, 77, 78, 146, 194, 265n.54

"spoiler state," 12, 24, 45, 55, 85, 225, 238n.6, 242n.29. *See also* state

Sputnik, 6

spy (the author as), 7, 236nn. 15 and 17

SRI. *See* Romanian Information Service

St. Dimitrie, 191, 233

Stalin, 3, 114, 232

Ständesstaat, 226, 227

Staniszkis, Jadwiga, 29, 33, 196, 210, 213, 226, 283n.48

Stark, David, 15, 211–13, 219, 220

state, 209, 220, 226, 240n.5; collapse of, 15, 161, 206, 207, 208, 209, 218; decentralization of, 205, 209, 211, 217, 227; encroaches on peasant households, 43, 48, 51, 223; ethnography of, 15, 209, 216, 220, 221, 226; "law-governed" (*see* law-governed state); nature of, 34, 46, 120–22, 166, 209, 214, 225, 226, 230; recentralization of, 161, 167, 197, 209, 211–15, 220, 224–27. *See also* autonomy; decentralization; Hungarians; law-governed state; legitimation; spoiler state

state farms (IASs) (in Romania): after 1989,

134, 136, 141–42, 150, 159–60, 264n.45; and rural elites, 137, 160, 211, 217–18; in Aurel Vlaicu, 88, 145, 154, 158, 162; in socialist period, 147–50, 165, 260n.2. *See also* collectivization; decollectivization; dividends; Law 18

State Property Agency (Hungary), 213

statues, 232

Stewart, Michael, 192

Stoica, Ioan (Romanian businessman), 169, 173–74, 179–80, 187, 191, 198, 200; about, 169, 172, 181, 272n.59; and Funar, 195–96; arrested, 174, 267n.8, 271n.50, 279nn. 145 and 146; sanctified, 189–91. *See also* Caritas; entrepratchiks; market economy; money; nationalism

"storming," 42, 54

subjection (ideological), 12, 24, 45, 46, 49, 50, 56, 57, 66, 223

suffering (as justification), 97, 107–9, 121, 122, 163. *See also* capital, moral

surveillance (in socialist systems). *See* Secret Police; Securitate

"suzerainties," 194, 201, 205–7, 216, 220

symbols, in political discourse, 91, 100, 105, 112–15, 116, 126–28, 221

Szakolczai, Árpád, 66

Szelényi, Ivan (Hungarian dissident sociologist), 106, 108

targets (in socialist economy), 20

Taussig, Michael, 192

teleological elites. *See* elites

teleology, 106, 227, 234

ten-hectare limit (on reconstituted farms), 136, 137, 261nn. 10 and 11. *See also* Law 18

theft, 27, 42, 51, 98, 99, 186. *See also* Caritas; collective farm; private plot

Thom, Françoise, 243n.44

Thompson, E. P., 13

time, 13, 36–37, 39–40, 77, 230, 274n.89, 286n.5; and Romanian regime, 43–53; and self, 41, 53–56; in socialism, 34–36, 42, 189, 243n.44; messianic/millenarian, 37, 56, 189; seizures of, 40, 43, 45–49; "wasted," 47, 241n.12, 242n.26

time-space compression, 35, 189

Tishkov, Valery, 86

Tőkés, László (Hungarian cleric in Transylvania), 123

topographic numbers (in Austrian Land Register), 139, 155, 225 "tradition," 69, 70, 79

"transition," 15

Transylvania, 152, 177, 200, 225, 246nn. 40 and 42, 271n.55; and Romanian elections, 100, 117, 118, 123, 126, 258n.36; ethnic group relations in, 86, 100, 117, 246n.42; historical dispute over, 69, 70, 74, 78, 90, 97, 100, 120, 122, 246n.40, 258n.42; property situation in, 138, 262n.14

Transylvanian Messenger, 171, 172, 174, 268n.21

trust, 190, 192

Tudor, Corneliu Vadim (Romanian nationalist politician), 104, 113, 123, 259n.54. *See also* Greater Romania Party; nationalist parties

22 (Romanian newspaper), 113, 114, 119

"typicality," 11, 262n.14

UDMR. *See* Hungarian Democratic Union of Romania

Ukraine, 173, 207

uncollectivized (hill) villages, 49, 139–40, 150–51. *See also* decollectivization; property

"unruly coalitions," 193–94, 197–201, 216, 230, 276n.114. *See also* Caritas; entrepratchiks; mafia

Urban, Jan, 94

"us" vs. "them," 23, 53, 55, 93–97, 107, 166. *See also* Communist Parties; nationalism; opposition; self

USAID (United States Agency for International Development), 224, 285n.78

usufruct (use rights), 133, 147. *See also* private plot; socialism

USSR. *See* Soviet Union

valuation (of state firms), 211–12, 283n.41

Vatra Românească ("Romanian Hearth"), 89, 91, 198

Vienna, 191

voucher privatization (in Romania), 212

waiting. *See* time

Wałęsa, Lech (Polish president), 108, 256n.11

Weber, Max, 106

weddings, 175, 271n.57

Wertrationalität, 106

"West," the, 16, 37, 38, 108

widows, 162, 163. *See also* gender

Wilson, Woodrow, 103

witchcraft, 220

Wolf, Eric R., 9, 237n.20

World Bank, 35, 177–79, 210

Yugoslavia, 6, 85, 87, 169, 208, 232, 267n.4

zadruga, 64, 245n.14

zadruga-state, 64–66, 68, 73, 78, 80

Zerubavel, Eviatar, 44, 54

Zilber, Herbert (Romanian Communist), 24

Zweckrationalität, 106

PRINCETON STUDIES IN
CULTURE/POWER/HISTORY

High Religion:
A Cultural and Political History of Sherpa Buddhism
by Sherry B. Ortner

A Place in History:
Social and Monumental Time in a Cretan Town
by Michael Herzfeld

The Textual Condition
by Jerome J. McGann

Regulating the Social:
The Welfare State and Local Politics in Imperial Germany
by George Steinmetz

Hanging without a Rope:
Narrative Experience in Colonial and Postcolonial Karoland
by Mary Margaret Steedly

Modern Greek Lessons:
A Primer in Historical Constructivism
by James Faubion

The Nation and Its Fragments:
Colonial and Postcolonial Histories
by Partha Chatterjee

Culture/Power/History:
A Reader in Contemporary Social Theory
edited by Nicholas B. Dirks, Geoff Eley, and Sherry B. Ortner

After Colonialism:
Imperial Histories and Postcolonial Displacements
edited by Gyan Prakash

Encountering Development:
The Making and Unmaking of the Third World
by Arturo Escobar

Social Bodies:
Science, Reproduction, and Italian Modernity
by David G. Horn

Revisioning History:
Film and the Construction of a New Past
edited by Robert A. Rosenstone

The History of Everyday Life:
Reconstructing Historical Experiences and Ways of Life
edited by Alf Lüdke

The Savage Freud and Other Essays on Possible
and Retrievable Selves
by Ashis Nandy

Children and the Politics of Culture
edited by Sharon Stephens

Intimacy and Exclusion:
Religious Politics in Pre-Revolutionary Baden
by Dagmar Herzog

What Was Socialism, and What Comes Next?
by Katherine Verdery

Non-Racial Apartheid:
Citizen and Subject in Contemporary Africa
by Mahmood Mamdani

KATHERINE VERDERY is a Professor of Anthropology at Johns Hopkins University. She is the author of *Transylvanian Villagers: Three Centuries of Political, Economic, and Ethnic Change* (California, 1983) and *National Ideology under Socialism: Identity and Cultural Politics in Ceaușescu's Romania* (California, 1991)